1195

WORD PICTURES
IN THE
NEW TESTAMENT

BOOKS BY PROFESSOR A. T. ROBERTSON

The English New Testament as a Whole:
SYLLABUS FOR NEW TESTAMENT STUDY
THE STUDENT'S CHRONOLOGICAL NEW TESTAMENT
STUDIES IN THE NEW TESTAMENT
NEW TESTAMENT HISTORY (AIRPLANE VIEW)

The Greek New Testament:
WORD PICTURES IN THE NEW TESTAMENT (IN SIX VOLS.)
A SHORT GRAMMAR OF THE GREEK NEW TESTAMENT
A GRAMMAR OF THE GREEK NEW TESTAMENT IN THE LIGHT
OF HISTORICAL RESEARCH
THE MINISTER AND HIS GREEK NEW TESTAMENT
AN INTRODUCTION TO THE TEXTUAL CRITICISM OF THE NEW
TESTAMENT
STUDIES IN THE TEXT OF THE NEW TESTAMENT

The Gospels and Jesus:
A HARMONY OF THE GOSPELS FOR STUDENTS OF THE LIFE OF
CHRIST
A COMMENTARY ON MATTHEW
STUDIES IN MARK'S GOSPEL
LUKE THE HISTORIAN IN THE LIGHT OF RESEARCH
A TRANSLATION OF LUKE'S GOSPEL
THE DIVINITY OF CHRIST IN THE GOSPEL OF JOHN
JOHN THE LOYAL (THE MINISTRY OF THE BAPTIST)
THE PHARISEES AND JESUS (STONE LECTURES FOR 1916)
EPOCHS IN THE LIFE OF JESUS
KEYWORDS IN THE TEACHING OF JESUS
THE TEACHING OF JESUS CONCERNING GOD THE FATHER
THE CHRIST OF THE LOGIA (PORTRAITS OF CHRIST IN Q AND
THE GOSPELS)
THE MOTHER OF JESUS: HER PROBLEMS AND HER GLORY

Paul:
PAUL AND THE INTELLECTUALS (EPISTLE TO THE COLOSSIANS)
EPOCHS IN THE LIFE OF PAUL
PAUL THE INTERPRETER OF CHRIST
PAUL'S JOY IN CHRIST (EPISTLE TO THE PHILIPPIANS)
THE GLORY OF THE MINISTRY (II COR. 2:12-6:10)
THE NEW CITIZENSHIP

Other Studies in the New Testament:
SOME MINOR CHARACTERS IN THE NEW TESTAMENT
STUDIES IN THE EPISTLE OF JAMES
MAKING GOOD IN THE MINISTRY (SKETCH OF JOHN MARK)
TYPES OF PREACHERS IN THE NEW TESTAMENT

Biography:
LIFE AND LETTERS OF JOHN ALBERT BROADUS

WORD PICTURES
IN THE
NEW TESTAMENT

BY

ARCHIBALD THOMAS ROBERTSON
A. M., D. D., LL. D., Litt. D.

PROFESSOR OF NEW TESTAMENT INTERPRETATION
IN THE
SOUTHERN BAPTIST THEOLOGICAL SEMINARY
OF
LOUISVILLE, KENTUCKY

VOLUME I

THE GOSPEL ACCORDING TO MATTHEW
THE GOSPEL ACCORDING TO MARK

BROADMAN PRESS
NASHVILLE, TENNESSEE

To
DR. ADOLF DEISSMANN
OF BERLIN
WHO HAS DONE SO MUCH
TO MAKE THE WORDS OF THE
NEW TESTAMENT GLOW WITH LIFE

PREFACE

It has now been forty years since Dr. Marvin R. Vincent wrote his most useful series of volumes entitled *Word Studies in the New Testament*. They are still helpful for those for whom they were designed, but a great deal of water has run under the mill in these years. More scientific methods of philology are now in use. No longer are Greek tenses and prepositions explained in terms of conjectural English translations or interchanged according to the whim of the interpreter. Comparative grammar has thrown a flood of light on the real meaning of New Testament forms and idioms. New Testament writers are no longer explained as using one construction "for" another. New light has come also from the papyri discoveries in Egypt. Unusual Greek words from the standpoint of the literary critic or classical scholar are here found in everyday use in letters and business and public documents. The New Testament Greek is now known to be not a new or peculiar dialect of the Greek language, but the very lingo of the time. The vernacular *Koiné*, the spoken language of the day, appears in the New Testament as in these scraps of Oxyrhynchus and Fayum papyri. There are specimens of the literary *Koiné* in the papyri as also in the writings of Luke, the Epistles of Paul, the Epistle to the Hebrews. A new Greek-English lexicon of the New Testament will come in due time which will take note of the many startling discoveries from the Greek papyri and inscriptions first brought to notice in their bearing on the New Testament by Dr. Adolf Deissmann, then of Heidelberg, now of Berlin. His *Bible Studies* (Translation by Alexander Grieve, 1901) and his *Light from the Ancient East* (Revised Edition translated by L. R. M. Strachan, 1927) are accessible to students unfamiliar with the German originals.

There is no doubt of the need of a new series of volumes today in the light of the new knowledge. Many ministers have urged me to undertake such a task and finally I have agreed to do it at the solicitation of my publishers. The readers of these volumes (six are planned) are expected to be primarily those who know no Greek or comparatively little and yet who are anxious to get fresh help from the study of words and phrases in the New Testament, men who do not have access to the technical books required, like Moulton and Milligan's *Vocabulary of the New Testament*. The critical student will appreciate the more delicate distinctions in words. But it is a sad fact that many ministers, laymen, and women, who took courses in Greek at college, university, or seminary, have allowed the cares of the world and the deceitfulness of riches to choke off the Greek that they once knew. Some, strangely enough, have done it even in the supposed interest of the very gospel whose vivid messages they have thus allowed to grow dim and faint. If some of these vast numbers can have their interest in the Greek New Testament revived, these volumes will be worth while. Some may be incited, as many have been by my volume, *The Minister and His Greek New Testament*, to begin the study of the Greek New Testament under the guidance of a book like Davis's *Beginner's Grammar of the Greek New Testament*. Others who are without a turn for Greek or without any opportunity to start the study will be able to follow the drift of the remarks and be able to use it all to profit in sermons, in Sunday school lessons, or for private edification.

The words of the Canterbury Version will be used, sometimes with my own rendering added, and the transliterated Greek put in parenthesis. Thus one who knows no Greek can read straight ahead and get the point simply by skipping the Greek words which are of great value to those who do know some Greek. The text of Westcott and Hort will be used though not slavishly. Those who know Greek are expected to keep the Greek text open as they read or study these volumes. The publishers insisted on the transliteration to cut down the cost of printing.

The six volumes will follow this order; Volume I, The Gospel according to Matthew and Mark; Vol. II, The Gospel according to Luke; Vol. III, The Acts of the Apostles; Vol. IV, The Pauline Epistles; Vol. V, The Gospel according to John and the Epistle to the Hebrews; Vol. VI, the general Epistles and the Revelation of John. For purely exegetical and expository development a more chronological order would be required. These volumes do not claim to be formal commentary. Nowhere is the whole text discussed, but everywhere those words are selected for discussion which seem to be richest for the needs of the reader in the light of present-day knowledge. A great deal of the personal equation is thus inevitable. My own remarks will be now lexical, now grammatical, now archaeological, now exegetical, now illustrative, anything that the mood of the moment may move me to write that may throw light here and there on the New Testament words and idioms. Another writer might feel disposed to enlarge upon items not touched upon here. But that is to be expected even in the more formal commentaries, useful as they are. To some extent it is true of lexicons. No one man knows everything, even in his chosen specialty, or has the wisdom to pick out what every reader wishes explained. But even diamonds in the rough are diamonds. It is for the reader to polish them as he will. He can turn the light this way and that. There is a certain amount of repetition at some points, part of it on purpose to save time and to emphasize the point.

I have called these volumes *Word Pictures* for the obvious reason that language was originally purely pictographic.

Children love to read by pictures either where it is all picture or where pictures are interspersed with simple words. The Rosetta Stone is a famous illustration. The Egyptian hieroglyphics come at the top of the stone, followed by the Demotic Egyptian language with the Greek translation at the bottom. By means of this stone the secret of the hieroglyphs or pictographs was unravelled. Chinese characters are also pictographic. The pictures were first for ideas, then for words, then for syllables, then for letters. Today in Alaska there are Indians who still use pictures alone for communicating their ideas. "Most words have been originally metaphors, and metaphors are continually falling into the rank of words" (Professor Campbell). Rather is it not true that words are metaphors, sometimes with the pictured flower still blooming, sometimes with the blossom blurred? Words have never gotten wholly away from the picture stage. These old Greek words in the New Testament are rich with meaning. They speak to us out of the past and with lively images to those who have eyes to see. It is impossible to translate all of one language into another. Much can be carried over, but not all. Delicate shades of meaning defy the translator. But some of the very words of Jesus we have still as he said: "The words that I have spoken unto you are spirit and are life" (John 6:63). We must never forget that in dealing with the words of Jesus we are dealing with things that have life and breath. That is true of all the New Testament, the most wonderful of all books of all time. One can feel the very throb of the heart of Almighty God in the New Testament if the eyes of his own heart have been enlightened by the Holy Spirit. May the Spirit of God take of the things of Christ and make them ours as we muse over the words of life that speak to us out of the New Covenant that we call the New Testament.

Louisville, Ky.

A. T. ROBERTSON.

BY WAY OF INTRODUCTION

The passing years do not make it any plainer who actually wrote our Greek Matthew. Papias records, as quoted by Eusebius, that Matthew wrote the *Logia* of Jesus in Hebrew (Aramaic). Is our present Matthew a translation of the Aramaic *Logia* along with Mark and other sources as most modern scholars think? If so, was the writer the Apostle Matthew or some other disciple? There is at present no way to reach a clear decision in the light of the known facts. There is no real reason why the Apostle Matthew could not have written both the Aramaic *Logia* and our Greek Matthew, unless one is unwilling to believe that he would make use of Mark's work on a par with his own. But Mark's book rests primarily on the preaching of Simon Peter. Scholfield has recently (1927) published *An Old Hebrew Text of St. Matthew's Gospel*. We know quite too little of the origin of the Synoptic Gospels to say dogmatically that the Apostle Matthew was not in any real sense the author.

If the book is genuine, as I believe, the date becomes a matter of interest. Here again there is nothing absolutely decisive save that it is later than the Gospel according to Mark which it apparently uses. If Mark is given an early date, between A.D. 50 to 60, then Matthew's book may be between 60 and 70, though many would place it between 70 and 80. It is not certain whether Luke wrote after Matthew or not, though that is quite possible. There is no definite use of Matthew by Luke that has been shown. One guess is as good as another and each decides by his own predilections. My own guess is that A.D. 60 is as good as any.

In the Gospel itself we find Matthew the publican (Matt.

9:9; 10:3) though Mark (2:14) and Luke (5:27) call him Levi
the publican. Evidently therefore he had two names like
John Mark. It is significant that Jesus called this man from
so disreputable a business to follow him. He was apparently
not a disciple of John the Baptist. He was specially chosen
by Jesus to be one of the Twelve Apostles, a business man
called into the ministry as was true of the fishermen James
and John, Andrew and Simon. In the lists of the Apostles
he comes either seventh or eighth. There is nothing definite
told about him in the Gospels apart from the circle of the
Twelve after the feast which he gave to his fellow publicans
in honor of Jesus.

Matthew was in the habit of keeping accounts and it is
quite possible that he took notes of the sayings of Jesus as
he heard them. At any rate he gives much attention to the
teachings of Jesus as, for instance, the Sermon on the Mount
in chapters 5 to 7, the parables in 13, the denunciation of the
Pharisees in 23, the great eschatological discourse in 24 and
25. As a publican in Galilee he was not a narrow Jew and so
we do not expect a book prejudiced in favor of the Jews and
against the Gentiles. He does seem to show that Jesus is
the Messiah of Jewish expectation and hope and so makes
frequent quotations from the Old Testament by way of confirmation and illustration. There is no narrow nationalism
in Matthew. Jesus is both the Messiah of the Jews and the
Saviour of the world.

There are ten parables in Matthew not in the other
Gospels: The Tares, the Hid Treasure, the Net, the Pearl
of Great Price, the Unmerciful Servant, the Labourers in the
Vineyard, the Two Sons, the Marriage of the King's Son, the
Ten Virgins, the Talents. The only miracles in Matthew
alone are the Two Blind Men, the Coin in the Mouth of the
Fish. But Matthew gives the narrative of the Birth of
Jesus from the standpoint of Joseph while Luke tells that
wonderful story from the standpoint of Mary. There are

details of the Death and Resurrection given by Matthew alone.

The book follows the same general chronological plan as that in Mark, but with various groups like the miracles in 8 and 9, the parables in 13.

The style is free from Hebraisms and has few individual peculiarities. The author is fond of the phrase the kingdom of heaven and pictures Jesus as the Son of man, but also as the Son of God. He sometimes abbreviates Mark's statements and sometimes expands them to be more precise.

Plummer shows the broad general plan of both Mark and Matthew to be the same as follows:

Introduction to the Gospel: Mark 1:1–13 = Matthew 3:1–4:11.

Ministry in Galilee: Mark 1:14–6:13 = Matthew 4:12–13:58.

Ministry in the Neighborhood: Mark 6:14–9:50 = Matthew 14:1–18:35.

Journey through Perea to Jerusalem: Mark 10:1–52 = Matthew 19:1–20:34.

Last week in Jerusalem: Mark 11:1–16:8 = Matthew 21:1–28:8.

The Gospel of Matthew comes first in the New Testament, though it is not so in all the Greek manuscripts. Because of its position it is the book most widely read in the New Testament and has exerted the greatest influence on the world. The book deserves this influence though it is later in date than Mark, not so beautiful as Luke, nor so profound as John. Yet it is a wonderful book and gives a just and adequate portraiture of the life and teachings of Jesus Christ as Lord and Saviour. The author probably wrote primarily to persuade Jews that Jesus is the fulfilment of their Messianic hopes as pictured in the Old Testament. It is thus a proper introduction to the New Testament story in comparison with the Old Testament prophecy.

THE TITLE

The Textus Receptus has "The Holy Gospel according to Matthew" (*to kata Matthaion hagion Euaggelion*), though the Elzevirs omit "holy," not agreeing here with Stephanus, Griesbach, and Scholz. Only minuscules (cursive Greek manuscripts) and all late have the adjective. Other minuscules and nine uncials including W (the Washington Codex of the fifth century), C of the fifth century (the palimpsest manuscript) and Delta of the ninth together with most Latin manuscripts have simply "Gospel according to Matthew" (*Euaggelion kata Matthaion*). But Aleph and B the two oldest and best Greek uncials of the fourth century have only "According to Matthew" (*Kata Maththaion*) (note double th) and the Greek uncial D of the fifth or sixth century follows Aleph and B as do some of the earliest Old Latin manuscripts and the Curetonian Syriac. It is clear, therefore, that the earliest form of the title was simply "According to Matthew." It may be doubted if Matthew (or the author, if not Matthew) had any title at all. The use of "according to" makes it plain that the meaning is not "the Gospel of Matthew," but the Gospel as given by Matthew, *secundum Matthaeum*, to distinguish the report by Matthew from that by Mark, by Luke, by John. Least of all is there any authority in the manuscripts for saying "Saint Matthew," a Roman Catholic practice observed by some Protestants.

The word Gospel (*Euaggelion*) comes to mean good news in Greek, though originally a reward for good tidings as in Homer's *Odyssey* XIV. 152 and in II Kings 4:10. In the New Testament it is the good news of salvation through Christ. The English word Gospel probably comes from the Anglo-Saxon Godspell, story or narrative of God, the life of Christ. It was early confused with the Anglo-Saxon godspell, good story, which seems like a translation of the

Greek *euaggelion*. But primarily the English word means the God story as seen in Christ which is the best news that the world has ever had. One thinks at once of the use of "word" (*Logos*) in John 1:1, 14. So then it is, according to the Greek, not the Good News of Matthew, but the Good News of God, brought to us in Christ the Word, the Son of God, the Image of the Father, the Message of the Father. We are to study this story first as presented by Matthew. The message is God's and it is as fresh to us today in Matthew's record as when he first wrote it.

CONTENTS

THE GOSPEL ACCORDING TO MATTHEW

CONTENTS

THE GOSPEL ACCORDING TO MARK

THE GOSPEL
ACCORDING TO MATTHEW

CHAPTER I

1. *The Book* (*biblos*). There is no article in the Greek, but the following genitives make it definite. It is our word Bible that is here used, *the* Book as Sir Walter Scott called it as he lay dying. The usual word for book is a diminutive form (*biblion*), a little book or roll such as we have in Luke 4:17, "The roll of the prophet Isaiah." The pieces of papyrus (*papuros*), our paper, were pasted together to make a roll of varying lengths according to one's needs. Matthew, of course, is not applying the word book to the Old Testament, probably not to his own book, but to "the genealogical table of Jesus Christ" (*biblos geneseōs Iēsou Christou*), "the birth roll of Jesus Christ" Moffatt translates it. We have no means of knowing where the writer obtained the data for this genealogy. It differs radically from that in Luke 3:23-38. One can only give his own theory of the difference. Apparently in Matthew we have the actual genealogy of Joseph which would be the legal pedigree of Jesus according to Jewish custom. In Luke we apparently have the actual genealogy of Mary which would be the real line of Jesus which Luke naturally gives as he is writing for the Gentiles. *Jesus Christ.* Both words are used. The first is the name (*Iēsous*) given by the angel to Mary (Matt. 1:21) which describes the mission of the child. The second was originally a verbal adjective (*christos*) meaning anointed from the verb to anoint (*chriō*). It was used often in the Septuagint as an adjective like "the anointed priest" (I Kings 2:10) and then as a substantive to translate the Hebrew word "Messiah" (*Messias*). So Andrew said to Simon: "We have found the Messiah, which is, being interpreted, Christ" (John 1:41). In the Gospels it is sometimes "the Anointed One," "the

3

Messiah," but finally just a proper name as here, Jesus
Christ.   Paul in his later Epistles usually has it "Christ
Jesus." *The Son of David, the son of Abraham (huiou
Daueid huiou Abraam).*   Matthew proposes to show that
Jesus Christ is on the human side the son of David, as the
Messiah was to be, and the son of Abraham, not merely a
real Jew and the heir of the promises, but the promise made
to Abraham.   So Matthew begins his line with Abraham
while Luke traces his line back to Adam.   The Hebrew and
Aramaic often used the word son (*bēn*) for the quality or
character, but here the idea is descent.   Christians are called
sons of God because Christ has bestowed this dignity upon
us (Rom. 8:14; 9:26; Gal. 3:26; 4:5-7).   Verse 1 is the description of the list in verses 2-17.   The names are given in
three groups, Abraham to David (2-6), David to Babylon
Removal (6-11), Jechoniah to Jesus (12-16).   The removal
to Babylon (*metoikesias Babulōnos*) occurs at the end of
verse 11, the beginning of verse 12, and twice in the résumé
in verse 17. This great event is used to mark off the two last
divisions from each other.   It is a good illustration of the
genitive as the case of genus or kind.   The Babylon removal
could mean either to Babylon or from Babylon or, indeed,
the removal of Babylon.   But the readers would know the
facts from the Old Testament, the removal of the Jews to
Babylon.   Then verse 17 makes a summary of the three
lists, fourteen in each by counting David twice and omitting
several, a sort of mnemonic device that is common enough.
Matthew does not mean to say that there were only fourteen
in actual genealogy.   The names of the women (Thamar,
Rahab, Ruth, Bathsheba the wife of Uriah) are likewise not
counted.   But it is a most interesting list.

2. *Begat (egennēsen).*   This word comes, like some of the
early chapters of Genesis, with regularity through verse 16,
until the birth of Jesus is reached when there is a sudden
change.   The word itself does not always mean immediate

parentage, but merely direct descent. In verse 16 we have "Joseph the husband of Mary, from whom was begotten Jesus who is called Christ" (*ton Iōsēph ton andra Marias ex hēs egennēthē Iēsous ho legomenos Christos*). The article occurs here each time with the object of "begat," but not with the subject of the verb to distinguish sharply the proper names. In the case of David the King (1:6) and Joseph the husband of Mary (1:16) the article is repeated. The mention of the brethren of Judah (1:2) and of both Phares and Zara (1:3) may show that Matthew was not copying a family pedigree but making his own table. All the Greek manuscripts give verse 16 as above save the Ferrar Group of minuscules which are supported by the Sinaitic Syriac Version. Because of this fact Von Soden, whose text Moffatt translates, deliberately prints his text "*Jacob begat Jesus*" (*Iōsēph de egennēsen Iēsoun*). But the Sinaitic Syriac gives the Virgin Birth of Jesus in Matt. 1:18–25. Hence it is clear that "begat" here in 1:16 must merely mean line of descent or the text has been tampered with in order to get rid of the Virgin Birth idea, but it was left untouched in 1:18–25. I have a full discussion of the problem in chapter XIV of *Studies in the Text of the New Testament.* The evidence as it now stands does not justify changing the text of the Greek uncials to suit the Sinaitic Syriac. The Virgin Birth of Jesus remains in 1:16. The spelling of these Hebrew names in English is usually according to the Hebrew form, not the Greek. In the Greek itself the Hebrew spelling is often observed in violation of the Greek rules for the ending of words with no consonants save *n, r, s.* But the list is not spelled consistently in the Greek, now like the Hebrew as in Abraham, Isaac, Jacob, now like the Greek as in Judah, Solomon, Hezekiah, though the Hebrew style prevails.

18. *The birth of Jesus Christ* (*tou [Iēsou] Christou hē genesis*). In the Greek Jesus Christ comes before birth as

the important matter after 1:16. It is not certain whether "Jesus" is here a part of the text as it is absent in the old Syriac and the Old Latin while the Washington Codex has only "Christ." The Vatican Codex has "Christ Jesus." But it is plain that the story of the birth of Jesus Christ is to be told briefly as follows, "on this wise" (*houtōs*), the usual Greek idiom. The oldest and best manuscripts have the same word genealogy (*genesis*) used in 1:1, not the word for birth (begotten) as in 1:16 (*gennēsis*). "It is in fact the word Genesis. The evangelist is about to describe, not the genesis of the heaven and the earth, but the genesis of Him who made the heaven and the earth, and who will yet make a new heaven and a new earth" (Morison).

Betrothed to Joseph (*Mnēsteutheisēs tōi Iōsēph*). Matthew proceeds to explain his statement in 1:16 which implied that Joseph, though the legal father of Jesus in the royal line, was not the actual father of Mary's Son. Betrothal with the Jews was a serious matter, not lightly entered into and not lightly broken. The man who betrothed a maiden was legally husband (Gen. 29:21; Deut. 22:23f.) and "an informal cancelling of betrothal was impossible" (McNeile). Though they did not live together as husband and wife till actual marriage, breach of faithfulness on the part of the betrothed was treated as adultery and punished with death. *The New Testament in Braid Scots* actually has "mairry't till Joseph" for "betrothed to Joseph." Matthew uses the genitive absolute construction here, a very common Greek idiom.

Of the Holy Ghost (*ek pneumatos hagiou*). The discovery that Mary was pregnant was inevitable and it is plain that she had not told Joseph. She "was found with child" (*heurethē en gastri echousa*). This way of putting it, the usual Greek idiom, plainly shows that it was the discovery that shocked Joseph. He did not as yet know what Matthew plainly asserts that the Holy Ghost, not Joseph and not any man, was responsible for the pregnancy of Mary. The

problem of the Virgin Birth of Jesus has been a disturbing
fact to some through all the ages and is today to those who
do not believe in the pre-existence of Christ, the Son of God,
before his Incarnation on earth. This is the primal fact
about the Birth of Christ. The Incarnation of Christ is
clearly stated by Paul (II Cor. 8:9; Phil. 2:5–11; and involved in Col. 1:15–19) and by John (John 1:14; 17:5). If
one frankly admits the actual pre-existence of Christ and the
real Incarnation, he has taken the longest and most difficult
step in the matter of the supernatural Birth of Christ. That
being true, no merely human birth without the supernatural
element can possibly explain the facts. Incarnation is far
more than the Indwelling of God by the Holy Spirit in the
human heart. To admit real incarnation and also full
human birth, both father and mother, creates a greater
difficulty than to admit the Virgin Birth of Jesus begotten
by the Holy Spirit, as Matthew here says, and born of the
Virgin Mary. It is true that only Matthew and Luke tell
the story of the supernatural birth of Jesus, though John
1:14 seems to refer to it. Mark has nothing whatever concerning the birth and childhood of Jesus and so cannot be
used as a witness on the subject. Both Matthew and Luke
present the birth of Jesus as not according to ordinary human birth. Jesus had no human father. There is such a
thing in nature as parthenogenesis in the lower orders of
life. But that scientific fact has no bearing here. We see
here God sending his Son into the world to be the world's
Saviour and he gave him a human mother, but not a human
father so that Jesus Christ is both Son of God and Son of
Man, the God Man. Matthew tells the story of the birth
of Jesus from the standpoint of Joseph as Luke gives it
from the standpoint of Mary. The two narratives harmo-
nize with each other. One credits these most wonderful of
all birth narratives according as he believes in the love and
power of Almighty God to do what he wills. There is no

miracle with God who has all power and all knowledge. The laws of nature are simply the expression of God's will, but he has not revealed all his will in the laws that we discover. God is Spirit. He is Person. He holds in his own power all life. John 3:16 is called the Little Gospel because it puts briefly the love of God for men in sending his own Son to live and die for us.

19. *A Righteous Man* (*dikaios*). Or just, not benignant or merciful. The same adjective is used of Zacharias and Elizabeth (Luke 1:6) and Simeon (Luke 2:25). "An upright man," the *Braid Scots* has it. He had the Jewish conscientiousness for the observance of the law which would have been death by stoning (Deut. 22:23). Though Joseph was upright, he would not do that. "As a good Jew he would have shown his zeal if he had branded her with public disgrace" (McNeile). *And yet not willing* (*kai mē thelōn*). So we must understand *kai* here, "and yet." Matthew makes a distinction here between "willing" (*thelōn*) and "wishing" (*eboulēthē*), that between purpose (*thelō*) and desire (*boulomai*) a distinction not always drawn, though present here. It was not his purpose to "make her a public example" (*deigmatisai*), from the root (*deiknumi* to show), a rare word (Col. 2:15). The Latin Vulgate has it *traducere*, the Old Latin *divulgare*, Wycliff *pupplische* (publish), Tyndale *defame*, Moffatt *disgrace*, Braid Scots "Be i the mooth o' the public." The substantive (*deigmatismos*) occurs on the Rosetta Stone in the sense of "verification." There are a few instances of the verb in the papyri though the meaning is not clear (Moulton and Milligan's *Vocabulary*). The compound form appears (*paradeigmatizō*) in Heb. 6:6 and there are earlier instances of this compound than of the uncompounded, curiously enough. But new examples of the simple verb, like the substantive, may yet be found. The papyri examples mean to furnish a sample (P Tebt. 5.75), to make trial of (P Ryl. I. 28.32). The substantive means exposure

in (P Ryl. I. 28.70). At any rate it is clear that Joseph "was minded to put her away privily." He could give her a bill of divorcement (*apolusai*), the *gêt* laid down in the Mishna, without a public trial. He had to give her the writ (*gêt*) and pay the fine (Deut. 24:1). So he proposed to do this privately (*lathrai*) to avoid all the scandal possible. One is obliged to respect and sympathize with the motives of Joseph for he evidently loved Mary and was appalled to find her untrue to him as he supposed. It is impossible to think of Joseph as the actual father of Jesus according to the narrative of Matthew without saying that Matthew has tried by legend to cover up the illegitimate birth of Jesus. The Talmud openly charges this sin against Mary. Joseph had "a short but tragic struggle between his legal conscience and his love" (McNeile).

20. *An angel of the Lord appeared unto him in a dream* (*aggelos kuriou kat' onar ephanē autōi*). This expression (*aggelos kuriou*) is without the article in the New Testament except when, as in 1:24, there is reference to the angel previously mentioned. Sometimes in the Old Testament Jehovah Himself is represented by this phrase. Surely Joseph needed God's help if ever man did. If Jesus was really God's Son, Joseph was entitled to know this supreme fact that he might be just to both Mary and her Child. It was in a dream, but the message was distinct and decisive for Joseph. He is called "Son of David" as had been shown by Matthew in 1:16. Mary is called his "wife" (*tēn gunaika sou*). He is told "not to become afraid" (ingressive first aorist passive subjunctive in prohibition, (*mē phobētheis*), "to take to his side" (*paralabein*, ingressive aorist active infinitive) her whom he had planned (*enthumēthentos*, genitive absolute again, from *en* and *thumos*) to send away with a writ of divorce. He had pondered and had planned as best he knew, but now God had called a halt and he had to decide whether he was willing to shelter Mary by marrying her and, if

necessary, take upon himself whatever stigma might attach to her. Joseph was told that the child was begotten of the Holy Spirit and thus that Mary was innocent of any sin. But who would believe it now if he told it of her? Mary knew the truth and had not told him because she could not expect him to believe it.

21. *Thou shalt call his name Jesus* (*Kalesies to onoma autou Iēsoun*). The rabbis named six whose names were given before birth: "Isaac, Ishmael, Moses, Solomon, Josiah, and the name of the Messiah, whom may the Holy One, blessed be His name, bring in our day." The angel puts it up to Joseph as the putative father to name the child. "Jesus is the same as Joshua, a contraction of Jehoshuah (Num. 13:16; I Chron. 7:27), signifying in Hebrew, 'Jehovah is helper,' or 'Help of Jehovah'" (Broadus). So Jesus is the Greek form of Joshua (Heb. 4:8). He is another Joshua to lead the true people of God into the Promised Land. The name itself was common enough as Josephus shows. Jehovah is Salvation as seen in Joshua for the Hebrews and in Jesus for all believers. "The meaning of the name, therefore, finds expression in the title *Saviour* applied to our Lord (Luke 1:47; 2:11; John 4:42)" (Vincent). He will save (*sōsei*) his people from their sins and so be their Saviour (*Sōtēr*). He will be prophet, priest, and king, but "Saviour" sums it all up in one word. The explanation is carried out in the promise, "for he is the one who (*autos*) will save (*sōsei* with a play on the name Jesus) his people from their sins." Paul will later explain that by the covenant people, the children of promise, God means the spiritual Israel, all who believe whether Jews or Gentiles. This wonderful word touches the very heart of the mission and message of the Messiah. Jesus himself will show that the kingdom of heaven includes all those and only those who have the reign of God in their hearts and lives. *From their sins* (*apo tōn hamartiōn autōn*). Both sins of omission and of commission.

The substantive (*hamartia*) is from the verb (*hamartanein*) and means missing the mark as with an arrow. How often the best of us fall short and fail to score. Jesus will save us away from (*apo*) as well as out of (*ex*) our sins. They will be cast into oblivion and he will cover them up out of sight.

22. *That it may be fulfilled* (*hina plērōthēi*). Alford says that "it is impossible to interpret *hina* in any other sense than in order that." That was the old notion, but modern grammarians recognize the non-final use of this particle in the *Koiné* and even the consecutive like the Latin *ut*. Some even argue for a causal use. If the context called for result, one need not hesitate to say so as in Mark 11:28; John 9:36; I John 1:9; Rev. 9:20; 13:13. See discussion in my *Grammar of the Greek New Testament in the Light of Historical Research*, pp. 997-9. All the same it is purpose here, God's purpose, Matthew reports the angel as saying, spoken "by (*hupo*, immediate agent) the Lord through (*dia*, intermediate agent) the prophet." "*All this has happened*" (*touto de holon gegonen*, present perfect indicative), stands on record as historical fact. But the Virgin Birth of Jesus is not due to this interpretation of Isaiah 7:14. It is not necessary to maintain (Broadus) that Isaiah himself saw anything more in his prophecy than that a woman then a virgin, would bear a son and that in the course of a few years Ahaz would be delivered from the king of Syria and Israel by the coming of the Assyrians. This historical illustration finds its richest fulfilment in the birth of Jesus from Mary. "Words of themselves are empty. They are useful only as vessels to convey things from mind to mind" (Morison). The Hebrew word for young woman is translated by virgin (*parthenos*), but it is not necessary to conclude that Isaiah himself contemplated the supernatural birth of Jesus. We do not have to say that the idea of the Virgin Birth of Jesus came from Jewish sources. Certainly it did not come from the pagan

myths so foreign to this environment, atmosphere and spirit. It is far simpler to admit the supernatural fact than try to explain the invention of the idea as a myth to justify the deification of Jesus. The birth, life, and death of Jesus throw a flood of light on the Old Testament narrative and prophecies for the early Christians. In Matthew and John in particular we often see "that the events of Christ's life were divinely ordered for the express purpose of fulfilling the Old Testament" (McNeile). See Matt. 2:15, 35; 4:14–17; 8:17; 12:17–21; 13:25; 21:4f.; John 12:38f.; 13:18; 19:24; 28:36f.

23. *They shall call* (*kalesousin*). Men, people, will call his name Immanuel, God with us. "The interest of the evangelist, as of all New Testament writers, in prophecy, was purely religious" (Bruce). But surely the language of Isaiah has had marvellous illustration in the Incarnation of Christ. This is Matthew's explanation of the meaning of Immanuel, a descriptive appellation of Jesus Christ and more than a mere motto designation. God's help, Jesus= the Help of God, is thus seen. One day Jesus will say to Philip: "He that has seen me has seen the Father" (John 14:9).

24. *Took unto him his wife* (*parelaben tēn gunaika autou*). The angel had told him not to be afraid to "take to his side" Mary his wife (1:20). So when he awoke from his sleep he promptly obeyed the angel and "took his wife home" (Moffatt). One can only imagine the relief and joy of Mary when Joseph nobly rose to his high duty toward her. I have tried to sketch Mary's problems in *Mary the Mother of Jesus: Her Problems and Her Glory.*

25. *And knew her not* (*kai ouk eginōsken autēn*). Note the imperfect tense, continuous or linear action. Joseph lived in continence with Mary till the birth of Jesus. Matthew does not say that Mary bore no other children than Jesus. "Her firstborn" is not genuine here, but is a part of the

text in Luke 2:7. The perpetual virginity of Mary is not taught here. Jesus had brothers and sisters and the natural meaning is that they were younger children of Joseph and Mary and not children of Joseph by a previous marriage. So Joseph "called his name Jesus" as the angel had directed and the child was born in wedlock. Joseph showed that he was an upright man in a most difficult situation.

CHAPTER II

1. *Now when Jesus was born (tou de Iēsou gennēthentos).*
The fact of the birth of Jesus is stated by the genitive absolute construction (first aorist passive participle of the same
verb *gennaō* used twice already of the birth of Jesus, 1:16, 20,
and used in the genealogy, 1:2–16). Matthew does not
propose to give biographic details of the supernatural birth
of Jesus, wonderful as it was and disbelieved as it is by some
today who actually deny that Jesus was born at all or ever
lived, men who talk of the Jesus Myth, the Christ Myth, etc.
"The main purpose is to show the reception given by the
world to the new-born Messianic King. Homage from afar,
hostility at home; foreshadowing the fortunes of the new
faith: reception by the Gentiles, rejection by the Jews"
(Bruce). *In Bethlehem of Judea (en Bēthleem tēs Ioudaias).*
There was a Bethlehem in Galilee seven miles northwest
of Nazareth (Josephus, *Antiquities* XIX. 15). This Bethlehem (house of bread, the name means) of Judah was the
scene of Ruth's life with Boaz (Ruth 1:1f.; Matt. 1:5) and
the home of David, descendant of Ruth and ancestor of
Jesus (Matt. 1:5). David was born here and anointed king
by Samuel (I Sam. 17:12). The town came to be called the
city of David (Luke 2:11). Jesus, who was born in this
House of Bread called himself the Bread of Life (John 6:35),
the true Manna from heaven. Matthew assumes the knowledge of the details of the birth of Jesus in Bethlehem which
are given in Luke 2:1–7 or did not consider them germane
to his purpose. Joseph and Mary went to Bethlehem from
Nazareth because it was the original family home for both
of them. The first enrolment by the Emperor Augustus as
the papyri show was by families (*kat' oikian*). Possibly

Joseph had delayed the journey for some reason till now it approached the time for the birth of the child. *In the days of Herod the King (en hēmerais Hērōidou tou Basileōs)*. This is the only date for the birth of Christ given by Matthew. Luke gives a more precise date in his Gospel (2:1-3), the time of the first enrolment by Augustus and while Cyrenius was ruler of Syria. More will be said of Luke's date when we come to his Gospel. We know from Matthew that Jesus was born while Herod was king, the Herod sometimes called Herod the Great. Josephus makes it plain that Herod died B.C. 4. He was first Governor of Galilee, but had been king of Judaea since B.C. 40 (by Antony and Octavius). I call him "Herod the Great Pervert" in *Some Minor Characters in the New Testament.* He was great in sin and in cruelty and had won the favour of the Emperor. The story in Josephus is a tragedy. It is not made plain by Matthew how long before the death of Herod Jesus was born. Our traditional date A.D. 1, is certainly wrong as Matthew shows. It seems plain that the birth of Jesus cannot be put later than B.C. 5. The data supplied by Luke probably call for B.C. 6 or 7.

Wise men from the east (magoi apo anatolōn). The etymology of *Magi* is quite uncertain. It may come from the same Indo-European root as *(megas) magnus,* though some find it of Babylonian origin. Herodotus speaks of a tribe of Magi among the Medians. Among the Persians there was a priestly caste of Magi like the Chaldeans in Babylon (Dan. 1:4). Daniel was head of such an order (Dan. 2:48). It is the same word as our "magician" and it sometimes carried that idea as in the case of Simon Magus (Acts 8:9, 11) and of Elymas Barjesus (Acts 13:6, 8). But here in Matthew the idea seems to be rather that of astrologers. Babylon was the home of astrology, but we only know that the men were from the east whether Arabia, Babylon, Persia, or elsewhere. The notion that they were kings arose

from an interpretation of Isa. 60:3; Rev. 21:24. The idea
that they were three in number is due to the mention of
three kinds of gifts (gold, frankincense, myrrh), but that
is no proof at all. Legend has added to the story that the
names were Caspar, Balthasar, and Melchior as in *Ben Hur*
and also that they represent Shem, Ham, and Japhet. A
casket in the Cologne Cathedral actually is supposed to contain the skulls of these three Magi. The word for east (*apo
anatolōn*) means "from the risings" of the sun.

2. *For we saw his star in the east* (*eidomen gar autou ton
astera en tēi anatolēi*). This does not mean that they saw
the star which was in the east. That would make them go
east to follow it instead of west from the east. The words
"in the east" are probably to be taken with "we saw" i.e.
we were in the east when we saw it, or still more probably
"we saw his star at its rising" or "when it rose" as Moffatt
puts it. The singular form here (*tēi anatolēi*) does sometimes
mean "east" (Rev. 21:13), though the plural is more common as in Matt. 2:1. In Luke 1:78 the singular means
dawn as the verb (*aneteilen*) does in Matt. 4:16 (Septuagint).
The Magi ask where is the one born king of the Jews. They
claim that they had seen his star, either a miracle or a combination of bright stars or a comet. These men may have
been Jewish proselytes and may have known of the Messianic hope, for even Vergil had caught a vision of it. The
whole world was on tiptoe of expectancy for something.
Moulton (*Journal of Theological Studies*, 1902, p. 524) "refers to the Magian belief that a star could be the *fravashi*,
the counterpart or angel (cf. Matt. 18:10) of a great man"
(McNeile). They came to worship the newly born king of
the Jews. Seneca (*Epistle* 58) tells of Magians who came to
Athens with sacrifices to Plato after his death. They had
their own way of concluding that the star which they had
seen pointed to the birth of this Messianic king. Cicero
(*De Divin.* i. 47) "refers to the constellation from which,

on the birthnight of Alexander, Magians foretold that the
destroyer of Asia was born" (McNeile). Alford is positive
that no miracle is intended by the report of the Magi or by
Matthew in his narrative. But one must be allowed to say
that the birth of Jesus, if really God's only Son who has
become Incarnate, is the greatest of all miracles. Even
the methods of astrologers need not disturb those who are
sure of this fact.

3. *He was troubled, and all Jerusalem with him* (*etara-
chthē kai pāsa Ierosoluma met' autou*). Those familiar with
the story of Herod the Great in Josephus can well understand the meaning of these words. Herod in his rage over
his family rivalries and jealousies put to death the two sons
of Mariamne (Aristobulus and Alexander), Mariamne herself, and Antipater, another son and once his heir, besides
the brother and mother of Mariamne (Aristobulus, Alex-
andra) and her grandfather John Hyrcanus. He had made
will after will and was now in a fatal illness and fury over
the question of the Magi. He showed his excitement and the
whole city was upset because the people knew only too well
what he could do when in a rage over the disturbance of his
plans. "The foreigner and usurper feared a rival, and the
tyrant feared the rival would be welcome" (Bruce). Herod
was a hated Idumaean.

4. *He inquired of them where the Christ should be born*
(*epunthaneto par' autōn pou ho Christos gennātai*). The
prophetic present (*gennātai*) is given, the very words of
Herod retained by Matthew's report. The imperfect tense
(*epunthaneto*) suggests that Herod inquired repeatedly,
probably of one and another of the leaders gathered together, both Sadducees (chief priests) and Pharisees (scribes).
McNeile doubts, like Holtzmann, if Herod actually called
together all the Sanhedrin and probably "he could easily
ask the question of a single scribe," because he had begun
his reign with a massacre of the Sanhedrin (Josephus, *Ant.*

XIV. ix. 4). But that was thirty years ago and Herod was desperately in earnest to learn what the Jews really expected about the coming of "the Messiah." Still Herod probably got together not the Sanhedrin since "elders" are not mentioned, but leaders among the chief priests and scribes, not a formal meeting but a free assembly for conference. He had evidently heard of this expected king and he would swallow plenty of pride to be able to compass the defeat of these hopes.

5. *And they said unto him* (*hoi de eipan autōi*). Whether the ecclesiastics had to search their scriptures or not, they give the answer that is in accord with the common Jewish opinion that the Messiah was to come from Bethlehem and of the seed of David (John 7:42). So they quote Micah 5:2, "a free paraphrase" Alford calls it, for it is not precisely like the Hebrew text or like the Septuagint. It may have come from a collection of *testimonia* with which J. Rendel Harris has made the world familiar. He had consulted the experts and now he has their answer. Bethlehem of Judah is the place. The use of the perfect passive indicative (*gegraptai*) is the common form in quoting scripture. It stands written. *Shall be shepherd* (*poimanei*). The Authorized Version had "shall rule," but "shepherd" is correct. "Homer calls kings 'the shepherds of the people' " (Vincent). In Heb. 13:20 Jesus is called "the great shepherd of the sheep." Jesus calls himself "the good shepherd" (John 10:11). Peter calls Christ "the chief shepherd" (I Peter 2:25). "The Lamb which is in the midst of the throne shall be their shepherd" (Rev. 7:17). Jesus told Peter to "shepherd" the lambs (John 21:16). Our word pastor means shepherd.

7. *Then Herod privily called the wise men* (*tote Hērōidēs lathrai kalesas tous magous*). He had manifestly not told members of the Sanhedrin why he was concerned about the Messiah. So he conceals his motives to the Magi. And yet

he "learned of them carefully" (*ekribōsen*), "learned exactly" or "accurately." He was anxious to see if the Jewish prophecy of the birthplace of the Messiah agreed with the indications of the star to the Magi. He kept to himself his purpose. The time of the appearing star (*ton chronon tou phainomenou asteros*) is not "the time when the star appeared," but the age of the star's appearance.

8. *Sent them to Bethlehem and said* (*pempsas autous eis Bēthleem eipen*). Simultaneous aorist participle, "sending said." They were to "search out accurately" (*exetasate akribōs*) concerning the child. Then "bring me word, that I also may come and worship him." The deceit of Herod seemed plausible enough and might have succeeded but for God's intervention to protect His Son from the jealous rage of Herod.

9. *Went before them* (*proēgen autous*). Imperfect tense, kept on in front of them, not as a guide to the town since they now knew that, but to the place where the child was, the inn according to Luke 2:7. Justin Martyr says that it was in a cave. The stall where the cattle and donkeys stayed may have been beneath the inn in the side of the hill.

10. *They rejoiced with exceeding great joy* (*echarēsan charan megalēn sphodra*). Second aorist passive indicative with cognate accusative. Their joy was due to the success of the search.

11. *Opening their treasures* (*anoixantes tous thēsaurous autōn*). Here "treasures" means "caskets" from the verb (*tithēmi*), receptacle for valuables. In the ancient writers it meant "treasury" as in I Macc. 3:29. So a "storehouse" as in Matt. 13:52. Then it means the things laid up in store, treasure in heaven (Matt. 6:20), in Christ (Col. 2:3). In their "caskets" the Magi had gold, frankincense, and myrrh, all found at that time in Arabia, though gold was found in Babylon and elsewhere.

12. *Warned in a dream* (*chrēmatisthentes kat' onar*). The

verb means to transact business (*chrēmatizō* from *chrēma*, and that from *chraomai*, to use. Then to consult, to deliberate, to make answer as of magistrates or an oracle, to instruct, to admonish. In the Septuagint and the New Testament it occurs with the idea of being warned by God and also in the papyri (Deissmann, *Bible Studies*, p. 122). Wycliff puts it here: "An answer taken in sleep."

15. *Until the death of Herod* (*heōs tēs teleutēs Hērōidou*). The Magi had been warned in a dream not to report to Herod and now Joseph was warned in a dream to take Mary and the child along (*mellei zētein tou apolesai* gives a vivid picture of the purpose of Herod in these three verbs). In Egypt Joseph was to keep Mary and Jesus till the death of Herod the monster. Matthew quotes Hosea 11:1 to show that this was in fulfilment of God's purpose to call his Son out of Egypt. He may have quoted again from a collection of *testimonia* rather than from the Septuagint. There is a Jewish tradition in the Talmud that Jesus "brought with him magic arts out of Egypt in an incision on his body" (*Shabb.* 104b). "This attempt to ascribe the Lord's miracles to Satanic agency seems to be independent of Matthew, and may have been known to him, so that one object of his account may have been to combat it" (McNeile).

16. *Slew all the male children that were in Bethlehem* (*aneilen pantas tous paidas tous en Bēthleem*). The flight of Joseph was justified, for Herod was violently enraged (*ethumōthē lian*) that he had been mocked by the Magi, deluded in fact (*enepaichthē*). Vulgate *illusus esset*. Herod did not know, of course, how old the child was, but he took no chances and included all the little boys (*tous paidas*, masculine article) in Bethlehem two years old and under, perhaps fifteen or twenty. It is no surprise that Josephus makes no note of this small item in Herod's chamber of horrors. It was another fulfilment of the prophecy in Jeremiah 31:15. The quotation (2:18) seems to be from the

Septuagint. It was originally written of the Babylonian captivity but it has a striking illustration in this case also. Macrobius (*Sat.* II. iv. 11) notes that Augustus said that it was better to be Herod's sow (*hus*) than his son (*huios*), for the sow had a better chance of life.

20. *For they are dead* (*tethnēkasin*). Only Herod had sought to kill the young child, but it is a general statement of a particular fact as is common with people who say: "They say." The idiom may be suggested by Exodus 4:19: "For all are dead that sought thy life."

22. *Warned in a dream* (*chrēmatistheis kat' onar*). He was already afraid to go to Judea because Archelaus was reigning (ruling, not technically king, *basileuei*). In a fret at last before his death Herod had changed his will again and put Archelaus, the worst of his living sons, in the place of Antipas. So Joseph went to Galilee. Matthew has had nothing about the previous dwelling of Joseph and Mary in Nazareth. We learn that from Luke who tells nothing of the flight into Egypt. The two narratives supplement one another and are in no sense contradictory.

23. *Should be called a Nazarene* (*Nazōraios klēthēsetai*). Matthew says "that it might be fulfilled which was spoken by the prophets" (*dia tōn prophētōn*). It is the plural and no single prophecy exists which says that the Messiah was to be called a Nazarene. It may be that this term of contempt (John 1:46; 7:52) is what is meant, and that several prophecies are to be combined like Ps. 22:6, 8; 69:11, 19; Isa. 53:2, 3, 4. The name Nazareth means a shoot or branch, but it is by no means certain that Matthew has this in mind. It is best to confess that we do not know. See Broadus on Matthew for the various theories. But, despised as Nazareth was at that time, Jesus has exalted its fame. The lowly Nazarene he was at first, but it is our glory to be the followers of the Nazarene. Bruce says that "in this case, therefore, we certainly know that the historic

fact suggested the prophetic reference, instead of the prophecy creating the history." The parallels drawn by Matthew between the history of Israel and the birth and infancy of Jesus are not mere fancy. History repeats itself and writers of history find frequent parallels. Surely Matthew is not beyond the bounds of reason or of fact in illustrating in his own way the birth and infancy of Jesus by the Providence of God in the history of Israel.

CHAPTER III

1. *And in those days cometh John the Baptist* (*en de tais hēmerais paraginetai Iōanēs ho Baptistēs*). Here the synoptic narrative begins with the baptism of John (Matt. 3:1; Mark 1:2; Luke 3:1) as given by Peter in Acts 1:22, "from the baptism of John, unto the day that he was received up from us" (cf. also Acts 10:37–43, Peter's summary to Cornelius very much like the outline of Mark's Gospel). Matthew does not indicate the date when John appeared as Luke does in ch. 3 (the fifteenth year of Tiberius's reign). It was some thirty years after the birth of John, precisely how long after the return of Joseph and Mary to Nazareth we do not know. Moffatt translates the verb (*paraginetai*) "came on the scene," but it is the historical present and calls for a vivid imagination on the part of the reader. There he is as he comes forward, makes his appearance. His name John means "Gift of Jehovah" (cf. German *Gotthold*) and is a shortened form of Johanan. He is described as "the Baptist," "the Baptizer" for that is the rite that distinguishes him. The Jews probably had proselyte baptism as I. Abrahams shows (*Studies in Pharisaism and the Gospels*, p. 37). But this rite was meant for the Gentiles who accepted Judaism. John is treating the Jews as Gentiles in demanding baptism at their hands on the basis of repentance.

Preaching in the wilderness of Judea (*Kērussōn en tēi erēmōi tēs Ioudaias*). It was the rough region in the hills toward the Jordan and the Dead Sea. There were some people scattered over the barren cliffs. Here John came in close touch with the rocks, the trees, the goats, the sheep, and the shepherds, the snakes that slipped before the burning

23

grass over the rocks.   He was the Baptizer, but he was also
the Preacher, heralding his message out in the barren hills
at first where few people were, but soon his startling message
drew crowds from far and near.   Some preachers start with
crowds and drive them away.

2. *Repent* (*metanoeite*).   Broadus used to say that this
is the worst translation in the New Testament.   The trouble
is that the English word "repent" means "to be sorry
again" from the Latin *repoenitet* (impersonal).   John did
not call on the people to be sorry, but to change (think
afterwards) their mental attitudes (*metanoeite*) and conduct.
The Vulgate has it "do penance" and Wycliff has followed
that.   The Old Syriac has it better: "Turn ye."   The French
(Geneva) has it "Amendez vous."   This is John's great
word (Bruce) and it has been hopelessly mistranslated.
The tragedy of it is that we have no one English word that
reproduces exactly the meaning and atmosphere of the Greek
word.   The Greek has a word meaning to be sorry (*metamelomai*) which is exactly our English word repent and it is used
of Judas (Matt. 27:3).   John was a new prophet with the
call of the old prophets: "Turn ye" (Joel 2:12; Isa. 55:7;
Ezek. 33:11, 15).

For the kingdom of heaven is at hand (*ēggiken gar hē Ba-
sileia tōn ouranōn*).   Note the position of the verb and the
present perfect tense.   It was a startling word that John
thundered over the hills and it re-echoed throughout the
land.   The Old Testament prophets had said that it would
come some day in God's own time.   John proclaims as the
herald of the new day that it has come, has drawn near.
How near he does not say, but he evidently means very
near, so near that one could see the signs and the proof.
The words "the kingdom of heaven" he does not explain.
The other Gospels use "the kingdom of God" as Matthew
does a few times, but he has "the kingdom of heaven"
over thirty times.   He means "the reign of God," not the

political or ecclesiastical organization which the Pharisees expected. His words would be understood differently by different groups as is always true of popular preachers. The current Jewish apocalypses had numerous eschatological ideas connected with the kingdom of heaven. It is not clear what sympathy John had with these eschatological features. He employs vivid language at times, but we do not have to confine John's intellectual and theological horizon to that of the rabbis of his day. He has been an original student of the Old Testament in his wilderness environment without any necessary contact with the Essenes who dwelt there. His voice is a new one that strikes terror to the perfunctory theologians of the temple and of the synagogue. It is the fashion of some critics to deny to John any conception of the spiritual content of his words, a wholly gratuitous criticism.

For this is he that was spoken of by Isaiah the prophet (*houtos gar estin ho rhētheis dia Esaiou tou prophētou*). This is Matthew's way of interpreting the mission and message of the Baptist. He quotes Isa. 40:3 where "the prophet refers to the return of Israel from the exile, accompanied by their God" (McNeile). He applies it to the work of John as "a voice crying in the wilderness" for the people to make ready the way of the Lord who is now near. He was only a voice, but what a voice he was. He can be heard yet across the centuries.

4. *Now John himself* (*autos de ho Iōanēs*). Matthew thus introduces the man himself and draws a vivid sketch of his dress (note *eichen*, imperfect tense), his habit, and his food. Would such an uncouth figure be welcome today in any pulpit in our cities? In the wilderness it did not matter. It was probably a matter of necessity with him, not an affectation, though it was the garb of the original Elijah (II Kings 1:8), rough sackcloth woven from the hair of camels. Plummer holds that "John consciously took Elijah as a model."

6. *And they were baptized* (*kai ebaptizonto*). It is the imperfect tense to show the repetition of the act as the crowds from Judea and the surrounding country kept going out to him (*exeporeueto*), imperfect again, a regular stream of folks going forth. Moffatt takes it as causative middle, "got baptized," which is possible. "The movement of course was gradual. It began on a small scale and steadily grew till it reached colossal proportions" (Bruce). It is a pity that baptism is now such a matter of controversy. Let Plummer, the great Church of England commentator on Matthew, speak here of John's baptising these people who came in throngs: "It is his office to bind them to a new life, symbolized by immersion in water." That is correct, symbolized, not caused or obtained. The word "river" is in the correct text, "river Jordan." They came "confessing their sins" (*exomologoumenoi*), probably each one confessing just before he was baptized, "making open confession" (Weymouth). Note *ex*. It was a never to be forgotten scene here in the Jordan. John was calling a nation to a new life. They came from all over Judea and even from the other side of El Ghor (the Jordan Gorge), Perea. Mark adds that finally all Jerusalem came.

7. *The Pharisees and Sadducees* (*tōn Pharisaiōn kai Saddoukaiōn*). These two rival parties do not often unite in common action, but do again in Matt. 16:1. "Here a strong attraction, there a strong repulsion, made them for the moment forget their differences" (McNeile). John saw these rival ecclesiastics "coming for baptism" (*erchomenous epi to baptisma*). Alford speaks of "the Pharisees representing hypocritical superstition; the Sadducees carnal unbelief." One cannot properly understand the theological atmosphere of Palestine at this time without an adequate knowledge of both Pharisees and Sadducees. The books are numerous besides articles in the Bible dictionaries. I have pictured the Pharisees in my first (1916) Stone Lectures, *The Pharisees*

and Jesus. John clearly grasped the significance of this movement on the part of the Pharisees and Sadducees who had followed the crowds to the Jordan. He had welcomed the multitudes, but right in the presence of the crowds he exposes the hypocrisy of the ecclesiastics. *Ye offspring of vipers (gennēmata echidnōn).* Jesus (Matt. 12:34; 23:33) will use the same language to the Pharisees. Broods of snakes were often seen by John in the rocks and when a fire broke out they would scurry (*phugein*) to their holes for safety. "The coming wrath" was not just for Gentiles as the Jews supposed, but for all who were not prepared for the kingdom of heaven (I Thess. 1:10). No doubt the Pharisees and Sadducees winced under the sting of this powerful indictment.

8. *Fruit worthy of repentance (Karpon axion tēs metanoias).* John demands proof from these men of the new life before he administers baptism to them. "The fruit is not the change of heart, but the acts which result from it" (McNeile). It was a bold deed for John thus to challenge as unworthy the very ones who posed as lights and leaders of the Jewish people. "Any one can do (*poiēsate*, *vide* Gen. 1:11) acts externally good but only a good man can grow a crop of right acts and habits" (Bruce).

9. *And think not to say within yourselves (kai mē doxēte legein en heautois).* John touched the tender spot, their ecclesiastical pride. They felt that the "merits of the fathers," especially of Abraham, were enough for all Israelites. At once John made clear that, reformer as he was, a breach existed between him and the religious leaders of the time. *Of these stones (ek tōn lithōn toutōn).* "Pointing, as he spoke to the pebbles on the beach of the Jordan" (Vincent).

10. *Is the axe laid (hē axinē keitai).* This verb *keitai* is used as the perfect passive of *tithēmi.* But the idea really is, "the axe lies at (*pros*, before) the root of the trees." It is

there ready for business. The prophetic present occurs
also with "is hewn down" and "cast."

11. *Mightier than I* (*ischuroteros mou*). Ablative after
the comparative adjective. His baptism is water baptism,
but the Coming One "will baptize in the Holy Spirit and
fire." "Life in the coming age is in the sphere of the Spirit.
Spirit and fire are coupled with one preposition as a double
baptism" (McNeile). Broadus takes "fire" in the sense
of separation like the use of the fan. As the humblest of
servants John felt unworthy to take off the sandals of the
Coming One. About *bastazō* see on Matt. 8:17.

12. *Will burn up with unquenchable fire* (*katakausei puri
asbestōi*). Note perfective use of *kata*. The threshing
floor, the fan, the wheat, the garner, the chaff (*achuron*,
chaff, straw, stubble), the fire furnish a life-like picture.
The "fire" here is probably judgment by and at the coming
of the Messiah just as in verse 11. The Messiah "will thoroughly cleanse" (*diakathariei*, Attic future of -*izō* and note
dia-). He will sweep from side to side to make it clean.

13. *Then cometh Jesus* (*tote paraginetai ho Iēsous*). The
same historical present used in 3:1. He comes all the
way from Galilee to Jordan "to be baptized by him" (*tou
baptisthēnai hupo autou*). The genitive articular infinitive
of purpose, a very common idiom. The fame of John had
reached Nazareth and the hour has come for which Jesus
has waited.

14. *Would have hindered* (*diekōluen*). Rather "tried to
prevent" as Moffatt has it. It is the conative imperfect.
The two men of destiny are face to face for the first time
apparently. The Coming One stands before John and he
recognizes him before the promised sign is given.

15. *To fulfil all righteousness* (*plērōsai pāsan dikaiosunēn*).
The explanation of Jesus satisfies John and he baptizes the
Messiah though he has no sins to confess. It was proper
(*prepon*) to do so else the Messiah would seem to hold aloof

from the Forerunner. Thus the ministries of the two are
linked together.

16. *The Spirit of God descending as a dove (pneuma theou
katabainon hōsei peristeran).* It is not certain whether
Matthew means that the Spirit of God took the form of a
dove or came upon Jesus as a dove comes down. Either
makes sense, but Luke (3:22) has it "in bodily form as a
dove" and that is probably the idea here. The dove in
Christian art has been considered the symbol of the Holy
Spirit.

17. *A voice out of the heavens (phōnē ek tōn ouranōn).*
This was the voice of the Father to the Son whom he identifies as His Son, "my beloved Son." Thus each person of
the Trinity is represented (Father, Son, Holy Spirit) at this
formal entrance of Jesus upon his Messianic ministry.
John heard the voice, of course, and saw the dove. It was
a momentous occasion for John and for Jesus and for the
whole world. The words are similar to Psa. 2:7 and the
voice at the Transfiguration (Matt. 17:5). The good
pleasure of the Father is expressed by the timeless aorist
(*eudokēsa*).

CHAPTER IV

1. *To be tempted of the devil (peirasthēnai hupo tou diabolou).* Matthew locates the temptation at a definite time, "then" (*tote*) and place, "into the wilderness" (*eis tēn erēmon*), the same general region where John was preaching. It is not surprising that Jesus was tempted by the devil immediately after his baptism which signified the formal entrance upon the Messianic work. That is a common experience with ministers who step out into the open for Christ. The difficulty here is that Matthew says that "Jesus was led up into the wilderness by the Spirit to be tempted by the devil." Mark (1:12) puts it more strongly that the Spirit "drives" (*ekballei*) Christ into the wilderness. It was a strong impulsion by the Holy Spirit that led Jesus into the wilderness to think through the full significance of the great step that he had now taken. That step opened the door for the devil and involved inevitable conflict with the slanderer (*tou diabolou*). Judas has this term applied to him (John 6:70) as it is to men (II Tim. 3:3; Tit. 2:3) and women (she devils, I Tim. 3:11) who do the work of the arch slanderer. There are those today who do not believe that a personal devil exists, but they do not offer an adequate explanation of the existence and presence of sin in the world. Certainly Jesus did not discount or deny the reality of the devil's presence. The word "tempt" here (*peirazō*) and in 4:3 means originally to test, to try. That is its usual meaning in the ancient Greek and in the Septuagint. Bad sense of *ekpeirazō* in 4:7 as in Deut. 6:16. Here it comes to mean, as often in the New Testament, to solicit to sin. The evil sense comes from its use for an evil purpose.

2. *Had fasted (nēsteusas).* No perfunctory ceremonial

fast, but of communion with the Father in complete abstention from food as in the case of Moses during forty days and
forty nights (Ex. 34:28). "The period of the fast, as in the
case of Moses was spent in a spiritual ecstasy, during which
the wants of the natural body were suspended" (Alford).
"He afterward hungered" and so at the close of the period
of forty days.

3. *If thou art the Son of God* (*ei huios ei tou theou*). More
exactly, "If thou art Son of God," for there is no article
with "Son." The devil is alluding to the words of the
Father to Jesus at the baptism: "This is my Son the Beloved." He challenges this address by a condition of the
first class which assumes the condition to be true and deftly
calls on Jesus to exercise his power as Son of God to appease
his hunger and thus prove to himself and all that he really
is what the Father called him. *Become bread* (*artoi genōntai*). Literally, "that these stones (round smooth stones
which possibly the devil pointed to or even picked up and
held) become loaves" (each stone a loaf). It was all so
simple, obvious, easy. It would satisfy the hunger of
Christ and was quite within his power. *It is written*
(*gegraptai*). Perfect passive indicative, stands written and
is still in force. Each time Jesus quotes Deuteronomy to
repel the subtle temptation of the devil. Here it is Deut.
8:3 from the Septuagint. Bread is a mere detail (Bruce)
in man's dependence upon God.

5. *Then the devil taketh him* (*tote paralambanei auton ho
diabolos*). Matthew is very fond of this temporal adverb
(*tote*). See already 2:7; 3:13; 4:1, 5. Note historic present
with vivid picturesqueness. Luke puts this temptation
third, the geographical order. But was the person of Christ
allowed to be at the disposal of the devil during these temptations? Alford so holds. *On the pinnacle of the temple*
(*epi to pterugion tou hierou*). Literally "wing?" the English
word "pinnacle" is from the Latin *pinnaculum,* a diminutive

of *pinna* (wing). "*The temple*" (*tou hierou*) here includes the whole temple area, not just the sanctuary (*ho naos*), the Holy Place and Most Holy Place. It is not clear what place is meant by "wing." It may refer to Herod's royal portico which overhung the Kedron Valley and looked down some four hundred and fifty feet, a dizzy height (Josephus, *Ant.* XV. xi. 5). This was on the south of the temple court. Hegesippus says that James the Lord's brother was later placed on the wing of the temple and thrown down therefrom.

6. *Cast thyself down* (*bale seauton katō*). The appeal to hurl himself down into the abyss below would intensify the nervous dread that most people feel at such a height. The devil urged presumptuous reliance on God and quotes Scripture to support his view (Psa. 91:11f.). So the devil quotes the Word of God, misinterprets it, omits a clause, and tries to trip the Son of God by the Word of God. It was a skilful thrust and would also be accepted by the populace as proof that Jesus was the Messiah if they should see him sailing down as if from heaven. This would be a sign from heaven in accord with popular Messianic expectation. The promise of the angels the devil thought would reassure Jesus. They would be a spiritual parachute for Christ.

7. *Thou shall not tempt* (*ouk ekpeiraseis*). Jesus quotes Deuteronomy again (6:16) and shows that the devil has wholly misapplied God's promise of protection.

8. *And showeth him* (*kai deiknusin autōi*). This wonderful panorama had to be partially mental and imaginative, since the devil caused to pass in review "all the kingdoms of the world and the glory of them." But this fact does not prove that all phases of the temptations were subjective without any objective presence of the devil. Both could be true. Here again we have the vivid historical present (*deiknusin*). The devil now has Christ upon a very high mountain whether the traditional Quarantania or not. It was from Nebo's summit that Moses caught the vision of

the land of Canaan (Deut. 34:1–3). Luke (4:5) says that the whole panorama was "in a moment of time" and clearly psychological and instantaneous.

9. *All these things will I give thee* (*tauta soi panta dōsō*). The devil claims the rule of the world, not merely of Palestine or of the Roman Empire. "The kingdoms of the cosmos" (4:8) were under his sway. This word for world brings out the orderly arrangement of the universe while *hē oikoumenē* presents the inhabited earth. Jesus does not deny the grip of the devil on the world of men, but the condition (*ean* and aorist subjunctive, second class undetermined with likelihood of determination), was spurned by Jesus. As Matthew has it Jesus is plainly to "fall down and worship me" (*pesōn prokunēseis moi*), while Luke (4:7) puts it, "worship before me" (*enōpion emou*), a less offensive demand, but one that really involved worship of the devil. The ambition of Jesus is thus appealed to at the price of recognition of the devil's primacy in the world. It was compromise that involved surrender of the Son of God to the world ruler of this darkness. "The temptation was threefold: to gain a temporal, not a spiritual, dominion; to gain it at once; and to gain it by an act of homage to the ruler of this world, which would make the self-constituted Messiah the vice-regent of the devil and not of God" (McNeile).

10. *Get thee hence, Satan* (*Hupage, Satanā*). The words "behind me" (*opisō mou*) belong to Matt. 16:23, not here. "Begone" Christ says to Satan. This temptation is the limit of diabolical suggestion and argues for the logical order in Matthew. "Satan" means the adversary and Christ so terms the devil here. The third time Jesus quotes Deuteronomy, this time 6:13, and repels the infamous suggestion by Scripture quotation. The words "him alone thou shalt serve" need be recalled today. Jesus will warn men against trying to serve God and mammon (Matt. 6:24). The devil as the lord of the evil world constantly tries to win men to

the service of the world and God. This is his chief camou-
flage for destroying a preacher's power for God. The word
here in Matt. 4:10 for serve is *latreuseis* from *latris* a hired
servant, one who works for hire, then render worship.

11. *Then the devil leaveth him* (*tote aphiēsin auton ho
diabolos*). Note the use of "then" (*tote*) again and the historical present. The movement is swift. "And behold"
(*kai idou*) as so often in Matthew carries on the life-like
picture. "*Angels came* (aorist tense *proselthon* punctiliar
action) *and were ministering* (*diēkonoun*, picturesque imperfect, linear action) *unto him.*" The victory was won in
spite of the fast of forty days and the repeated onsets of the
devil who had tried every avenue of approach. The angels
could cheer him in the inevitable nervous and spiritual reac-
tion from the strain of conflict, and probably also with food
as in the case of Elijah (I Kings 19:6f.). The issues at stake
were of vast import as the champions of light and darkness
grappled for the mastery of men. Luke 4:13 adds, that the
devil left Jesus only "until a good opportunity" (*achri
kairou*).

12. *Now when he heard* (*akousas de*). The reason for
Christ's return to Galilee is given here to be that John had
been delivered up into prison. The Synoptic Gospels skip
from the temptation of Jesus to the Galilean ministry, a
whole year. But for John 1:19–3:36 we should know nothing of the "year of obscurity" (Stalker). John supplies
items to help fill in the picture. Christ's work in Galilee
began after the close of the active ministry of the Baptist
who lingered on in prison for a year or more.

13. *Dwelt in Capernaum* (*Katōikēsen eis Kapharnaoum*).
He went first to Nazareth, his old home, but was rejected
there (Luke 4:16–31). In Capernaum (probably the modern *Tell Hûm*) Jesus was in a large town, one of the centres
of Galilean political and commercial life, a fishing mart,
where many Gentiles came. Here the message of the king-

dom would have a better chance than in Jerusalem with its ecclesiastical prejudices or in Nazareth with its local jealousies. So Jesus "made his home" (*katōikēsen*) here.

16. *Saw a great light* (*phōs eiden mega*).   Matthew quotes Isa. 9:1f., and applies the words about the deliverer from Assyria to the Messiah. "The same district lay in spiritual darkness and death and the new era dawned when Christ went thither" (McNeile). Light sprang up from those who were sitting in the region and shadow of death (*en chorāi kai skiāi thanatou*). Death is personified.

17. *Began Jesus to preach* (*ērxato ho Iēsous kērussein*). In Galilee. He had been preaching for over a year already elsewhere. His message carries on the words of the Baptist about "repentance" and the "kingdom of heaven" (Matt. 3:2) being at hand. The same word for "preaching" (*kērussein*) from *kērux*, herald, is used of Jesus as of John. Both proclaimed the good news of the kingdom. Jesus is more usually described as the Teacher, (*ho didaskalos*) who taught (*edidasken*) the people. He was both herald and teacher as every preacher should be.

18. *Casting a net into the sea* (*ballantas amphiblēstron eis tēn thalassan*). The word here for net is a casting-net (compare *amphiballō* in Mark. 1:16, casting on both sides). The net was thrown over the shoulder and spread into a circle (*amphi*). In 4:20 and 21 another word occurs for nets (*diktua*), a word used for nets of any kind. The large drag-net (*sagēnē*) appears in Matthew 13:47.

19. *Fishers of men* (*haleeis anthrōpōn*). Andrew and Simon were fishers by trade. They had already become disciples of Jesus (John 1:35–42), but now they are called upon to leave their business and to follow Jesus in his travels and work. These two brothers promptly (*eutheōs*) accepted the call and challenge of Jesus.

21. *Mending their nets* (*katartizontas ta diktua autōn*). These two brothers, James and John, were getting their nets

ready for use. The verb (*katartizō*) means to adjust, to articulate, to mend if needed (Luke 6:40; Rom. 9:22; Gal. 6:1). So they promptly left their boat and father and followed Jesus. They had also already become disciples of Jesus. Now there are four who follow him steadily.

23. *Went about in all Galilee* (*periēgen en holēi tēi Galilaiai*). Literally Jesus "was going around (imperfect) in all Galilee." This is the first of the three tours of Galilee made by Jesus. This time he took the four fishermen whom he had just called to personal service. The second time he took the twelve. On the third he sent the twelve on ahead by twos and followed after them. He was teaching and preaching the gospel of the kingdom in the synagogues chiefly and on the roads and in the streets where Gentiles could hear. *Healing all manner of diseases and all manner of sickness* (*therapeuōn pāsan noson kai pāsan malakian*). The occasional sickness is called *malakian*, the chronic or serious disease *noson*.

24. *The report of him went forth into all Syria* (*apēlthen hē akoē autou eis holēn tēn Syrian*). Rumour (*akoē*) carries things almost like the wireless or radio. The Gentiles all over Syria to the north heard of what was going on in Galilee. The result was inevitable. Jesus had a moving hospital of patients from all over Galilee and Syria. "*Those that were sick*" (*tous kakōs echontas*), literally "those who had it bad," cases that the doctors could not cure. "*Holden with divers diseases and torments*" (*poikilais nosois kai basanois sunechomenous*). "Held together" or "compressed" is the idea of the participle. The same word is used by Jesus in Luke 12:50 and by Paul in Phil. 1:23 and of the crowd pressing on Jesus (Luke 8:45). They brought these difficult and chronic cases (present tense of the participle here) to Jesus. Instead of "divers" say "various" (*poikilais*) like fever, leprosy, blindness. The adjective means literally many colored or variegated like flowers, paintings, jaundice, etc.

Some had "torments" (*basanois*). The word originally (oriental origin) meant a touchstone, "Lydian stone" used for testing gold because pure gold rubbed on it left a peculiar mark. Then it was used for examination by torture. Sickness was often regarded as "torture." These diseases are further described "in a descending scale of violence" (McNeile) as "demoniacs, lunatics, and paralytics" as Moffatt puts it, "demoniacs, epileptics, paralytics" as Weymouth has it (*daimonizomenous kai seleniazomenous kai paralutikous*), people possessed by demons, lunatics or "moon-struck" because the epileptic seizures supposedly followed the phases of the moon (Bruce) as shown also in Matt. 17:15, paralytics (our very word). Our word "lunatic" is from the Latin *luna* (moon) and carries the same picture as the Greek *seleniazomai* from *selene* (moon). These diseases are called "torments."

25. *Great multitudes* (*ochloi polloi*). Note the plural, not just one crowd, but crowds and crowds. And from all parts of Palestine including Decapolis, the region of the Ten Greek Cities east of the Jordan. No political campaign was equal to this outpouring of the people to hear Jesus and to be healed by Jesus.

CHAPTER V

1. *He went up into the mountain (anebē eis to oros).*
Not "a" mountain as the Authorized Version has it. The
Greek article is poorly handled in most English versions.
We do not know what mountain it was. It was the one
there where Jesus and the crowds were. "Delitzsch calls
the Mount of Beatitudes the Sinai of the New Testament"
(Vincent). He apparently went up to get in closer contact
with the disciples, "seeing the multitudes." Luke (6:12)
says that he went out into the mountain to pray, Mark
(3:13) that he went up and called the twelve. All three
purposes are true. Luke adds that after a whole night in
prayer and after the choice of the twelve Jesus came down
to a level place on the mountain and spoke to the multitudes from Judea to Phoenicia. The crowds are great in
both Matthew and in Luke and include disciples and the
other crowds. There is no real difficulty in considering the
Sermon on the Mount in Matthew and the Sermon on the
Plain in Luke as one and the same. See full discussion in
my *Harmony of the Gospels.*

2. *Taught them (edidasken).* Inchoative imperfect, began
to teach. He sat down on the mountain side as the Jewish rabbis did instead of standing. It was a most impressive
scene as Jesus opened his mouth wide and spoke loud enough
for the great throng to hear him. The newly chosen twelve
apostles were there, "a great number of disciples and a great
number of the people" (Luke 6:17).

3. *Blessed (makarioi).* The English word "blessed" is
more exactly represented by the Greek verbal *eulogētoi* as
in Luke 1:68 of God by Zacharias, or the perfect passive
participle *eulogēmenos* as in Luke 1:42 of Mary by Eliza-

beth and in Matt. 21:9. Both forms come from *eulogeō*, to
speak well of (*eu, logos*). The Greek word here (*makarioi*)
is an adjective that means "happy" which in English
etymology goes back to hap, chance, good-luck as seen in
our words haply, hapless, happily, happiness. "Blessedness
is, of course, an infinitely higher and better thing than mere
happiness" (Weymouth). English has thus ennobled
"blessed" to a higher rank than "happy." But "happy"
is what Jesus said and the *Braid Scots New Testament* dares
to say "Happy" each time here as does the *Improved Edition
of the American Bible Union Version*. The Greek word is as
old as Homer and Pindar and was used of the Greek gods
and also of men, but largely of outward prosperity. Then it
is applied to the dead who died in the Lord as in Rev. 14:13.
Already in the Old Testament the Septuagint uses it of moral
quality. "Shaking itself loose from all thoughts of outward
good, it becomes the express symbol of a happiness identified with pure character. Behind it lies the clear cognition
of sin as the fountain-head of all misery, and of holiness as
the final and effectual cure for every woe. For knowledge
as the basis of virtue, and therefore of happiness, it substi-
tutes faith and love" (Vincent). Jesus takes this word
"happy" and puts it in this rich environment. "This is
one of the words which have been transformed and ennobled
by New Testament use; by association, as in the Beatitudes,
with unusual conditions, accounted by the world miserable,
or with rare and difficult" (Bruce). It is a pity that we have
not kept the word "happy" to the high and holy plane where
Jesus placed it. "If you know these things, happy (*makarioi*) are you if you do them" (John 13:17). "Happy
(*makarioi*) are those who have not seen and yet have believed" (John 20:29). And Paul applies this adjective to
God, "according to the gospel of the glory of the happy
(*makariou*) God" (I Tim. 1:11. Cf. also Tit. 2: 13). The
term "Beatitudes" (Latin *beatus*) comes close to the mean-

ing of Christ here by *makarioi*. It will repay one to make a
careful study of all the "beatitudes" in the New Testament
where this word is employed. It occurs nine times here
(3 to 11), though the beatitudes in verses 10 and 11 are
very much alike. The copula is not expressed in either of
these nine beatitudes. In each case a reason is given for the
beatitude, "for" (*hoti*), that shows the spiritual quality
involved. Some of the phrases employed by Jesus here
occur in the Psalms, some even in the Talmud (itself later
than the New Testament, though of separate origin). That
is of small moment. "The originality of Jesus lies in putting
the due value on these thoughts, collecting them, and making
them as prominent as the Ten Commandments. No
greater service can be rendered to mankind than to rescue
from obscurity neglected moral commonplaces" (Bruce).
Jesus repeated his sayings many times as all great teachers
and preachers do, but this sermon has unity, progress, and
consummation. It does not contain all that Jesus taught
by any means, but it stands out as the greatest single sermon
of all time, in its penetration, pungency, and power. *The
poor in spirit* (*hoi ptōchoi tōi pneumati*). Luke has only
"the poor," but he means the same by it as this form in
Matthew, "the pious in Israel, for the most part poor, whom
the worldly rich despised and persecuted" (McNeile). The
word used here (*ptōchoi*) is applied to the beggar Lazarus
in Luke 16:20, 22 and suggests spiritual destitution (from
ptōssō to crouch, to cower). The other word *penēs* is from
penomai, to work for one's daily bread and so means one
who works for his living. The word *ptōchos* is more frequent in the New Testament and implies deeper poverty
than *penēs*. "The kingdom of heaven" here means the
reign of God in the heart and life. This is the *summum
bonum* and is what matters most.

4. *They that mourn* (*hoi penthountes*). This is another
paradox. This verb "is most frequent in the LXX for

mourning for the dead, and for the sorrows and sins of others" (McNeile). "There can be no comfort where there is no grief" (Bruce). Sorrow should make us look for the heart and hand of God and so find the comfort latent in the grief.

5. *The meek* (*hoi praeis*). Wycliff has it "Blessed be mild men." The ancients used the word for outward conduct and towards men. They did not rank it as a virtue anyhow. It was a mild equanimity that was sometimes negative and sometimes positively kind. But Jesus lifted the word to a nobility never attained before. In fact, the Beatitudes assume a new heart, for the natural man does not find in happiness the qualities mentioned here by Christ. The English word "meek" has largely lost the fine blend of spiritual poise and strength meant by the Master. He calls himself "meek and lowly in heart" (Matt. 11:29) and Moses is also called meek. It is the gentleness of strength, not mere effeminacy. By "the earth" (*tēn gēn*) Jesus seems to mean the Land of Promise (Psa. 37:11) though Bruce thinks that it is the whole earth. Can it be the solid earth as opposed to the sea or the air?

6. *They that hunger and thirst after righteousness* (*hoi peinōntes kai dipsōntes tēn dikaiosunēn*). Here Jesus turns one of the elemental human instincts to spiritual use. There is in all men hunger for food, for love, for God. It is passionate hunger and thirst for goodness, for holiness. The word for "filled" (*chortasthēsontai*) means to feed or to fatten cattle from the word for fodder or grass like Mark 6:39 "green grass" (*chortos chlōros*).

7. *Obtain mercy* (*eleēthēsontai*) "Sal win pitie theirsels" (*Braid Scots*). "A self-acting law of the moral world" (Bruce).

8. *Shall see God* (*ton theon opsontai*). Without holiness no man will see the Lord in heaven (Heb. 12:14). The Beatific Vision is only possible here on earth to those with

pure hearts. No other can see the King now. Sin befogs
and beclouds the heart so that one cannot see God. Purity
has here its widest sense and includes everything.

9. *The peacemakers* (*hoi eirēnopoioi*). Not merely "peace-
able men" (Wycliff) but "makkers up o' strife" (*Braid
Scots*). It is hard enough to keep the peace. It is still more
difficult to bring peace where it is not. "The perfect peace-
maker is the Son of God (Eph. 2:14f.)" (McNeile). Thus
we shall be like our Elder Brother.

10. *That have been persecuted for righteousness' sake* (*hoi
dediōgmenoi heneken dikaiosunēs*). Posing as persecuted is a
favourite stunt. The kingdom of heaven belongs only to
those who suffer for the sake of goodness, not who are guilty
of wrong.

11. *Falsely, for my sake* (*pseudomenoi heneken emou*).
Codex Bezae changes the order of these last Beatitudes, but
that is immaterial. What does matter is that the bad things
said of Christ's followers shall be untrue and that they are
slandered for Christ's sake. Both things must be true before
one can wear a martyr's crown and receive the great reward
(*misthos*) in heaven. No prize awaits one there who deserves
all the evil said of him and done to him here.

13. *Lost its savour* (*mōranthēi*). The verb is from *mōros*
(dull, sluggish, stupid, foolish) and means to play the
fool, to become foolish, of salt become tasteless, insipid
(Mark 9:50). It is common in Syria and Palestine to see
salt scattered in piles on the ground because it has lost its
flavour, "hae tint its tang" (*Braid Scots*), the most worthless
thing imaginable. Jesus may have used here a current
proverb.

15. *Under the bushel* (*hupo ton modion*). Not *a* bushel.
"The figure is taken from lowly cottage life. There was a
projecting stone in the wall on which the lamp was set. The
house consisted of a single room, so that the tiny light suf-
ficed for all" (Bruce). It was not put under the bushel

(the only one in the room) save to put it out or to hide it. The bushel was an earthenware grain measure. "*The stand*" (*tēn luchnian*), not "candlestick." It is "lamp-stand" in each of the twelve examples in the Bible. There was the one lamp-stand for the single room.

16. *Even so* (*houtōs*). The adverb points backward to the lamp-stand. Thus men are to let their light shine, not to glorify themselves, but "your Father in heaven." Light shines to see others by, not to call attention to itself.

17. *I came not to destroy, but to fulfil* (*ouk ēlthon katalusai alla plērōsai*). The verb "destroy" means to "loosen down" as of a house or tent (II Cor. 5:1). Fulfil is to fill full. This Jesus did to the ceremonial law which pointed to him and the moral law he kept. "He came to fill the law, to reveal the full depth of meaning that it was intended to hold" (McNeile).

18. *One jot or one tittle* (*iōta hen ē mia kerea*). "Not an iota, not a comma" (Moffatt), "not the smallest letter, not a particle" (Weymouth). The iota is the smallest Greek vowel, which Matthew here uses to represent the Hebrew *yod* (jot), the smallest Hebrew letter. "Tittle" is from the Latin *titulus* which came to mean the stroke above an abbreviated word, then any small mark. It is not certain here whether *kerea* means a little horn, the mere point which distinguishes some Hebrew letters from others or the "hook" letter *Vav*. Sometimes *yod* and *vav* were hardly distinguishable. "In *Vay. R.* 19 the guilt of altering one of them is pronounced so great that if it were done the world would be destroyed" (McNeile).

19. *Shall do and teach* (*poiēsei kai didaxei*). Jesus puts practice before preaching. The teacher must apply the doctrine to himself before he is qualified to teach others. The scribes and Pharisees were men who "say and do not" (Matt. 23:3), who preach but do not perform. This is Christ's test of greatness.

20. *Shall exceed* (*perisseusei pleion*). Overflow like a river out of its banks and then Jesus adds "more" followed by an unexpressed ablative (*tēs dikaiosunēs*), brachylogy. A daring statement on Christ's part that they had to be better than the rabbis. They must excel the scribes, the small number of regular teachers (5:21–48), and the Pharisees in the Pharisaic life (6:1–18) who were the separated ones, the orthodox pietists.

22. *But I say unto you* (*egō de legō humin*). Jesus thus assumes a tone of superiority over the Mosaic regulations and proves it in each of the six examples. He goes further than the Law into the very heart. "*Raca*" (*Raka*) and "*Thou fool*" (*Mōre*). The first is probably an Aramaic word meaning "Empty," a frequent word for contempt. The second word is Greek (dull, stupid) and is a fair equivalent of "raca." It is urged by some that *mōre* is a Hebrew word, but Field (*Otium Norvicense*) objects to that idea. "*Raca* expresses contempt for a man's head = you stupid! *Mōre* expresses contempt for his heart and character=you scoundrel" (Bruce). "*The hell of fire*" (*tēn geennan tou puros*), "the Gehenna of fire," the genitive case (*tou puros*) as the genus case describing Gehenna as marked by fire. Gehenna is the Valley of Hinnom where the fire burned continually. Here idolatrous Jews once offered their children to Molech (II Kings 23:10). Jesus finds one cause of murder to be abusive language. Gehenna "should be carefully distinguished from Hades (*hāidēs*) which is never used for the place of punishment, but for *the place of departed spirits*, without reference to their moral condition" (Vincent). The place of torment is in Hades (Luke 16:23), but so is heaven.

24. *First be reconciled* (*prōton diallagēthi*). Second aorist passive imperative. Get reconciled (ingressive aorist, take the initiative). Only example of this compound in the New Testament where usually *katallassō* occurs. Deissmann (*Light from the Ancient East*, p. 187, New Ed.) gives a

papyrus example second century A.D. A prodigal son, Longinus, writes to his mother Nilus: "I beseech thee, mother, be reconciled (*dialagēti*) with me." The boy is a poor speller, but with a broken heart he uses the identical form that Jesus does. "The verb denotes mutual concession after mutual hostility, an idea absent from *katallassō*" (Lightfoot). This because of *dia* (two, between two).

25. *Agree with* (*isthi eunoōn*). A present periphrastic active imperative. The verb is from *eunoos* (friendly, kindly disposed). "Mak up wi' yere enemy" (*Braid Scots*). Compromise is better than prison where no principle is involved, but only personal interest. It is so easy to see principle where pride is involved.

The officer (*tōi hupēretēi*). This word means "under rower" on the ship with several ranks of rowers, the bottom rower (*hupo* under and *ēressō*, to row), the galley-slave, then any servant, the attendant in the synagogue (Luke 4:20). Luke so describes John Mark in his relation to Barnabas and Saul (Acts 13:5). Then it is applied to the "ministers of the word" (Luke 1:2).

26. *The last farthing* (*ton eschaton kodrantēn*). A Latin word, *quadrans*, ¼ of an *as* (*assarion*) or two mites (Mark 12:42), a vivid picture of inevitable punishment for debt. This is emphasized by the strong double negative *ou mē* with the aorist subjunctive.

27. *Thou shalt not commit adultery* (*ou moicheuseis*). These quotations (verses 21, 27, 33) from the Decalogue (Ex. 20 and Deut. 5) are from the Septuagint and use *ou* and the future indicative (volitive future, common Greek idiom). In 5:43 the positive form, volitive future, occurs (*agapēseis*). In 5:41 the third person (*dotō*) singular second aorist active imperative is used. In 5:38 no verb occurs.

28. *In his heart* (*en tēi kardiāi autou*). Not just the centre of the blood circulation though it means that. Not just the emotional part of man's nature, but here the inner

man including the intellect, the affections, the will. This word is exceedingly common in the New Testament and repays careful study always. It is from a root that means to quiver or palpitate. Jesus locates adultery in the eye and heart before the outward act. Wünsche (*Beiträge*) quotes two pertinent rabbinical sayings as translated by Bruce: "The eye and the heart are the two brokers of sin." "Passions lodge only in him who sees." Hence the peril of lewd pictures and plays to the pure.

29. *Causeth thee to stumble* (*skandalizei se*). This is far better than the Authorized Version "*Offend thee*." *Braid Scots* has it rightly "ensnare ye." It is not the notion of giving offence or provoking, but of setting a trap or snare for one. The substantive (*skandalon*, from *skandalēthron*) means the stick in the trap that springs and closes the trap when the animal touches it. Pluck out the eye when it is a snare, cut off the hand, even the right hand. These vivid pictures are not to be taken literally, but powerfully plead for self-mastery. Bengel says: *Non oculum, sed scandalizentem oculum.* It is not mutilating of the body that Christ enjoins, but control of the body against sin. The man who plays with fire will get burnt. Modern surgery finely illustrates the teaching of Jesus. The tonsils, the teeth, the appendix, to go no further, if left diseased, will destroy the whole body. Cut them out in time and the life will be saved. Vincent notes that "the words scandal and slander are both derived from *skandalon*. And Wyc. renders, 'if thy right eye *slander* thee.' " Certainly slander is a scandal and a stumbling-block, a trap, and a snare.

31. *A writing of divorcement* (*apostasion*), "a divorce certificate" (Moffatt), "a written notice of divorce" (Weymouth). The Greek is an abbreviation of *biblion apostasiou* (Matt. 19:7; Mark. 10:4). Vulgate has here *libellum repudii*. The papyri use *suggraphē apostasiou* in commercial transactions as "a bond of release" (see Moulton

and Milligan's *Vocabulary*, etc.)   The written notice (*biblion*)
was a protection to the wife against an angry whim of the
husband who might send her away with no paper to show
for it.

32. *Saving for the cause of fornication* (*parektos logou
porneias*).   An unusual phrase that perhaps means "except
for a matter of unchastity."   "Except on the ground of unchastity" (Weymouth), "except unfaithfulness" (Goodspeed), and is equivalent to *mē epi porneiāi* in Matt. 19:9.
McNeile denies that Jesus made this exception because
Mark and Luke do not give it.   He claims that the early
Christians made the exception to meet a pressing need,
but one fails to see the force of this charge against Matthew's report of the words of Jesus.   It looks like criticism
to meet modern needs.

34. *Swear not at all* (*mē omosai holōs*).   More exactly
"not to swear at all" (indirect command, and aorist infinitive).   Certainly Jesus does not prohibit oaths in a court of
justice for he himself answered Caiaphas on oath.   Paul
made solemn appeals to God (I Thess. 5:27; I Cor. 15:31).
Jesus prohibits all forms of profanity.   The Jews were past-
masters in the art of splitting hairs about allowable and forbidden oaths or forms of profanity just as modern Christians employ a great variety of vernacular "cuss-words"
and excuse themselves because they do not use the more
flagrant forms.

38. *An eye for an eye, and a tooth for a tooth* (*ophthalmon
anti ophthalmou kai odonta anti odontos*).   Note *anti* with
the notion of exchange or substitution.   The quotation is
from Ex. 21:24; Deut. 19:21; Lev. 24:20.   Like divorce this
jus talionis is a restriction upon unrestrained vengeance.
"It limited revenge by fixing an exact compensation for an
injury" (McNeile).   A money payment is allowed in the
Mishna.   The law of retaliation exists in Arabia today.

39. *Resist not him that is evil* (*me antistēnai tōi ponērōi*).

Here again it is the infinitive (second aorist active) in indirect command. But is it "the evil man" or the "evil deed"? The dative case is the same form for masculine and neuter. Weymouth puts it "not to resist a (the) wicked man," Moffatt "not to resist an injury," Goodspeed "not to resist injury." The examples will go with either view. Jesus protested when smitten on the cheek (John 18:22). And Jesus denounced the Pharisees (Matt. 23) and fought the devil always. The language of Jesus is bold and picturesque and is not to be pressed too literally. Paradoxes startle and make us think. We are expected to fill in the other side of the picture. One thing certainly is meant by Jesus and that is that personal revenge is taken out of our hands, and that applies to "lynch-law." Aggressive or offensive war by nations is also condemned, but not necessarily defensive war or defence against robbery and murder. Professional pacifism may be mere cowardice.

40. *Thy coat . . . thy cloke also* (*ton chitōna sou kai to himation*). The "coat" is really a sort of shirt or undergarment and would be demanded at law. A robber would seize first the outer garment or cloke (one coat). If one loses the undergarment at law, the outer one goes also (the more valuable one).

41. *Shall compel thee* (*aggareusei*). The Vulgate has *angariaverit*. The word is of Persian origin and means public couriers or mounted messengers (*aggaroi*) who were stationed by the King of Persia at fixed localities, with horses ready for use, to send royal messages from one to another. So if a man is passing such a post-station, an official may rush out and compel him to go back to another station to do an errand for the king. This was called impressment into service. This very thing was done to Simon of Cyrene who was thus compelled to carry the cross of Christ (Matt. 27:32, *ēggareusan*).

42. *Turn not thou away* (*mē apostraphēis*). Second aorist

passive subjunctive in prohibition. "This is one of the
clearest instances of the necessity of accepting the spirit
and not the letter of the Lord's commands (see *vv.* 32, 34, 38).
Not only does indiscriminate almsgiving do little but injury to society, but the words must embrace far more than
almsgiving" (McNeile). Recall again that Jesus is a popular teacher and expects men to understand his paradoxes.
In the organized charities of modern life we are in danger of
letting the milk of human kindness dry up.

43. *And hate thine enemy* (*kai miseseis*). This phrase
is not in Lev. 19:18, but is a rabbinical inference which
Jesus repudiates bluntly. The Talmud says nothing of love
to enemies. Paul in Rom. 12:20 quotes Prov. 25:22 to prove
that we ought to treat our enemies kindly. Jesus taught us
to pray for our enemies and did it himself even when he hung
upon the cross. Our word "neighbour" is "nigh-bor," one
who is nigh or near like the Greek word *plesion* here. But
proximity often means strife and not love. Those who have
adjoining farms or homes may be positively hostile in spirit.
The Jews came to look on members of the same tribe as
neighbours as even Jews everywhere. But they hated the
Samaritans who were half Jews and lived between Judea
and Galilee. Jesus taught men how to act as neighbours by
the parable of the Good Samaritan (Luke 10:29ff.).

48. *Perfect* (*teleioi*). The word comes from *telos*, end,
goal, limit. Here it is the goal set before us, the absolute
standard of our Heavenly Father. The word is used also
for relative perfection as of adults compared with children.

CHAPTER VI

1. *Take heed* (*prosechete*). The Greek idiom includes "mind" (*noun*) which is often expressed in ancient Greek and once in the Septuagint (Job 7:17). In the New Testament the substantive *nous* is understood. It means to "hold the mind on a matter," take pains, take heed. "Righteousness" (*dikaiosunēn*) is the correct text in this verse. Three specimens of the Pharisaic "righteousness" are given (alms, prayer, fasting). *To be seen* (*theathēnai*). First aorist passive infinitive of purpose. Our word *theatrical* is this very word, spectacular performance. *With your Father* (*para tōi patri humōn*). Literally "beside your Father," standing by his side, as he looks at it.

2. *Sound not a trumpet* (*mē salpisēis*). Is this literal or metaphorical? No actual instance of such conduct has been found in the Jewish writings. McNeile suggests that it may refer to the blowing of trumpets in the streets on the occasion of public fasts. Vincent suggests the thirteen trumpet-shaped chests of the temple treasury to receive contributions (Luke 21:2). But at Winona Lake one summer a missionary from India named Levering stated to me that he had seen Hindu priests do precisely this very thing to get a crowd to see their beneficences. So it looks as if the rabbis could do it also. Certainly it was in keeping with their love of praise. And Jesus expressly says that "the hypocrites" (*hoi hupokritai*) do this very thing. This is an old word for actor, interpreter, one who personates another, from *hupokrinomai* to answer in reply like the Attic *apokrinomai*. Then to pretend, to feign, to dissemble, to act the hypocrite, to wear a mask. This is the hardest word that

Jesus has for any class of people and he employs it for these pious pretenders who pose as perfect. *They have received their reward (apechousin ton misthon autōn).* This verb is common in the papyri for receiving a receipt, "they have their receipt in full," all the reward that they will get, this public notoriety. "They can sign the receipt of their reward" (Deissmann, *Bible Studies*, p. 229). So *Light from the Ancient East*, pp. 110f. *Apochē* means "receipt." So also in 6:5.

4. *In secret (tōi kruptōi).* The Textus Receptus added the words *en tōi phanerōi* (openly) here and in 6:6, but they are not genuine. Jesus does not promise a *public* reward for private piety.

5. *In the synagogues and in the corners of the streets (en tais sunagōgais kai en tais gōniais tōn plateiōn).* These were the usual places of prayer (synagogues) and the street corners where crowds stopped for business or talk. If the hour of prayer overtook a Pharisee here, he would strike his attitude of prayer like a modern Moslem that men might see that he was pious.

6. *Into thy closet (eis to tameion).* The word is a late syncopated form of *tamieion* from *tamias* (steward) and the root *tam-* from *temnō*, to cut. So it is a store-house, a separate apartment, one's private chamber, closet, or "den" where he can withdraw from the world and shut the world out and commune with God.

7. *Use not vain repetitions (mē battalogēsēte).* Used of stammerers who repeat the words, then mere babbling or chattering, empty repetition. The etymology is uncertain, but it is probably onomatopoetic like "babble." The worshippers of Baal on Mount Carmel (I Kings 8:26) and of Diana in the amphitheatre at Ephesus who yelled for two hours (Acts 19:34) are examples. The Mohammedans may also be cited who seem to think that they "will be heard for their much speaking" (*en tēi polulogiāi*). Vincent adds

"and the Romanists with their *paternosters* and *aves*." The Syriac Sinaitic has it: "Do not be saying idle things." Certainly Jesus does not mean to condemn all repetition in prayer since he himself prayed three times in Gethsemane "saying the same words again" (Matt. 26:44). "As the Gentiles do," says Jesus. "The Pagans thought that by endless repetitions and many words they would inform their gods as to their needs and weary them (*'fatigare deos'*) into granting their requests" (Bruce).

9. *After this manner therefore pray ye* (*houtōs oun proseuchesthe humeis*). "You" expressed in contrast with "the Gentiles." It should be called "The Model Prayer" rather than "The Lord's Prayer." "Thus" pray as he gives them a model. He himself did not use it as a liturgy (cf. John 17). There is no evidence that Jesus meant it for liturgical use by others. In Luke 11:2-4 practically the same prayer though briefer is given at a later time by Jesus to the apostles in response to a request that he teach them how to pray. McNeile argues that the form in Luke is the original to which Matthew has made additions: "The tendency of liturgical formulas is towards enrichment rather than abbreviation." But there is no evidence whatever that Jesus designed it as a set formula. There is no real harm in a liturgical formula if one likes it, but no one sticks to just one formula in prayer. There is good and not harm in children learning and saying this noble prayer. Some people are disturbed over the words "Our Father" and say that no one has a right to call God Father who has not been "born again." But that is to say that an unconverted sinner cannot pray until he is converted, an absurd contradiction. God is the Father of all men in one sense; the recognition of Him as the Father in the full sense is the first step in coming back to him in regeneration and conversion.

Hallowed be thy name (*hagiasthētō to onoma sou*). In the Greek the verb comes first as in the petitions in verse 10.

They are all aorist imperatives, punctiliar action expressing urgency.

11. *Our daily bread* (*ton arton hēmōn ton epiousion*). This adjective "daily" (*epiousion*) coming after "Give us this day" (*dos hēmin sēmeron*) has given expositors a great deal of trouble. The effort has been made to derive it from *epi* and *ōn* (*ousa*). It clearly comes from *epi* and *iōn* (*epi* and *eimi*) like *tēi epiousēi* ("on the coming day," "the next day," Acts 16:12). But the adjective *epiousios* is rare and Origen said it was made by the Evangelists Matthew and Luke to reproduce the idea of an Aramaic original. Moulton and Milligan, *Vocabulary* say: "The papyri have as yet shed no clear light upon this difficult word (Matt. 6:11; Luke. 11:3), which was in all probability a new coinage by the author of the Greek Q to render his Aramaic Original" (this in 1919). Deissmann claims that only about fifty purely New Testament or "Christian" words can be admitted out of the more than 5,000 used. "But when a word is not recognizable at sight as a Jewish or Christian new formation, we must consider it as an ordinary Greek word until the contrary is proved. *Epiousios* has all the appearance of a word that originated in trade and traffic of the everyday life of the people (cf. my hints in *Neutestamentliche Studien Georg Heinrici dargebracht*, Leipzig, 1914, pp. 118f.). The opinion here expressed has been confirmed by A. Debrunner's discovery (*Theol. Lit. Ztg.* 1925, Col. 119) of *epiousios* in an ancient housekeeping book" (*Light from the Ancient East*, New ed. 1927, p. 78 and note 1). So then it is not a word coined by the Evangelist or by Q to express an Aramaic original. The word occurs also in three late MSS. after II Macc. 1:8, *tous epiousious* after *tous artous*. The meaning, in view of the kindred participle (*epiousēi*) in Acts 16:12, seems to be "for the coming day," a daily prayer for the needs of the next day as every housekeeper understands like the housekeeping book discovered by Debrunner.

12. *Our debts* (*ta opheilēmata hēmōn*). Luke (11:4) has "sins" (*hamartias*). In the ancient Greek *opheilēma* is common for actual legal debts as in Rom. 4:4, but here it is used of moral and spiritual debts to God. "Trespasses" is a mistranslation made common by the Church of England Prayer Book. It is correct in verse 14 in Christ's argument about prayer, but it is not in the Model Prayer itself. See Matt. 18:28, 30 for sin pictured again by Christ "as debt and the sinner as a debtor" (Vincent). We are thus described as having wronged God. The word *opheilē* for moral obligation was once supposed to be peculiar to the New Testament. But it is common in that sense in the papyri (Deismann, *Bible Studies*, p. 221; *Light from the Ancient East*, New ed., p. 331). We ask forgiveness "in proportion as" (*hōs*) we *also* have forgiven those in debt to us, a most solemn reflection. *Aphēkamen* is one of the three k aorists (*ethēka, edōka, hēka*). It means to send away, to dismiss, to wipe off.

13. *And bring us not into temptation* (*kai mē eisenegkēis eis peirasmon*). "Bring" or "lead" bothers many people. It seems to present God as an active agent in subjecting us to temptation, a thing specifically denied in James 1:13. The word here translated "temptation" (*peirasmon*) means originally "trial" or "test" as in James 1:2 and Vincent so takes it here. *Braid Scots* has it: "And lat us no be siftit." But God does test or sift us, though he does not tempt us to evil. No one understood temptation so well as Jesus for the devil tempted him by every avenue of approach to all kinds of sin, but without success. In the Garden of Gethsemane Jesus will say to Peter, James, and John: "Pray that ye enter not into temptation" (Luke 22:40). That is the idea here. Here we have a "Permissive imperative" as grammarians term it. The idea is then: "Do not allow us to be led into temptation." There is a way out (I Cor. 10:13), but it is a terrible risk.

From the evil one (apo tou ponērou). The ablative case
in the Greek obscures the gender. We have no way of knowing whether it is *ho ponēros* (the evil one) or *to ponēron* (the
evil thing). And if it is masculine and so *ho ponēros*, it can
either refer to the devil as the Evil One *par excellence* or the
evil man whoever he may be who seeks to do us ill. The
word *ponēros* has a curious history coming from *ponos*
(toil) and *poneō* (to work). It reflects the idea either that
work is bad or that this particular work is bad and so the
bad idea drives out the good in work or toil, an example of
human depravity surely.

The Doxology is placed in the margin of the Revised Version. It is wanting in the oldest and best Greek manuscripts.
The earliest forms vary very much, some shorter, some longer
than the one in the Authorized Version. The use of a doxology arose when this prayer began to be used as a liturgy
to be recited or to be chanted in public worship. It was
not an original part of the Model Prayer as given by
Jesus.

14. *Trespasses (paraptōmata)*. This is no part of the
Model Prayer. The word "trespass" is literally "falling
to one side," a lapse or deviation from truth or uprightness.
The ancients sometimes used it of intentional falling or
attack upon one's enemy, but "slip" or "fault" (Gal. 6:1)
is the common New Testament idea. *Parabasis* (Rom.
5:14) is a positive violation, a transgression, conscious
stepping aside or across.

16. *Of a sad countenance (skuthrōpoi)*. Only here and
Luke 24:17 in the N.T. It is a compound of *skuthros* (sullen)
and *ops* (countenance). These actors or hypocrites "put
on a gloomy look" (Goodspeed) and, if necessary, even
"disfigure their faces" (*aphanizousin ta prosōpa autōn*), that
they may look like they are fasting. It is this pretence of
piety that Jesus so sharply ridicules. There is a play on the
Greek words *aphanizousi* (disfigure) and *phanōsin* (figure).

They conceal their real looks that they may seem to be fasting, conscious and pretentious hypocrisy.

18. *In secret* (*en tōi kruphaiōi*). Here as in 6:4 and 6 the Textus Receptus adds *en tōi phanerōi* (openly), but it is not genuine. The word *kruphaios* is here alone in the New Testament, but occurs four times in the Septuagint.

19. *Lay not up for yourselves treasures* (*mē thēsaurizete hūmin thēsaurous*). Do not have this habit (*mē* and the present imperative). See on Matt. 2:11 for the word "treasure." Here there is a play on the word, "treasure not for yourselves treasures." Same play in verse 20 with the cognate accusative. In both verses *hūmin* is dative of personal interest and is not reflexive, but the ordinary personal pronoun. Wycliff has it: "Do not treasure to you treasures." *Break through* (*diorussousin*). Literally "dig through." Easy to do through the mud walls or sun-dried bricks. Today they can pierce steel safes that are no longer safe even if a foot thick. The Greeks called a burglar a "mud-digger" (*toichoruchos*).

20. *Rust* (*brōsis*). Something that "eats" (*bibrōskō*) or "gnaws" or "corrodes."

22. *Single* (*haplous*). Used of a marriage contract when the husband is to repay the dowry "pure and simple" (*tēn phernēn haplēn*), if she is set free; but in case he does not do so promptly, he is to add interest also (Moulton and Milligan's *Vocabulary*, etc.). There are various other instances of such usage. Here and in Luke 11:34 the eye is called "single" in a moral sense. The word means "without folds" like a piece of cloth unfolded, *simplex* in Latin. Bruce considers this parable of the eye difficult. "The figure and the ethical meaning seem to be mixed up, moral attributes ascribed to the physical eye which with them still gives light to the body. This confusion may be due to the fact that the eye, besides being the organ of vision, is the seat of expression, revealing inward dispositions." The "evil"

eye (*ponēros*) may be diseased and is used of stinginess in the LXX and so *haplous* may refer to liberality as Hatch argues (*Essays in Biblical Greek*, p. 80). The passage may be elliptical with something to be supplied. If our eyes are healthy we see clearly and with a single focus (without astigmatism). If the eyes are diseased (bad, evil), they may even be cross-eyed or cock-eyed. We see double and confuse our vision. We keep one eye on the hoarded treasures of earth and roll the other proudly up to heaven. Seeing double is double-mindedness as is shown in verse 24.

24. *No man can serve two masters* (*oudeis dunatai dusi kuriois douleuein*). Many try it, but failure awaits them all. Men even try "to be slaves to God and mammon" (*Theōi douleuein kai mamōnāi*). Mammon is a Chaldee, Syriac, and Punic word like *Plutus* for the money-god (or devil). The slave of mammon will obey mammon while pretending to obey God. The United States has had a terrible revelation of the power of the money-god in public life in the Sinclair-Fall-Teapot-Air-Dome-Oil case. When the guide is blind and leads the blind, both fall into the ditch. The man who cannot tell road from ditch sees falsely as Ruskin shows in *Modern Painters. He will hold to one* (*henos anthexetai*). The word means to line up face to face (*anti*) with one man and so against the other.

25. *Be not anxious for your life* (*mē merimnate tēi psuchēi hūmōn*). This is as good a translation as the Authorized Version was poor; "Take no thought for your life." The old English word "thought" meant anxiety or worry as Shakespeare says:

> "The native hue of resolution
> Is sicklied o'er with the pale cast of thought."

Vincent quotes Bacon (Henry VII): "Harris, an alderman of London, was put in trouble and died with thought and anguish." But words change with time and now this passage is actually quoted (Lightfoot) "as an objection to the moral teaching of the Sermon on the Mount, on the ground that it encouraged, nay, commanded, a reckless neglect of the future." We have narrowed the word to mere planning without any notion of anxiety which is in the Greek word. The verb *merimnaō* is from *meris, merizō,* because care or anxiety distracts and divides. It occurs in Christ's rebuke to Martha for her excessive solicitude about something to eat (Luke 10:41). The notion of proper care and forethought appears in I Cor. 7:32; 12:25; Phil. 2:20. It is here the present imperative with the negative, a command not to have the habit of petulant worry about food and clothing, a source of anxiety to many housewives, a word for women especially as the command not to worship mammon may be called a word for men. The command can mean that they must stop such worry if already indulging in it. In verse 31 Jesus repeats the prohibition with the ingressive aorist subjunctive: "Do not become anxious," "Do not grow anxious." Here the direct question with the deliberative subjunctive occurs with each verb (*phagōmen, piōmen, peribalōmetha*). This deliberative subjunctive of the direct question is retained in the indirect question employed in verse 25. A different verb for clothing occurs, both in the indirect middle (*peribalōmetha,* fling round ourselves in 31, *endusēsthe,* put on yourselves in 25). *For your life (tēi psuchēi).* "Here *psuchē* stands for the life principle common to man and beast, which is embodied in the *sōma:* the former needs food, the latter clothing" (McNeile). *Psuchē* in the Synoptic Gospels occurs in three senses (McNeile): either the life principle in the body as here and which man may kill (Mark 3:4) or the seat of the thoughts and emotions on a par with *kardia* and *dianoia* (Matt. 22:37) and *pneuma* (Luke 1:46; cf. John 12:27 and 13:21) or something higher that makes up the real self (Matt. 10:28; 16:26). In Matt. 16:25 (Luke 9:25) *psuchē* appears in two senses paradoxical use, saving life and losing it.

27. *Unto his stature* (*epi tēn hēlikian autou*).   The word *hēlikian* is used either of height (stature) or length of life (age).   Either makes good sense here, though probably "stature" suits the context best.   Certainly anxiety will not help either kind of growth, but rather hinder by auto-intoxication if nothing more.   This is no plea for idleness, for even the birds are diligent and the flowers grow.

28. *The lilies of the field* (*ta krina tou agrou*).   The word may include other wild flowers besides lilies, blossoms like anemones, poppies, gladioli, irises (McNeile).

29. *Was not arrayed* (*oude periebaleto*).   Middle voice and so "did not clothe himself," "did not put around himself."

30. *The grass of the field* (*ton chorton tou agrou*).   The common grass of the field.   This heightens the comparison.

33. *First his kingdom* (*prōton tēn basileian*).   This in answer to those who see in the Sermon on the Mount only ethical comments.   Jesus in the Beatitudes drew the picture of the man with the new heart.   Here he places the Kingdom of God and his righteousness before temporal blessings (food and clothing).

34. *For the morrow* (*eis tēn aurion*).   The last resort of the anxious soul when all other fears are allayed.   The ghost of tomorrow stalks out with all its hobgoblins of doubt and distrust.

CHAPTER VII

1. *Judge not* (*mē krinete*). The habit of censoriousness, sharp, unjust criticism. Our word critic is from this very word. It means to separate, distinguish, discriminate. That is necessary, but pre-judice (pre-judgment) is unfair, captious criticism.

3. *The mote* (*to karphos*). Not dust, but a piece of dried wood or chaff, splinter (Weymouth, Moffatt), speck (Goodspeed), a very small particle that may irritate. *The beam* (*tēn dokon*). A log on which planks in the house rest (so papyri), joist, rafter, plank (Moffatt), pole sticking out grotesquely. Probably a current proverb quoted by Jesus like our people in glass houses throwing stones. Tholuck quotes an Arabic proverb: "How seest thou the splinter in thy brother's eye, and seest not the cross-beam in thine eye?"

5. *Shalt thou see clearly* (*diablepseis*). Only here and Luke 6:42 and Mark 8:25 in the New Testament. Look through, penetrate in contrast to *blepeis,* to gaze at, in verse 3. Get the log out of your eye and you will see clearly how to help the brother get the splinter out (*ekbalein*) of his eye.

6. *That which is holy unto the dogs* (*to hagion tois kusin*). It is not clear to what "the holy" refers, to ear-rings or to amulets, but that would not appeal to dogs. Trench (*Sermon on the Mount*, p. 136) says that the reference is to meat offered in sacrifice that must not be flung to dogs: "It is not that the dogs would not eat it, for it would be welcome to them; but that it would be a profanation to give it to them, thus to make it a *skubalon*, Exod. 22:31." The yelping dogs would jump at it. Dogs are kin to wolves and infest the streets of oriental cities. *Your pearls before the swine* (*tous margaritas hūmōn emprosthen tōn choirōn*). The word

60

pearl we have in the name Margarita (Margaret). Pearls
look a bit like peas or acorns and would deceive the hogs
until they discovered the deception. The wild boars haunt
the Jordan Valley still and are not far removed from bears
as they trample with their feet and rend with their tusks
those who have angered them.

9. *Loaf—stone* (*arton—lithon*). Some stones look like
loaves of bread. So the devil suggested that Jesus make
loaves out of stones (Matt. 4:3).

10. *Fish—serpent* (*ichthun—ophin*). Fish, common article of food, and water-snakes could easily be substituted.
Anacoluthon in this sentence in the Greek.

11. *How much more* (*posōi mallon*). Jesus is fond of the
a fortiori argument.

12. *That men should do unto you* (*hina poiōsin hūmīn hoi
anthrōpoi*). Luke (6:31) puts the Golden Rule parallel with
Matt. 5:42. The negative form is in Tobit 4:15. It was
used by Hillel, Philo, Isocrates, Confucius. "The Golden
Rule is the distilled essence of that 'fulfilment' (5:17) which
is taught in the sermon" (McNeile). Jesus puts it in positive form.

13. *By the narrow gate* (*dia tēs stenēs pulēs*). The
Authorized Version "at the strait gate" misled those who
did not distinguish between "strait" and "straight." The
figure of the Two Ways had a wide circulation in Jewish
and Christian writings (cf. Deut. 30:19; Jer. 21:8; Psa. 1).
See the *Didache* i–vi; Barnabas xviii–xx. "The narrow gate"
is repeated in verse 14 and *straitened the way* (*tethlim-
menē hē hodos*) added. The way is "compressed," narrowed as in a defile between high rocks, a tight place like
stenochōria in Rom. 8:35. "The way that leads to life involves straits and afflictions" (McNeile). Vincent quotes
the *Pinax* or *Tablet* of Cebes, a contemporary of Socrates:
"Seest thou not, then, a little door, and a way before the
door, which is not much crowded, but very few travel it?

This is the way that leadeth unto true culture." "The broad way" (*euruchōros*) is in every city, town, village, with the glaring white lights that lure to destruction.

15. *False prophets* (*tōn pseudoprophētōn*). There were false prophets in the time of the Old Testament prophets. Jesus will predict "false Messiahs and false prophets" (Matt. 24:24) who will lead many astray. They came in due time posing as angels of light like Satan, Judaizers (II Cor. 11:13ff.) and Gnostics (I John 4: 1; I Tim. 4:1). Already false prophets were on hand when Jesus spoke on this occasion (cf. Acts 13:6; II Pet. 2:1). In outward appearance they look like sheep in the sheep's clothing which they wear, but within they are "ravening wolves" (*lukoi harpages*), greedy for power, gain, self. It is a tragedy that such men and women reappear through the ages and always find victims. Wolves are more dangerous than dogs and hogs.

16 and 20. *By their fruits ye shall know them* (*apo tōn karpōn autōn epignōsesthe*). "From their fruits you will recognize them." The verb "know" (*ginōskō*) has *epi* added, fully know. The illustrations from the trees and vines have many parallels in ancient writers.

21. *Not—but* (*ou—all'*). Sharp contrast between the mere talker and the doer of God's will.

22. *Did we not prophesy in thy name?* (*ou tōi sōi onomati eprophēteusamen;*). The use of *ou* in the question expects the affirmative answer. They claim to have prophesied (preached) in Christ's name and to have done many miracles. But Jesus will tear off the sheepskin and lay bare the ravening wolf. "I never knew you" (*oudepote egnōn hūmās*). "I was never acquainted with you" (experimental knowledge). Success, as the world counts it, is not a criterion of one's knowledge of Christ and relation to him. "I will profess unto them" (*homologēsō autois*), the very word used of profession of Christ before men (Matt. 10:32). This

word Jesus will use for public and open announcement of their doom.

24. *And doeth them (kai poiei autous).* That is the point in the parable of the wise builder, "who digged and went deep, and laid a foundation upon the rock" (Luke 6:48).

25. *Was founded (tethemeliōto).* Past perfect indicative passive state of completion in the past. It had been built upon the rock and it stood. No augment.

26. *And doeth them not (kai mē poiōn autous).* The foolish builder put his house on the sands that could not hold in the storm. One is reminded of the words of Jesus at the beginning of the Sermon in 5:19 about the one "who does and teaches." Hearing sermons is a dangerous business if one does not put them into practice.

28. *The multitudes were astonished (exeplēssonto hoi ochloi).* They listened spell-bound to the end and were left amazed. Note the imperfect tense, a buzz of astonishment. The verb means literally "were struck out of themselves."

29. *And not as their scribes (kai ouch hōs hoi grammateis autōn).* They had heard many sermons before from the regular rabbis in the synagogues. We have specimens of these discourses preserved in the Mishna and Gemara, the Jewish Talmud when both were completed, the driest, dullest collection of disjointed comments upon every conceivable problem in the history of mankind. The scribes quoted the rabbis before them and were afraid to express an idea without bolstering it up by some predecessor. Jesus spoke with the authority of truth, the reality and freshness of the morning light, and the power of God's Spirit. This sermon which made such a profound impression ended with the tragedy of the fall of the house on the sand like the crash of a giant oak in the forest. There was no smoothing over the outcome.

CHAPTER VIII

2. *If thou wilt* (*ean theleis*). The leper knew that Jesus had the power to heal him. His doubt was about his willingness. "Men more easily believe in miraculous power than in miraculous love" (Bruce). This is a condition of the third class (undetermined, but with prospect of being determined), a hopeful doubt at any rate. Jesus accepted his challenge by "I will." The command to "tell no one" was to suppress excitement and prevent hostility.

5. *Unto him* (*autōi*). Dative in spite of the genitive absolute *eiselthontos autou* as in verse 1, a not infrequent Greek idiom, especially in the *koiné*.

6. *Grievously tormented* (*deinōs basanizomenos*). Participle present passive from root *basanos* (see on Matt. 4:24). The boy (*pais*), slave (*doulos*, Luke 7.2), was a bedridden (*beblētai*, perfect passive indicative of *ballō*) paralytic.

7. *I will come and heal him* (*egō elthōn therapeusō auton*). Future indicative, not deliberative subjunctive in question (McNeile). The word here for heal (*therapeusō*) means first to serve, give medical attention, then cure, restore to health. The centurion uses the more definite word for healing (*iathē-setai* 8:8) as Matthew does in 8:13 (*iathē*). Luke (9:11), like a physician, says that Jesus healed (*iato*) those in need of treatment (*therapeias*), but the distinction is not always observed. In Acts 28:8 Luke uses *iasato* of the miraculous healings in Malta by Paul while he employs *etherapeuonto* (28:10) apparently of the practice of Luke the physician (so W. M. Ramsay). Matthew represents the centurion himself as speaking to Jesus while Luke has it that two committees from the centurion brought the messages, apparently

a more detailed narrative. What one does through others he does himself as Pilate "scourged Jesus" (had him scourged).

9. *For I also am a man under authority* (*kai gar egō anthrōpos hupo exousian*). "Also" is in the text, though the *kai* here may mean "even," even I in my subordinate position have soldiers under me. As a military man he had learned obedience to his superiors and so expected obedience to his commands, instant obedience (aorist imperatives and aoristic present indicatives). Hence his faith in Christ's power over the illness of the boy even without coming. Jesus had only to speak with a word (8:8), say the word, and it would be done.

10. *So great faith* (*tosautēn pistin*). In a Roman centurion and greater than in any of the Jews. In like manner Jesus marvelled at the great faith of the Canaanitish woman (Matt. 15:28).

11. *Sit down* (*anaklithēsontai*). Recline at table on couches as Jews and Romans did. Hence Leonardo da Vinci's famous picture of the Last Supper is an anachronism with all seated at table in modern style.

12. *The sons of the kingdom* (*hoi huioi tēs basileias*). A favourite Hebrew idiom like "son of hell" (Matt. 23:15), "sons of this age" (Luke 16:8). The Jews felt that they had a natural right to the privileges of the kingdom because of descent from Abraham (Matt. 3:9). But mere natural birth did not bring spiritual sonship as the Baptist had taught before Jesus did.

Into the outer darkness (*eis to skotos to exōteron*). Comparative adjective like our "further out," the darkness outside the limits of the lighted palace, one of the figures for hell or punishment (Matt. 23:13; 25:30). The repeated article makes it bolder and more impressive, "the darkness the outside," there where the wailing and gnashing of teeth is heard in the thick blackness of night.

14. *Lying sick of a fever* (*biblēmenēn kai puressousan*). Two participles, bedridden (perfect passive of *ballō*) and

burning with fever (present active). How long the fever had
had her we have no means of knowing, possibly a sudden and
severe attack (Mark. 1:30), as they tell Jesus about her on
reaching the house of Peter. We are not told what kind of
fever it was. Fever itself was considered a disease. "Fever"
is from German feuer (fire) like the Greek *pur*.

15. *Touched her hand* (*hēpsato tēs cheiros autēs*). In loving sympathy as the Great Physician and like any good
doctor today.

Ministered (*diēkonei*). "Began to minister" (conative
imperfect) at once to Jesus at table in gratitude and love.

16. *When even was come* (*opsias genomenēs*). Genitive
absolute. A beautiful sunset scene at the close of the Sabbath day (Mark 1:21). Then the crowds came as Jesus stood
in the door of Peter's house (Mark 1:33; Matt. 8:14) as all the
city gathered there with the sick, "all those who had it bad"
(see on Matt. 4:24) and he healed them "with a word" (*logōi*).
It was a never to be forgotten memory for those who saw it.

17. *Himself took our infirmities and bare our diseases* (*autos
tas astheneias elaben kai tas nosous ebastasen*). A quotation from Isa. 53:4. It is not clear in what sense Matthew
applies the words in Isaiah whether in the precise sense of
the Hebrew or in an independent manner. Moffatt translates it: "He took away our sicknesses, and bore the burden
of our diseases." Goodspeed puts it: "He took our sickness
and carried away our diseases." Deissmann (*Bible Studies*,
pp. 102f.) thinks that Matthew has made a free interpretation
of the Hebrew, has discarded the translation of the Septuagint, and has transposed the two Hebrew verbs so that
Matthew means: "He took upon himself our pains, and
bore our diseases." Plummer holds that "It is impossible,
and also unnecessary, to understand what the Evangelist
understood by 'took' (*elaben*) and 'bare' (*ebastasen*). It at
least must mean that Christ removed their sufferings from
the sufferers. He can hardly have meant that the diseases

were transferred to Christ." *Bastazō* occurs freely in the
papyri with the sense of lift, carry, endure, carry away (the
commonest meaning, Moulton and Milligan, *Vocabulary*),
pilfer. In Matt. 3:11 we have the common vernacular use
to take off sandals. The Attic Greek did not use it in the
sense of carrying off. "This passage is the cornerstone of
the faith-cure theory, which claims that the atonement of
Christ includes provision for *bodily* no less than for spiritual
healing, and therefore insists cn translating 'took away'"
(Vincent). We have seen that the word *bastazō* will possibly
allow that meaning, but I agree with McNeile: "The passage, *as Mt. employs it*, has no bearing on the doctrine of the
atonement." But Jesus does show his sympathy with us.
"Christ's sympathy with the sufferers was so intense that
he really felt their weaknesses and pains." In our burdens
Jesus steps under the load with us and helps us to carry on.

19. *A scribe* (*heis grammateus*). One (*heis*) = "a," indefinite article. Already a disciple as shown by "another
of the disciples" (*heteros tōn mathētōn*) in 8:21. He calls
Jesus "Teacher" (*didaskale*), but he seems to be a "bumptious" brother full of self-confidence and self-complacency.
"Even one of that most unimpressionable class, in spirit
and tendency utterly opposed to the ways of Jesus" (Bruce).
Yet Jesus deals gently with him.

20. *Holes* (*phōleous*). A lurking hole, burrow. *Nests*
(*kataskēnōseis*). "Roosts, i.e. leafy, *skēnai* for settling at
night (*tabernacula, habitacula*), not nests" (McNeile). In
the Septuagint it is used of God tabernacling in the Sanctuary. The verb (*kataskēnoō*) is there used of birds (Ps. 103:12).

The Son of man (*ho huios tou anthrōpou*). This remarkable expression, applied to himself by Jesus so often, appears
here for the first time. There is a considerable modern literature devoted to it. "It means much for the Speaker, who
has chosen it deliberately, in connection with private re-
flections, at whose nature we can only guess, by study of the

many occasions on which the name is used" (Bruce). Often
it means the Representative Man. It may sometimes stand
for the Aramaic *barnasha*, the man, but in most instances that
idea will not suit. Jesus uses it as a concealed Messianic
title. It is possible that this scribe would not understand
the phrase at all. Bruce thinks that here Jesus means "the
unprivileged Man," worse off than the foxes and the birds.
Jesus spoke Greek as well as Aramaic. It is inconceivable
that the Gospels should never call Jesus "the Son of man"
and always credit it to him as his own words if he did not
so term himself, about eighty times in all, thirty-three in
Matthew. Jesus in his early ministry, except at the very
start in John 4, abstains from calling himself Messiah. This
term suited his purpose exactly to get the people used to his
special claim as Messiah when he is ready to make it openly.

21. *And bury my father* (*kai thapsai ton patera mou*).
The first man was an enthusiast. This one is overcautious.
It is by no means certain that the father was dead. Tobit
urged his son Tobias to be sure to bury him: "Son, when I
am dead, bury me" (Tobit 4:3). The probability is that this
disciple means that, after his father is dead and buried, he
will then be free to follow Jesus. "At the present day, an
Oriental, with his father sitting by his side, has been known
to say respecting his future projects: 'But I must first bury
my father!'" (Plummer). Jesus wanted first things first.
But even if his father was not actually dead, service to
Christ comes first.

22. *Leave the dead to bury their own dead* (*aphes tous nekrous thapsai tous heautōn nekrous*). The spiritually dead are
always on hand to bury the physically dead, if one's real
duty is with Jesus. Chrysostom says that, while it is a good
deed to bury the dead, it is a better one to preach Christ.

24. *But he was asleep* (*autos de ekatheuden*). Imperfect,
was sleeping. Picturesque scene. The Sea of Galilee is 680
feet below the Mediterranean Sea. These sudden squalls

come down from the summit of Hermon with terrific force
(*seismos megas*) like an earthquake. Mark (4:37) and Luke
(8:23) term it a whirlwind (*lailaps*) in furious gusts.

25. *Save, Lord; we perish* (*Kurie, sōson, apollumetha*).
More exactly, "Lord, save us at once (aorist), we are perishing (present linear)."

27. *Even the winds and the sea obey him* (*Kai hoi anēmoi
kai hē thalassa autōi hupakouousin*). A nature miracle. Even
a sudden drop in the wind would not at once calm the sea.
"J. Weiss explains that by 'an astonishing coincidence' the
storm happened to lull at the moment that Jesus spoke!"
(McNeile). Some minds are easily satisfied by their own
stupidities.

28. *The country of the Gadarenes* (*tēn chōran tōn Gada-
rēnōn*). This is the correct text in Matthew while in Mark
5:1 and Luke 8:26 it is "the country of the Gerasenes."
Dr. Thomson discovered by the lake the ruins of Khersa
(Gerasa). This village is in the district of the city of Gadara
some miles southeastward so that it can be called after
Gerasa or Gadara. So Matthew speaks of "two demoniacs"
while Mark and Luke mention only one, the leading one.
"*The tombs*" (*tōn mnēmeiōn*) were chambers cut into the
mountain side common enough in Palestine then and now.
On the eastern side of the lake the precipitous cliffs are of
limestone formation and full of caves. It is one of the proofs
that one is a maniac that he haunts the tombs. People
shunned the region as dangerous because of the madmen.

29. *Thou Son of God* (*huie tou theou*). The recognition
of Jesus by the demons is surprising. The whole subject of
demonology is difficult. Some hold that it is merely the
ancient way of describing disease. But that does not explain
the situation here. Jesus is represented as treating the demons as real existences separate from the human personality.
Missionaries in China today claim that they have seen demons cast out. The devil knew Jesus clearly and it is not

strange that Jesus was recognized by the devil's agents. They know that there is nothing in common between them and the Son of God (*hēmin kai soi*, ethical dative) and they fear torment "before the time" (*pro kairou*). Usually *ta daimonia* is the word in the New Testament for demons, but in 8:31 we have *hoi daimones* (the only example in the N.T.). *Daimonion* is a diminutive of *daimōn*. In Homer *daimōn* is used synonymously with *theos* and *thea*. Hesiod employed *daimōn* of men of the golden age as tutelary deities. Homer has the adjective *daimonios* usually in an evil sense. Empedocles considered the demons both bad and good. They were thus used to relieve the gods and goddesses of much rascality. Grote (*History of Greece*) notes that the Christians were thus by pagan usage justified in calling idolatry the worship of demons. See I Cor. 10-20f.; I Tim. 4:1; Rev. 9:20; 16:13f. In the Gospels demons are the same as unclean spirits (Mark 5:12, 15; 3:22, 30; Luke 4:33). The demons are disturbers (Vincent) of the whole life of man (Mark 5:2f.; 7:25; Matt. 12:45; Luke 13:11, 16).

32. *Rushed down the steep* (*hōrmēsen kata tou krēmnou*). Down from the cliff (ablative case) into the sea. Constative aorist tense. The influence of mind on matter is now understood better than formerly, but we have the mastery of the mind of the Master on the minds of the maniacs, the power of Christ over the demons, over the herd of hogs. Difficulties in plenty exist for those who see only folk-lore and legend, but plain enough if we take Jesus to be really Lord and Saviour. The incidental destruction of the hogs need not trouble us when we are so familiar with nature's tragedies which we cannot comprehend.

34. *That he would depart* (*hopōs metabēi*). The whole city was excited over the destruction of the hogs and begged Jesus to leave, forgetful of the healing of the demoniacs in their concern over the loss of property. They cared more for hogs than for human souls, as often happens today.

CHAPTER IX

1. *His own city* (*tēn idian polin*). Capernaum (Mark 2:1; Matt. 4:13).

2. *They brought* (*prosepheron*). Imperfect, "were bringing," graphic picture made very vivid by the details in Mark 2:1–4 and Luke 5:17. "*Lying on a bed*" (stretched on a couch), perfect passive participle, a little bed or couch (*klinidion*) in Luke 5:19, "a pallet" (*krabatos*) in Mark 2:4, 9, 11. *Thy sins are forgiven* (*aphientai*). Present passive indicative (aoristic present). Luke (5:21) has *apheōntai*, Doric and Ionic perfect passive indicative for the Attic *apheintai*, one of the dialectical forms appearing in the *Koiné*.

3. *This man blasphemeth* (*houtos blasphēmei*). See the sneer in "this fellow." "The prophet always is a scandalous, irreverent blasphemer from the conventional point of view" (Bruce).

6. *That ye may know* (*hina eidēte*). Jesus accepts the challenge in the thoughts of the scribes and performs the miracle of healing the paralytic, who so far only had his sins forgiven, to prove his Messianic power on earth to forgive sins even as God does. The word *exousia* may mean either power or authority. He had both as a matter of fact. Note same word in 9:8. *Then saith he to the sick of the palsy* (*tote legei tōi paralutikōi*). These words of course, were not spoken by Jesus. Curiously enough Matthew interjects them right in the midst of the sayings of Jesus in reply to the scorn of the scribes. Still more remarkable is the fact that Mark (2:10) has precisely the same words in the same place save that Matthew has added *tote*, of which he is fond, to what Mark already had. Mark, as we know, largely reports Peter's words and sees with Peter's eyes. Luke has

the same idea in the same place without the vivid historical present *legei* (*eipen tōi paralelumenōi*) with the participle in place of the adjective. This is one of the many proofs that both Matthew and Luke made use of Mark's Gospel each in his own way. *Take up thy bed* (*āron sou tēn klinēn*). Pack up at once (aorist active imperative) the rolled-up pallet.

9. *At the place of toll* (*epi to telōnion*). The tax-office or custom-house of Capernaum placed here to collect taxes from the boats going across the lake outside of Herod's territory or from people going from Damascus to the coast, a regular caravan route. "*Called Matthew*" (*Maththaion legomenon*) and in 10:3 Matthew the publican is named as one of the Twelve Apostles. Mark (2:14) and Luke (5:27) call this man Levi. He had two names as was common, Matthew Levi. The publicans (*telōnai*) get their name in English from the Latin *publicanus* (a man who did public duty), not a very accurate designation. They were detested because they practised graft. Even Gabinius the proconsul of Syria was accused by Cicero of relieving Syrians and Jews of legitimate taxes for graft. He ordered some of the tax-officers removed. Already Jesus had spoken of the publican (5:46) in a way that shows the public disfavour in which they were held.

10. *Publicans and sinners* (*telōnai kai hamartōloi*). Often coupled together in common scorn and in contrast with the righteous (*dikaioi* in 9:13). It was a strange medley at Levi's feast (Jesus and the four fisher disciples, Nathanael and Philip; Matthew Levi and his former companions, publicans and sinners; Pharisees with their scribes or students as on-lookers; disciples of John the Baptist who were fasting at the very time that Jesus was feasting and with such a group). The Pharisees criticize sharply "your teacher" for such a social breach of "reclining" together with publicans at Levi's feast.

12. *But they that are sick (alla hoi kakōs echontes).* Probably a current proverb about the physician. As a physician of body and soul Jesus was bound to come in close touch with the social outcasts.

13. *But go ye and learn (poreuthentes de mathete).* With biting sarcasm Jesus bids these preachers to learn the meaning of Hos. 6:6. It is repeated in Matt. 12:7. Ingressive aorist imperative *(mathete).*

14. *The disciples of John (hoi mathētai Iōanou).* One is surprised to find disciples of the Baptist in the rôle of critics of Christ along with the Pharisees. But John was languishing in prison and they perhaps were blaming Jesus for doing nothing about it. At any rate John would not have gone to Levi's feast on one of the Jewish fast-days. "The strict asceticism of the Baptist (11:18) and of the Pharisaic rabbis (Luke 18:12) was imitated by their disciples" (McNeile).

15. *The sons of the bride-chamber (hoi huioi tou numphōnos).* It is a late Hebrew idiom for the wedding guests, "the friends of the bridegroom and all the sons of the bride-chamber" *(Tos. Berak.* ii. 10). Cf. John 2:29.

16. *Undressed cloth (rhakous agnaphou).* An unfulled, raw piece of woollen cloth that will shrink when wet and tear a bigger hole than ever. *A worse rent (cheiron schisma).* Our word "schism." The *"patch" (plērōma,* filling up) thus does more harm than good.

17. *Old wineskins (askous palaious).* Not glass *"bottles,"* but wineskins used as bottles as is true in Palestine yet, goatskins with the rough part inside. "Our word *bottle* originally carried the true meaning, being a bottle of leather. In Spanish *bota* means a *leather bottle,* a *boot,* and a *butt.* In Spain wine is still brought to market in pig-skins" (Vincent). The new wine will ferment and crack the dried-up old skins. *The wine is spilled (ekcheitai),* poured out.

18. *Is even now dead (arti eteleutēsen).* Aorist tense with

arti and so better, "just now died," "just dead" (Moffatt).
Mark (5:23) has it "at the point of death," Luke (8:42)
"lay a dying." It is not always easy even for physicians
to tell when actual death has come. Jesus in 9:24 pointedly
said, "The damsel is not dead, but sleepeth," meaning that
she did not die to stay dead.

20. *The border of his garment* (*tou kraspedou tou hima-
tiou*). The hem or fringe of a garment, a tassel or tuft hanging from the edge of the outer garment according to Numbers 15:38. It was made of twisted wool. Jesus wore the
dress of other people with these fringes at the four corners of
the outer garment. The Jews actually counted the words
Jehovah One from the numbers of the twisted white threads,
a refinement that Jesus had no concern for. This poor
woman had an element of superstition in her faith as many
people have, but Jesus honours her faith and cures her.

23. *The flute-players* (*tous auletas*). The girl was just
dead, but already a crowd "making a tumult" (*thoruboumenon*) with wild wailing and screaming had gathered in
the outer court, "brought together by various motives,
sympathy, money, desire to share in the meat and drink going at such a time" (Bruce). Besides the several flute-players
(voluntary or hired) there were probably "some hired mourning women (Jer. 9:17) *praeficae*, whose duty it was to sing
naenia in praise of the dead" (Bruce). These when put
out by Jesus, "laughed him to scorn" (*kategelon*), in a sort
of loud and repeated (imperfect) guffaw of scorn. Jesus
overcame all this repellent environment.

27. *As Jesus passed by* (*paragonti Iēsou*). Associative
instrumental case with *ēkolouthēsan*. It was the supreme
opportunity of these two blind men. Note two demoniacs
in Matt. 8:28 and two blind men in Matt. 20:30. See the
same word *paragōn* used of Jesus in 9:9.

29. *Touched their eyes* (*hēpsato tōn ophthalmōn*). The men
had faith (9:28) and Jesus rewards their faith and yet he

touched their eyes as he sometimes did with kindly sympathy.

30. *Were opened* (*ēneōichthēsan*). Triple augment (on *oi* = *ōi*, *e* and then on preposition *an* = *ēn*). *Strictly charged them* (*enebrimēthē autois*). A difficult word, compound of *en* and *brimaomai* (to be moved with anger). It is used of horses snorting (Aeschylus, *Theb.* 461), of men fretting or being angry (Dan. 11:30). Allen notes that it occurs twice in Mark (1:43; 14:5) when Matthew omits it. It is found only here in Matthew. John has it twice in a different sense (John 11:33 with *en heautōi*). Here and in Mark 1:32 it has the notion of commanding sternly, a sense unknown to ancient writers. Most manuscripts have the middle *enebrimēsato*, but Aleph and B have the passive *enebrimēthē* which Westcott and Hort accept, but without the passive sense (cf. *apekrithē*). "The word describes rather a rush of deep feeling which in the synoptic passages showed itself in a vehement injunctive and in John 11:33 in look and manner" (McNeile). Bruce translates Euthymius Zigabenus on Mark 1:32: "Looked severely, contracting His eyebrows, and shaking His head at them as they are wont to do who wish to make sure that secrets will be kept." "See to it, let no one know it" (*horate, mēdeis ginōsketō*). Note elliptical change of persons and number in the two imperatives.

32. *A dumb man* (*kōphon*). Literally blunted in tongue as here and so dumb, in ear as in Matt. 11:5 and so deaf. Homer used it of a blunted dart (*Iliad* xi. 390). Others applied it to mental dulness.

34. *By the prince of the devils* (*en tōi archonti tōn daimoniōn*). Demons, not devils. The codex Bezae omits this verse, but it is probably genuine. The Pharisees are becoming desperate and, unable to deny the reality of the miracles, they seek to discredit them by trying to connect Jesus with the devil himself, the prince of the demons.

They will renew this charge later (Matt. 12:24) when Jesus will refute it with biting sarcasm.

35. *And Jesus went about* (*kai periēgen ho Iēsous*). Imperfect tense descriptive of this third tour of all Galilee.

36. *Were distressed and scattered* (*ēsan eskulmenoi kai erimmenoi*). Periphrastic past perfect indicative passive. A sad and pitiful state the crowds were in. Rent or mangled as if by wild beasts. *Skullō* occurs in the papyri in sense of plunder, concern, vexation. "Used here of the common people, it describes their religious condition. They were harassed, importuned, bewildered by those who should have taught them; hindered from entering into the kingdom of heaven (23:13), laden with the burdens which the Pharisees laid upon them (23:3). *Erimmenoi* denotes men cast down and prostrate on the ground, whether from drunkenness, Polyb. v. 48.2, or from mortal wounds" (Allen): This perfect passive participle from *rhiptō*, to throw down. The masses were in a state of mental dejection. No wonder that Jesus was moved with compassion (*esplagchnisthē*).

38. *That he send forth labourers* (*hopōs ekbalēi ergatas*). Jesus turns from the figure of the shepherdless sheep to the harvest field ripe and ready for the reapers. The verb *ekballō* really means to drive out, to push out, to draw out with violence or without. Prayer is the remedy offered by Jesus in this crisis for a larger ministerial supply. How seldom do we hear prayers for more preachers. Sometimes God literally has to push or force a man into the ministry who resists his known duty.

CHAPTER X

1. *His twelve disciples (tous dōdeka mathētas autou).* First mention of the group of "learners" by Matthew and assumed as already in existence (note the article) as they were (Mark 3:14). They were chosen before the Sermon on the Mount was delivered, but Matthew did not mention it in connection with that sermon.

Gave them authority (edōken autois exousian). "Power" (Moffatt, Goodspeed). One may be surprised that here only the healing work is mentioned, though Luke (9:2) has it "to preach the kingdom of God, and to heal the sick." And Matthew says (10:7), "And as ye go, preach." Hence it is not fair to say that Matthew knows only the charge to heal the sick, important as that is. The physical distress was great, but the spiritual even greater. Power is more likely the idea of *exousia* here. This healing ministry attracted attention and did a vast deal of good. Today we have hospitals and skilled physicians and nurses, but we should not deny the power of God to bless all these agencies and to cure disease as he wills. Jesus is still the master of soul and body. But intelligent faith does not justify us in abstaining from the help of the physician who must not be confounded with the quack and the charlatan.

2. *The names of the twelve apostles (tōn dōdeka apostolōn ta onomata).* This is the official name (missionaries) used here by Matthew for the first time. The names are given here, but Matthew does not say that they were chosen at this time. Mark (3:13–19) and Luke (6:12–16) state that Jesus "chose" them, "appointed" them after a night of prayer in the mountain and came down with them and then delivered the Sermon (Luke 6:17). Simon heads the list (*prōtos*) in all

four lists including Acts 1:13f. He came to be first and foremost at the great Pentecost (Acts 2 and 3). The apostles disputed a number of times as to which was greatest. Judas Iscariot comes last each time save that he is absent in Acts, being already dead. Matthew calls him the betrayer (*ho paradidous*). Iscariot is usually explained as "man of Kerioth" down near Edom (Josh. 15:25). Philip comes fifth and James the son of Alphaeus the ninth. Bartholomew is the name for Nathanael. Thaddaeus is Judas the brother of James. Simon Zelotes is also called Simon the Canaanean (Zealous, Hebrew word). This is apparently their first preaching and healing tour without Jesus. He sends them forth by twos (Mark 6:7). Matthew names them in pairs, probably as they were sent out.

5. *These twelve Jesus sent forth* (*toutous tous dōdeka apesteilen ho Iēsous*). The word "sent forth" (*apesteilen*) is the same root as "apostles." The same word reappears in 10:16. *Way of the Gentiles* (*hodon ethnōn*). Objective genitive, way leading to the Gentiles. This prohibition against going among the Gentiles and the Samaritans was for this special tour. They were to give the Jews the first opportunity and not to prejudice the cause at this stage. Later Jesus will order them to go and disciple all the Gentiles (Matt. 28:19).

6. *The lost sheep* (*ta probata ta apolōlota*). The sheep, the lost ones. Mentioned here first by Matthew. Jesus uses it not in blame, but in pity (Bruce). Bengel notes that Jesus says "lost" more frequently than "led astray." "If the Jewish nation could be brought to repentance the new age would dawn" (McNeile).

7. *As ye go, preach* (*poreuomenoi kērussete*). Present participle and present imperative. They were itinerant preachers on a "preaching tour," heralds (*kērukes*) proclaiming good news. The summary message is the same as that of the Baptist (3:2) that first startled the country, "the kingdom of heaven has drawn nigh." He echoed it up and

down the Jordan Valley. They are to shake Galilee with it as Jesus had done (4:17). That same amazing message is needed today. But "the apprentice apostles" (Bruce) could tell not a little about the King of the Kingdom who was with them.

9. *Get you no gold* (*mē ktēsesthe*). It is not, "Do not possess" or "own," but "do not acquire" or "procure" for yourselves, indirect middle aorist subjunctive. Gold, silver, brass (copper) in a descending scale (nor even bronze). *In your purses* (*eis tas zōnas hūmōn*). In your girdles or belts used for carrying money.

10. *No wallet* (*mē pēran*). Better than "scrip." It can be either a travelling or bread bag. Deissmann (*Light from the Ancient East*, pp. 108f.) shows that it can mean the beggar's collecting bag as in an inscription on a monument at Kefr Hanar in Syria: "While Christianity was still young the beggar priest was making his rounds in the land of Syria on behalf of the national goddess." Deissmann also quotes a pun in the *Didaskalia = Const. Apost.* 3, 6 about some itinerant widows who said that they were not so much *chērai* (spouseless) as *pērai* (pouchless). He cites also Shakespeare, *Troilus and Cressida* III. iii. 145: "Time hath, my lord, a wallet at his back, wherein he puts alms for oblivion." *For the labourer is worthy of his food* (*axios gar ho ergatēs tēs trophēs autou*). The sermon is worth the dinner, in other words. Luke in the charge to the seventy (10:7) has the same words with *misthou* (reward) instead of *trophēs* (food). In I Tim. 5:18 Paul quotes Luke's form as scripture (*hē graphē*) or as a well-known saying if confined to the first quotation. The word for workman here (*ergatēs*) is that used by Jesus in the prayer for labourers (Matt. 9:38). The well-known *Didachē* or *Teaching of the Twelve* (xiii) shows that in the second century there was still a felt need for care on the subject of receiving pay for preaching. The travelling sophists added also to the embarrassment of the situation. The wisdom of these restrictions was justified in Galilee at

this time. Mark (6:6–13) and Luke (9:1–6) vary slightly from Matthew in some of the details of the instructions of Jesus.

13. *If the house be worthy* (*ean ēi hē oikia axia*). Third class condition. What makes a house worthy? "It would naturally be readiness to receive the preachers and their message" (McNeile). Hospitality is one of the noblest graces and preachers receive their share of it. The apostles are not to be burdensome as guests.

14. *Shake off the dust* (*ektinaxate ton koniorton*). Shake out, a rather violent gesture of disfavour. The Jews had violent prejudices against the smallest particles of Gentile dust, not as a purveyor of disease of which they did not know, but because it was regarded as the putrescence of death. If the apostles were mistreated by a host or hostess, they were to be treated as if they were Gentiles (cf. Matt. 18:17; Acts 18:6). Here again we have a restriction that was for this special tour with its peculiar perils.

15. *More tolerable* (*anektoteron*). The papyri use this adjective of a convalescent. People in their vernacular today speak of feeling "tolerable." The Galileans were having more privileges than Sodom and Gomorrah had.

16. *As sheep in the midst of wolves* (*hōs probata en mesōi lukōn*). The presence of wolves on every hand was a fact then and now. Some of these very sheep (10:6) at the end will turn out to be wolves and cry for Christ's crucifixion. The situation called for consummate wisdom and courage. The serpent was the emblem of wisdom or shrewdness, intellectual keenness (Gen. 3:1; Psa. 58:5), the dove of simplicity (Hosea 7:11). It was a proverb, this combination, but one difficult of realization. Either without the other is bad (rascality or gullibility). The first clause with *arnas* for *probata* is in Luke 10:3 and apparently is in a *Fragment of a Lost Gospel* edited by Grenfell and Hunt. The combination of wariness and innocence is necessary for the protec-

tion of the sheep and the discomfiture of the wolves.   For "harmless" (*akeraioi*) Moffatt and Goodspeed have "guileless," Weymouth "innocent." The word means "unmixed" (*a* privative and *kerannumi*), "unadulterated," "simple," "unalloyed."

17. *Beware of men* (*prosechete apo tōn anthrōpōn*). Ablative case with *apo*. Hold your mind (*noun* understood) away from. The article with *anthrōpōn* points back to *lukōn* (wolves) in 10:16.

To councils (*eis sunedria*). The local courts of justice in every Jewish town. The word is an old one from Herodotus on for any deliberative body (*concilium*). The same word is used for the Sanhedrin in Jerusalem. *In their synagogues* (*en tois sunagōgais autōn*). Here not merely as the place of assembly for worship, but as an assembly of justice exercising discipline as when the man born blind was cast out of the synagogue (John 9:35). They were now after the exile in every town of any size where Jews were.

19. *Be not anxious* (*mē merimnēsēte*). Ingressive aorist subjunctive in prohibition. "Do not become anxious" (Matt. 6:31). "Self-defence before Jewish kings and heathen governors would be a terrible ordeal for humble Galileans. The injunction applied to cases when preparation of a speech would be impossible" (McNeile). "It might well alarm the bravest of these simple fishermen to be told that they would have to answer for their doings on Christ's behalf before Jewish councils and heathen courts" (Plummer). Christ is not talking about preparation of sermons. *"In that hour"* (*en ekeinēi tēi hōrāi*), if not before. The Spirit of your Father will speak to you and through you (10:20). Here is no posing as martyr or courting a martyr's crown, but real heroism with full loyalty to Christ.

22. *Ye shall be hated* (*esesthe misoumenoi*). Periphrastic future passive, linear action. It will go on through the ages. *For my name's sake* (*dia to onoma mou*). In the O.T. as

in the Targums and the Talmud "the name" as here stands
for the person (Matt. 19:29; Acts 5:41; 9:16; 15:26). "He
that endureth to the end" (*ho hupomeinas eis telos*). Effective aorist participle with future indicative.

23. *Till the Son of man be come* (*heōs elthēi ho huios tou
anthrōpou*). Moffatt puts it "before the Son of man arrives"
as if Jesus referred to this special tour of Galilee. Jesus
could overtake them. Possibly so, but it is by no means
clear. Some refer it to the Transfiguration, others to the
coming of the Holy Spirit at Pentecost, others to the Second
Coming. Some hold that Matthew has put the saying in
the wrong context. Others bluntly say that Jesus was mistaken, a very serious charge to make in his instructions to
these preachers. The use of *heōs* with aorist subjunctive
for a future event is a good Greek idiom.

25. *Beelzebub* (*beezeboul* according to B, *beelzeboul* by most
Greek MSS., *beelzeboub* by many non-Greek MSS.). The
etymology of the word is also unknown, whether "lord of a
dwelling" with a pun on "the master of the house" (*oikodes-
potēn*) or "lord of flies" or "lord of dung" or "lord of idolatrous sacrifices." It is evidently a term of reproach. "An
opprobrious epithet; exact form of the word and meaning
of the name have given more trouble to commentators than
it is all worth" (Bruce). See Matt. 12:24.

26. *Fear them not therefore* (*mē oun phobēthēte autous*).
Repeated in verses 28 and 31 (*mē phobeisthe* present middle
imperative here in contrast with aorist passive subjunctive
in the preceding prohibitions). Note also the accusative
case with the aorist passive subjunctive, transitive though
passive. See same construction in Luke 12:5. In Matthew
10:28 the construction is with *apo* and the ablative, a translation Hebraism as in Luke 12:4 (Robertson, *Grammar of the
Greek N.T. in the Light of Historical Research*, p. 577).

28. *Destroy both soul and body in hell* (*kai psuchēn kai
sōma apolesai en geennēi*). Note "soul" here of the eternal

spirit, not just life in the body. "Destroy" here is not annihilation, but eternal punishment in Gehenna (the real hell) for which see on 5:22. Bruce thinks that the devil as the tempter is here meant, not God as the judge, but surely he is wrong. There is no more needed lesson today than the fear of God.

29. *Two sparrows* (*duo strouthia*). Diminutive of *strouthos* and means any small bird, sparrows in particular. They are sold today in the markets of Jerusalem and Jaffa. "For a farthing" (*assariou*) is genitive of price. Only here and Luke 12:6 in the N.T. Diminutive form of the Roman *as*, slightly more than half an English penny. *Without your Father* (*aneu tou patros hūmōn*). There is comfort in this thought for us all. Our father who knows about the sparrows knows and cares about us.

31. *Than many sparrows* (*pollōn strouthiōn*). Ablative case of comparison with *diapherete* (our differ).

32. *Shall confess me* (*homologēsei en emoi*). An Aramaic idiom, not Hebrew, see also Luke 12:8. So also here, "him will I also confess" (*homologēsō kagō en autōi*). Literally this Aramaic idiom reproduced in the Greek means "confess in me," indicating a sense of unity with Christ and of Christ with the man who takes the open stand for him.

33. *Shall deny me* (*arnēsētai me*). Aorist subjunctive here with *hostis*, though future indicative *homologēsei* above. Note accusative here (case of extension), saying "no" to Christ, complete breach. This is a solemn law, not a mere social breach, this cleavage by Christ of the man who repudiates him, public and final.

34. *I came not to send peace, but a sword* (*ouk ēlthon balein eirēnēn, alla machairan*). A bold and dramatic climax. The aorist infinitive means a sudden hurling of the sword where peace was expected. Christ does bring peace, not as the world gives, but it is not the force of compromise with evil, but of conquest over wrong, over Satan, the triumph of

the cross. Meanwhile there will be inevitably division in families, in communities, in states. It is no namby-pamby sentimentalism that Christ preaches, no peace at any price. The Cross is Christ's answer to the devil's offer of compromise in world dominion. For Christ the kingdom of God is virile righteousness, not mere emotionalism.

35. *Set at variance* (*dichasai*). Literally divide in two, *dicha*. Jesus uses Micah 7:1-6 to describe the rottenness of the age as Micah had done. Family ties and social ties cannot stand in the way of loyalty to Christ and righteous living.

The daughter-in-law (*numphēn*). Literally bride, the young wife who is possibly living with the mother-in-law. It is a tragedy to see a father or mother step between the child and Christ.

38. *Doth not take his cross* (*ou lambanei ton stauron autou*). The first mention of cross in Matthew. Criminals were crucified in Jerusalem. It was the custom for the condemned person to carry his own cross as Jesus did till Simon of Cyrene was impressed for that purpose. The Jews had become familiar with crucifixion since the days of Antiochus Epiphanes and one of the Maccabean rulers (Alexander Jannaeus) had crucified 800 Pharisees. It is not certain whether Jesus was thinking of his own coming crucifixion when he used this figure, though possible, perhaps probable. The disciples would hardly think of that outcome unless some of them had remarkable insight.

39. *Shall lose it* (*apolesei autēn*). This paradox appears in four forms according to Allen (1) Matt. 10:39 (2) Mark 8:35 = Matt. 16:25 = Luke 9:24 (3) Luke 17:33 (4) John 12:25. *The Wisdom of Sirach* (Hebrew text) in 51:26 has: "He that giveth his life findeth her (wisdom)." It is one of the profound sayings of Christ that he repeated many times. Plato (*Gorgias* 512) has language somewhat similar though not so sharply put. The article and aorist participles here (*ho*

heurōn, ho apolesas) are timeless in themselves just like *ho dechomenos* in verses 40 and 41.

41. *In the name of a prophet* (*eis onoma prophētou*). "Because he is a prophet" (Moffatt). In an Oxyrhynchus Papyrus 37 (A.D. 49) we find *onomati eleutherou* in virtue of being free-born. "He that receiveth a prophet from no ulterior motive, but simply *qua* prophet (*ut prophetam*, Jer.) would receive a reward in the coming age equal to that of his guest" (McNeile). The use of *eis* here is to be noted. In reality *eis* is simply *en* with the same meaning. It is not proper to say that *eis* has always to be translated "into." Besides these examples of *eis onoma* in verses 41 and 43 see Matt. 12:41 *eis to kērugma Iōnā* (see Robertson's *Grammar*, p. 593). *Unto one of these little ones* (*hena tōn mikrōn toutōn*). Simple believers who are neither apostles, prophets, or particularly righteous, just "learners," "in the name of a disciple" (*eis onoma mathētou*). Alford thinks that some children were present (cf. Matt. 18:2-6).

CHAPTER XI

1. *He departed thence to teach and preach* (*metebē ekeithen tou didaskein kai kērussein*). In five instances (7:28; 11:1; 13:53; 19:1; 26:1) after great discourses by Jesus "the transition to what follows is made with the formula, 'And it came to pass when Jesus had ended'" (McNeile). This is a wrong chapter division, for 11:1 belongs with the preceding section. "*Commanding*" (*diatassōn*, complementary participle with *etelesen*), means giving orders in detail (*dia-*) for each of them. Note both "teach and preach" as in 4:23. Where did Jesus go? Did he follow behind the twelve as he did with the seventy "whither he himself was about to come" (Luke 10:1)? Bruce holds with Chrysostom that Jesus avoided the places where they were, giving them room and time to do their work. But, if Jesus himself went to the chief cities of Galilee on this tour, he would be compelled to touch many of the same points. Jesus would naturally follow behind at some distance. At the end of the tour the apostles come together in Capernaum and tell Jesus all that they had done and that they had taught (Mark 6:30). Matthew follows the general outline of Mark, but the events are not grouped in chronological order here.

2. *John heard in the prison* (*ho de Iōanēs akousas en tōi desmōtēriōi*). Probably (Luke 7:18) the raising of the son of the widow of Nain. The word for prison here is the place where one was kept bound (Acts 5:21, 23; 16:26). See Matt. 4:12. It was in Machaerus east of the Dead Sea which at this time belonged to the rule of Herod Antipas (Jos. *Ant.* XVIII. v. 2). John's disciples had access to him. So he sent word by (*dia*, not *duo* as in Luke 7:19) them to Jesus.

3. *He that cometh* (*ho erchomenos*). This phrase refers to

the Messiah (Mark 11:9; Luke 13:35; 19:38; Heb. 10:37; Psa. 118:26; Dan. 7:13). Some rabbis applied the phrase to some forerunner of the kingdom (McNeile). Was there to be "another" (*heteron*) after Jesus? John had been in prison "long enough to develop a *prison mood*" (Bruce). It was once clear enough to him, but his environment was depressing and Jesus had done nothing to get him out of Machaerus (see chapter IX in my *John the Loyal*). John longed for reassurance.

4. *The things which ye do hear and see* (*ha akouete kai blepete*). This symbolical message was for John to interpret, not for them.

5. *And the dead are raised up* (*kai nekroi egeirontai*). Like that of the son of the widow of Nain. Did he raise the dead also on this occasion? "Tell John your story over again and remind him of these prophetic texts, Isa. 35:5; 61:1" (Bruce). The items were convincing enough and clearer than mere eschatological symbolism. "The poor" in particular have the gospel, a climax.

6. *Whosoever shall find none occasion of stumbling in me* (*hos an mē skandalisthēi en emoi*). Indefinite relative clause with first aorist passive subjunctive. This beatitude is a rebuke to John for his doubt even though in prison. Doubt is not a proof of superior intellect, scholarship, or piety. John was in the fog and that is the time not to make serious decisions. "In some way even the Baptist had found some occasion of stumbling in Jesus" (Plummer).

7. *As these went their way* (*toutōn poreuomenōn*). Present participle genitive absolute. The eulogy of Jesus was spoken as the two disciples of John were going away. Is it a matter of regret that they did not hear this wondrous praise of John that they might cheer him with it? "It may almost be called the funeral oration of the Baptist, for not long afterwards Herodias compassed his death" (Plummer). *A reed shaken by the wind* (*kalamon hupo anemou saleuo-*

menon). Latin *calamus*. Used of the reeds that grew in plenty in the Jordan Valley where John preached, of a staff made of a reed (Matt. 27:29), as a measuring rod (Rev. 11:1), of a writer's pen (III John 13). The reeds by the Jordan bent with the wind, but not so John.

9. *And much more than a prophet* (*kai perissoteron prophētou*). Ablative of comparison after *perissoteron* itself comparative though meaning exceeding (surrounded by, overflowing). John had all the great qualities of the true prophet: "Vigorous moral conviction, integrity, strength of will, fearless zeal for truth and righteousness" (Bruce). And then he was the Forerunner of the Messiah (Mal. 3:1).

11. *He that is but little* (*ho mikroteros*). The Authorized Version here has it better, "he that is least." The article with the comparative is a growing idiom in the vernacular *Koiné* for the superlative as in the modern Greek it is the only idiom for the superlative (Robertson, *Grammar of the Greek N.T.*, p. 668). The papyri and inscriptions show the same construction. The paradox of Jesus has puzzled many. He surely means that John is greater (*meizōn*) than all others in character, but that the least in the kingdom of heaven surpasses him in privilege. John is the end of one age, "until John" (11:14), and the beginning of the new era. All those that come after John stand upon his shoulders. John is the mountain peak between the old and the new.

12. *Suffereth violence* (*biazetai*). This verb occurs only here and in Luke 16:16 in the N.T. It seems to be middle in Luke and Deissmann (*Bible Studies*, p. 258) quotes an inscription "where *biazomai* is without doubt reflexive and absolute" as in Luke 16:16. But there are numerous papyri examples where it is passive (Moulton and Milligan, *Vocabulary*, etc.) so that "there seems little that promises decisive help for the difficult Logion of Matt. 11:12 = Luke 16:16." So then in Matt. 11:12 the form can be either middle or passive and either makes sense, though a different sense. The

passive idea is that the kingdom is forced, is stormed, is taken by men of violence like "men of violence take it by force" (*biastai harpazousin autēn*) or seize it like a conquered city. The middle voice may mean "experiences violence" or "forces its way" like a rushing mighty wind (so Zahn holds). These difficult words of Jesus mean that the preaching of John "had led to a violent and impetuous thronging to gather round Jesus and his disciples" (Hort, *Judaistic Christianity*, p. 26).

14. *This is Elijah* (*autos estin Eleias*). Jesus here endorses John as the promise of Malachi. The people understood Malachi 4:1 to mean the return of Elijah in person. This John denied as to himself (John 1:21). But Jesus affirms that John is the Elijah of promise who has come already (Matt. 17:12). He emphasizes the point: "He that hath ears to hear, let him hear."

17. *Children sitting in the market places* (*paidiois kathēmenois en tais agorais*). This parable of the children playing in the market place is given also in Luke 7:31f. Had Jesus as a child in Nazareth not played games with the children? He had certainly watched them often since. The interest of Christ in children was keen. He has really created the modern child's world out of the indifference of the past. They would not play wedding or funeral in a peevish fret. These metaphors in the Gospels are vivid to those with eyes to see. The *agora* was originally the assembly, then the forum or public square where the people gathered for trade or for talk as in Athens (Acts 17:17) and in many modern towns. So the Roman Forum. The oriental bazaars today are held in streets rather than public squares. Even today with all the automobiles children play in the streets. In English the word "cheap" (Cheapside) meant only barter and price, not cheap in our sense. The word for mourn (*ekopsasthe*) means to beat the heart, direct middle, after the fashion of eastern funeral lamentations.

19. *Wisdom is justified by her works* (*edikaiōthē apo tōn ergōn autēs*). A timeless aorist passive (Robertson, *Grammar*, p. 836f.). The word "justified" means "set right." Luke (7:35) has "by all her children" as some MSS. have here to make Matthew like Luke. These words are difficult, but understandable. God's wisdom has planned the different conduct of both John and Jesus. He does not wish all to be just alike in everything. "This generation" (verse 16) is childish, not childlike, and full of whimsical inconsistencies in their faultfinding. They exaggerate in each case. John did not have a demon and Jesus was not a glutton or a winebibber. "And, worse than either, for *philos* is used in a sinister sense and implies that Jesus was the comrade of the worst characters, and like them in conduct. A malicious nickname at first, it is now a name of honour: the sinner's lover" (Bruce). Cf. Luke 15:2. The plan of God is justified by results.

20. *Most of his mighty works* (*hai pleistai dunameis autou*). Literally, "His very many mighty works" if elative as usual in the papyri (Moulton, *Prolegomena*, p. 79; Robertson, *Grammar*, p. 670). But the usual superlative makes sense here as the Canterbury translation has it. This word *dunamis* for miracle presents the notion of *power* like our *dynamite*. The word *teras* is wonder, portent, *miraculum* (miracle) as in Acts 2:19. It occurs only in the plural and always with *sēmeia*. The word *sēmeion* means sign (Matt. 12:38) and is very common in John's Gospel as well as the word *ergon* (work) as in John 5:36. Other words used are *paradoxon*, our word *paradox*, strange (Luke 5:26), *endoxon*, glorious (Luke 13:17), *thaumasion*, wonderful (Matt. 21:15).

21. *Chorazin* (*Chorazein*). Mentioned only here and in Luke 10:13. Proof of "the meagreness of our knowledge of Judaism in the time of Christ" (Plummer) and of the many things not told in our Gospels (John 21:25). We know something of Bethsaida and more about Capernaum as

places of privilege. But (*plēn*, howbeit) neither of these cities repented, changed their conduct. Note condition of the second class, determined as unfulfilled in verses 21 and 23.

25. *At that season Jesus answered and said* (*en ekeinōi tōi kairōi apokritheis eipen*). Spoke to his Father in audible voice. The time and place we do not know. But here we catch a glimpse of Jesus in one of his moods of worship. "It is usual to call this golden utterance a prayer, but it is at once prayer, praise, and self-communing in a devout spirit" (Bruce). Critics are disturbed because this passage from the Logia of Jesus or Q of Synoptic criticism (Matt. 11:25–30 = Luke 10:21–24) is so manifestly Johannine in spirit and very language, "the Father" (*ho patēr*), "the son" (*ho huios*), whereas the Fourth Gospel was not written till the close of the first century and the Logia was written before the Synoptic Gospels. The only satisfying explanation lies in the fact that Jesus did have this strain of teaching that is preserved in John's Gospel. Here he is in precisely the same mood of elevated communion with the Father that we have reflected in John 14 to 17. Even Harnack is disposed to accept this Logion as a genuine saying of Jesus. The word "thank" (*homologoumai*) is better rendered "praise" (Moffatt). Jesus praises the Father "not that the *sophoi* were ignorant, but that the *nēpioi* knew" (McNeile).

26. *Wellpleasing in thy sight* (*eudokia emprosthen sou*). "For such has been thy gracious will" (Weymouth).

27. *All things have been delivered unto me of my Father* (*panta moi paredothē hupo tou patros mou*). This sublime claim is not to be whittled down or away by explanations. It is the timeless aorist like *edothē* in 28:18 and "points back to a moment in eternity, and implies the pre-existence of the Messiah" (Plummer). The Messianic consciousness of Christ is here as clear as a bell. It is a moment of high fellowship. Note *epiginōskei* twice for "fully know." Note also *boulētai*

=wills, is willing. The Son retains the power and the will
to reveal the Father to men.

28. *Come unto me (deute pros me)*. Verses 28 to 30 are
not in Luke and are among the special treasures of Matthew's Gospel. No sublimer words exist than this call of
Jesus to the toiling and the burdened (*pephortismenoi*, perfect
passive participle, state of weariness) to come to him. He
towers above all men as he challenges us. "I will refresh
you" (*kagō anapausō hūmas*). Far more than mere rest,
rejuvenation. The English slang expression "rest up" is
close to the idea of the Greek compound *ana-pauō*. It is
causative active voice.

29. *Take my yoke upon you and learn of me (arate ton
zugon mou eph' humas kai mathete ap' emou)*. The rabbis used
yoke for school as many pupils find it now a yoke. The
English word "school" is Greek for leisure (*scholē*). But
Jesus offers refreshment (*anapausin*) in his school and promises to make the burden light, for he is a meek and humble
teacher. Humility was not a virtue among the ancients. It
was ranked with servility. Jesus has made a virtue of this
vice. He has glorified this attitude so that Paul urges it
(Phil. 2:3), "in lowliness of mind each counting other better
than himself." In portions of Europe today people place
yokes on the shoulders to make the burden easier to carry.
Jesus promises that we shall find the yoke kindly and the
burden lightened by his help. "Easy" is a poor translation
of *chrēstos*. Moffatt puts it "kindly." That is the meaning
in the Septuagint for persons. We have no adjective that
quite carries the notion of kind and good. The yoke of Christ
is useful, good, and kindly. Cf. Song of Solomon 1:10.

CHAPTER XII

1. *On the sabbath day through the cornfields* (*tois sabbasin dia tōn sporimōn*). This paragraph begins exactly like 11:25 "at that season" (*en ekeinōi tōi kairōi*), a general statement with no clear idea of time. So also 14:1. The word *kairos* means a definite and particular time, but we cannot fix it. The word "cornfields" does not mean our maize or Indian corn, but simply fields of grain (wheat or even barley).

2. *Thy disciples do* (*hoi mathētai sou poiousin*). These critics are now watching a chance and they jump at this violation of their Pharisaic rules for Sabbath observance. The disciples were plucking the heads of wheat which to the Pharisees was reaping and were rubbing them in their hands (Luke 6:1) which was threshing.

3. *What David did* (*ti epoiēsen Daueid*). From the necessity of hunger. The first defence made by Christ appeals to the conduct of David (I Sam. 21:6). David and those with him did "what was not lawful" (*ho ouk exon ēn*) precisely the charge made against the disciples (*ho ouk exestin* in verse 2).

6. *One greater than the temple* (*tou hierou meizon*). Ablative of comparison, *tou hierou*. The Textus Receptus has *meizōn*, but the neuter is correct. Literally, "something greater than the temple." What is that? It may still be Christ, or it may be: "The work and His disciples were of more account than the temple" (Plummer). "If the temple was not subservient to Sabbath rules, how much less the Messiah! " (Allen).

7. *The guiltless* (*tous anaitious*). So in verse 5. Common in ancient Greek. No real ground against, it means *an* + *aitios*. Jesus quotes Hosea 6:6 here as he did in Matt.

9:13. A pertinent prophecy that had escaped the notice of the sticklers for ceremonial literalness and the letter of the law.

9. *Lord of the Sabbath (kurios tou sabbatou).* This claim that he as the Son of Man is master of the Sabbath and so above the Pharisaic regulations angered them extremely. By the phrase "the Son of man" here Jesus involves the claim of Messiahship, but as the Representative Man he affirms his solidarity with mankind, "standing for the human interest" (Bruce) on this subject.

10. *Is it lawful? (ei exestin).* The use of *ei* in direct questions is really elliptical and seems an imitation of the Hebrew (Robertson, *Grammar*, p. 916). See also Matt. 19:3. It is not translated in English.

12. *How much then is a man (posōi oun diapherei anthrōpos).* Another of Christ's pregnant questions that goes to the roots of things, an *a fortiori* argument. "By how much does a human being differ from a sheep? That is the question which Christian civilization has not even yet adequately answered" (Bruce). The poor pettifogging Pharisees are left in the pit.

13. *Stretch forth thy hand (ekteinon sou tēn cheira).* Probably the arm was not withered, though that is not certain. But he did the impossible. "He stretched it forth," straight, I hope, towards the Pharisees who were watching Jesus (Mark 3:2).

14. *Took counsel against him (sumboulion elabon kat' autou).* An imitation of the Latin *concilium capere* and found in papyri of the second century A.D. (Deissmann, *Bible Studies*, p. 238.) This incident marks a crisis in the hatred of the Pharisees toward Jesus. They bolted out of the synagogue and actually conspired with their hated rivals, the Herodians, how to put Jesus to death (Mark 3:6 = Matt. 12:14 = Luke 6:11). By "destroy" (*apolesōsin*) they meant "kill."

15. *Perceiving* (*gnous*). Second aorist active participle
of *ginōskō*. Jesus read their very thoughts. They were
now plain to any one who saw their angry countenances.

17. *That it might be fulfilled* (*hina plērōthēi*). The final
use of *hina* and the sub-final just before (verse 16). The
passage quoted is Isa. 42:1–4 "a very free reproduction of
the Hebrew with occasional side glances at the Septuagint"
(Bruce), possibly from an Aramaic collection of *Testimonia*
(McNeile). Matthew applies the prophecy about Cyrus to
Christ.

18. *My beloved* (*ho agapētos mou*). This phrase reminds
one of Matt. 3:17 (the Father's words at Christ's baptism).

20. *A bruised reed* (*kalamon suntetrimmenon*). Perfect
passive participle of *suntribō*. A crushed reed he will not
break. The curious augment in *kateaxei* (future active indicative) is to be noted. The copyists kept the augment
where it did not belong in this verb (Robertson, *Grammar*,
p. 1212) even in Plato. "Smoking flax" (*linon tuphomenon*).
The wick of a lamp, smoking and flickering and going out.
Only here in N.T. Flax in Ex. 9:31. Vivid images that
picture Jesus in the same strain as his own great words in
Matt. 11:28–30.

23. *Is this the Son of David?* (*mēti houtos estin ho huios
Daueid?*). The form of the question expects the answer
"no," but they put it so because of the Pharisaic hostility
towards Jesus. The multitudes "were amazed" or "stood
out of themselves" (*existanto*), imperfect tense, vividly
portraying the situation. They were almost beside themselves with excitement.

24. *The Pharisees* (*hoi de Pharisaioi*). Already (Matt.
9:32–34) we have had in Matthew the charge that Jesus is
in league with the prince of demons, though the incident
may be later than this one. See on 10:25 about "Beelzebub."
The Pharisees feel that the excited condition of the crowds
and the manifest disposition to believe that Jesus is the

Messiah (the Son of David) demand strenuous action on their part. They cannot deny the fact of the miracles for the blind and dumb men both saw and spoke (12:22). So in desperation they suggest that Jesus works by the power of Beelzebub the prince of the demons.

25. *Knowing their thoughts* (*eidōs de tas enthumēseis autōn*). What they were revolving in their minds. They now find out what a powerful opponent Jesus is. By parables, by a series of conditions (first class), by sarcasm, by rhetorical question, by merciless logic, he lays bare their hollow insincerity and the futility of their arguments. Satan does not cast out Satan. Note timeless aorist passive *emeristhē* in 26, *ephthasen* in 28 (simple sense of arriving as in Phil. 3:16 from *phthanō*). Christ is engaged in deathless conflict with Satan the strong man (29). "Goods" (*skeuē*) means house-gear, house furniture, or equipment as in Luke 17:36 and Acts 27:17, the tackling of the ship.

30. *He that is not with me* (*ho mē ōn met' emou*). With these solemn words Jesus draws the line of cleavage between himself and his enemies then and now. Jesus still has his enemies who hate him and all noble words and deeds because they sting what conscience they have into fury. But we may have our choice. We either gather with (*sunagōn*) Christ or scatter (*skorpizei*) to the four winds. Christ is the magnet of the ages. He draws or drives away. "Satan is the arch-waster, Christ the collector, Saviour" (Bruce).

31. *But the blasphemy against the Spirit* (*hē de tou pneumatos blasphēmia*). Objective genitive. This is the unpardonable sin. In 32 we have *kata tou pneumatos tou hagiou* to make it plainer. What is the blasphemy against the Holy Spirit? These Pharisees had already committed it. They had attributed the works of the Holy Spirit by whose power Jesus wrought his miracles (12:28) to the devil. That sin was without excuse and would not be forgiven in their age or in the coming one (12:32). People often ask

if they can commit the unpardonable sin. Probably some do who ridicule the manifest work of God's Spirit in men's lives and attribute the Spirit's work to the devil.

34. *Ye offspring of vipers* (*gennēmata echidnōn*). These same terrible words the Baptist had used to the Pharisees and Sadducees who came to his baptism (Matt. 3:7). But these Pharisees had deliberately made their choice and had taken Satan's side. The charge against Jesus of being in league with Satan reveals the evil heart within. The heart "spurts out" (*ekballei*) good or evil according to the supply (treasure, *thēsaurou*) within. Verse 33 is like Matt. 7:17-19. Jesus often repeated his crisp pungent sayings as every teacher does.

36. *Every idle word* (*pan rhēma argon*). An ineffective, useless word (*a* privative and *ergon*). A word that does no good and so is pernicious like pernicious anaemia. It is a solemn thought. Jesus who knows our very thoughts (12:25) insists that our words reveal our thoughts and form a just basis for the interpretation of character (12:37). Here we have judgment by words as in 25:31-46 where Jesus presents judgment by deeds. Both are real tests of actual character. Homer spoke of "winged words" (*pteroenta epea*). And by the radio our words can be heard all round the earth. Who knows where they stop?

38. *A sign from thee* (*apo sou sēmeion*). One wonders at the audacity of scribes and Pharisees who accused Jesus of being in league with Satan and thus casting out demons who can turn round and blandly ask for a "sign from thee." As if the other miracles were not signs! "The demand was impudent, hypocritical, insulting" (Bruce).

39. *An evil and adulterous generation* (*genea ponēra kai moichalis*). They had broken the marriage tie which bound them to Jehovah (Plummer). See Psa. 73:27; Isa. 57:3ff.; 62:5; Ezek. 23:27; James 4:4; Rev. 2:20. What is "the sign of Jonah?"

40. *The whale* (*tou kētous*). Sea-monster, huge fish. In Jonah 2:1 the LXX has *kētei megalōi*. "Three days and three nights" may simply mean three days in popular speech. Jesus rose "on the third day" (Matt. 16:21), not "on the fourth day." It is just a fuller form for "after three days" (Mark 8:31; 10:34).

41. *In the judgment* (*en tēi krisei*). Except here and in the next verse Matthew has "day of judgment" (*hēmera kriseōs*) as in 10:15; 11:22, 24; 12:36. Luke (10:14) has *en tēi krisei*. *They repented at the preaching of Jonah* (*metenoēson eis to kērugma Iōna*). Note this use of *eis* just like *en*. Note also *pleion* (neuter), not *pleiōn* (masc.). See the same idiom in 12:6 and 12:48. Jesus is something greater than the temple, than Jonah, than Solomon. "You will continue to disbelieve in spite of all I can say or do, and at last you will put me to death. But I will rise again, a sign for your confusion, if not for your conversion" (Bruce).

44. *Into my house* (*eis ton oikon mou*). So the demon describes the man in whom he had dwelt. "The demon is ironically represented as implying that he left his victim voluntarily, as a man leaves his house to go for a walk" (McNeile). "Worse than the first" is a proverb.

46. *His mother and his brothers* (*hē mētēr kai hoi adelphoi autou*). Brothers of Jesus, younger sons of Joseph and Mary. The charge of the Pharisees that Jesus was in league with Satan was not believed by the disciples of Jesus, but some of his friends did think that he was beside himself (Mark 3:21) because of the excitement and strain. It was natural for Mary to want to take him home for rest and refreshment. So the mother and brothers are pictured standing outside the house (or the crowd). They send a messenger to Jesus.

47. Aleph, B, L, Old Syriac, omit this verse as do Westcott and Hort. It is genuine in Mark 3:32 = Luke 8:20. It was probably copied into Matthew from Mark or Luke.

49. *Behold my mother and my brothers* (*idou hē mētēr mou kai hoi adelphoi mou*). A dramatic wave of the hand towards his disciples (learners) accompanied these words. Jesus loved his mother and brothers, but they were not to interfere in his Messianic work. The real spiritual family of Jesus included all who follow him. But it was hard for Mary to go back to Nazareth and leave Jesus with the excited throng so great that he was not even stopping to eat (Mark 3:20).

CHAPTER XIII

1. *On that day* (*en tēi hēmerai ekeinēi*). So this group of parables is placed by Matthew on the same day as the blasphemous accusation and the visit of the mother of Jesus. It is called "the Busy Day," not because it was the only one, but simply that so much is told of this day that it serves as a specimen of many others filled to the full with stress and strain. *Sat by the seaside* (*ekathēto para tēn thalassan*). The accusative case need give no difficulty. Jesus came out of the stuffy house and took his seat (*ekathēto*, imperfect) along the shore with the crowds stretched up and down, a picturesque scene.

2. *And all the multitude stood on the beach* (*kai pas ho ochlos epi ton aigialon histēkei*). Past perfect tense of *histēmi* with imperfect sense, had taken a stand and so stood. Note accusative also with *epi* upon the beach where the waves break one after the other (*aigialos* is from *hals*, sea, and *agnumi*, to break, or from *aissō*, to rush). Jesus had to get into a boat and sit down in that because of the crush of the crowd.

3. *Many things in parables* (*polla en parabolais*). It was not the first time that Jesus had used parables, but the first time that he had spoken so many and some of such length. He will use a great many in the future as in Luke 12 to 18 and Matt. 24 and 25. The parables already mentioned in Matthew include the salt and the light (5:13–16), the birds and the lilies (6:26–30), the splinter and the beam in the eye (7:3–5), the two gates (7:13f.), the wolves in sheep's clothing (7:15), the good and bad trees (7:17–19), the wise and foolish builders (7:24–27), the garment and the wineskins (9:16f.), the children in the market places (11:

16f.). It is not certain how many he spoke on this occasion. Matthew mentions eight in this chapter (the Sower, the Tares, the Mustard Seed, the Leaven, the Hid Treasure, the Pearl of Great Price, the Net, the Householder). Mark adds the Parable of the Lamp (4:21 = Luke 8:16), the Parable of the Seed Growing of Itself (4:26–29), making ten of which we know. But both Mark (4:33) and Matthew (13: 34) imply that there were many others. "Without a parable spake he nothing unto them" (Matt. 13:34), on this occasion, we may suppose. The word parable (*parabolē* from *paraballō*, to place alongside for measurement or comparison like a yardstick) is an objective illustration for spiritual or moral truth. The word is employed in a variety of ways (a) as for sententious sayings or proverbs (Matt. 15:15; Mark 3:23; Luke 4:23; 5:36–9; 6:39), for a figure or type (Heb. 9:9; 11:19); (b) a comparison in the form of a narrative, the common use in the Synoptic Gospels like the Sower; (c) "A narrative illustration not involving a comparison" (Broadus), like the Rich Fool, the Good Samaritan, etc. "The oriental genius for picturesque speech found expression in a multitude of such utterances" (McNeile). There are parables in the Old Testament, in the Talmud, in sermons in all ages. But no one has spoken such parables as these of Jesus. They hold the mirror up to nature and, as all illustrations should do, throw light on the truth presented. The fable puts things as they are not in nature, Aesop's Fables, for instance. The parable may not be actual fact, but it could be so. It is harmony with the nature of the case. The allegory (*allēgoria*) is a speaking parable that is self-explanatory all along like Bunyan's *Pilgrim's Progress*. All allegories are parables, but not all parables are allegories. The Prodigal Son is an allegory, as is the story of the Vine and Branches (John 15). John does not use the word parable, but only *paroimia*, a saying by the way (John 10:6; 16:25, 29). As a rule the parables of Jesus illustrate one main point and the details are more or less incidental, though sometimes Jesus himself explains these. When he does not do so, we should be slow to interpret the minor details. Much heresy has come from fantastic interpretations of the parables. In the case of the Parable of the Sower (13:3–8) we have also the careful exposition of the story by Jesus (18–23) as well as the reason for the use of parables on this occasion by Jesus (9–17). *Behold, the sower went forth* (*idou ēlthen ho speirōn*). Matthew is very fond of this exclamation *idou*. It is "the sower," not "a sower." Jesus expects one to see the man as he stepped forth to begin scattering with his hand. The parables of Jesus are vivid word pictures. To understand them one must see them, with the eyes of Jesus if he can. Christ drew his parables from familiar objects.

4. *As he sowed* (*en tōi speirein auton*). Literally, "in the sowing as to him," a neat Greek idiom unlike our English temporal conjunction. Locative case with the articular present infinitive. *By the wayside* (*para tēn hodon*). People will make paths along the edge of a ploughed field or even across it where the seed lies upon the beaten track. *Devoured* (*katephagen*). "Ate down." We say, "ate up." Second aorist active indicative of *katesthiō* (defective verb).

5. *The rocky places* (*ta petrōdē*). In that limestone country ledges of rock often jut out with thin layers of soil upon the layers of rock. *Straightway they sprang up* (*eutheōs exaneteilen*). "Shot up at once" (Moffatt). Double compound (*ex*, out of the ground, *ana*, up). Ingressive aorist of *exanatellō*.

6. *The sun was risen* (*hēliou anateilantos*). Genitive absolute. "The sun having sprung up" also, same verb except the absence of *ex* (*anatellō, exanatellō*).

7. *The thorns grew up* (*anebēsan hai akanthai*). Not "sprang up" as in verse 5, for a different verb occurs meaning "came up" out of the ground, the seeds of the thorns being already in the soil, "upon the thorns" (*epi tas akanthas*)

rather than "among the thorns." But the thorns got a
quick start as weeds somehow do and "choked them"
(*apepnixan auta*, effective aorist of *apopnigō*), "choked
them off" literally. Luke (8:33) uses it of the hogs in the
water. Who has not seen vegetables and flowers and corn
made yellow by thorns and weeds till they sicken and die?

8. *Yielded fruit* (*edidou karpon*). Change to imperfect tense of *didōmi*, to give, for it was continuous fruit-
bearing. *Some a hundredfold* (*ho men hekaton*). Variety,
but fruit. This is the only kind that is worth while. The
hundredfold is not an exaggeration (cf. Gen. 26:12). Such
instances are given by Wetstein for Greece, Italy, and
Africa. Herodotus (i. 93) says that in Babylonia grain
yielded two hundredfold and even to three hundredfold.
This, of course, was due to irrigation as in the Nile Valley.

9. *He that hath ears let him hear* (*ho echōn ōta akouetō*).
So also in 11:15 and 13:43. It is comforting to teachers and
preachers to observe that even Jesus had to exhort people
to listen and to understand his sayings, especially his parables. They will bear the closest thought and are often
enigmatical.

10. *Why speakest thou unto them in parables?* (*dia ti
en parabolais laleis autois*). Already the disciples are puzzled over the meaning of this parable and the reason for
giving them to the people. So they "came up" closer to
Jesus and asked him. Jesus was used to questions and surpassed all teachers in his replies.

11. *To know the mysteries* (*gnōnai ta mustēria*). Second aorist active infinitive of *ginōskō*. The word *mustērion*
is from *mustēs*, one initiated, and that from *mueō* (*muō*), to
close or shut (Latin, *mutus*). The mystery-religions of the
east had all sorts of secrets and signs as secret societies do
today. But those initiated knew them. So the disciples
have been initiated into the secrets of the kingdom of heaven.
Paul will use it freely of the mystery once hidden, but now

revealed, now made known in Christ (Rom. 16:25; I Cor. 2:7, etc.). In Phil. 4:12 Paul says: "I have learned the secret or been initiated" (*memuēmai*). So Jesus here explains that his parables are open to the disciples, but shut to the Pharisees with their hostile minds. In the Gospels *mustērion* is used only here and in the parallel passages (Mark 4:11 = Luke 8:10).

13. *Because seeing* (*hoti blepontes*). In the parallel passages in Mark 4:12 and Luke 8:10 we find *hina* with the subjunctive. This does not necessarily mean that in Mark and Luke *hina* = *hoti* with the causal sense, though a few rare instances of such usage may be found in late Greek. For a discussion of the problem see my chapter on "The Causal Use of *Hina*" in *Studies in Early Christianity* (1928) edited by Prof. S. J. Case. Here in Matthew we have first "an adaptation of Isa. 6:9f. which is quoted in full in v. 14f." (McNeile). Thus Matthew presents "a striking paradox, 'though they see, they do not (really) see' " (McNeile). Cf. John 9:41. The idiom here in Matthew gives no trouble save in comparison with Mark and Luke which will be discussed in due turn. The form *suniousin* is an omega verb form (*suniō*) rather than the *mi* verb (*suniēmi*) as is common in the *Koiné*.

14. *Is fulfilled* (*anaplēroutai*). Aoristic present passive indicative. Here Jesus points out the fulfilment and not with Matthew's usual formula (*hina* or *hopōs plōrethēi to rhēthen* (see 1:22). The verb *anaplēroō* occurs nowhere else in the Gospels, but occurs in the Pauline Epistles. It means to fill up like a cup, to fill another's place (I Cor. 14:16), to fill up what is lacking (Phil. 2:30). Here it means that the prophecy of Isaiah is fully satisfied in the conduct of the Pharisees and Jesus himself points it out. Note two ways of reproducing the Hebrew idiom (infinitive absolute), one by *akoēi* the other by *blepontes*. Note also the strong negative *ou mē* with aorist subjunctive.

15. *Is waxed gross* (*epachunthē*). Aorist passive tense. From *pachus*, thick, fat, stout. Made callous or dull—even fatty degeneration of the heart. *Dull of hearing* (*tois ōsin bareōs ēkousan*). Another aorist. Literally, "They heard (or hear) heavily with their ears." The hard of hearing are usually sensitive. *Their eyes they have closed* (*tous ophthalmous autōn ekammusan*). The epic and vernacular verb *kammuō* is from *katamuō* (to shut down). We say shut up of the mouth, but the eyes really shut down. The Hebrew verb in Isa. 6:10 means to smear over. The eyes can be smeared with wax or cataract and thus closed. "Sealing up the eyes was an oriental punishment" (Vincent). See Isa. 29:10; 44:18. *Lest* (*mēpote*). This negative purpose as a judgment is left in the quotation from Isaiah. It is a solemn thought for all who read or hear the word of God. *And I should heal them* (*kai iasomai autous*). Here the LXX changes to the future indicative rather than the aorist subjunctive as before.

16. *Blessed are your eyes* (*humōn de makarioi hoi ophthalmoi*). A beatitude for the disciples in contrast with the Pharisees. Note position of "Happy" here also as in the Beatitudes in Matt. 5.

18. *Hear then ye the parable* (*humeis oun akousate tēn parabolēn*). Jesus has given in 13:13 one reason for his use of parables, the condemnation which the Pharisees have brought on themselves by their spiritual dulness: "Therefore I speak to them in parables" (*dia touto en parabōlais antois lalō*). He can go on preaching the mysteries of the kingdom without their comprehending what he is saying, but he is anxious that the disciples really get personal knowledge (*gnōnai*, verse 11) of these same mysteries. So he explains in detail what he means to teach by the Parable of the Sower. He appeals to them (note position of *humeis*) to listen as he explains.

19. *When anyone heareth* (*pantos akouontos*). Genitive

absolute and present participle, "while everyone is listening and not comprehending" (*mē sunientos*), "not putting together" or "not grasping." Perhaps at that very moment Jesus observed a puzzled look on some faces. *Cometh the evil one and snatcheth away* (*erchetai ho ponēros kai harpazei*). The birds pick up the seeds while the sower sows. The devil is busy with his job of snatching or seizing like a bandit or rogue the word of the kingdom before it has time even to sprout. How quickly after the sermon the impression is gone. "This is he" (*houtos estin*). Matthew, like Mark, speaks of the people who hear the words as the seed itself. That creates some confusion in this condensed form of what Jesus actually said, but the real point is clear. *The seed sown in his heart* (*to esparmenon en tēi kardiāi autou*, perfect passive participle of *speirō*, to sow) and "the man sown by the wayside" (*ho para tēn hodon spareis*, aorist passive participle, along the wayside) are identified. The seed in the heart is not of itself responsible, but the man who lets the devil snatch it away.

21. *Yet hath he not root in himself* (*ouk echei de rhizan en heautōi*). Cf. Col. 2:7 and Eph. 3:18 *errizōmemoi*. Stability like a tree. Here the man has a mushroom growth and "endureth for a while" (*proskairos*), temporary, quick to sprout, quick to stumble (*skandalizetai*). What a picture of some converts in our modern revivals. They drop away overnight because they did not have the root of the matter in them. This man does not last or hold out.

21. *Tribulation* (*thlipseōs*). From *thlibō*, to press, to oppress, to squeeze (cf. 7:14). The English word is from the Latin *tribulum*, the roller used by the Romans for pressing wheat. Cf. our "steam roller" Trench (*Synonyms of the N.T.*, pp. 202-4): "When, according to the ancient law of England, those who wilfully refused to plead, had heavy weights placed on their breasts, and were pressed and

crushed to death, this was literally *thlipsis*." The iron cage
was *stenochōria*.

22. *Choke the word* (*sunpnigei ton logon*). We had *apepnixan* (choked off) in 13:7. Here it is *sunpnigei* (choke
together), historical present and singular with both subjects lumped together. "Lust for money and care go together and between them spoil many an earnest religious
nature" (Bruce), "thorns" indeed. The thorns flourish
and the character sickens and dies, choked to death for lack
of spiritual food, air, sunshine.

23. *Verily beareth fruit* (*dē karpophorei*). Who in reality
(*dē*) does bear fruit (cf. Matt. 7:16–20). The fruit reveals
the character of the tree and the value of the straw
for wheat. Some grain must come else it is only chaff,
straw, worthless. The first three classes have no frūit and
so show that they are unfruitful soil, unsaved souls and lives.
There is variety in those who do bear fruit, but they have
some fruit. The lesson of the parable as explained by Jesus
is precisely this, the variety in the results of the seed sown
according to the soil on which it falls. Every teacher and
preacher knows how true this is. It is the teacher's task as
the sower to sow the right seed, the word of the kingdom.
The soil determines the outcome. There are critics today
who scout this interpretation of the parable by Jesus as too
allegorical with too much detail and probably not that really
given by Jesus since modern scholars are not agreed on the
main point of the parable. But the average Christian sees
the point all right. This parable was not meant to explain
all the problems of human life.

24. *Set he before them* (*parethēken*). So again in 13:31.
He placed another parable beside (*para*) the one already
given and explained. The same verb (*paratheinai*) occurs
in Luke 9:16. *Is likened* (*hōmoiōthē*). Timeless aorist
passive and a common way of introducing these parables
of the kingdom where a comparison is drawn (18:23;

22:2; 25:1). The case of *anthrōpoi* is associative instrumental.

25. *While men slept* (*en tōi katheudein tous anthrōpous*). Same use of the articular present infinitive with *en* and the accusative as in 13:4. *Sowed tares also* (*epespeiren ta zizania*). Literally "sowed upon," "resowed" (Moffatt). The enemy deliberately sowed "the darnel" (*zizania* is not "tares," but "darnel," a bastard wheat) over (*epi*) the wheat, "in the midst of the wheat." This bearded darnel, *lolium temulentum*, is common in Palestine and resembles wheat except that the grains are black. In its earlier stages it is indistinguishable from the wheat stalks so that it has to remain till near the harvest. Modern farmers are gaining more skill in weeding it out.

26. *Then appeared also* (*tote ephanē kai*). The darnel became plain (*ephanē*, second aorist passive, effective aorist of *phainō* to show) by harvest.

29. *Ye root up the wheat with them* (*ekrizōsēte hama autois ton siton*). Literally, "root out." Easy to do with the roots of wheat and darnel intermingled in the field. So *sullegontes* is not "gather up," but "gather together," here and verses 28 and 30. Note other compound verbs here, "grow together" (*sunauxanesthai*), "burn up" (*katakausai*, burn down or completely), "bring together" (*sunagete*).

30. *My barn* (*tēn apothēkēn mou*). See already 3:12; 6:26. Granary, storehouse, place for putting things away.

31. *Is like* (*homoia estin*). Adjective for comparison with associative instrumental as in 13:13, 44, 45, 47, 52. *Grain of mustard seed* (*kokkōi sinapeōs*). Single grain in contrast with the collective *sperma* (17:20). *Took and sowed* (*labōn espeiren*). Vernacular phrasing like Hebrew and all conversational style. In *Koinē*.

32. *A tree* (*dendron*). "Not in nature, but in size" (Bruce). "An excusable exaggeration in popular discourse."

33. *Is like unto leaven* (*homoia estin zumēi*). In its

pervasive power. Curiously enough some people deny that
Jesus here likens the expanding power of the Kingdom of
heaven to leaven, because, they say, leaven is the symbol
of corruption. But the language of Jesus is not to be explained away by such exegetical jugglery. The devil is
called like a lion by Peter (I Pet. 5:8) and Jesus in Revelation
is called the Lion of the Tribe of Judah (Rev. 5:5). The
leaven permeates all the "wheaten meal" (*aleurou*) till the
whole is leavened. There is nothing in the "three meas-
ures," merely a common amount to bake. Dr. T. R. Glover
in his *Jesus of History* suggests that Jesus used to notice his
mother using that amount of wheat flour in baking bread.
To find the Trinity here is, of course, quite beside the mark.
The word for leaven, *zumē*, is from *zeō*, to boil, to seethe, and
so pervasive fermentation.

35. *I will utter* (*ereuxomai*). To cast forth like a river,
to gurgle, to disgorge, the passion of a prophet. From Psa.
19:2; 78:2. The Psalmist claims to be able to utter "things
hidden from the foundation of the world" and Matthew
applies this language to the words of Jesus. Certain it is
that the life and teaching of Jesus throw a flood of light on
the purposes of God long kept hidden (*kekrummena*).

36. *Explain unto us* (*diasaphēson hēmin*). Also in 18:31.
"Make thoroughly clear right now" (aorist tense of
urgency). The disciples waited till Jesus left the crowds
and got into the house to ask help on this parable. Jesus
had opened up the Parable of the Sower and now they pick
out this one, passing by the mustard seed and the leaven.

38. *The field is the world* (*ho de agros estin ho kosmos*).
The article with both "field" and "world" in Greek means
that subject and predicate are coextensive and so inter-
changeable. It is extremely important to understand that
both the good seed and the darnel (tares) are sown in the
world, not in the Kingdom, not in the church. The separation comes at the consummation of the age (*sunteleia*

aiōnos, 39), the harvest time. They all grow together in the field (the world).

41. *Out of his kingdom* (*ek tēs basileias autou*). Out from the midst of the kingdom, because in every city the good and the bad are scattered and mixed together. Cf. *ek mesou tōn dikaiōn* in 13:49 "from the midst of the righteous." What this means is that, just as the wheat and the darnel are mixed together in the field till the separation at harvest, so the evil are mixed with the good in the world (the field). Jesus does not mean to say that these "stumbling-blocks" (*ta skandala*) are actually in the Kingdom of heaven and really members of the Kingdom. They are simply mixed in the field with the wheat and God leaves them in the world till the separation comes. Their destiny is "the furnace of fire" (*tēn kaminon tou puros*).

43. *Shine forth* (*eklampsousin*). Shine out as the sun comes from behind a cloud (Vincent) and drive away the darkness after the separation has come (cf. Dan. 12:3).

44. *And hid* (*kai ekrupsen*). Not necessarily bad morality. "He may have hid it to prevent it being stolen, or to prevent himself from being anticipated in buying a field" (Plummer). But if it was a piece of sharp practice, that is not the point of the parable. That is, the enormous wealth of the Kingdom for which any sacrifice, all that one has, is not too great a price to pay.

46. *He went and sold* (*apelthōn pepraken*). Rather eagerly and vividly told thus, "He has gone off and sold." The present perfect indicative, the dramatic perfect of vivid picture. Then he bought it. Present perfect, imperfect, aorist tenses together for lively action. *Emporoi* is a merchant, one who goes in and out, travels like a drummer.

47. *A net* (*sagēnēi*). Drag-net. Latin, *sagena*, English, seine. The ends were stretched out and drawn together. Only example of the word in the N.T. Just as the field is the world, so the drag-net catches all the fish that are in

the sea. The separation comes afterwards. Vincent per-
tinently quotes Homer's *Odyssey* (xxii. 384-389) where the
slain suitors in the halls of Ulysses are likened to fishes on the
shore caught by nets with myriad meshes.

48. *Vessels* (*aggē*). Here only in the N.T.   In Matt. 25:4
we have *aggeia*.

52. *Made a disciple to the kingdom of heaven* (*mathe-
teutheis tēi basileiāi tōn ouranōn*).   First aorist passive participle. The verb is transitive in 28:19. Here a scribe is
made a learner to the kingdom. "The mere scribe, Rabbinical in spirit, produces only the old and stale. The disciple
of the kingdom like the Master, is always fresh-minded,
yet knows how to value all old spiritual treasures of Holy
Writ, or Christian tradition" (Bruce). So he uses things
fresh (*kaina*) and ancient (*palaia*). "He hurls forth" (*ekballei*) both sorts.

54. *Is not this the carpenter's son?* (*ouch houtos estin ho tou
tektōnos huios?*).   The well-known, the leading, or even for a
time the only carpenter in Nazareth till Jesus took the place
of Joseph as the carpenter. What the people of Nazareth
could not comprehend was how one with the origin and environment of Jesus here in Nazareth could possess the
wisdom which he appeared to have in his teaching (*edidasken*). That has often puzzled people how a boy whom they
knew could become the man he apparently is after leaving
them. They knew Joseph, Mary, the brothers (four of them
named) and sisters (names not given). Jesus passed here as
the son of Joseph and these were younger brothers and
sisters (half brothers and sisters technically).

57. *And they were offended in him* (*kai eskandalizonto
en autōi*).   Graphic imperfect passive. Literally, "They
stumbled at him," "They were repelled by him" (Moffatt),
"They turned against him" (Weymouth). It was unpardonable for Jesus not to be commonplace like themselves.
Not without honour (*ouk estin atimos*).   This is a proverb

found in Jewish, Greek, and Roman writers. Seen also in the *Logia of Jesus* (*Oxyr. Papyri* i. 3).

58. *Mighty works* (*dunameis*). Powers. The "disbelief" (*apistian*) of the townspeople blocked the will and the power of Jesus to work cures.

CHAPTER XIV

1. *Herod the tetrarch* (*Hērōides tetraarchēs*). Herod Antipas ruler of Galilee and Perea, one-fourth of the dominion of Herod the Great. *The report concerning Jesus* (*tēn akouēn Iēsou*). See on 4:24. Cognate accusative, heard the hearing (rumour), objective genitive. It is rather surprising that he had not heard of Jesus before.

2. *His servants* (*tois paisin autou*). Literally "boys," but here the courtiers, not the menials of the palace. *Work in him* (*energousin*). Cf. our "energize." "The powers of the invisible world, vast and vague in the king's imagination" (Bruce). John wrought no miracles, but one *redivivus* might be under the control of the unseen powers. So Herod argued. A guilty conscience quickened his fears. Possibly he could see again the head of John on a charger. "The King has the Baptist on the brain" (Bruce). Cf. Josephus (*War*, I. xxx. 7) for the story that the ghosts of Alexander and Aristobulus haunted the palace of Herod the Great. There were many conjectures about Jesus as a result of this tour of Galilee and Herod Antipas feared this one.

3. *For the sake of Herodias* (*dia Hērōidiada*). The death of John had taken place some time before. The Greek aorists here (*edēsen, apetheto*) are not used for past perfects. The Greek aorist simply narrates the event without drawing distinctions in past time. This Herodias was the unlawful wife of Herod Antipas. She was herself a descendant of Herod the Great and had married Herod Philip of Rome, not Philip the Tetrarch. She had divorced him in order to marry Herod Antipas after he had divorced his wife, the daughter of Aretas King of Arabia. It was a nasty mess equal to any of our modern divorces. Her first husband was still alive

and marriage with a sister-in-law was forbidden to Jews
(Lev. 18:16).   Because of her Herod Antipas had put John
in the prison at Machaerus.   The bare fact has been mentioned in Matt. 4:12 without the name of the place.   See
11:2 also for the discouragement of John *en tōi desmōtēriōi*
(place of bondage), here *en tēi phulakēi* (the guard-house).
Josephus (*Ant.* xviii. 5. 2) tells us that Machaerus is the name
of the prison.   On a high hill an impregnable fortress had
been built.   Tristram (*Land of Moab*) says that there are
now remains of "two dungeons, one of them deep and its
sides scarcely broken in" with "small holes still visible in
the masonry where staples of wood and iron had once been
fixed.   One of these must surely have been the prison-
house of John the Baptist."   "On this high ridge Herod the
Great built an extensive and beautiful palace" (Broadus).
"The windows commanded a wide and grand prospect, including the Dead Sea, the course of the Jordan, and Jerusalem" (Edersheim, *Life and Times of Jesus*).

4. *For John said unto him* (*elegen gar Iōanēs autōi*).
Possibly the Pharisees may have put Herod up to inveigling
John to Machaerus on one of his visits there to express an
opinion concerning his marriage to Herodias (Broadus) and
the imperfect tense (*elegen*) probably means that John said
it repeatedly.   It was a blunt and brave thing that John
said.   It cost him his head, but it is better to have a head
like John's and lose it than to have an ordinary head and
keep it.   Herod Antipas was a politician and curbed his
resentment toward John by his fear of the people who still
held (*eichon*, imperfect tense) him as a prophet.

6. *When Herod's birthday came* (*genesiois genomenois tou
Hērōidou*).   Locative of time (cf. Mark 6:21) without the
genitive absolute.   The earlier Greeks used the word *genesia*
for funeral commemorations (birthdays of the dead), *geneth-
lia* being the word for birthday celebrations of living persons.
But that distinction has disappeared in the papyri.   The

word *genesia* in the papyri (*Fayum Towns*, 114[20], 115[8], 119[30])
is always a birthday feast as here in Matthew and Mark.
Philo used both words of birthday feasts. Persius, a Roman
satirist (*Sat.* V. 180–183), describes a banquet on Herod's
Day. *Danced in the midst* (*ōrchēsato en tōi mesōi*). This
was Salome, daughter of Herodias by her first marriage.
The root of the verb means some kind of rapid motion.
"Leaped in the middle," Wycliff puts it. It was a shameful
exhibition of lewd dancing prearranged by Herodias to
compass her purpose for John's death. Salome had stooped
to the level of an *almeh*, or common dancer.

7. *Promised with an oath* (*meta horkou hōmologēsen*).
Literally, "confessed with an oath." For this verb in the
sense of promise, see Acts 7:17. Note middle voice of *aitēsētai*
(ask for herself). Cf. Esther 5:3; 7:2.

8. *Put forward* (*probibastheisa*). See Acts 19:33 for a
similar verb (*probalontōn*), "pushing forward." Here (Acts)
the Textus Receptus uses *probibazō*. "It should require a
good deal of 'educating' to bring a young girl to make such a
grim request" (Bruce). *Here* (*hōde*). On the spot. Here
and now. *In a charger* (*epi pinaki*). Dish, plate, platter.
Why the obsolete "charger"?

9. *Grieved* (*lupētheis*). Not to hurt, for in verse 5 we
read that he wanted (*thelōn*) to put him to death (*apokteinai*). Herod, however, shrank from so dastardly a deed
as this public display of brutality and bloodthirstiness.
Men who do wrong always have some flimsy excuses for
their sins. A man here orders a judicial murder of the most
revolting type "for the sake of his oath" (*dia tous horkous*).
"More like profane swearing than deliberate utterance once
for all of a solemn oath" (Bruce). He was probably maudlin
with wine and befuddled by the presence of the guests.

10. *Beheaded John* (*apekephalisen Iōanēn*). That is, he
had John beheaded, a causative active tense of a late verb
apokephalizō. Took his head off.

11. *She brought it to her mother* (*ēnegken tēi mētri autēs*). A gruesome picture as Herodias with fiendish delight witnesses the triumph of her implacable hatred of John for daring to reprove her for her marriage with Herod Antipas. A woman scorned is a veritable demon, a literal she-devil when she wills to be. Kipling's "female of the species" again. Legends actually picture Salome as in love with John, sensual lust, of which there is no proof.

12. *And they went and told Jesus* (*kai elthontes apēggeilan tōi Iēsou*). As was meet after they had given his body decent burial. It was a shock to the Master who alone knew how great John really was. The fate of John was a prophecy of what was before Jesus. According to Matt. 14:13 the news of the fate of John led to the withdrawal of Jesus to the desert privately, an additional motive besides the need for rest after the strain of the recent tour.

13. *In a boat* (*en ploiōi*), "on foot" (*pezēi*, some MSS. *pezoi*). Contrast between the lake and the land route.

14. *Their sick* (*tous arrōstous autōn*). "Without strength" (*rhōnnumi* and *a* privative). *Esplagchnisthē* is a deponent passive. The verb gives the oriental idea of the bowels (*splagchna*) as the seat of compassion.

15. *When even was come* (*opsias genomenēs*). Genitive absolute. Not sunset about 6 P.M. as in 8:16 and as in 14:23, but the first of the two "evenings" beginning at 3 P.M. *The place is desert* (*erēmos estin ho topos*). Not a desolate region, simply lonely, comparatively uninhabited with no large towns near. There were "villages" (*kōmas*) where the people could buy food, but they would need time to go to them. Probably this is the idea of the disciples when they add: *The time is already past* (*hē hōra ēdē parēlthen*). They must hurry.

16. *Give ye them to eat* (*dote autois hūmeis phagein*). The emphasis is on *hūmeis* in contrast (note position) with their "send away" (*apoluson*). It is the urgent aorist of

instant action (*dote*). It was an astounding command. The disciples were to learn that "no situation appears to Him desperate, no crisis unmanageable" (Bruce).

17. *And they say unto him* (*hoi de legousin autōi*). The disciples, like us today, are quick with reasons for their inability to perform the task imposed by Jesus.

18. *And he said* (*ho de eipen*). Here is the contrast between the helpless doubt of the disciples and the confident courage of Jesus. He used "*the* five loaves and' two fishes" which they had mentioned as a reason for doing nothing. "Bring them hither unto me." They had overlooked the power of Jesus in this emergency.

19. *To sit down on the grass* (*anaklithēnai epi tou chortou*). "Recline," of course, the word means, first aorist passive infinitive. A beautiful picture in the afternoon sun on the grass on the mountain side that sloped westward. The orderly arrangement (Mark) made it easy to count them and to feed them. Jesus stood where all could see him "break" (*klasas*) the thin Jewish cakes of bread and give to the disciples and they to the multitudes. This is a nature miracle that some men find it hard to believe, but it is recorded by all four Gospels and the only one told by all four. It was impossible for the crowds to misunderstand and to be deceived. If Jesus is in reality Lord of the universe as John tells us (John 1:1-18) and Paul holds (Col. 1:15-20), why should we balk at this miracle? He who created the universe surely has power to go on creating what he wills to do.

20. *Were filled* (*echortasthēsan*). Effective aorist passive indicative of *chortazō*. See Matt. 5:6. From the substantive *chortos* grass. Cattle were filled with grass and people usually with other food. They all were satisfied. *Broken pieces* (*tōn klasmatōn*). Not the scraps upon the ground, but the pieces broken by Jesus and still in the "twelve baskets" (*dōdeka kophinous*) and not eaten. Each

of the twelve had a basketful left over (*to perisseuon*). One hopes that the boy (John 6:9) who had the five loaves and two fishes to start with got one of the basketsful, if not all of them. Each of the Gospels uses the same word here for baskets (*kophinos*), a wicker-basket, called "coffins" by Wycliff. Juvenal (*Sat.* iii. 14) says that the grove of Numa near the Capenian gate of Rome was "let out to Jews whose furniture is a basket (*cophinus*) and some hay" (for a bed). In the feeding of the Four Thousand (Matthew and Mark) the word *sphuris* is used which was a sort of hamper or large provisions basket.

21. *Beside women and children* (*chōris gunaikōn kai paidiōn*). Perhaps on this occasion there were not so many as usual because of the rush of the crowd around the head of the lake. Matthew adds this item and does not mean that the women and children were not fed, but simply that "the eaters" (*hoi esthiontes*) included five thousand men (*andres*) besides the women and children.

22. *Constrained* (*ēnagkasen*). Literally, "compelled" or "forced." See this word also in Luke 14:23. The explanation for this strong word in Mark 6:45 and Matt. 14:22 is given in John 6:15. It is the excited purpose of the crowd to take Jesus by force and to make him national king. This would be political revolution and would defeat all the plans of Jesus about his kingdom. Things have reached a climax. The disciples were evidently swept off their feet by the mob psychology for they still shared the Pharisaic hope of a political kingdom. With the disciples out of the way Jesus could handle the crowd more easily, *till he should send the multitudes away* (*heōs hou apolusēi tous ochlous*). The use of the aorist subjunctive with *heōs* or *heōs hou* is a neat and common Greek idiom where the purpose is not yet realized. So in 18:30; 26:36. "While" sometimes renders it well. The subjunctive is retained after a past tense instead of the change to the optative of the ancient Attic.

The optative is very rare anyhow, but Luke uses it with *prin ē* in Acts 25:16.

23. *Into the mountain* (*eis to oros*).   After the dismissal of the crowd Jesus went up alone into the mountain on the eastern side of the lake to pray as he often did go to the mountains to pray. If ever he needed the Father's sympathy, it was now. The masses were wild with enthusiasm and the disciples wholly misunderstood him. The Father alone could offer help now.

24. *Distressed* (*basanizomenon*).   Like a man with demons (8:29). One can see, as Jesus did (Mark 6:48), the boat bobbing up and down in the choppy sea.

25. *Walking upon the sea* (*peripatōn epi tēn thalassan*). Another nature miracle. Some scholars actually explain it all away by urging that Jesus was only walking along the beach and not on the water, an impossible theory unless Matthew's account is legendary. Matthew uses the accusative (extension) with *epi* in verse 25 and the genitive (specifying case) in 26.

26. *They were troubled* (*etarachthēsan*).   Much stronger than that. They were literally "terrified" as they saw Jesus walking on the sea. *An apparition* (*phantasma*), or "ghost," or "spectre" from *phantazō* and that from *phainō*. They cried out "from fear" (*apo tou phobou*) as any one would have done. "A little touch of sailor superstition" (Bruce).

28. *Upon the waters* (*epi ta hudata*).   The impulsiveness of Peter appears as usual. Matthew alone gives this Peter episode.

30. *Seeing the wind* (*blepōn ton anemon*). Cf. Ex. 20:18 and Rev. 1:12 "to see the voice" (*tēn phōnēn*). "It is one thing to see a storm from the deck of a stout ship, another to see it in the midst of the waves" (Bruce). Peter was actually beginning to sink (*katapontizesthai*) to plunge down into the sea, "although a fisherman and a good swimmer"

(Bengel). It was a dramatic moment that wrung from Peter the cry: "Lord, save me" (*Kurie, sōson me*), and do it quickly the aorist means. He could walk on the water till he saw the wind whirl the water round him.

31. *Didst thou doubt? (edistasas?).* Only here and 28:17 in the N.T. From *distazō* and that from *dis* (twice). Pulled two ways. Peter's trust in the power of Christ gave way to his dread of the wind and waves. Jesus had to take hold of Peter (*epelabeto*, middle voice) and pull him up while still walking on the water.

32. *Ceased (ekopasen).* From *kopos*, toil. The wind grew weary or tired, exhausted itself in the presence of its Master (cf. Mark 4:39). Not a mere coincidence that the wind ceased now.

33. *Worshipped him (prosekunēsan autōi).* And Jesus accepted it. They were growing in appreciation of the person and power of Christ from the attitude in 8:27. They will soon be ready for the confession of 16:16. Already they can say: "Truly God's Son thou art." The absence of the article here allows it to mean a Son of God as in 27:54 (the centurion). But they probably mean "the Son of God" as Jesus was claiming to them to be.

34. *Gennesaret (Gennēsaret).* A rich plain four miles long and two broad. The first visit of Jesus apparently with the usual excitement at the cures. People were eager to touch the hem of Christ's mantle like the woman in 9:20. Jesus honoured their superstitious faith and "as many as touched were made whole" (*hosoi hēpsanto diesōthēsan*), completely (*di-*) healed.

CHAPTER XV

1. *From Jerusalem (apo Ierosolumōn).* Jerusalem is the headquarters of the conspiracy against Jesus with the Pharisees as the leaders in it. Already we have seen the Herodians combining with the Pharisees in the purpose to put Jesus to death (Mark 3:6 = Matt. 12:14 = Luke 6:11). Soon Jesus will warn the disciples against the Sadducees also (Matt. 16:6). Unusual order here, "Pharisees and scribes." "The guardians of tradition in the capital have their evil eye on Jesus and co-operate with the provincial rigorists" (Bruce), if the Pharisees were not all from Jerusalem.

2. *The tradition of the elders (tēn paradosin tōn presbuterōn).* This was the oral law, handed down by the elders of the past in *ex cathedra* fashion and later codified in the Mishna. Handwashing before meals is not a requirement of the Old Testament. It is, we know, a good thing for sanitary reasons, but the rabbis made it a mark of righteousness for others at any rate. This item was magnified at great length in the oral teaching. The washing (*niptontai,* middle voice, note) of the hands called for minute regulations. It was commanded to wash the hands before meals, it was one's duty to do it after eating. The more rigorous did it between the courses. The hands must be immersed. Then the water itself must be "clean" and the cups or pots used must be ceremonially "clean." Vessels were kept full of clean water ready for use (John 2:6–8). So it went on *ad infinitum.* Thus a real issue is raised between Jesus and the rabbis. It was far more than a point of etiquette or of hygienics. The rabbis held it to be a mortal sin. The incident may have happened in a Pharisee's house.

3. *Ye also (kai hūmeis).* Jesus admits that the disciples

had transgressed the rabbinical traditions. Jesus treats
it as a matter of no great importance in itself save as
they had put the tradition of the elders in the place of the
commandment of God. When the two clashed, as was often
the case, the rabbis transgress the commandment of God "because of your tradition" (*dia tēn paradosin hūmōn*). The accusative with *dia* means that, not "by means of." Tradition
is not good or bad in itself. It is merely what is handed on
from one to another. Custom tended to make these traditions binding like law. The Talmud is a monument of their
struggle with tradition. There could be no compromise on
this subject and Jesus accepts the issue. He stands for real
righteousness and spiritual freedom, not for bondage to mere
ceremonialism and tradition. The rabbis placed tradition
(the oral law) above the law of God.

5. *But ye say* (*hūmeis de legete*). In sharp contrast to
the command of God. Jesus had quoted the fifth commandment (Ex. 20:12, 16) with the penalty "die the death"
(*thanatōi teleutatō*), "go on to his end by death," in imitation
of the Hebrew idiom. They dodged this command of God
about the penalty for dishonouring one's father or mother by
the use of "Corban" (*korban*) as Mark calls it (7:11). All
one had to do to evade one's duty to father or mother was
to say "Corban" or "Gift" (*Dōron*) with the idea of using
the money for God. By an angry oath of refusal to help
one's parents, the oath or vow was binding. By this magic
word one set himself free (*ou mē timēsei*, he shall not honour)
from obedience to the fifth commandment. Sometimes un-
filial sons paid graft to the rabbinical legalists for such
dodges. Were some of these very faultfinders guilty?

6. *Ye have made void the word of God* (*ekurōsate ton logon
tou theou*). It was a stinging indictment that laid bare
the hollow pretence of their quibbles about handwashing.
Kuros means force or authority, *akuros* is without authority,
null and void. It is a late verb, *akuroō* but in the LXX, Gal.

3:17; and in the papyri Adjective, verb, and substantive occur
in legal phraseology like cancelling a will, etc. The moral
force of God's law is annulled by their hairsplitting techni-
calities and immoral conduct.

7. *Well did Isaiah prophesy of you* (*kalōs eprophēteusen
peri hūmōn Esaias*). There is sarcasm in this pointed application of Isaiah's words (Is. 29:13) to these rabbis. He
"beautifully pictured" them. The portrait was to the very
life, "teaching as their doctrines the commandments of
men." They were indeed far from God if they imagined
that God would be pleased with such gifts at the expense
of duty to one's parents.

11. *This defileth the man* (*touto koinoi ton anthrōpon*).
This word is from *koinos* which is used in two senses, either
what is "common" to all and general like the *Koiné* Greek,
or what is unclean and "common" either ceremonially or in
reality. The ceremonial "commonness" disturbed Peter on
the housetop in Joppa (Acts 10:14). See also Acts 21:28;
Heb. 9:13. One who is thus religiously common or unclean
is cut off from doing his religious acts. "Defilement" was a
grave issue with the rabbinical ceremonialists. Jesus appeals
to the crowd here: *Hear and understand* (*akouete kai suniete*).
He has a profound distinction to draw. Moral uncleanness
is what makes a man common, defiles him. That is what
is to be dreaded, not to be glossed over. "This goes beyond
the tradition of the elders and virtually abrogates the Levitical distinctions between clean and unclean" (Bruce). One
can see the pettifogging pretenders shrivel up under these
withering words.

12. *Were offended* (*eskandalisthēsan*). First aorist passive.
"Were caused to stumble," "have taken offence" (Moffatt),
"have turned against you" (Weymouth), "were shocked"
(Goodspeed), "War ill-pleased" (Braid Scots). They took
umbrage at the public rebuke and at such a scorpion sting
in it all. It cut to the quick because it was true. It showed

in the glowering countenances of the Pharisees so plainly
that the disciples were uneasy. See on 5:29.

14. *They are blind guides* (*tuphloi eisin hodēgoi*). Graphic
picture. Once in Cincinnati a blind man introduced me
to his blind friend. He said that he was showing him
the city. Jesus is not afraid of the Pharisees. Let them
alone to do their worst. Blind leaders and blind victims will land in the ditch. A proverbial expression in
the O.T.

15. *Declare unto us the parable* (*phrason hūmin tēn parabolēn*). Explain the parable (pithy saying) in verse 11,
not in verse 14. As a matter of fact, the disciples had been
upset by Christ's powerful exposure of the "Corban" duplic-
ity and the words about "defilement" in verse 11.

16. *Are ye also even yet without understanding?* (*Akmēn
kai hūmeis asunetoi este*). *Akmēn* is an adverbial accusative
(classic *aichmē*, point (of a weapon) = *akmēn chronou* at this
point of time, just now = *eti*. It occurs in papyri and inscriptions, though condemned by the old grammarians. "In
spite of all my teaching, are ye also like the Pharisees without spiritual insight and grasp?" One must never forget
that the disciples lived in a Pharisaic environment. Their
religious world-outlook was Pharisaic. They were lacking in spiritual intelligence or sense, "totally ignorant"
(Moffatt).

17. *Perceive ye not?* (*ou noeite*). Christ expects us to
make use of our *nous*, intellect, not for pride, but for insight.
The mind does not work infallibly, but we should use it for
its God-given purpose. Intellectual laziness or flabbiness
is no credit to a devout soul.

18. *Out of the mouth* (*ek tou stomatos*). Spoken words
come out of the heart and so are a true index of character.
By "heart" (*kardias*) Jesus means not just the emotional nature, but the entire man, the inward life of "evil thoughts"
(*dialogismoi ponēroi*) that issue in words and deeds. "These

defile the man," not "eating with unwashed hands." The captious quibblings of the Pharisees, for instance, had come out of evil hearts.

22. *A Canaanitish woman* (*gunē Chananaia*). The Phoenicians were descended from the Canaanites, the original inhabitants of Palestine. They were of Semitic race, therefore, though pagan. *Have pity on me* (*eleēson me*). She made her daughter's case her own, "badly demonized."

23. *For she crieth after us* (*hoti krazei opisthen hēmōn*). The disciples greatly disliked this form of public attention, a strange woman crying after them. They disliked a sensation. Did they wish the woman sent away with her daughter healed or unhealed?

24. *I was not sent* (*ouk apestalēn*). Second aorist passive indicative of *apostellō*. Jesus takes a new turn with this woman in Phoenicia. He makes a test case of her request. In a way she represented the problem of the Gentile world. He calls the Jews "the lost sheep of the house of Israel" in spite of the conduct of the Pharisees.

27. *Even the dogs* (*kai ta kunaria*). She took no offence at the implication of being a Gentile dog. The rather she with quick wit took Christ's very word for little dogs (*kunaria*) and deftly turned it to her own advantage, for the little dogs eat of the crumbs (*psichiōn*, little morsels, diminutive again) that fall from the table of their masters (*kuriōn*), the children.

28. *As thou wilt* (*hōs theleis*). Her great faith and her keen rejoinder won her case.

29. *And sat there* (*ekathēto ekei*). "Was sitting there" on the mountain side near the sea of Galilee, possibly to rest and to enjoy the view or more likely to teach.

30. *And they cast them down at his feet* (*kai eripsan autous para tous podas autou*). A very strong word, flung them down, "not carelessly, but in haste, because so many

were coming on the same errand" (Vincent). It was a great day for "they glorified the God of Israel."

32. *Three days* (*hēmerai treis*). A parenthetic nominative (Robertson, *Grammar*, p. 460). *What to eat* (*ti phagōsin*). Indirect question with the deliberative subjunctive retained. In the feeding of the five thousand Jesus took compassion on the people and healed their sick (14:14). Here the hunger of the multitude moves him to compassion (*splagchnizomai*, in both instances). So he is unwilling (*ou thelō*) to send them away hungry. *Faint* (*ekluthōsin*). Unloosed, (*ekluō*) exhausted.

33. *And the disciples say to him* (*kai legousin autōi hoi mathētai*). It seems strange that they should so soon have forgotten the feeding of the five thousand (Matt. 14:13–21), but they did. Soon Jesus will remind them of both these demonstrations of his power (16:9 and 10). They forgot both of them, not just one. Some scholars scout the idea of two miracles so similar as the feeding of the five thousand and the four thousand, though both are narrated in detail by both Mark and Matthew and both are later mentioned by Jesus. Jesus repeated his sayings and wrought multitudes of healings. There is no reason in itself why Jesus should not on occasion repeat a nature miracle like this elsewhere. He is in the region of Decapolis, not in the country of Philip (*Trachonitis*).

34. *A few small fishes* (*oliga ichthudia*, diminutive again).

35. *On the ground* (*epi tēn gēn*). No mention of "grass" as in 14:19 for this time, midsummer, the grass would be parched and gone.

36. *Gave thanks* (*eucharistēsas*). In 14:19 the word used for "grace" or "blessing" is *eulogēsen*. Vincent notes that the Jewish custom was for the head of the house to say the blessing only if he shared the meal unless the guests were his own household. But we need not think of Jesus as bound by the peccadilloes of Jewish customs.

39. *The borders of Magadan (eis ta horia Magadan).* On the eastern side of the Sea of Galilee and so in Galilee again. Mark terms it Dalmanutha (8:10). Perhaps after all the same place as Magdala, as most manuscripts have it.

CHAPTER XVI

1. *The Pharisees and Sadducees* (*hoi Pharisaioi kai Saddoukaioi*). The first time that we have this combination of the two parties who disliked each other exceedingly. Hate makes strange bedfellows. They hated Jesus more than they did each other. Their hostility has not decreased during the absence of Jesus, but rather increased. *Tempting him* (*peirazontes*). Their motive was bad. *A sign from heaven* (*sēmeion ek tou ouranou*). The scribes and Pharisees had already asked for a sign (12:38). Now this new combination adds "from heaven." What did they have in mind? They may not have had any definite idea to embarrass Jesus. The Jewish apocalypses did speak of spectacular displays of power by the Son of Man (the Messiah). The devil had suggested that Jesus let the people see him drop down from the pinnacle of the temple and the people expected the Messiah to come from an unknown source (John 7:27) who would do great signs (John 7:31). Chrysostom (*Hom.* liii.) suggests stopping the course of the sun, bridling the moon, a clap of thunder.

2. *Fair weather* (*eudia*). An old poetic word from *eu* and *Zeus* as the ruler of the air and giver of fair weather. So men today say "when the sky is red at sunset." It occurs on the Rosetta Stone and in a fourth century A.D. Oxyr. papyrus for "calm weather" that made it impossible to sail the boat. Aleph and B and some other MSS. omit verses 2 and 3. W omits part of verse 2. These verses are similar to Luke 12:54–56. McNeile rejects them here. Westcott and Hort place in brackets. Jesus often repeated his sayings. Zahn suggests that Papias added these words to Matthew.

3. *Lowring* (*stugnazōn*). A sky covered with clouds. Used

also of a gloomy countenance as of the rich young ruler in
Mark 10:22. Nowhere else in the New Testament. This
very sign of a rainy day we use today. The word for "foul
weather" (*cheimōn*) is the common one for winter and a
storm. *The signs of the times* (*ta sēmeia tōn kairōn*). How
little the Pharisees and Sadducees understood the situation.
Soon Jerusalem would be destroyed and the Jewish state
overturned. It is not always easy to discern (*diakrinein*,
discriminate) the signs of our own time. Men are numerous
with patent keys to it all. But we ought not to be blind
when others are gullible.

4. Same words in 12:39 except *tou prophētou*, a real
doublet.

5. *Came* (*elthontes*). Probably = "went" as in Luke 15:
20 (*ire*, not *venire*). So in Mark 8:13 *apēlthen*. *Forgot*
(*epelathonto*). Perhaps in the hurry to leave Galilee, probably in the same boat by which they came across from
Decapolis.

7. *They reasoned* (*dielogizonto*). It was pathetic, the
almost jejune inability of the disciples to understand the
parabolic warning against "the leaven of the Pharisees and
Sadducees" (verse 6) after the collision of Christ just before
with both parties in Magadan. They kept it up, imperfect
tense. It is "loaves" (*artous*) rather than "bread."

8. Jesus asks four pungent questions about the intellectual dulness, refers to the feeding of the five thousand and
uses the word *kophinous* (14:20) for it and *sphuridas* for
the four thousand (15:37), and repeats his warning (16:11).
Every teacher understands this strain upon the patience of
this Teacher of teachers.

12. *Then understood they* (*tote sunēkan*). First aorist active
indicative of *suniēmi*, to grasp, to comprehend. They saw
the point after this elaborate rebuke and explanation that
by "leaven" Jesus meant "teaching."

13. *Caesarea Philippi* (*Kaisarias tēs Philippou*). Up

on a spur of Mt. Hermon under the rule of Herod Philip.
He asked (*ērōtā*). Began to question, inchoative imperfect
tense. He was giving them a test or examination. The
first was for the opinion of men about the Son of Man.

14. *And they said* (*hoi de eipan*). They were ready to
respond for they knew that popular opinion was divided on
that point (14:1f.). They give four different opinions. It
is always a risky thing for a pastor to ask for people's opinions of him. But Jesus was not much concerned by their
answers to this question. He knew by now that the Pharisees and Sadducees were bitterly hostile to him. The masses
were only superficially following him and they looked for a
political Messiah and had vague ideas about him. How
much did the disciples understand and how far have they
come in their development of faith? Are they still loyal?

15. *But who say ye that I am?* (*hūmeis de tina me legete
einai?*). This is what matters and what Jesus wanted to
hear. Note emphatic position of *hūmeis*, "But *you*, who
say ye that I am?"

16. Peter is the spokesman now: "Thou art the Christ,
the Son of the living God" (*Su ei ho Christos ho huios tou
theou tou zōntos*). It was a noble confession, but not a new
claim by Jesus. Peter had made it before (John 6:69) when
the multitude deserted Jesus in Capernaum. Since the early
ministry (John 4) Jesus had avoided the word Messiah because of its political meaning to the people. But now Peter
plainly calls Jesus the Anointed One, the Messiah, the Son
of the God the living one (note the four Greek articles).
This great confession of Peter means that he and the other
disciples believe in Jesus as the Messiah and are still true to
him in spite of the defection of the Galilean populace
(John 6).

17. *Blessed art thou* (*makarios ei*). A beatitude for
Peter. Jesus accepts the confession as true. Thereby Jesus
on this solemn occasion solemnly claims to be the Messiah,

the Son of the living God, his deity in other words. The
disciples express positive conviction in the Messiahship
or Christhood of Jesus as opposed to the divided opinions
of the populace. "The terms in which Jesus speaks of Peter
are characteristic—warm, generous, unstinted. The style
is not that of an ecclesiastical editor laying the foundation for church power, and prelatic pretentions, but of a
noble-minded Master eulogizing in impassioned terms a
loyal disciple" (Bruce). The Father had helped Peter get
this spiritual insight into the Master's Person and Work.

18. *And I also say unto thee* (*kagō de soi legō*). "The
emphasis is not on 'Thou art Peter' over against 'Thou art
the Christ,' but on *Kagō:* 'The Father hath revealed to thee
one truth, and I also tell you another" (McNeile). Jesus
calls Peter here by the name that he had said he would have
(John 1:42). Peter (*Petros*) is simply the Greek word for
Cephas (Aramaic). Then it was prophecy, now it is fact.
In verse 17 Jesus addresses him as "Simon Bar-Jonah," his
full patronymic (Aramaic) name. But Jesus has a purpose
now in using his nickname "Peter" which he had himself
given him. Jesus makes a remarkable play on Peter's name,
a pun in fact, that has caused volumes of controversy and
endless theological strife. *On this rock* (*epi tautēi tēi pe-
trāi*) Jesus says, a ledge or cliff of rock like that in 7:24 on
which the wise man built his house. *Petros* is usually a
smaller detachment of the massive ledge. But too much
must not be made of this point since Jesus probably spoke
Aramaic to Peter which draws no such distinction (*Kēphā*).
What did Jesus mean by this word-play? *I will build my
church* (*oikodomēsō mou tēn ekklēsian*). It is the figure of a
building and he uses the word *ekklēsian* which occurs in the
New Testament usually of a local organization, but sometimes in a more general sense. What is the sense here in
which Jesus uses it? The word originally meant "assembly"
(Acts 19:39), but it came to be applied to an "unassembled

assembly" as in Acts 8:3 for the Christians persecuted by
Saul from house to house. "And the name for the new
Israel, *ekklēsia*, in His mouth is not an anachronism. It is
an old familiar name for the congregation of Israel found in
Deut. (18:26; 23:2) and Psalms (22:36), both books well
known to Jesus" (Bruce). It is interesting to observe that
in Psalm 89 most of the important words employed by
Jesus on this occasion occur in the LXX text. So *oikodomēsō* in 89:5; *ekklēsia* in 6; *katischuō* in 22; *Christos* in 39, 52;
hāidēs in 49 (*ek cheiros hāidou*). If one is puzzled over the
use of "building" with the word *ekklēsia* it will be helpful
to turn to I Pet. 2:5. Peter, the very one to whom Jesus is
here speaking, writing to the Christians in the five Roman
provinces in Asia (I Pet. 1:1), says: "You are built a spiritual house" (*oikodomeisthe oikos pneumatikos*). It is difficult
to resist the impression that Peter recalls the words of Jesus
to him on this memorable occasion. Further on (2:9) he
speaks of them as an elect race, a royal priesthood, a holy
nation, showing beyond controversy that Peter's use of building a spiritual house is general, not local. This is undoubtedly the picture in the mind of Christ here in 16:18. It is a
great spiritual house, Christ's Israel, not the Jewish nation,
which he describes. What is the rock on which Christ will
build his vast temple? Not on Peter alone or mainly or primarily. Peter by his confession was furnished with the
illustration for the rock on which His church will rest. It is
the same kind of faith that Peter has just confessed. The
perpetuity of this church general is guaranteed. *The gates
of Hades* (*pulai hāidou*) *shall not prevail against it* (*ou
katischusousin autēs*). Each word here creates difficulty.
Hades is technically the unseen world, the Hebrew Sheol,
the land of the departed, that is death. Paul uses *thanate*
in I Cor. 15:55 in quoting Hosea 13:14 for *hāidē*. It is not
common in the papyri, but it is common on tombstones in
Asia Minor, "doubtless a survival of its use in the old Greek

religion" (Moulton and Milligan, *Vocabulary*). The ancient
pagans divided Hades (*a* privative and *idein*, to see, abode
of the unseen) into Elysium and Tartarus as the Jews put
both Abraham's bosom and Gehenna in Sheol or Hades
(cf. Luke 16:25). Christ was in Hades (Acts 2:27, 31), not
in Gehenna. We have here the figure of two buildings, the
Church of Christ on the Rock, the House of Death (Hades).
"In the Old Testament the 'gates of Hades' (Sheol) never
bears any other meaning (Isa. 38:10; Wisd. 16:3; III Macc.
5:51) than death," McNeile claims. See also Psa. 9:13;
107:18; Job 38:17 (*pulai thanatou pulōroi hāidou*). It is not
the picture of Hades *attacking* Christ's church, but of death's
possible victory over the church. "The *ekklēsia* is built
upon the Messiahship of her master, and death, the gates of
Hades, will not prevail against her by keeping Him impris-
oned. It was a mysterious truth, which He will soon tell
them in plain words (verse 21); it is echoed in Ac. 2:24:31"
(McNeile). Christ's church will prevail and survive because He will burst the gates of Hades and come forth
conqueror. He will ever live and be the guarantor of the
perpetuity of His people or church. The verb *katischuō*
(literally have strength against, *ischuō* from *ischus* and *kat-*)
occurs also in Luke 21:36 and 23:23. It appears in the ancient Greek, the LXX, and in the papyri with the accusative
and is used in the modern Greek with the sense of gaining the
mastery over. The wealth of imagery in Matt. 16:18 makes
it difficult to decide each detail, but the main point is clear.
The *ekklēsia* which consists of those confessing Christ as
Peter has just done will not cease. The gates of Hades or
bars of Sheol will not close down on it. Christ will rise and
will keep his church alive. *Sublime Porte* used to be the
title of Turkish power in Constantinople.

19. *The Keys of the kingdom* (*tas kleidas tēs basileias*).
Here again we have the figure of a building with keys to
open from the outside. The question is raised at once if

Jesus does not here mean the same thing by "kingdom" that he did by "church" in verse 18. In Rev. 1:18; 3:7 Christ the Risen Lord has "the keys of death and of Hades." He has also "the keys of the kingdom of heaven" which he here hands over to Peter as "gatekeeper" or "steward" (*oikonomos*) provided we do not understand it as a special and peculiar prerogative belonging to Peter. The same power here given to Peter belongs to every disciple of Jesus in all the ages. Advocates of papal supremacy insist on the primacy of Peter here and the power of Peter to pass on this supposed sovereignty to others. But this is all quite beside the mark. We shall soon see the disciples actually disputing again (Matt. 18:1) as to which of them is the greatest in the kingdom of heaven as they will again (20:21) and even on the night before Christ's death. Clearly neither Peter nor the rest understood Jesus to say here that Peter was to have supreme authority. What is added shows that Peter held the keys precisely as every preacher and teacher does. To "bind" (*dēsēis*) in rabbinical language is to forbid, to "loose" (*lusēis*) is to permit. Peter would be like a rabbi who passes on many points. Rabbis of the school of Hillel "loosed" many things that the school of Schammai "bound." The teaching of Jesus is the standard for Peter and for all preachers of Christ. Note the future perfect indicative (*estai dedemenon, estai lelumenon*), a state of completion. All this assumes, of course, that Peter's use of the keys will be in accord with the teaching and mind of Christ. The binding and loosing is repeated by Jesus to all the disciples (18:18). Later after the Resurrection Christ will use this same language to all the disciples (John 20:23), showing that it was not a special prerogative of Peter. He is simply first among equals, *primus inter pares*, because on this occasion he was spokesman for the faith of all. It is a violent leap in logic to claim power to forgive sins, to pronounce absolution, by reason of the technical rabbinical language that Jesus employed about binding and loosing. Every preacher uses the keys of the kingdom when he proclaims the terms of salvation in Christ. The proclamation of these terms when accepted by faith in Christ has the sanction and approval of God the Father. The more personal we make these great words the nearer we come to the mind of Christ. The more ecclesiastical we make them the further we drift away from him.

20. *That they should tell no man* (*hina mēdeni eipōsin*). Why? For the very reason that he had himself avoided this claim in public. He was the Messiah (*ho Christos*), but the people would inevitably take it in a political sense. Jesus was plainly profoundly moved by Peter's great confession on behalf of the disciples. He was grateful and confident of the final outcome. But he foresaw peril to all. Peter had confessed him as the Messiah and on this rock of faith thus confessed he would build his church or kingdom. They will all have and use the keys to this greatest of all buildings, but for the present they must be silent.

21. *From that time began* (*apo tote ērxato*). It was a suitable time for the disclosure of the greatest secret of his death. It is now just a little over six months before the cross. They must know it now to be ready then. The great confession of Peter made this seem an appropriate time. He will repeat the warnings (17:22f. with mention of betrayal; 20:17–19 with the cross) which he now "began." So the necessity (*dei*, must) of his suffering death at the hands of the Jerusalem ecclesiastics who have dogged his steps in Galilee is now plainly stated. Jesus added his resurrection "on the third day" (*tēi tritēi hēmerāi*), not "on the fourth day," please observe. Dimly the shocked disciples grasped something of what Jesus said.

22. *Peter took him* (*proslabomenos auton ho Petros*). Middle voice, "taking to himself," aside and apart, "as if by a right of his own. He acted with greater familiarity

after the token of acknowledgment had been given. Jesus,
however, reduces him to his level" (Bengel). "Peter here
appears in a new character; a minute ago speaking under
inspiration from heaven, now under inspiration from the
opposite quarter" (Bruce). Syriac Sinaitic for Mark 8:32
has it "as though pitying him." But this exclamation and
remonstrance of Peter was soon interrupted by Jesus. *God
have mercy on thee* (*hileōs*. Supply *eiē* or *estō ho theos*).
This shall never be (*ou mē estai soi touto*). Strongest kind
of negation, as if Peter would not let it happen. Peter had
perfect assurance.

23. *But he turned* (*ho de strapheis*). Second aorist passive participle, quick ingressive action, away from Peter in
revulsion, and toward the other disciples (Mark 8:33 has
epistrapheis and *idōn tous mathētas autou*). *Get thee behind
me, Satan* (*Hupage opisō mou, Satanā*). Just before Peter
played the part of a rock in the noble confession and was
given a place of leadership. Now he is playing the part of
Satan and is ordered to the rear. Peter was tempting Jesus
not to go on to the cross as Satan had done in the wilderness.
"None are more formidable instruments of temptation than
well-meaning friends, who care more for our comfort than
for our character" (Bruce). "In Peter the banished Satan
had once more returned" (Plummer). *A stumbling-block
unto me* (*skandalon ei emou*). Objective genitive. Peter was
acting as Satan's catspaw, in ignorance, surely, but none
the less really. He had set a trap for Christ that would undo
all his mission to earth. "Thou art not, as before, a noble
block, lying in its right position as a massive foundation
stone. On the contrary, thou art like a stone quite out of
its proper place, and lying right across the road in which I
must go—lying as a stone of stumbling" (Morison). *Thou
mindest not* (*ou phroneis*). "Your outlook is not God's,
but man's" (Moffatt). You do not think God's thoughts.
Clearly the consciousness of the coming cross is not a new

idea with Jesus. We do not know when he first foresaw
this outcome any more than we know when first the Messianic consciousness appeared in Jesus. He had the glimmer-
ings of it as a boy of twelve, when he spoke of "My Father's
house." He knows now that he must die on the cross.

24. *Take up his cross* (*aratō ton stauron autou*). Pick up
at once, aorist tense. This same saying in 10:38, which
see. But pertinent here also in explanation of Christ's
rebuke to Peter. Christ's own cross faces him. Peter had
dared to pull Christ away from his destiny. He would do
better to face squarely his own cross and to bear it after
Jesus. The disciples would be familiar with cross-bearing
as a figure of speech by reason of the crucifixion of criminals
in Jerusalem. *Follow* (*akaloutheitō*). Present tense. Keep
on following.

25. *Save his life* (*tēn psuchēn autou sōsai*). Paradoxical
play on word "life" or "soul," using it in two senses. So
about "saving" and "losing" (*apolesei*).

26. *Gain* (*kerdēsēi*) and *profit* (*zēmiōthēi*). Both aorist
subjunctives (one active, the other passive) and so punctiliar action, condition of third class, undetermined, but
with prospect of determination. Just a supposed case.
The verb for "forfeit" occurs in the sense of being fined or
mulcted of money. So the papyri and inscriptions. *Exchange* (*antallagma*). As an exchange, accusative in apposition with *ti*. The soul has no market price, though the devil
thinks so. "A man must give, surrender, his life, and nothing less to God; no *antallagma* is possible" (McNeile). This
word *antallagma* occurs twice in the *Wisdom of Sirach:*
"There is no exchange for a faithful friend" (6:15); "There
is no exchange for a well-instructed soul" (26:14).

28. *Some of them that stand here* (*tines tōn hode hestōtōn*).
A *crux interpretum* in reality. Does Jesus refer to the
Transfiguration, the Resurrection of Jesus, the great Day
of Pentecost, the Destruction of Jerusalem, the Second

Coming and Judgment? We do not know, only that Jesus was certain of his final victory which would be typified and symbolized in various ways. The apocalyptic eschatological symbolism employed by Jesus here does not dominate his teaching. He used it at times to picture the triumph of the kingdom, not to set forth the full teaching about it. The kingdom of God was already in the hearts of men. There would be climaxes and consummations.

CHAPTER XVII

1. *After six days* (*meth' hēmerās hex*). This could be on the sixth day, but as Luke (9:28) puts it "about eight days" one naturally thinks of a week as the probable time, though it is not important. *Taketh with him* (*paralambanei*). Literally, *takes along*. Note historical present. These three disciples form an inner group who have shown more understanding of Jesus. So at Gethsemane. *Apart* (*kat' idian*) means "by themselves" (*alone, monous,* Mark has it) up (*anapherei*) into a high mountain, probably Mount Hermon again, though we do not really know. "The Mount of Transfiguration does not concern geography" (Holtzmann).

2. *He was transfigured before them* (*metemorphōthē emprosthen autōn*). The word is the same as the metamorphoses (cf. Ovid) of pagan mythology. Luke does not use it. The idea is change (*meta-*) of form (*morphē*). It really presents the essence of a thing as separate from the *schēma* (fashion), the outward accident. So in Rom. 12:2 Paul uses both verbs, *sunschematizesthe* (be not fashioned) and *metamorphousthe* (be ye transformed in your inner life). So in I Cor. 7:31 *schēma* is used for the fashion of the world while in 16:12 *morphē* is used of the form of Jesus after his resurrection. The false apostles are described by *metaschēmatisomai* in II Cor. 11:13–15. In Phil. 2:6 we have *en morphēi* used of the Preincarnate state of Christ and *morphēn doulou* of the Incarnate state (2:7), while *schēmati hōs anthrōpos* emphasizes his being found "in fashion as a man." But it will not do in Matt. 17:2 to use the English transliteration *metamorphōsis* because of its pagan associations. So the Latin *transfigured* (Vulgate *transfiguratus est*) is better. "The

139

deeper force of *metamorphousthai* is seen in II Cor. 3:18 (with reference to the shining on Moses' face), Rom. 12:2" (McNeile). The word occurs in a second-century papyrus of the pagan gods who are invisible. Matthew guards against the pagan idea by adding and explaining about the face of Christ "as the sun" and his garments "as the light."

3. *There appeared* (*ōphthē*). Singular aorist passive verb with Moses (to be understood also with Elijah), but the participle *sunlalountes* is plural agreeing with both. "Sufficient objectivity is guaranteed by the vision being enjoyed by all three" (Bruce). The Jewish apocalypses reveal popular expectations that Moses and Elijah would reappear. Both had mystery connected with their deaths. One represented law, the other prophecy, while Jesus represented the gospel (grace). They spoke of his decease (Luke 9:31), the cross, the theme uppermost in the mind of Christ and which the disciples did not comprehend. Jesus needed comfort and he gets it from fellowship with Moses and Elijah.

4. *And Peter answered* (*apokritheis de ho Petros*). "Peter to the front again, but not greatly to his credit" (Bruce). It is not clear what Peter means by his saying: "It is good for us to be here" (*kalon estin hēmās hōde einai*). Luke (9:33) adds "not knowing what he said," as they "were heavy with sleep." So it is not well to take Peter too seriously on this occasion. At any rate he makes a definite proposal. *I will make* (*paiēsō*). Future indicative though aorist subjunctive has same form. *Tabernacles* (*skēnas*), booths. The Feast of Tabernacles was not far away. Peter may have meant that they should just stay up here on the mountain and not go to Jerusalem for the feast.

5. *Overshadowed* (*epeskiasen*). They were up in cloudland that swept round and over them. See this verb used of Mary (Luke 1:35) and of Peter's shadow (Acts 5:15). *This is* (*houtos estin*). At the baptism (Matt. 3:17) these

words were addressed to Jesus. Here the voice out of the bright cloud speaks to them about Jesus. *Hear ye him* (*akouete autou*). Even when he speaks about his death. A sharp rebuke to Peter for his consolation to Jesus about his death.

7. *And touched them* (*kai hapsamenos autōn*). Tenderness in their time of fear.

8. *Lifting up their eyes* (*eparantes tous ophthalmous autōn*). After the reassuring touch of Jesus and his words of cheer. *Jesus only* (*Iēsoun monon*). Moses and Elijah were gone in the bright cloud.

9. *Until* (*heōs hou*). This conjunction is common with the subjunctive for a future event as his Resurrection (*egerthēi*) was. Again (Mark 9:10) they were puzzled over his meaning. Jesus evidently hopes that this vision of Moses and Elijah and his own glory might stand them in good stead at his death.

10. *Elijah must first come* (*Ēleian dei elthein prōton*). So this piece of theology concerned them more than anything else. They had just seen Elijah, but Jesus the Messiah had come before Elijah. The scribes used Mal. 3:24; 4:5. Jesus had also spoken again of his death (resurrection). So they are puzzled.

12. *Elijah is come already* (*Ēleias ēdē ēlthen*). Thus Jesus identifies John the Baptist with the promise in Malachi, though not the real Elijah in person which John denied (John 1:26). *They knew him not* (*ouk epignōsan auton*). Second aorist active indicative of *epiginōskō*, to recognize. Just as they do not know Jesus now (John 1:26). They killed John as they will Jesus the Son of Man.

13. *Then understood* (*tote sunēkan*). One of the three k aorists. It was plain enough even for them. John was Elijah in spirit and had prepared the way for the Messiah.

15. *Epileptic* (*selēniazetai*). Literally, "moonstruck," "lunatic." The symptoms of epilepsy were supposed to be

aggravated by the changes of the moon (cf. 4:24). *He has it bad* (*kakōs echei*) as often in the Synoptic Gospels.

17. *Perverse* (*diestrammenē*). Distorted, twisted in two, corrupt. Perfect passive participle of *diastrephō*.

20. *Little faith* (*oligopistian*). A good translation. It was less than "a grain of mustard seed" (*kokkon sinapeōs*). See 13:31 for this phrase. They had no miracle faith. Bruce holds "this mountain" to be the Mount of Transfiguration to which Jesus pointed. Probably so. But it is a parable. Our trouble is always with "this mountain" which confronts our path. Note the form *metaba* (*meta* and *bēthi*).

23. *And they were exceeding sorry* (*kai elupēthēsan sphodra*). So they at last understood that he was talking about his death and resurrection.

24. *They that received the half-shekel* (*hoi ta didrachma lambanontes*). This temple tax amounted to an Attic drachma or the Jewish half-shekel, about one-third of a dollar. Every Jewish man twenty years of age and over was expected to pay it for the maintenance of the temple. But it was not a compulsory tax like that collected by the publicans for the government. "The tax was like a voluntary church-rate; no one could be compelled to pay" (Plummer). The same Greek word occurs in two Egyptian papyri of the first century A.D. for the receipt for the tax for the temple of Suchus (Milligan and Moulton's *Vocabulary*). This tax for the Jerusalem temple was due in the month Adar (our March) and it was now nearly six months overdue. But Jesus and the Twelve had been out of Galilee most of this time. Hence the question of the tax-collectors. The payment had to be made in the Jewish coin, half-shekel. Hence the money-changers did a thriving business in charging a small premium for the Jewish coin, amounting to some forty-five thousand dollars a year, it is estimated. It is significant that they approached Peter rather than Jesus, perhaps not wishing to embarrass "Your Teacher," "a

roundabout hint that the tax was overdue" (Bruce). Evidently Jesus had been in the habit of paying it (Peter's).

25. *Jesus spake first to him (proephthasen auton ho Iēsous legōn).* Here only in the N.T. One example in a papyrus B.C. 161 (Moulton and Milligan, *Vocabulary*). The old idiomatic use of *phthanō* with the participle survives in this example of *prophthanō* in Matt. 17:25, meaning to anticipate, to get before one in doing a thing. The *Koinê* uses the infinitive thus with *phthanō* which has come to mean simply to arrive. Here the anticipation is made plain by the use of *pro-*. See Robertson's *Grammar*, p. 1120. The "prevent" of the Authorized Version was the original idea of *praevenire*, to go before, to anticipate. Peter felt obliged to take the matter up with Jesus. But the Master had observed what was going on and spoke to Peter first. *Toll or tribute (telē ē kēnson).* Customs or wares collected by the publicans (like *phoros*, Rom. 13:7) and also the capitation tax on persons, indirect and direct taxation. *Kēnsos* is the Latin *census*, a registration for the purpose of the appraisement of property like *hē apographē* in Luke 2:2; Acts 5:37. By this parable Jesus as the Son of God claims exemption from the temple tax as the temple of his Father just as royal families do not pay taxes, but get tribute from the foreigners or aliens, subjects in reality.

26. *The sons (hoi huioi).* Christ, of course, and the disciples also in contrast with the Jews. Thus a reply to Peter's prompt "Yes." Logically *(arage)* free from the temple tax, but practically not as he proceeds to show.

27. *Lest we cause them to stumble (hina mē skandalisōmen autous).* He does not wish to create the impression that he and the disciples despise the temple and its worship. Aorist tense (punctiliar single act) here, though some MSS. have present subjunctive (linear). "A hook" *(agkistron)*. The only example in the N.T. of fishing with a hook. From an unused verb *agkizō*, to angle, and that from *agkos*, a curve

(so also *agkalē* the inner curve of the arm, Luke 2:38). *First cometh up* (*ton anabanta prōton ichthun*). More correctly, "the first fish that cometh up." *A shekel* (*statēra*). Greek stater = four drachmae, enough for two persons to pay the tax. *For me and thee* (*anti emou kai sou*). Common use of *anti* in commercial transactions, "in exchange for." Here we have a miracle of foreknowledge. Such instances have happened. Some try to get rid of the miracle by calling it a proverb or by saying that Jesus only meant for Peter to sell the fish and thus get the money, a species of nervous anxiety to relieve Christ and the Gospel of Matthew from the miraculous. "All the attempts have been in vain which were made by the older Rationalism to put a non-miraculous meaning into these words" (B. Weiss). It is not stated that Peter actually caught such a fish though that is the natural implication. Why provision is thus only made for Peter along with Jesus we do not know.

CHAPTER XVIII

1. *Who then is greatest (tis ara meizōn estin)*. The *ara* seems to point back to the tax-collection incident when Jesus had claimed exemption for them all as "sons" of the Father. But it was not a new dispute, for jealousy had been growing in their hearts. The wonderful words of Jesus to Peter on Mount Hermon (Matt. 16:17–19) had evidently made Peter feel a fresh sense of leadership on the basis of which he had dared even to rebuke Jesus for speaking of his death (16:22). And then Peter was one of the three (James and John also) taken with the Master up on the Mount of Transfiguration. Peter on that occasion had spoken up promptly. And just now the tax-collectors had singled out Peter as the one who seemed to represent the group. Mark (9:33) represents Jesus as asking them about their dispute on the way into the house, perhaps just after their question in Matt. 18:1. Jesus had noticed the wrangling. It will break out again and again (Matt. 20:20–28; Luke 22:24). Plainly the primacy of Peter was not yet admitted by the others. The use of the comparative *meizōn* (so *ho meizōn* in verse 4) rather than the superlative *megistos* is quite in accord with the *Koinē* idiom where the comparative is displacing the superlative (Robertson, *Grammar*, pp. 667ff.). But it is a sad discovery to find the disciples chiefly concerned about their own places (offices) in the political kingdom which they were expecting.

2. *Called to him (proskalesamenos)*. Indirect middle voice aorist participle. It may even be Peter's "little child" (*paidion*) as it was probably in Peter's house (Mark 9:33). *Set him (estēsen)*. Transitive first aorist active indicative, not intransitive second aorist, *estē*. *In the midst of them*

145

(*en mesōi autōn*).   Luke adds (9:47) "by his side" (*par'* *heautōi*).   Both are true.

3. *Except ye turn and become* (*ean mē straphēte kai* *genēsthe*).   Third-class condition, undetermined but with prospect of determination.   *Straphēte* is second aorist passive subjunctive and *genēsthe* second aorist middle subjunctive.   They were headed in the wrong direction with their selfish ambition.   "His tone at this time is markedly severe, as much as when He denounces the Pharisaism in the bud He had to deal with" (Bruce).   The strong double negative *ou mē eiselthēte* means that they will otherwise not get into the kingdom of heaven at all, let alone have big places in it.

4. *This little child* (*to paidion touto*).   This saying about humbling oneself Jesus repeated a number of times as for instance in Matt. 23:12.   Probably Jesus pointed to the child by his side.   The ninth-century story that the child was Ignatius is worthless.   It is not that the child humbled himself, but that the child is humble from the nature of the case in relation to older persons.   That is true, however "bumptious" the child himself may be.   Bruce observes that to humble oneself is "the most difficult thing in the world for saint as for sinner."

5. *In my name* (*epi tōi onomati mou*).   For "one such little child" (any believer in Christ) Luke (9:48) has "this little child" as a representative or symbol.   "On the basis or ground of my name," "for my sake."   Very much like *eis onoma* in 10:41 which does not differ greatly from *en onomati* (Acts 10:48).

6. *These little ones* (*tōn mikrōn toutōn*).   In the same sense as "one such little one" above.   The child is the type of believers.   *A great millstone* (*mulos onikos*), literally, "a millstone turned by an ass."   The upper millstone was turned by an ass (*onos*).   There were no examples of the adjective *onikos* (turned by an ass) outside the N.T. until

the papyri revealed several for loads requiring an ass to carry them, stones requiring an ass to move them, etc. Deissmann (*Light from the Ancient East*, p. 81) notes it also in papyri examples about the sale of an ass and tax for an ass's burden of goods. *The depth of the sea* (*tōi pelagei tēs thalassēs*). "The sea of the sea." *Pelagos* probably from *plēsso*, to beat, and so the beating, splashing waves of the sea. "Far out into the open sea, a vivid substitute for *eis tēn thalassan*" (McNeile).

7. *Through whom* (*di' ou*). Jesus recognizes the inevitableness of stumbling-blocks, traps, hindrances, the world being as it is, but he does not absolve the man who sets the trap (cf. Luke 17:1).

8. In verses 8 and 9 we have one of the dualities or doublets in Matthew (5:29-30). Jesus repeated his pungent sayings many times. Instead of *eis geennan* (5:29) we have *eis to pur to aiōnion* and at the end of verse 9 *tou puros* is added to *tēn geennan*. This is the first use in Matthew of *aiōnios*. We have it again in 19:16, 29 with *zoē*, in 25:41 with *pur*, in 25:46 with *kolasin* and *zoēn*. The word means ageless, without beginning or end as of God (Rom. 16:26), without beginning as in Rom. 16:25, without end as here and often. The effort to make it mean "*aeonian*" fire will make it mean "*aeonian*" life also. If the punishment is limited, *ipso facto* the life is shortened. In verse 9 also *monophthalmon* occurs. It is an Ionic compound in Herodotus that is condemned by the Atticists, but it is revived in the vernacular *Koinē*. Literally one-eyed. Here only and Mark 9:47 in the New Testament.

10. *Despise* (*kataphronēsēte*). Literally, "think down on," with the assumption of superiority. *Their angels* (*hoi aggeloi autōn*). The Jews believed that each nation had a guardian angel (Dan. 10:13, 20f.; 12:1). The seven churches in Revelation (1:20) have angels, each of them, whatsoever the meaning is. Does Jesus mean to teach here

that each little child or child of faith had a special angel who appears in God's presence, "see the face of my Father" (*blepousin to prosōpon tou patros mou*) in special intimacy? Or does he simply mean that the angels do take an interest in the welfare of God's people (Heb. 1:14)? There is comfort to us in that thought. Certainly Jesus means that the Father takes special care of his "little ones" who believe in Him. There are angels in God's presence (Luke 1:19).

12. *Leave the ninety and nine* (*aphēsei ta enenēkonta ennea epi ta orē kai poreutheis zētei to planōmenon?*). This is the text of Westcott and Hort after BL, etc. This text means: "Will he not leave the ninety and nine upon the mountains and going does he not seek (change to present tense) the wandering one?" On the high pastures where the sheep graze at will one has wandered afield. See this parable later in Luke 15:4–7. Our word "planet" is from *planaomai*, wandering (moving) stars they were called as opposed to fixed stars. But now we know that no stars are fixed. They are all moving and rapidly.

14. *The will of your Father* (*thelēma emprosthen*). Observe that Westcott and Hort read *mou* here rather than *hūmōn* after B Sahidic Coptic. Either makes good sense, though "your" carries on the picture of God's care for "each one of these little ones" (*hen tōn mikrōn toutōn*) among God's children. The use of *emprosthen* with *thelēma* is a Hebraism like *emprosthen sou* in 11:25 with *eudokia*, "before the face" of God.

15. *If thy brother sin against thee* (*ean hamartēsēi adelphos sou*). Literally, commit a sin (ingressive aorist subjunctive of *hamartanō*). Aleph B Sahidic do not have "against thee" (*eis se*). *Shew him his fault* (*elegxon*). Such private reproof is hard to do, but it is the way of Christ. *Thou hast gained* (*ekerdēsas*). Aorist active indicative of *kerdainō* in conclusion of a third-class condition, a sort of timeless aorist, a blessed achievement already made.

16. *Take with thee* (*paralabe meta sou*). Take alone (*para*) with (*meta*) thee.

17. *Refuse to hear* (*parakousēi*). Like Isa. 65:12. Many papyri examples for ignoring, disregarding, hearing without heeding, hearing aside (*para-*), hearing amiss, overhearing (Mark 5:36). *The church* (*tēi ekklēsiāi*). The local body, not the general as in Matt. 16:18 which see for discussion. The problem here is whether Jesus has in mind an actual body of believers already in existence or is speaking prophetically of the local churches that would be organized later (as in Acts). There are some who think that the Twelve Apostles constituted a local *ekklēsia*, a sort of moving church of preachers. That could only be true in essence as they were a band of ministers and not located in any one place. Bruce holds that they were "the nucleus" of a local church at any rate.

18. *Shall be bound in heaven* (*estai dedemena en ouranōi*). Future passive periphrastic perfect indicative as in "shall be loosed" (*estai lelumena*). In 16:19 this same unusual form occurs. The finding and the loosing is there addressed to Peter, but it is here repeated for the church or for the disciples as the case may be.

19. *Shall agree* (*sumphōnēsōsin*). Our word "symphony" is this very root. It is no longer looked at as a concord of voices, a chorus in harmony, though that would be very appropriate in a church meeting rather than the rasping discord sometimes heard even between two brethren or sisters. *Of my Father* (*para tou patros mou*). From the side of, "by my Father."

20. *There am I* (*ekei eimi*). This blessed promise implies that those gathered together are really disciples with the spirit of Christ as well as "in his name" (*eis to emon onoma*). One of the Oxyrhynchus *Sayings of Our Lord* is: "Wherever there are (two) they are not without God, and wherever there is one alone I say I am with him." Also this:

"Raise the stone and there thou shalt find me, cleave the wood and there am I." See Mal. 3:16.

21. *Until seven times?* (*heōs heptakis?*) Peter thought that he was generous as the Jewish rule was three times (Amos 1:6). His question goes back to verse 15. "Against me" is genuine here. "The man who asks such a question does not really know what forgiveness means" (Plummer).

22. *Until seventy times seven* (*heōs hebdomēkontakis hepta*). It is not clear whether this idiom means seventy-seven or as the Revised Version has it (490 times). If *heptakis* were written it would clearly be 490 times. The same ambiguity is seen in Gen. 4:24, the LXX text by omitting *kai*. In the *Test. of the Twelve Patriarchs*, *Benj.* vii. 4, it is used in the sense of seventy times seven. But it really makes little difference because Jesus clearly means unlimited forgiveness in either case. "The unlimited revenge of primitive man has given place to the unlimited forgiveness of Christians" (McNeile).

23. *Make a reckoning* (*sunārai logon*). Seen also in 25:19. Perhaps a Latinism, *rationes conferre*. First aorist active infinitive of *sunairō*, to cast up accounts, to settle, to compare accounts with. Not in ancient Greek writers, but in two papyri of the second century A.D. in the very sense here and the substantive appears in an ostracon from Nubia of the early third century (Deissmann, *Light from the Ancient East*, p. 117).

24. *Ten thousand talents* (*muriōn talantōn*). A talent was 6,000 denarii or about a thousand dollars or 240 pounds. Ten thousand times this is about ten or twelve million dollars, an enormous sum for that period. We live today in the age of national debts of billions of dollars or even of pounds sterling. The imperial taxes of Judea, Idumea, and Samaria for one year were only 600 talents while Galilee and Perea paid 200 (Josephus, *Ant.* xi. 4). But oriental kings

were free in the use of money and in making debts like the
native kings of India today.

25. *Had not wherewith to pay* (*mē echontos autou apodou-
nai*). There is no "wherewith" in the Greek. This idiom is
seen in Luke 7:42; 14:14; Heb. 6:13. Genitive absolute
though *auton* in the same clause as often in the N.T. *To be
sold* (*prathēnai*). First aorist passive infinitive of *pipraskō*.
This was according to the law (Ex. 22:3; Lev. 25:39, 47).
Wife and children were treated as property in those primitive times.

27. *The debt* (*to danion*). The loan. Common in the
papyri for a loan. The interest had increased the debt
enormously. "This heavy oriental usury is of the scenery
of the parable" (McNeile).

28. *A hundred pence* (*hekaton dēnaria*). A denarius was
worth about eight and a half pence. The hundred denarii
here were equal to some "fifty shillings" (Bruce), "about 4
pounds" (McNeile), "twenty pounds" (Moffatt), "twenty
dollars" (Goodspeed), "100 shillings" (Weymouth). These
are various efforts to represent in modern language the small
amount of this debt compared with the big one. *Took him
by the throat* (*epnigen*). "Held him by the throat" (Allen).
It is imperfect, probably inchoative, "began to choke or
throttle him." The Roman law allowed this indignity.
Vincent quotes Livy (iv. 53) who tells how the necks were
twisted (*collum torsisset*) and how Cicero (*Pro Cluentio*, xxi.)
says: "Lead him to the judgment seat with twisted neck
(*collo obtorto*)." *What thou owest* (*ei ti opheileis*). Literally,
"if thou owest anything," however little. He did not
even know how much it was, only that he owed him something. "The 'if' is simply the expression of a pitiless logic"
(Meyer).

30. *And he would not* (*ho de ouk ēthelen*). Imperfect
tense of persistent refusal. *Till he should pay* (*heōs
apodōi*). This futuristic aorist subjunctive is the rule with

heōs for a future goal. He was to stay in prison till he should pay. "He acts on the instinct of a base nature, and also doubtless in accordance with long habits of harsh tyrannical behaviour towards men in his power" (Bruce). On imprisonment for debt among the Greeks and Romans see Deissmann, *Light from the Ancient East*, pp. 270, 330.

31. *Told* (*diesaphēsan*). Made wholly clear to their own lord. That is the usual result in the long run. There is a limit to what people will put up with.

33. *Shouldst thou not?* (*ouk edei se?*) "Was it not necessary?" The king fits the cap on this wicked slave that he put on the poor debtor.

34. *The tormentors* (*tois basanistais*). Not to prison simply, but to terrible punishment. The papyri give various instances of the verb *basanizō*, to torture, used of slaves and others. "Livy (ii. 23) pictures an old centurion complaining that he was taken by his creditor, not into servitude, but to a workhouse and torture, and showing his back scarred with fresh wounds" (Vincent). *Till he should pay all* (*heōs* [*hou*] *apodōi pan*). Just as in verse 30, his very words. But this is not purgatorial, but punitive, for he could never pay back that vast debt.

35. *From your hearts* (*apo tōn kardiōn hūmōn*). No sham or lip pardon, and as often as needed. This is Christ's full reply to Peter's question in 18:21. This parable of the unmerciful servant is surely needed today.

CHAPTER XIX

1. *He departed* (*meteren*). Literally, to lift up, change something to another place. Transitive in the LXX and in a Cilician rock inscription. Intransitive in 13:53 and here, the only N.T. instances. Absence of *hoti* or *kai* after *kai egeneto*, one of the clear Hebraisms in the N.T. (Robertson, *Grammar*, pp. 1042f.). This verse is a sort of formula in Matthew at the close of important groups of *logia* as in 7:28; 11:1; 13:53. *The borders of Judea beyond Jordan* (*eis ta horia tēs Ioudaias peran tou Iordanou*). This is a curious expression. It apparently means that Jesus left Galilee to go to Judea by way of Perea as the Galileans often did to avoid Samaria. Luke (17:11) expressly says that he passed through Samaria and Galilee when he left Ephraim in Northern Judea (John 11:54). He was not afraid to pass through the edge of Galilee and down the Jordan Valley in Perea on this last journey to Jerusalem. McNeile is needlessly opposed to the trans-Jordanic or Perean aspect of this phase of Christ's work.

3. *Pharisees tempting him* (*Pharisaioi peirazontes auton*). They "could not ask a question of Jesus without sinister motives" (Bruce). See 4:1 for the word (*peirazō*). *For every cause* (*kata pasan aitian*). This clause is an allusion to the dispute between the two theological schools over the meaning of Deut. 24:1. The school of Shammai took the strict and unpopular view of divorce for unchastity alone while the school of Hillel took the liberal and popular view of easy divorce for any passing whim if the husband saw a prettier woman (modern enough surely) or burnt his biscuits for breakfast. It was a pretty dilemma and meant to do Jesus harm with the people. There is no real trouble

about the use of *kata* here in the sense of *propter* or because of (Robertson, *Grammar*, p. 509).

5. *Shall cleave* (*kollēthēsetai*). First future passive, "shall be glued to," the verb means. *The twain shall become one flesh* (*esontai hoi duo eis sarka mian*). This use of *eis* after *eimi* is an imitation of the Hebrew, though a few examples occur in the older Greek and in the papyri. The frequency of it is due to the Hebrew and here the LXX is a direct translation of the Hebrew idiom.

6. *What therefore God hath joined together* (*ho oun ho theos sunezeuxen*). Note "what," not "whom." The marriage relation God has made. "The creation of sex, and the high doctrine as to the cohesion it produces between man and woman, laid down in Gen., interdict separation" (Bruce). The word for "joined together" means "yoked together," a common verb for marriage in ancient Greek. It is the timeless aorist indicative (*sunezeuxen*), true always. *Bill* (*biblion*). A little *biblos* (see on 1:1), a scroll or document (papyrus or parchment). This was some protection to the divorced wife and a restriction on laxity.

8. *For your hardness of heart* (*pros tēn sklērokardian hūmōn*). The word is apparently one of the few Biblical words (LXX and the N.T.). It is a heart dried up (*sklēros*), hard and tough. *But from the beginning it hath not been so* (*ap' archēs de ouk gegonen houtōs*). The present perfect active of *ginomai* to emphasize the permanence of the divine ideal. "The original ordinance has never been abrogated nor superseded, but continues in force" (Vincent). "How small the Pharisaic disputants must have felt in presence of such holy teaching, which soars above the partisan view of controversialists into the serene region of ideal, universal, eternal truth" (Bruce).

9. *Except for fornication* (*parektos logou porneias*). This is the marginal reading in Westcott and Hort which also adds "maketh her an adulteress" (*poiei autēn moicheu-*

thēnai) and also these words: "and he that marrieth her
when she is put away committeth adultery" (*kai ho apole-
lumenēn gamēsas moichatai*).   There seems to be a certain
amount of assimilation in various manuscripts between this
verse and the words in 5:32.   But, whatever reading is
accepted here, even the short one in Westcott and Hort
(*mē epi porneiāi*, not for fornication), it is plain that Matthew
represents Jesus in both places as allowing divorce for fornication as a general term (*porneia*) which is technically adultery
(*moicheia* from *moichaō* or *moicheuō*).   Here, as in 5:31f., a
group of scholars deny the genuineness of the exception
given by Matthew alone.   McNeile holds that "the addition
of the saving clause is, in fact, opposed to the spirit of the
whole context, and must have been made at a time when the
practice of divorce for adultery had already grown up."
That in my opinion is gratuitous criticism which is unwilling
to accept Matthew's report because it disagrees with one's
views on the subject of divorce.   He adds: "It cannot be
supposed that Matthew wished to represent Jesus as siding
with the school of Shammai."   Why not, if Shammai on
this point agreed with Jesus?   Those who deny Matthew's
report are those who are opposed to remarriage at all.   Jesus
by implication, as in 5:31, does allow remarriage of the
innocent party, but not of the guilty one.   Certainly Jesus
has lifted the whole subject of marriage and divorce to a new
level, far beyond the petty contentions of the schools of
Hillel and Shammai.

10. *The disciples say unto him* (*legousin autōi hoi mathētai*).   "Christ's doctrine on marriage not only separated
Him *toto caelo* from Pharisaic opinions of all shades, but
was too high even for the Twelve" (Bruce).   *The case*
(*hē aitia*).   The word may refer to the use in verse 3 "for
every cause."   It may have a vague idea here = *res*, condition.   But the point clearly is that "it is not expedient to
marry" (*ou sumpherei gamēsai*) if such a strict view is held.

If the bond is so tight a man had best not commit matrimony. It is a bit unusual to have *anthrōpos* and *gunē* contrasted rather than *anēr* and *gunē*.

11. *But they to whom it is given* (*all' hois dedotai*). A neat Greek idiom, dative case of relation and perfect passive indicative. The same idea is repeated at the close of verse 12. It is a voluntary renunciation of marriage for the sake of the kingdom of heaven. "Jesus recognizes the severity of the demand as going beyond the capacity of all but a select number." It was a direct appeal to the spiritual intelligence of the disciples not to misconceive his meaning as certainly the monastic orders have done.

13. *Rebuked them* (*epetimēsen autois*). No doubt people did often crowd around Jesus for a touch of his hand and his blessing. The disciples probably felt that they were doing Jesus a kindness. How little they understood children and Jesus. It is a tragedy to make children feel that they are in the way at home and at church. These men were the twelve apostles and yet had no vision of Christ's love for little children. The new child world of today is due directly to Jesus.

14. *Suffer* (*aphete*). "Leave them alone." Second aorist active imperative. *Forbid them not* (*mē kōluete*). "Stop hindering them." The idiom of *mē* with the present imperative means just that. *Of such* (*tōn toioutōn*). The childlike as in 18:3f.

16. *What good thing* (*ti agathon*). Mark (10:17) has the adjective "good" with "Teacher." *May have* (*schō*). Ingressive aorist subjunctive, "may get," "may acquire."

17. *Concerning that which is good* (*peri tou agathou*). He had asked Jesus in verse 16 "what good thing" he should do. He evidently had a light idea of the meaning of *agathos*. "This was only a teacher's way of leading on a pupil" (Bruce). So Jesus explains that "One there is who is good," one alone who is really good in the absolute sense.

20. *What lack I yet?* (*ti eti husterō?*) Here is a psychological paradox. He claims to have kept all these commandments and yet he was not satisfied. He had an uneasy conscience and Jesus called him to something that he did not have. He thought of goodness as quantitative (a series of acts) and not qualitative (of the nature of God). Did his question reveal proud complacency or pathetic despair? A bit of both most likely.

21. *If thou wouldest be perfect* (*ei theleis teleios einai*). Condition of the first class, determined as fulfilled. Jesus assumes that the young man really desires to be perfect (a big adjective that, perfect as God is the goal, 5:48). *That thou hast* (*sou ta huparchonta*). "Thy belongings." The Greek neuter plural participle used like our English word "belongings." It was a huge demand, for he was rich.

22. *Went away sorrowful* (*apēlthen lupoumenos*). "Went away grieved." He felt that Jesus had asked too much of him. He worshipped money more than God when put to the test. Does Jesus demand this same test of every one? Not unless he is in the grip of money. Different persons are in the power of different sins. One sin is enough to keep one away from Christ.

23. *It is hard* (*duskolōs*). With difficulty. Adverb from *duskolos*, hard to find food, fastidious, faultfinding, then difficult.

24. *It is easier for a camel to go through a needle's eye* (*eukopōteron estin kamēlon dia trēmatos rhaphidos eiselthein*). Jesus, of course, means by this comparison, whether an eastern proverb or not, to express the impossible. The efforts to explain it away are jejune like a ship's cable, *kamilon* or *rhaphis* as a narrow gorge or gate of entrance for camels which recognized stooping, etc. All these are hopeless, for Jesus pointedly calls the thing "impossible" (verse 26). The Jews in the Babylonian Talmud did have a proverb that a man even in his dreams did not see an elephant **pass**

through the eye of a needle (Vincent). The Koran speaks of the wicked finding the gates of heaven shut "till a camel shall pass through the eye of a needle." But the Koran may have got this figure from the New Testament. The word for an ordinary needle is *rhaphis*, but, Luke (18:25) employs *belonē*, the medical term for the surgical needle not elsewhere in the N.T.

25. *Were astonished* (*exeplēssonto*). Imperfect descriptive of their blank amazement. They were literally "struck out."

26. *Looking on them* (*emblepsas*). Jesus saw their amazement.

27. *What then shall we have?* (*ti ara estai hēmin?*) A pathetic question of hopeless lack of comprehension.

28. *In the regeneration* (*en tēi palingenesiāi*). The new birth of the world is to be fulfilled when Jesus sits on his throne of glory. This word was used by the Stoics and the Pythagoreans. It is common also in the mystery religions (Angus, *Mystery Religions and Christianity*, pp. 95ff.). It is in the papyri also. We must put no fantastic ideas into the mouth of Jesus. But he did look for the final consummation of his kingdom. What is meant by the disciples also sitting on twelve thrones is not clear.

29. *A hundredfold* (*hekatonplasiona*). But Westcott and Hort read *pollaplasiona*, manifold. Eternal life is the real reward.

30. *The last first and the first last* (*hoi eschatoi prōtoi kai hoi prōtoi eschatoi*). This paradoxical enigma is probably in the nature of a rebuke to Peter and refers to ranks in the kingdom. There are many other possible applications. The following parable illustrates it.

CHAPTER XX

1. *For* (*gar*). The parable of the house illustrates the aphorism in 19:30. *A man that is a householder* (*anthrōpōi oikodespotēi*). Just like *anthrōpōi basilei* (18:23). Not necessary to translate *anthrōpōi*, just "a householder."

Early in the morning (*hama prōi*). A classic idiom. *Hama* as an "improper" preposition is common in the papyri. *Prōi* is just an adverb in the locative. At the same time with early dawn, break of day, country fashion for starting to work. *To hire* (*misthōsasthai*). The middle voice aorist tense, to hire for oneself.

2. *For a penny a day* (*ek dēnariou tēn hēmeran*). See on 18:28. "Penny" is not adequate, "shilling" Moffatt has it. The *ek* with the ablative represents the agreement (*sunphōnēsas*) with the workmen (*ergatōn*). "The day" the Greek has it, an accusative of extent of time.

3. *Standing in the marketplace idle* (*hestōtas agorāi argous*). The market place was the place where men and masters met for bargaining. At Hamadan in Persia, Morier in *Second Journey through Persia*, as cited by Trench in his *Parables*, says: "We observed every morning, before the sun rose, that a numerous band of peasants were collected, with spades in their hands, waiting to be hired for the day to work in the surrounding fields."

4. *Whatsoever is right* (*ho ean ēi dikaion*). "Is fair" (Allen), not anything he pleased, but a just proportionate wage. Indefinite relative with subjunctive *ean = an*.

6. *All the day idle* (*holēn tēn hēmeran argoi*). Extent of time (accusative) again. *Argoi* is *a* privative and *ergon*, work, no work. The problem of the unemployed.

10. *Every man a penny* (*ana dēnarion kai autoi*). Lit-

erally, "themselves also a denarius apiece" (distributive use of *ana*). Bruce asks if this householder was a humorist when he began to pay off the last first and paid each one a denarius according to agreement. False hopes had been raised in those who came first who got only what they had agreed to receive.

11. *They murmured* (*egogguzon*). Onomatopoetic word, the meaning suiting the sound. Our words murmur and grumble are similar. Probably here inchoative imperfect, began to grumble. It occurs in old Ionic and in the papyri.

12. *Equal unto us* (*isous autous hēmin*). Associative instrumental case *hēmin* after *isous*. It was a regular protest against the supposed injustice of the householder. *The burden of the day and the scorching wind* (*to baros tēs hēmeras kai ton kausōna*). These last "did" work for one hour. Apparently they worked as hard as any while at it. A whole day's work on the part of these sweat-stained men who had stood also the sirocco, the hot, dry, dust-laden east wind that blasted the grain in Pharaoh's dream (Gen. 41:6), that withered Jonah's gourd (Jonah 4:8), that blighted the vine in Ezekiel's parable (Ezek. 17:10). They seemed to have a good case.

13. *To one of them* (*heni autōn*). Evidently the spokesman of the group. "Friend" (*hetaire*). Comrade. So a kindly reply to this man in place of an address to the whole gang. Gen. 31:40; Job 27:21; Hos. 13:1;. The word survives in modern Greek.

14. *Take up* (*aron*). First aorist active imperative of *airō*. Pick up, as if he had saucily refused to take it from the table or had contemptuously thrown the denarius on the ground. If the first had been paid first and sent away, there would probably have been no murmuring, but "the murmuring is needed to bring out the lesson" (Plummer). The *dēnarius* was the common wage of a day labourer at that time. *What I will* (*ho thelō*). This is the point of the

parable, the *will* of the householder. *With mine own* (*en tois emois*). In the sphere of my own affairs. There is in the *Koinê* an extension of the instrumental use of *en*.

15. *Is thine eye evil?* (*ho ophthalmos sou ponēros estin?*) See on 6:22-24 about the evil eye and the good eye. The complainer had a grudging eye while the householder has a liberal or generous eye. See Rom. 5:7 for a distinction between *dikaios* and *agathos*.

16. *The last first and the first last* (*hoi eschātoi prōtoi kai hoi prōtoi eschatoi*). The adjectives change places as compared with 19:30. The point is the same, though this order suits the parable better. After all one's work does not rest wholly on the amount of time spent on it. "Even so hath Rabbi Bun bar Chija in twenty-eight years wrought more than many studious scholars in a hundred years" (Jer. *Berak.* ii. 5c).

17. *Apart* (*kat' idian*). This is the prediction in Matthew of the cross (16:21; 17:22; 20:17). "Aside by themselves" (Moffatt). The verb is *parelaben*. Jesus is having his inward struggle (Mark 10:32) and makes one more effort to get the Twelve to understand him.

19. *And to crucify* (*kai staurōsai*). The very word now. The details fall on deaf ears, even the point of the resurrection on the third day.

20. *Then* (*tote*). Surely an inopportune time for such a request just after the pointed prediction of Christ's crucifixion. Perhaps their minds had been preoccupied with the words of Jesus (19:28) about their sitting on twelve thrones taking them in a literal sense. The mother of James and John, probably Salome, possibly a sister of the Master's mother (John 19:25), apparently prompted her two sons because of the family relationship and now speaks for them. *Asking a certain thing* (*aitousa ti*). "Asking something," "plotting perhaps when their Master was predicting" (Bruce). The "something" put forward as a small matter

was simply the choice of the two chief thrones promised by Jesus (19:28).

22. *Ye know not what ye ask* (*ouk oidate ti aiteisthe*). How often that is true. *Aiteisthe* is indirect middle voice, "ask for yourselves," "a selfish request." *We are able* (*dunametha*). Amazing proof of their ignorance and self-confidence. Ambition had blinded their eyes. They had not caught the martyr spirit.

23. *Ye shall drink* (*piesthe*). Future middle from *pinō*. Christ's cup was martyrdom. James was the first of the Twelve to meet the martyr's death (Acts 12:2) and John the last if reports are true about him. How little they knew what they were saying.

24. *Moved with indignation* (*ēganaktēsan*). A strong word for angry resentment. In the papyri. The ten felt that James and John had taken advantage of their relation to Jesus.

25. *Called them unto him* (*proskalesamenos autous*). Indirect middle again, calling to him.

26. *Would become great* (*hos an thelēi megas genesthai*). Jesus does not condemn the desire to become great. It is a laudable ambition. There are "great ones" (*megaloi*) among Christians as among pagans, but they do not "lord it over" one another (*katakurieuousin*), a LXX word and very expressive, or "play the tyrant" (*katexousiazousin*), another suggestive word. *Your minister* (*humōn diakonos*). This word may come from *dia* and *konis* (dust), to raise a dust by one's hurry, and so to minister. It is a general word for servant and is used in a variety of ways including the technical sense of our "deacon" in Phil. 1:1. But it more frequently is applied to ministers of the Gospel (I Cor. 3:5). The way to be "first" (*prōtos*), says Jesus, is to be your "servant" (*doulos*), "bond-servant" (verse 27). This is a complete reversal of popular opinion then and now.

28. *A ransom for many* (*lutron anti pollōn*). The Son

of man is the outstanding illustration of this principle of
self-abnegation in direct contrast to the self-seeking of
James and John. The word translated "ransom" is the
one commonly employed in the papyri as the price paid
for a slave who is then set free by the one who bought him,
the purchase money for manumitting slaves. See examples
in Moulton and Milligan's *Vocabulary* and Deissmann's
Light from the Ancient East, pp. 328f. There is the notion
of exchange also in the use of *anti*. Jesus gave his own life
as the price of freedom for the slaves of sin. There are those
who refuse to admit that Jesus held this notion of a substitu-
tionary death because the word in the N.T. occurs only
here and the corresponding passage in Mark 10:45. But
that is an easy way to get rid of passages that contradict
one's theological opinions. Jesus here rises to the full consciousness of the significance of his death for men.

29. *From Jericho* (*apo Iereichō*). So Mark 10:46. But
Luke (18:35) places the incident as they were drawing near
to Jericho (*eis Iereichō*). It is probable that Mark and
Matthew refer to the old Jericho, the ruins of which have
been discovered, while Luke alludes to the new Roman
Jericho. The two blind men were apparently between the
two towns. Mark (10:46) and Luke (18:35) mention only
one blind man, Bartimaeus (Mark). In Kentucky there
are two towns about a half mile apart both called Pleasureville (one Old Pleasureville, the other New Pleasureville).

30. *That Jesus was passing by* (*hoti Iēsous paragei*).
These men "were sitting by the wayside" (*kathēmenoi para
tēn hodon*) at their regular stand. They heard the crowd
yelling that Jesus of Nazareth was passing by (*paragei*,
present indicative of direct discourse retained in the indirect). It was their one opportunity, now or never. They
had heard of what he had done for other blind men. They
hail him as "the son of David" (the Messiah). It is just
one of many such incidents when Jesus stood still and

opened their eyes, so many that even the multitude was impatient with the cries of these poor men that their eyes be opened (*anoigōsin*, second aorist passive subjunctive).

34. *Touched their eyes* (*hēpsato tōn ommatōn*). A synonym for *ophthalmōn* in Mark 8:23 and here alone in the N.T. In the LXX and a common poetic word (Euripides) and occurs in the papyri. In modern Greek *matia mou* (abbreviation) means "light of my eye," "my darling." The verb *haptomai* is very common in the Synoptic Gospels. The touch of Christ's hand would sooth the eyes as they were healed.

CHAPTER XXI

1. *Unto Bethphage (eis Bethphagē).* An indeclinable Aramaic name here only in O.T. or N.T. (=Mark 11:1 = Luke 19:29). It means "house of unripe young figs." It apparently lay on the eastern slope of Olivet or at the foot of the mountain, a little further from Jerusalem than Bethany. Both Mark and Luke speak of Christ's coming "unto Bethphage and Bethany" as if Bethphage was reached first. It is apparently larger than Bethany. *Unto the Mount of Olives (eis to oros tōn Elaiōn).* Matthew has thus three instances of *eis* with Jerusalem, Mount of Olives. Mark and Luke use *pros* with Mount of Olives, the Mount of Olive trees (*elaiōn* from *elaia*, olive tree), the mountain covered with olive trees.

2. *Into the village that is over against you (eis tēn kōmēn tēn katenanti hūmōn).* Another use of *eis.* If it means "into" as translated, it could be Bethany right across the valley and this is probably the idea. *And a colt with her (kai pōlon met' autēs).* The young of any animal. Here to come with the mother and the more readily so.

3. *The Lord (ho kurios).* It is not clear how the word would be understood here by those who heard the message though it is plain that Jesus applies it to himself. The word is from *kuros*, power or authority. In the LXX it is common in a variety of uses which appear in the N.T. as master of the slave (Matt. 10:24), of the harvest (9:38), of the vineyard (20:8), of the emperor (Acts 13:27), of God (Matt. 11:20; 11:25), and often of Jesus as the Messiah (Acts 10:36). Note Matt. 8:25. This is the only time in Matthew where the words *ho kurios* are applied to Jesus except the doubtful passage in 28:6. A similar usage is shown by Moulton and

Milligan's *Vocabulary* and Deissmann's *Light from the Ancient East*. Particularly in Egypt it was applied to "the Lord Serapis" and Ptolemy and Cleopatra are called "the lords, the most great gods" (*hoi kurioi theoi megistoi*). Even Herod the Great and Herod Agrippa I are addressed as "Lord King." In the west the Roman emperors are not so termed till the time of Domitian. But the Christians boldly claimed the word for Christ as Jesus is here represented as using it with reference to himself. It seems as if already the disciples were calling Jesus "Lord" and that he accepted the appellative and used it as here.

4. *By the prophet* (*dia tou prophētou*). The first line is from Isa. 62:11, the rest from Zech. 9:9. John (12:14f.) makes it clear that Jesus did not quote the passage himself. In Matthew it is not so plain, but probably it is his own comment about the incident. It is not Christ's intention to fulfil the prophecy, simply that his conduct did fulfil it.

5. *The daughter of Zion* (*tēi thugatri Siōn*). Jerusalem as in Isa. 22:4 (daughter of my people). So Babylon (Isa. 47:1), daughter of Tyre for Tyre (Psa. 45:12). *Riding* (*epibebēkōs*). Perfect active participle of *epibainō*, "having gone upon." *And upon a colt the foal of an ass* (*kai epi pōlon huion hupozugiou*). These words give trouble if *kai* is here taken to mean "and." Fritzsche argues that Jesus rode alternately upon each animal, a possible, but needless interpretation. In the Hebrew it means by common Hebrew parallelism "upon an ass, even upon a colt." That is obviously the meaning here in Matthew. The use of *hupozugiou* (a beast of burden, under a yoke) for ass is common in the LXX and in the papyri (Deissmann, *Bible Studies* p. 161).

7. *And he sat thereon* (*kai epekathisen epanō autōn*), Mark (11:7) and Luke (19:35) show that Jesus rode the colt. Matthew does not contradict that, referring to the garments (*ta himatia*) put on the colt by "them" (*autōn*). not to the two asses. The construction is somewhat loose,

but intelligible. The garments thrown on the animals were the outer garments (*himatia*), Jesus "took his seat" (*epekathisen*, ingressive aorist active) upon the garments.

8. *The most part of the multitude* (*ho pleistos ochlos*). See 11:20 for this same idiom, article with superlative, a true superlative (Robertson, *Grammar*, p. 670). *In the way* (*en tēi hodōi*). This the most of the crowd did. The disciples put their garments on the asses. Note change of tenses (constative aorist *estrōsan*, descriptive imperfects *ekopton kai estrōnnuon* showing the growing enthusiasm of the crowd). When the colt had passed over their garments, they would pick the garments up and spread them again before.

9. *That went before him and that followed* (*hoi proagontes auton kai hoi akolouthountes*). Note the two groups with two articles and the present tense (linear action) and the imperfect *ekrazon* "were crying" as they went. *Hosanna to the Son of David* (*Hosanna tōi huiōi Daueid*). They were now proclaiming Jesus as the Messiah and he let them do it. "Hosanna" means "Save, we pray thee." They repeat words from the *Hallel* (Psa. 148:1) and one recalls the song of the angelic host when Jesus was born (Luke 2:14). "Hosanna in the highest" (heaven) as well as here on earth.

10. *Was stirred* (*eseisthē*). Shaken as by an earthquake. "Even Jerusalem frozen with religious formalism and socially undemonstrative, was stirred with popular enthusiasm as by a mighty wind or by an earthquake" (Bruce).

12. *Cast out* (*exebalen*). Drove out, assumed authority over "the temple of God" (probably correct text with *tou theou*, though only example of the phrase). John (2:14) has a similar incident at the beginning of the ministry of Jesus. It is not impossible that he should repeat it at the close after three years with the same abuses in existence again. It is amazing how short a time the work of reformers lasts. The traffic went on in the court of the Gentiles and to a certain

extent was necessary. Here the tables of *the money-changers* (*tōn kollubistōn*, from *kollubos*, a small coin) were overturned. See on 17:24 for the need of the change for the temple tax. The doves were the poor man's offering.

13. *A den of robbers* (*spēlaion lēistōn*). By charging exorbitant prices.

15. *The children* (*tous paidas*). Masculine and probably boys who had caught the enthusiasm of the crowd.

16. *Hearest thou* (*akoueis*). In a rage at the desecration of the temple by the shouts of the boys they try to shame Jesus, as responsible for it.

16. *Thou hast perfected* (*katērtisō*). The quotation is from Psa. 8:3 (LXX text). See 4:21 where the same verb is used for mending nets. Here it is the timeless aorist middle indicative with the perfective use of *kata-*. It was a stinging rebuke.

17. *To Bethany* (*eis Bēthanian*). House of depression or misery, the Hebrew means. But the home of Martha and Mary and Lazarus there was a house of solace and comfort to Jesus during this week of destiny. He *lodged there* (*ēulisthē ekei*) whether at the Bethany home or out in the open air. It was a time of crisis for all.

18. *He hungered* (*epeinasen*). Ingressive aorist indicative, became hungry, felt hungry (Moffatt). Possibly Jesus spent the night out of doors and so had no breakfast.

19. *A fig tree* (*sukēn mian*). "A single fig tree" (Margin of Rev. Version). But *heis* was often used = *tis* or like our indefinite article. See Matt. 8:10; 26:69. The Greek has strictly no indefinite article as the Latin has no definite article. *Let there be no fruit from thee henceforward for ever* (*ou mēketi sou karpos genētai eis ton aiōna*). Strictly speaking this is a prediction, not a prohibition or wish as in Mark 11:14 (optative *phagoi*). "On you no fruit shall ever grow again" (Weymouth). The double negative *ou mē* with the aorist subjunctive (or future indicative) is the strongest

kind of negative prediction. It sometimes amounts to a prohibition like *ou* and the future indicative (Robertson, *Grammar*, pp. 926f.). The early figs start in spring before the leaves and develop after the leaves. The main fig crop was early autumn (Mark 11:14). There should have been figs on the tree with the crop of leaves. It was a vivid object lesson. Matthew does not distinguish between the two mornings as Mark does (Mark 11:13, 20), but says "immediately" (*parachrēma*) twice (21:19, 20). This word is really *para to chrēma* like our "on the spot" (Thayer). It occurs in the papyri in monetary transactions for immediate cash payment.

21. *Doubt not* (*mē diakrithēte*). First aorist passive subjunctive, second-class condition. To be divided in mind, to waver, to doubt, the opposite of "faith" (*pistin*), trust, confidence. *What is done to the fig tree* (*to tēs sukēs*). The Greek means "the matter of the fig tree," as if a slight matter in comparison with *this mountain* (*tōi orei toutōi*). Removing a mountain is a bigger task than blighting a fig tree. "The cursing of the fig-tree has always been regarded as of symbolic import, the tree being in Christ's mind an emblem of the Jewish people, with a great show of religion and no fruit of real godliness. This hypothesis is very credible" (Bruce). Plummer follows Zahn in referring it to the Holy City. Certainly "this mountain" is a parable and one already reported in Matt. 17:20 (cf. sycamine tree in Luke 17:6). Cf. Zech. 17:4.

22. *Believing* (*pisteuontes*). This is the point of the parable of the mountain, "faith in the efficacy of prayer" (Plummer).

24. *One question* (*logon hena*). Literally "one word" or "a word." The answer to Christ's word will give the answer to their query. The only human ecclesiastical authority that Jesus had came from John.

25. *The baptism of John* (*to baptisma to Iōanou*). This

represents his relation to Jesus who was baptized by him. At once the ecclesiastical leaders find themselves in a dilemma created by their challenge of Christ. *They reasoned with themselves (dielogizonto).* Picturesque imperfect tense describing their hopeless quandary.

29. *I will not (ou thelō).* So many old manuscripts, though the Vatican manuscript (B) has the order of the two sons reversed. Logically the "I, sir" *(egō, kurie)* suits better for the second son (verse 30) with a reference to the blunt refusal of the first. So also the manuscripts differ in verse 31 between the first *(ho prōtos)* and the last *(ho husteros or eschatos).* But the one who actually did the will of the father is the one who *repented and went (metameletheis apēlthen).* This word really means "repent," to be sorry afterwards, and must be sharply distinguished from the word *metanoeō* used 34 times in the N.T. as in Matt. 3:2 and *metanoia* used 24 times as in Matt. 3:8. The verb *metamelomai* occurs in the N.T. only five times (Matt. 21:29, 32; 27:3; II Cor. 7:8; Heb. 7:21 from Psa. 109:4). Paul distinguishes sharply between mere sorrow and the act "repentance" which he calls *metanoian* (II Cor. 7:9). In the case of Judas (Matt. 27:3) it was mere remorse. Here the boy got sorry for his stubborn refusal to obey his father and went and obeyed. Godly sorrow leads to repentance *(metanoian)*, but mere sorrow is not repentance.

31. *Go before you (proagousin).* "In front of you" (Weymouth). The publicans and harlots march ahead of the ecclesiastics into the kingdom of heaven. It is a powerful indictment of the complacency of the Jewish theological leaders.

32. *In the way of righteousness (en hodōi dikaiosunēs).* In the path of righteousness. Compare the two ways in Matt. 7:13 and 14 and "the way of God" (22:16).

33. *A hedge (phragmon).* Or fence as a protection against wild beasts. *Digged a winepress (ōruxen lēnon).* Out of the

solid rock to hold the grapes and wine as they were crushed.
Such wine-vats are to be seen today in Palestine. *Built a
tower* (*ōikodomēsen purgon*). This for the vinedressers and
watchmen (II Chron. 26:10). Utmost care was thus taken.
Note "a booth in a vineyard" (Isa. 1:8). See also Isa. 24:20;
Job. 27:18. *Let it out* (*exedeto, exedoto* the usual form).
For hire, the terms not being given. The lease allowed
three forms, money-rent, a proportion of the crop, or a definite amount of the produce whether it was a good or bad
year. Probably the last form is that contemplated here.

34. *His servants* (*tous doulous autou*). These slaves are
distinguished from *the husbandmen* (*geōrgoi*, workers of the
soil) or workers of the vineyard who had leased it from the
householder before he went away. The conduct of the husbandmen towards the householder's slaves portrays the
behaviour of the Jewish people and the religious leaders in
particular towards the prophets and now towards Christ.
The treatment of God's prophets by the Jews pointedly
illustrates this parable.

35. *They will reverence my son* (*entrapēsontai ton huion
mou*). Second future passive from *entrepō*, to turn at, but
used transitively here as though active or middle. It is the
picture of turning with respect when one worthy of it appears.

38. *Take his inheritance* (*schōmen tēn klēronomian autou*).
Ingressive aorist active subjunctive (hortatory, volitive) of
echō. Let us get his inheritance.

41. *He will miserably destroy those miserable men* (*kakous
kakōs apolesei autous*). The paronomasia or assonance is
very clear. A common idiom in literary Greek. "He will
put the wretches to a wretched death" (Weymouth).
Which (*hoitines*). Who, which very ones of a different character.

42. *The stone which* (*lithon hon*). Inverse attraction of
the antecedent into the case of the relative. *The builders*

rejected (*apedokimasan hoi oikodomountes*). From Psa. 118:
22. A most telling quotation. These experts in building
God's temple had rejected the corner-stone chosen by God
for his own house. But God has the last word and sets aside
the building experts and puts his Son as the Head of the
corner. It was a withering indictment.

43. *Shall be taken away from you* (*arthēsetai aph' hūmōn*).
Future passive indicative of *airō*. It was the death-knell of
the Jewish nation with their hopes of political and religious
world leadership.

44. *Shall be broken to pieces* (*sunthlasthēsetai*). Some
ancient manuscripts do not have this verse. But it graphically pictures the fate of the man who rejects Christ. The
verb means to shatter. We are familiar with an automobile
that dashes against a stone wall, a tree, or a train and the
ruin that follows. *Will scatter him as dust* (*likmēsei*). The
verb was used of winnowing out the chaff and then of grind-
ing to powder. This is the fate of him on whom this Rejected Stone falls.

45. *Perceived* (*egnōsan*). Ingressive second aorist active
of *ginōskō*. There was no mistaking the meaning of these
parables. The dullest could see the point.

46. *Took him* (*eichon*). Descriptive imperfect of *echō*,
to hold. This fear of the people was all that stayed the
hands of the rabbis on this occasion. Murderous rage was
in their hearts towards Jesus. People do not always grasp
the application of sermons to themselves.

CHAPTER XXII

1. *Again in parables* (*palin en parabolais*). Matthew has already given two on this occasion (The Two Sons, The Wicked Husbandmen). He alone gives this Parable of the Marriage Feast of the King's Son. It is somewhat similar to that of The Supper in Luke 14:16–23 given on another occasion. Hence some scholars consider this merely Matthew's version of the Lucan parable in the wrong place because of Matthew's habit of grouping the sayings of Jesus. But that is a gratuitous indictment of Matthew's report which definitely locates the parable here by *palin*. Some regard it as not spoken by Jesus at all, but an effort on the part of the writer to cover the sin and fate of the Jews, the calling of the Gentiles, and God's demand for righteousness. But here again it is like Jesus and suits the present occasion.

2. *A marriage feast* (*gamous*). The plural, as here (2, 3, 4, 9), is very common in the papyri for the wedding festivities (the several acts of feasting) which lasted for days, seven in Judges 14:17. The very phrase here, *gamous poiein*, occurs in the Doric of Thera about B.C. 200. The singular *gamos* is common in the papyri for the wedding contract, but Field (*Notes*, p. 16) sees no difference between the singular here in 22:8 and the plural (see also Gen. 29:22; Esther 9:22; Macc. 10:58).

3. *To call them that were bidden* (*kalesai tous keklēmenous*). "Perhaps an unconscious play on the words, lost in both A.V. and Rev., *to call the called*" (Vincent). It was a Jewish custom to invite a second time the already invited (Esther 5:8; 6:14). The prophets of old had given God's invitation to the Jewish people. Now the Baptist and Jesus had given the second invitation that the feast was ready. *And*

they would not come (kai ouk ēthelon elthein). This negative imperfect characterizes the stubborn refusal of the Jewish leaders to accept Jesus as God's Son (John 1:11). This is "The Hebrew Tragedy" (Conder).

4. *My dinner (to ariston mou)*. It is breakfast, not dinner. In Luke 14:12 both *ariston* (breakfast) and *deipnon* (dinner) are used. This noon or midday meal, like the French breakfast at noon, was sometimes called *deipnon mesēmbrinon* (midday dinner or luncheon). The regular dinner (*deipnon*) came in the evening. The confusion arose from applying *ariston* to the early morning meal and then to the noon meal (some not eating an earlier meal). In John 21:12, 15 *aristaō* is used of the early morning meal, "Break your fast" (*aristēsate*). When *ariston* was applied to luncheon, like the Latin *prandium*, *akratisma* was the term for the early breakfast. *My fatlings (ta sitista)*. Verbal from *sitizō*, to feed with wheat or other grain, to fatten. Fed-up or fatted animals.

5. *Made light of it (amelēsantes)*. Literally, neglecting, not caring for. They may even have ridiculed the invitation, but the verb does not say so. However, to neglect an invitation to a wedding feast is a gross discourtesy. *One to his own farm (hos men eis ton idion agron)* or field, *another to his merchandise (hos de epi tēn emporian autou)* only example in the N.T., from *emporos*, merchant, one who travels for traffic (*emporeuomai*), a drummer.

7. *Armies (strateumata)*. Bands of soldiers, not grand armies.

9. *The partings of the highways (tas diexodous tōn hodōn)*. Vulgate, *exitus viarum*. *Diodoi* are cross-streets, while *diexodoi* (double compound) seem to be main streets leading out of the city where also side-streets may branch off, "byways."

10. *The wedding (ho gamos)*. But Westcott and Hort rightly read here *ho numphōn*, marriage dining hall. The same word in 9:15 means the bridechamber.

12. *Not having a wedding-garment (mē echōn enduma gamou).* *Mē* is in the *Koinē* the usual negative with participles unless special emphasis on the negative is desired as in *ouk endedumenon.* There is a subtle distinction between *mē* and *ou* like our subjective and objective notions. Some hold that the wedding-garment here is a portion of a lost parable separate from that of the Wedding Feast, but there is no evidence for that idea. Wünsche does report a parable by a rabbi of a king who set no time for his feast and the guests arrived, some properly dressed waiting at the door; others in their working clothes did not wait, but went off to work and, when the summons suddenly came, they had no time to dress properly and were made to stand and watch while the others partook of the feast.

13. *Was speechless (epsimōthē).* Was muzzled, dumb from confusion and embarrassment. It is used of the ox (I Tim. 5:18). *The outer darkness (to skotos to exōteron).* See Matt. 8:12. All the blacker from the standpoint of the brilliantly lighted banquet hall. *There shall be (ekei estai).* Out there in the outer darkness.

14. *For many are called, but few chosen (polloi gar eisin klētoi oligoi de eklektoi).* This crisp saying of Christ occurs in various connections. He evidently repeated many of his sayings many times as every teacher does. There is a distinction between the called (*klētoi*) and the chosen (*eklektoi*) called out from the called.

15. *Went (poreuthentes).* So-called deponent passive and redundant use of the verb as in 9:13: "Go and learn." *Took counsel (sumboulion elabon).* Like the Latin *consilium capere* as in 12:14. *Ensnare in his talk (pagideusōsin en logōi).* From *pagis,* a snare or trap. Here only in the N.T. In the LXX (I Kings 28:9; Eccles. 9:12; Test. of Twelve Patriarchs, *Joseph* 7:1). Vivid picture of the effort to trip Jesus in his speech like a bird or wild beast.

16. *Their disciples (tous mathētas autōn).* Students, pupils,

of the Pharisees as in Mark 2:18. There were two Pharisaic theological seminaries in Jerusalem (Hillel, Shammai). *The Herodians* (*tōn Herōidianōn*). Not members of Herod's family or Herod's soldiers, but partisans or followers of Herod. The form in *-ianos* is a Latin termination like that in *Christianos* (Acts 11:26). Mentioned also in Mark 3:6 combining with the Pharisees against Jesus. *The person of men* (*prosōpon anthrōpōn*). Literally, face of men. Paying regard to appearance is the sin of partiality condemned by James (2:1, 9) when *prosōpolēmpsia, prosōpolēmptein* are used, in imitation of the Hebrew idiom. This suave flattery to Jesus implied "that Jesus was a reckless simpleton" (Bruce).

19. *Tribute money* (*to nomisma tou kēnsou*). *Kēnsos*, Latin *census*, was a capitation tax or head-money, *tributum capitis*, for which silver denaria were struck, with the figure of Caesar and a superscription, e.g. "Tiberiou Kaisaros" (McNeile). *Nomisma* is the Latin *numisma* and occurs here only in the N.T., is common in the old Greek, from *nomizō* sanctioned by law or custom.

20. *This image and superscription* (*hē eikōn hautē kai hē epigraphē*). Probably a Roman coin because of the image (picture) on it. The earlier Herods avoided this practice because of Jewish prejudice, but the Tetrarch Philip introduced it on Jewish coins and he was followed by Herod Agrippa I. This coin was pretty certainly stamped in Rome with the image and name of Tiberius Caesar on it.

21. *Render* (*apodote*). "Give back" to Caesar what is already Caesar's.

24. *Shall marry* (*epigambreusei*). The Sadducees were "aiming at amusement rather than deadly mischief" (Bruce). It was probably an old conundrum that they had used to the discomfiture of the Pharisees. This passage is quoted from Deut. 25:5 and 6. The word appears here only in the N.T. and elsewhere only in the LXX. It is used of

any connected by marriage as in Gen. 34:9; I Sam. 18:22.
But in Gen. 38:8 and Deut. 25:5 it is used specifically of one
marrying his brother's widow.

33. *They were astonished* (*exeplēssonto*). Descriptive imperfect passive showing the continued amazement of the
crowds. They were struck out (literally).

34. *He had put the Sadducees to silence* (*ephimōsen tous
Saddoukaious*). Muzzled the Sadducees. The Pharisees
could not restrain their glee though they were joining with
the Sadducees in trying to entrap Jesus. *Gathered themselves
together* (*sunēchthēsan epi to auto*). First aorist passive,
were gathered together. *Epi to auto* explains more fully
sun-. See also Acts 2:47. "Mustered their forces" (Moffatt).

36. *The great commandment in the law* (*entolē megalē en
tōi nomōi*). The positive adjective is sometimes as high in
rank as the superlative. See *megas* in Matt. 5:19 in contrast
with *elachistos*. The superlative *megistos* occurs in the N.T.
only in II Pet. 1:4. Possibly this scribe wishes to know which
commandment stood first (Mark 12:28) with Jesus. "The
scribes declared that there were 248 affirmative precepts,
as many as the members of the human body; and 365 negative precepts, as many as the days in the year, the total being 613, the number of letters in the Decalogue" (Vincent).
But Jesus cuts through such pettifogging hair-splitting to the
heart of the problem.

42. *The Christ* (*tou Christou*). The Messiah, of course,
not Christ as a proper name of Jesus. Jesus here assumes
that Psalm 110 refers to the Messiah. By his pungent
question about the Messiah as David's son and Lord he
really touches the problem of his Person (his Deity and his
Humanity). Probably the Pharisees had never faced that
problem before. They were unable to answer.

CHAPTER XXIII

2. *Sit on Moses' seat (epi tēs Mōuseōs kathedras ekathisan).* The gnomic or timeless aorist tense, *ekathisan*, not the aorist "for" the perfect. The "seat of Moses" is a brief form for the chair of the professor whose function it is to interpret Moses. "The heirs of Moses' authority by an unbroken tradition can deliver *ex cathedra* pronouncements on his teaching" (McNeile).

3. *For they say and do not (legousin kai ou poiousin).* "As teachers they have their place, but beware of following their example" (Bruce). So Jesus said: "Do not ye after their works" (*mē poieite*). Do not practice their practices. They are only preachers. Jesus does not here disapprove any of their teachings as he does elsewhere. The point made here is that they are only teachers (or preachers) and do not practice what they teach as God sees it.

4. *With their finger (tōi daktulōi autōn).* A picturesque proverb. They are taskmasters, not burden-bearers, not sympathetic helpers.

5. *To be seen of men (pros to theathēnai tois anthrōpois).* See 6:1 where this same idiom occurs. Ostentation regulates the conduct of the rabbis. *Phylacteries (phulaktēria).* An adjective from *phulaktēr, phulassō* (to guard). So a fortified place, station for garrison, then a safeguard, protecting charm or amulet. The rabbis wore *tephillin* or prayer-fillets, small leather cases with four strips of parchment on which were written the words of Ex. 13:1–10; 11–16; Deut. 6:4–9; 11:13–21. They took literally the words about "a sign unto thy hand," "a memorial between thine eyes," and "front-lets." "That for the head was to consist of a box with four compartments, each containing a slip of parchment in-

scribed with one of the four passages.   Each of these strips
was to be tied up with a well-washed hair from a calf's tail;
lest, if tied with wool or thread, any fungoid growth should
ever pollute them.   The phylactery of the arm was to contain a single slip, with the same four passages written in
four columns of seven lines each.   The black leather straps
by which they were fastened were wound seven times round
the arm and three times round the hand.   They were rever-
enced by the rabbis as highly as the scriptures, and, like
them, might be rescued from the flames on a sabbath.   They
profanely imagined that God wore the *tephillin*" (Vincent).
It is small wonder that Jesus ridiculed such minute concern
for pretentious externalism and literalism.   These *tephillin*
"are still worn at the present day on the forehead and left
arm by Jews at the daily Morning Prayer" (McNeile).
"The size of the phylacteries indexed the measure of zeal,
and the wearing of large ones was apt to take the place of
obedience" (Bruce).   Hence they made them "broad."
The superstitious would wear them as mere charms to ward
off evil.   *Enlarge the borders (megalunousin ta kraspeda).*   In
9:20 we see that Jesus, like the Jews generally, wore a tassel
or tuft, hem or border, a fringe on the outer garment according to Num. 15:38.   Here again the Jewish rabbi had
minute rules about the number of the fringes and the knots
(see on 9:20).   They made a virtue of the size of the fringes
also.   "Such things were useful as reminders; they were fatal
when they were regarded as charms" (Plummer).

6. *The chief place at feasts (tēn prōtoklisian en tois deip-*
nois).   Literally, the first reclining place on the divan at
the meal.   The Persians, Greeks, Romans, Jews differed in
their customs, but all cared for the post of honour at formal
functions as is true of us today.   Hostesses often solve the
point by putting the name of each guest at the table.   At
the last passover meal the apostles had an ugly snarl over
this very point of precedence (Luke 22:24; John 13:2–11),

just two days after this exposure of the Pharisees in the presence of the apostles. *The chief seats in the synagogues* (*tas prōtokathedrias en tais sunagōgais*). "An insatiable hunger for prominence" (Bruce). These chief seats (Zuchermandel) were on the platform looking to the audience and with the back to the chest in which were kept the rolls of scripture. The Essenes had a different arrangement. People today pay high prices for front seats at the theatre, but at church prefer the rear seats out of a curious mock-humility. In the time of Jesus the hypocrites boldly sat up in front. Now, if they come to church at all, they take the rear seats.

7. *Salutations* (*aspasmous*). The ordinary courtiers were coveted because in public. They had an itch for notice. There are occasionally today ministers who resent it if they are not called upon to take part in the services at church. They feel that their ministerial dignity has not been recognized.

8. *But be not ye called Rabbi* (*hūmeis de mē klēthēte Rabbei*). An apparent aside to the disciples. Note the emphatic position of *hūmeis*. Some even regard verses 8 to 10 as a later addition and not part of this address to the Pharisees, but the apostles were present. Euthymius Zigabenus says: "Do not seek to be called (ingressive aorist subjunctive), if others call you this it will not be your fault." This is not far from the Master's meaning. Rabbi means "my great one," "my Master," apparently a comparatively new title in Christ's time.

9. *Call no man your father* (*patera mē kalesēte hūmōn*). Jesus meant the full sense of this noble word for our heavenly Father. "Abba was not commonly a mode of address to a living person, but a title of honour for Rabbis and great men of the past" (McNeile). In Gethsemane Jesus said: "Abba, Father" (Mark 14:36). Certainly the ascription of "Father" to pope and priest seems out of harmony with

what Jesus here says. He should not be understood to be condemning the title to one's real earthly father. Jesus often leaves the exceptions to be supplied.

10. *Masters* (*kathēgētai*). This word occurs here only in the N.T. It is found in the papyri for teacher (Latin, *doctor*). It is the modern Greek word for professor. "While *didaskalos* represents *Rab*, *kathēgētēs* stands for the more honourable Rabbān, -bōn" (McNeile). Dalman (*Words of Jesus*, p. 340) suggests that the same Aramaic word may be translated by either *didaskalos* or *kathēgētēs*. *The Christ* (*ho Christos*). The use of these words here by Jesus like "Jesus Christ" in his Prayer (John 17:3) is held by some to show that they were added by the evangelist to what Jesus actually said, since the Master would not have so described himself. But he commended Peter for calling him "the Christ the Son of the living God" (Matt. 16:16f.). We must not empty the consciousness of Jesus too much.

12. *Exalt himself* (*hupsōsei heauton*). Somewhat like 18:4; 20:26. Given by Luke in other contexts (14:11; 18:14). Characteristic of Christ.

13. *Hypocrites* (*hupokritai*). This terrible word of Jesus appears first from him in the Sermon on the Mount (Matt. 6:2, 5,16; 7:5), then in 15:7 and 22:18. Here it appears "with terrific iteration" (Bruce) save in the third of the seven woes (23:13, 15, 23, 25, 27, 29). The verb in the active (*hupokrinō*) meant to separate slowly or slightly subject to gradual inquiry. Then the middle was to make answer, to take up a part on the stage, to act a part. It was an easy step to mean to feign, to pretend, to wear a masque, to act the hypocrite, to play a part. This hardest word from the lips of Jesus falls on those who were the religious leaders of the Jews (Scribes and Pharisees), who had justified this thunderbolt of wrath by their conduct toward Jesus and their treatment of things high and holy. The *Textus Receptus* has eight woes, adding verse 14 which the Revised Version

places in the margin (called verse 13 by Westcott and Hort
and rejected on the authority of Aleph B D as a manifest
gloss from Mark 12:40 and Luke 20:47). The MSS. that
insert it put it either before 13 or after 13. Plummer cites
these seven woes as another example of Matthew's fondness
for the number seven, more fancy than fact for Matthew's
Gospel is not the Apocalypse of John. These are all illustrations of Pharisaic saying and not doing (Allen). *Ye
shut the kingdom of heaven* (*kleiete tēn basileian tōn ouranōn*).
In Luke 11:52 the lawyers are accused of keeping the door
to the house of knowledge locked and with flinging away
the keys so as to keep themselves and the people in ignorance.
These custodians of the kingdom by their teaching obscured
the way to life. It is a tragedy to think how preachers and
teachers of the kingdom of God may block the door for those
who try to enter in (*tous eiserchomenous*, conative present
middle participle). *Against* (*emprosthen*). Literally, before.
These door-keepers of the kingdom slam it shut in men's
faces and they themselves are on the outside where they
will remain. They hide the key to keep others from
going in.

15. *Twofold more a son of hell than yourselves* (*huion
geennēs diploteron hūmōn*). It is a convert to Pharisaism
rather than Judaism that is meant by "one proselyte"
(*hena prosēluton*), from *proserchomai*, newcomers, aliens.
There were two kinds of proselytes: of the gate (not actual
Jews, but God-fearers and well-wishers of Judaism, like
Cornelius), of righteousness who received circumcision and
became actual Jews. But a very small per cent of the latter
became Pharisees. There was a Hellenistic Jewish literature
(Philo, Sibylline Oracles, etc.) designed to attract Gentiles
to Judaism. But the Pharisaic missionary zeal (compass,
periagēte, go around) was a comparative failure. And
success was even worse, Jesus says with pitiless plainness.
The "son of Gehenna" means one fitted for and so destined

for Gehenna. "The more converted the more perverted" (H. J. Holtzmann). The Pharisees claimed to be in a special sense sons of the kingdom (Matt. 8:12). They were more partisan than pious. *Diplous* (twofold, double) is common in the papyri. The comparative here used, as if from *diplos*, appears also in Appian. Note the ablative of comparison *hūmōn*. It was a withering thrust.

16. *Ye blind guides* (*hodēgoi tuphloi*). Note omission of "Scribes and Pharisees, hypocrites" with this third woe. In 15:14 Jesus had already called the Pharisees "blind guides" (leaders). They split hairs about oaths, as Jesus had explained in 5:33-37, between the temple and the gold of the temple. *He is a debtor* (*opheilei*). He owes his oath, is bound by his oath. A.V., *is guilty*, is old English, obsolete sense of guilt as fine or payment.

17. *Ye fools* (*mōroi*). In 5:22 Jesus had warned against calling a man *mōros* in a rage, but here he so terms the blind Pharisees for their stupidity, description of the class. "It shows that not the word but the spirit in which it is uttered is what matters" (McNeile).

23. *Ye tithe* (*apodekatoute*). The tithe had to be paid upon "all the increase of thy seed" (Deut. 14:22; Lev. 27:30). The English word tithe is tenth. These small aromatic herbs, mint (*to hēduosmon*, sweet-smelling), anise or dill (*anēthon*), cummin (*kuminon*, with aromatic seeds), show the Pharisaic scrupulous conscientiousness, all marketable commodities. "The Talmud tells of the ass of a certain Rabbi which had been so well trained as to refuse corn of which the tithes had not been taken" (Vincent). *These ye ought* (*tauta edei*). Jesus does not condemn tithing. What he does condemn is doing it to the neglect of the *weightier matters* (*ta barutera*). The Pharisees were externalists; cf. Luke 11:39-44.

24. *Strain out the gnat* (*diulizontes ton kōnōpa*). By filtering through (*dia*), not the "straining at" in swallowing so

crudely suggested by the misprint in the A.V. *Swallow the camel* (*tēn de kamēlon katapinontes*). Gulping or drinking down the camel. An oriental hyperbole like that in 19:24. See also 5:29, 30; 17:20; 21:21. Both insects and camels were ceremonially unclean (Lev. 11:4, 20, 23, 42). "He that kills a flea on the Sabbath is as guilty as if he killed a camel" (Jer. *Shabb.* 107).

25. *From extortion and excess* (*ex harpagēs kai akrasias*). A much more serious accusation. These punctilious observers of the external ceremonies did not hesitate at robbery (*harpagēs*) and graft (*akrasias*), lack of control. A modern picture of wickedness in high places both civil and ecclesiastical where the moral elements in life are ruthlessly trodden under foot. Of course, the idea is for both the outside *ektos* and the inside (*entos*) of the cup and the platter (fine side dish). But the inside is the more important. Note the change to singular in verse 26 as if Jesus in a friendlier tone pleads with a Pharisee to mend his ways.

27. *Whited sepulchre* (*taphois kekoniamenois*). The perfect passive participle is from *koniaō* and that from *konia*, dust or lime. Whitened with powdered lime dust, the sepulchres of the poor in the fields or the roadside. Not the rock-hewn tombs of the well-to-do. These were whitewashed a month before the passover that travellers might see them and so avoid being defiled by touching them (Num. 19:16). In Acts 23:3 Paul called the high priest a whited wall. When Jesus spoke the sepulchres had been freshly whitewashed. We today speak of whitewashing moral evil.

29. *The tombs of the prophets* (*tous taphous tōn prophētōn*). Cf. Luke 11:48–52. They were bearing witness against themselves (*heautois*, verse 31) to "the murder-taint in your blood" (Allen). "These men who professed to be so distressed at the murdering of the Prophets, were themselves compassing the death of Him who was far greater

than any Prophet" (Plummer). There are four monuments
called Tombs of the Prophets (Zechariah, Absalom, Jehosha-
phat, St. James) at the base of the Mount of Olives. Some
of these may have been going up at the very time that Jesus
spoke. In this seventh and last woe Jesus addresses the
Jewish nation and not merely the Pharisees.

32. *Fill ye up* (*plērōsate*). The keenest irony in this command has been softened in some MSS. to the future indicative
(*plērōsete*). "Fill up the measure of your fathers; crown
their misdeeds by killing the prophet God has sent to you.
Do at last what has long been in your hearts. The hour is
come" (Bruce).

33. *Ye serpents, ye offspring of vipers* (*opheis gennēmata
echidnōn*). These blistering words come as a climax and
remind one of the Baptist (3:17) and of the time when the
Pharisees accused Jesus of being in league with Beelzebub
(12:34). They cut to the bone like whip-cords. *How shall
ye escape* (*pōs phugēte*). Deliberate subjunctive. There is
a curse in the Talmud somewhat like this: "Woe to the
house of Annas! Woe to their serpent-like hissings."

35. *Zachariah son of Barachiah* (*Zachariou huiou Bar-
achiou*). Broadus gives well the various alternatives in
understanding and explaining the presence of "son of
Barachiah" here which is not in Luke 11:51. The usual
explanation is that the reference is to Zachariah the son of
Jehoiada the priest who was slain in the court of the temple
(II Chron. 24:20ff.). How the words, "son of Barachiah,"
got into Matthew we do not know. A half-dozen possibil-
ities can be suggested. In the case of Abel a reckoning for
the shedding of his blood was foretold (Gen. 4:10) and the
same thing was true of the slaying of Zachariah (II Chron.
24:22).

37. *How often would I have gathered* (*posakis ēthelēsa
episunagein*). More exactly, how often did I long to gather
to myself (double compound infinitive). The same verb

(*episunagei*) is used of the hen with the compound preposition *hupokatō*. Everyone has seen the hen quickly get together the chicks under her wings in the time of danger. These words naturally suggest previous visits to Jerusalem made plain by John's Gospel.

CHAPTER XXIV

1. *Went out from the temple (exelthōn apo tou hierou)*. All the discourses since Matt. 21:23 have been in the temple courts (*hieron*, the sacred enclosure). But now Jesus leaves it for good after the powerful denunciation of the scribes and Pharisees in chapter 23. His public teaching is over. It was a tragic moment. As he was going out (*eporeueto*, descriptive imperfect, the disciples, as if to relieve the thought of the Master came to him (*proselthon*) to show (*epideixai*, ingressive aorist infinitive) the buildings of the temple (*tas oikodomas tou hierou*). They were familiar to Jesus and the disciples, but beautiful like a snow mountain (Josephus, *Wars* V, 5, 6), the monument that Herod the Great had begun and that was not yet complete (John 2:20). Great stones were there of polished marble.

2. *One stone upon another (lithos epi lithon)*. Stone upon stone. A startling prediction showing that the gloomy current of the thoughts of Jesus were not changed by their words of admiration for the temple.

3. *As he sat (kathēmenou)*. Genitive absolute. Picture of Jesus sitting on the Mount of Olives looking down on Jerusalem and the temple which he had just left. After the climb up the mountain four of the disciples (Peter, James, John, Andrew) come to Jesus with the problem raised by his solemn words. They ask these questions about the destruction of Jerusalem and the temple, his own second coming (*parousia*, presence, common in the papyri for the visit of the emperor), and the end of the world. Did they think that they were all to take place simultaneously? There is no way to answer. At any rate Jesus treats all three in this great eschatological discourse, the most difficult problem in the

187

Synoptic Gospels. Many theories are advanced that impugn
the knowledge of Jesus or of the writers or of both. It is
sufficient for our purpose to think of Jesus as using the destruction of the temple and of Jerusalem which did happen
in that generation in A.D. 70, as also a symbol of his own
second coming and of the end of the world (*sunteleias tou
aiōnos*) or consummation of the age. In a painting the artist
by skilful perspective may give on the same surface the
inside of a room, the fields outside the window, and the sky
far beyond. Certainly in this discourse Jesus blends in
apocalyptic language the background of his death on the
cross, the coming destruction of Jerusalem, his own second
coming and the end of the world. He now touches one, now
the other. It is not easy for us to separate clearly the various
items. It is enough if we get the picture as a whole as it is
here drawn with its lessons of warning to be ready for his
coming and the end. The destruction of Jerusalem came as
he foretold. There are some who would date the Synoptic
Gospels after A.D. 70 in order to avoid the predictive element
involved in the earlier date. But that is to limit the foreknowledge of Jesus to a merely human basis. The word
parousia occurs in this chapter alone (3, 27, 37, 39) in the
Gospels, but often in the Epistles, either of presence as opposed to absence (Phil. 2:12) or the second coming of Christ
(II Thess. 2:1).

4. *Lead you astray* (*hūmās planēsēi*). This warning runs
all through the discourse. It is amazing how successful
deceivers have been through the ages with their eschatological programs. The word in the passive appears in 18:12
when the one sheep wanders astray. Here it is the active
voice with the causative sense to lead astray. Our word
planet comes from this root.

5. *In my name* (*epi tōi onomati mou*). They will arrogate
to themselves false claims of Messiahship in (on the basis of)
the name of Christ himself. Josephus (*Wars* VI, 54) gives

there false Christs as one of the reasons for the explosion against Rome that led to the city's destruction. Each new hero was welcomed by the masses including Barcochba. "I am the Messiah," each would say. Forty odd years ago two men in Illinois claimed to be Messiah, each with followers (Schlatter, Schweinfurth). In more recent years Mrs. Annie Besant has introduced a theosophical Messiah and Mrs. Eddy made claims about herself on a par with those of Jesus.

6. *See that ye be not troubled* (*horate mē throeisthe*). Asyndeton here with these two imperatives as Mark 8:15 *orate blepete* (Robertson, *Grammar*, p. 949). Look out for the wars and rumours of wars, but do not be scared out of your wits by them. *Throeō* means to cry aloud, to scream, and in the passive to be terrified by an outcry. Paul uses this very verb (*mēde throeisthai*) in II Thess. 2:2 as a warning against excitement over false reports that he had predicted the immediate second coming of Christ. *But the end is not yet* (*all' oupō estin to telos*). It is curious how people overlook these words of Jesus and proceed to set dates for the immediate end. That happened during the Great War and it has happened since.

8. *The beginning of travail* (*archē odinōn*). The word means birth-pangs and the Jews used the very phrase for the sufferings of the Messiah which were to come before the coming of the Messiah (Book of Jubilees, 23:18; Apoc. of Baruch 27-29). But the word occurs with no idea of birth as the pains of death (Psa. 18:5; Acts 2:24). These woes, says Jesus, are not a proof of the end, but of the beginning.

9. *Ye shall be hated* (*esesthe misoumenoi*). Periphrastic future passive to emphasize the continuous process of the linear action. For tribulation (*thlipsin* see 13:21), a word common in the Acts, Epistles, and Apocalypse for the oppression (pressure) that the Christians received. *For my name's sake* (*dia to onoma mou*). The most glorious name

in the world today, but soon to be a byword of shame (Acts 5:41). The disciples would count it an honour to be dishonoured for the Name's sake.

11. *False prophets* (*pseudoprophētai*). Jesus had warned against them in the Sermon on the Mount (7:15). They are still coming.

12. *Shall wax cold* (*psugēsetai*). Second future passive indicative from *psuchō*. To breathe cool by blowing, to grow cold, "spiritual energy blighted or chilled by a malign or poisonous wind" (Vincent). *The love of many* (*hē agapē tōn pollōn*). Love of the brotherhood gives way to mutual hatred and suspicion.

14. *Shall be preached* (*keruchthēsetai*). Heralded in all the inhabited world. *En holēi tēi oikoumenēi* supply *gēi*. It is not here said that all will be saved nor must this language be given too literal and detailed an application to every individual.

15. *The abomination of desolation* (*to bdelugma tēs eremōseōs*). An allusion to Dan. 9:27; 11:31; 12:11. Antiochus Epiphanes erected an altar to Zeus on the altar of Jehovah (I Macc. 1:54, 59; 6:7; II Macc. 6:1–5). The desolation in the mind of Jesus is apparently the Roman army (Luke 21:20) in the temple, an application of the words of Daniel to this dread event. The verb *bdelussomai* is to feel nausea because of stench, to abhor, to detest. Idolatry was a stench to God (Luke 16:15; Rev. 17:4). Josephus tells us that the Romans burned the temple and offered sacrifices to their ensigns placed by the eastern gate when they proclaimed Titus as Emperor.

16. *Let him that readeth understand* (*ho anaginoskōn noeitō*). This parenthesis occurs also in Mark 13:14. It is not to be supposed that Jesus used these words. They were inserted by Mark as he wrote his book and he was followed by Matthew.

16. *Flee unto the mountains* (*pheugetōsan eis ta orē*). The

mountains east of the Jordan. Eusebius (H. E. iii, 5, 3) says that the Christians actually fled to Pella at the foot of the mountains about seventeen miles south of the Sea of Galilee. They remembered the warning of Jesus and fled for safety.

17. *On the housetop* (*epi tou dōmatos*). They could escape from roof to roof and so escape, "the road of the roofs," as the rabbis called it. There was need for haste.

18. *In the field* (*en tōi agrōi*). The peasant worked in his time and left his mantle at home then as now.

20. *In winter nor on a sabbath* (*cheimōnos*, genitive of time, *mēde sabbatōi*, locative of time). In winter because of the rough weather. On a sabbath because some would hesitate to make such a journey on the sabbath. Josephus in his *Wars* gives the best illustration of the horrors foretold by Jesus in verse 21.

22. *Had been shortened* (*ekolobōthēsan*). From *kolobos*, lopped, mutilated, as the hands, the feet. It is a second-class condition, determined as unfulfilled. It is a prophetic figure, the future regarded as past. *For the elect's sake* (*dia tous eklektous*). See Matt. 22:14 for another use of this phrase by Jesus and also 24:31. The siege was shortened by various historical events like the stopping of the strengthening of the walls by Herod Agrippa by orders from the Emperor, the sudden arrival of Titus, the neglect of the Jews to prepare for a long siege. "Titus himself confessed that God was against the Jews, since otherwise neither his armies nor his engines would have availed against their defences" (Vincent).

23. *Lo, here is the Christ, or here* (*idou hōde ho Christos ē hōde*). The false prophets (24:11) create the trouble and now false Christs (*pseudo-Christoi*, verse 24) offer a way out of these troubles. The deluded victims raise the cries of "Lo, here," when these false Messiahs arise with their panaceas for public ills (political, religious, moral, and spiritual).

24. *Great signs and wonders* (*sēmeia megala kai terata*). Two of the three words so often used in the N.T. about the works (*erga*) of Jesus, the other being *dunameis* (powers). They often occur together of the same work (John 4:48; Acts 2:22; 4:30; II Cor. 12:12; Heb. 2:4). *Teras* is a wonder or prodigy, *dunamis*, a mighty work or power, *sēmeion*, a sign of God's purpose. Miracle (*miraculum*) presents only the notion of wonder or portent. The same deed can be looked at from these different angles. But the point to note here is that mere "signs and wonders" do not of themselves prove the power of God. These charlatans will be so skilful that they will, *if possible* (*ei dunaton*), lead astray the very elect. The implication is that it is not possible. People become excited and are misled and are unable to judge of results. Often it is *post hoc, sed non propter hoc*. Patent-medicine men make full use of the credulity of people along this line as do spiritualistic mediums. Sleight-of-hand men can deceive the unwary.

26. *In the wilderness* (*en tēi erēmōi*). Like Simon son of Gioras (Josephus, *War*, IV, 9, 5, & 7). *In the inner chambers* (*en tois tameiois*). Like John of Giscala (Josephus, *War* V, 6, 1). False Messiahs act the rôle of the Great Unseen and Unknown.

27. *As seen* (*phainetai*). Visible in contrast to the invisibility of the false Messiahs. Cf. Rev. 1:7. Like a flash of lightning.

28. *Carcase* (*ptōma*). As in 14:12, the corpse. Originally a fallen body from *piptō*, to fall, like Latin *cadaver* from *cado*, to fall. The proverb here as in Luke 17:37, is like that in Job 39:30; Prov. 30:17. *Eagles* (*aetoi*). Perhaps the griffon vulture, larger than the eagle, which (Aristotle) was often seen in the wake of an army and followed Napoleon's retreat from Russia.

29. *Immediately* (*eutheōs*). This word, common in Mark's Gospel as *euthus*, gives trouble if one stresses the time ele-

ment. The problem is how much time intervenes between "the tribulation of those days" and the vivid symbolism of verse 29. The use of *en tachei* in Rev. 1:1 should make one pause before he decides. Here we have a prophetic panorama like that with foreshortened perspective. The apocalyptic pictures in verse 29 also call for sobriety of judgment. One may compare Joel's prophecy as interpreted by Peter in Acts 21:16–22. Literalism is not appropriate in this apocalyptic eschatology.

30. *The sign of the Son of Man in heaven* (*to sēmeion tou huiou tou anthrōpou en ouranōi*). Many theories have been suggested like the cross in the sky, etc. Bruce sees a reference to Dan. 7:13 "one like the Son of man" and holds that Christ himself is the sign in question (the genitive of apposition). This is certainly possible. It is confirmed by the rest of the verse: "They shall see the Son of man coming." See Matt. 16:27; 26:64. The Jews had repeatedly asked for such a sign (Broadus) as in Matt. 12:38; 16:1; John 2:18.

31. *With a great sound of a trumpet* (*meta salpiggos phōnēs megalēs*). Some MSS. omit (*phōnēs*) "sound." The trumpet was the signal employed to call the hosts of Israel to march as to war and is common in prophetic imagery (Isa. 27:13). Cf. the seventh angel (Rev. 11:15). Clearly "the coming of the son of man is not to be identified with the judgment of Jerusalem but rather forms its preternatural background" (Bruce).

32. *Putteth forth its leaves* (*ta phulla ekphuēi*). Present active subjunctive according to Westcott and Hort. If accented *ekphuēi* (last syllable), it is second aorist passive subjunctive (Erasmus).

34. *This generation* (*hē genea hautē*). The problem is whether Jesus is here referring to the destruction of Jerusalem or to the second coming and end of the world. If to the destruction of Jerusalem, there was a literal fulfilment.

In the Old Testament a generation was reckoned as forty years. This is the natural way to take verse 34 as of 33 (Bruce), "all things" meaning the same in both verses.

36. *Not even the Son* (*oude ho huios*). Probably genuine, though absent in some ancient MSS. The idea is really involved in the words "but the Father only" (*ei mē ho patēr monos*). It is equally clear that in this verse Jesus has in mind the time of his second coming. He had plainly stated in verse 34 that those events (destruction of Jerusalem) would take place in that generation. He now as pointedly states that no one but the Father knows the day or the hour when these things (the second coming and the end of the world) will come to pass. One may, of course, accuse Jesus of hopeless confusion or extend his confession of ignorance of the date of the second coming to the whole chain of events. So McNeile: "It is impossible to escape the conclusion that Jesus as Man, expected the End, within the lifetime of his contemporaries." And that after his explicit denial that he knew anything of the kind! It is just as easy to attribute ignorance to modern scholars with their various theories as to Jesus who admits his ignorance of the date, but not of the character of the coming.

37. *The days of Noah* (*hai hēmerai tou Nōe*). Jesus had used this same imagery before to the Pharisees (Luke 17: 26–30). In Noah's day there was plenty of warning, but utter unpreparedness. Most people are either indifferent about the second coming or have fanciful schemes or programs about it. Few are really eager and expectant and leave to God the time and the plans.

38. *Were eating* (*ēsan trōgontes*). Periphrastic imperfect. The verb means to chew raw vegetables or fruits like nuts or almonds.

41. *At the mill* (*en tōi mulōi*). So Westcott and Hort and not *mulōni* (millhouse) Textus Receptus. The millstone and then hand-mill which was turned by two women (*alē-*

thousai) as in Ex. 11:5. This verb is a late form for *aleō*. There was a handle near the edge of the upper stone.

42. *Watch therefore* (*grēgoreite oun*). A late present imperative from the second perfect *egrēgora* from *egeirō*. Keep awake, be on the watch "therefore" because of the uncertainty of the time of the second coming. Jesus gives a half dozen parables to enforce the point of this exhortation (the Porter, the Master of the House, the Faithful Servant and the Evil Servants, the Ten Virgins, the Talents, the Sheep and the Goats). Matthew does not give the Parable of the Porter (Mark 13:35-37).

43. *In what watch* (*poiāi phulakēi*). As in 14:25 (four watches of the night). *Broken through* (*dioruchthēnai*). Digged through the tile roof or under the floor (dirt in the poorer houses).

44. *That ye think not* (*hēi ou dokeite hōrāi*). It is useless to set the day and hour for Christ's coming. It is folly to neglect it. This figure of the thief will be used also by Paul concerning the unexpectedness of Christ's second coming (I Thess. 5:2). See also Matt. 24:50 for the unexpectedness of the coming with punishment for the evil servant.

48. *My lord tarrieth* (*chronizei mou ho kurios*). That is the temptation and to give way to indulge in fleshly appetites or to pride of superior intellect. Within a generation scoffers will be asking where is the promise of the coming of Christ (II Peter 3:4). They will forget that God's clock is not like our clock and that a day with the Lord may be a thousand years or a thousand years as one day (3:8).

CHAPTER XXV

1. *Ten virgins* (*deka parthenois*). No special point in the number ten. The scene is apparently centered round the house of the bride to which the bridegroom is coming for the wedding festivities. But Plummer places the scene near the house of the bridegroom who has gone to bring the bride home. It is not pertinent to the point of the parable to settle it. *Lamps* (*lampadas*). Probably torches with a wooden staff and a dish on top in which was placed a piece of rope or cloth dipped in oil or pitch. But sometimes *lampas* has the meaning of oil lamp (*luchnos*) as in Acts 20:8. That may be the meaning here (Rutherford, *New Phrynichus*).

3. *Took no oil with them* (*ouk elabon meth' heautōn elaion*). Probably none at all, not realizing their lack of oil till they lit the torches on the arrival of the bridegroom and his party.

4. *In their vessels* (*en tois aggeiois*). Here alone in the N.T., through *aggē* in 13:48. Extra supply in these receptacles besides the oil in the dish on top of the staff.

5. *They all slumbered and slept* (*enustaxan pāsai kai ekatheudon*). They dropped off to sleep, nodded (ingressive aorist) and then went on sleeping (imperfect, linear action), a vivid picture drawn by the difference in the two tenses. Many a preacher has seen this happen while he is preaching.

6. *There is a cry* (*kraugē gegonen*). A cry has come. Dramatic use of the present perfect (second perfect active) indicative, not the perfect for the aorist. It is not *estin*, but *gegonen* which emphasizes the sudden outcry which has rent the air. The very memory of it is preserved by this tense with all the bustle and confusion, the rushing to the oil-venders. *Come ye forth to meet him* (*exerchesthe eis apan-*

tēsin). Or, Go out for meeting him, dependent on whether
the cry comes from outside the house or inside the house
where they were sleeping because of the delay. It was a
ceremonial salutation neatly expressed by the Greek phrase.

7. *Trimmed* (*ekosmēsan*). Put in order, made ready. The
wicks were trimmed, the lights being out while they slept,
fresh oil put in the dish, and lit again. A marriage ceremony
in India is described by Ward (*View of the Hindoos*) in
Trench's *Parables:* "After waiting two or three hours, at
length near midnight it was announced, as in the very words
of Scripture, 'Behold the bridegroom cometh; go ye out to
meet him.'"

8. *Are going out* (*sbennuntai*). Present middle indicative
of linear action, not punctiliar or aoristic. When the five
foolish virgins lit their lamps, they discovered the lack of oil.
The sputtering, flickering, smoking wicks were a sad revelation. "And *perhaps* we are to understand that there is
something in the coincidence of the lamps going out just
as the Bridegroom arrived. Mere outward religion is found
to have no illuminating power" (Plummer).

9. *Peradventure there will not be enough for us and you*
(*mēpote ou mē arkesei hēmīn kai humīn*). There is an elliptical construction here that is not easy of explanation.
Some MSS. ℵ A L Z have *ouk* instead of *ou mē*. But even
so *mē pote* has to be explained either by supplying an imperative like *ginesthō* or by a verb of fearing like *phoboumetha*
(this most likely). Either *ouk* or *ou mē* would be proper
with the futuristic subjunctive *arkesei* (Moulton, *Prolegomena*, p. 192; Robertson, *Grammar*, pp. 1161, 1174).
"We are afraid that there is no possibility of there being
enough for us both." This is a denial of oil by the wise
virgins because there was not enough for both. "It was
necessary to show that the foolish virgins could not have the
consequences of their folly averted at the last moment"
(Plummer). It is a courteous reply, but it is decisive. The

compound Greek negatives are very expressive, *mēpote—ou mē.*

10. *And while they went away* (*aperchomenōn de autōn*). Present middle participle, genitive absolute, while they were going away, descriptive linear action. Picture of their inevitable folly. *Was shut* (*ekleisthē*). Effective aorist passive indicative, shut to stay shut.

11. *Afterward* (*husteron*). And find the door shut in their faces. *Lord, Lord, open to us* (*Kurie, Kurie, anoixon hēmin*). They appeal to the bridegroom who is now master whether he is at the bride's house or his own.

12. *I know you not* (*ouk oida humās*). Hence there was no reason for special or unusual favours to be granted them. They must abide the consequences of their own negligence.

13. *Watch therefore* (*grēgoreite oun*). This is the refrain with all the parables. Lack of foresight is inexcusable. Ignorance of the time of the second coming is not an excuse for neglect, but a reason for readiness. Every preacher goes up against this trait in human nature, putting off till another time what should be done today.

14. *Going into another country* (*apodēmōn*). About to go away from one's people (*dēmos*), on the point of going abroad. This word in ancient use in this sense. There is an ellipse here that has to be supplied, *It is as when* or *The kingdom of heaven is as when.* This Parable of the Talents is quite similar to the Parable of the Pounds in Luke 19:11-28, but they are not variations of the same story. Some scholars credit Jesus with very little versatility. *His goods* (*ta huparchonta autou*). His belongings, neuter participle used as a substantive.

15. *To one* (*hōi men, hōi de, hōi de*). Demonstrative *hos*, not the relative. Neat Greek idiom. *According to his several ability* (*kata tēn idian dunamin*). According to his own ability. Each had all that he was capable of handling. The use that one makes of his opportunities is the measure of his

capacity for more. One talent represented a considerable amount of money at that time when a *denarius* was a day's wage. See on 18:24 for the value of a talent.

16. *Straightway (eutheōs)*. Beginning of verse 16, not the end of verse 15. The business temper of this slave is shown by his promptness. *With them (en autois)*. Instrumental use of *en*. He worked (*ērgasato*), did business, traded with them. "The virgins wait, the servants work" (Vincent). *Made (epoiēsen)*. But Westcott and Hort read *ekerdēsen*, gained, as in verse 17. *Kerdos* means interest. This gain was a hundred per cent.

19. *Maketh a reckoning (sunairei logon)*. As in 18:23. Deissmann (*Light from the Ancient East*, p. 117) gives two papyri quotations with this very business idiom and one Nubian ostracon with it. The ancient Greek writers do not show it.

21. *The joy of thy lord (tēn charin tou kuriou sou)*. The word *chara* or joy may refer to the feast on the master's return. So in verse 23.

24. *That had received the one talent (ho to talenton eilēphōs)*. Note the perfect active participle to emphasize the fact that he still had it. In verse 20 we have *ho—labōn* (aorist active participle). *I knew thee (egnōn se)*. Second aorist active indicative. Experimental knowledge (*ginōskō*) and proleptical use of *se*. *A hard man (sklēros)*. Harsh, stern, rough man, worse than *austēros* in Luke 19:21, grasping and ungenerous. *Where thou didst not scatter (hothen ou dieskorpisas)*. But this scattering was the chaff from which wheat was winnowed, not the scattering of seed.

26. *Thou wicked and slothful servant (ponēre doule kai oknēre)*. From *ponos* (work, annoyance, disturbance, evil) and *okneō* (to be slow, "poky," slothful). Westcott and Hort make a question out of this reply to the end of verse 26. It is sarcasm.

27. *Thou oughtest therefore (edei se oun)*. His very words

of excuse convict him. It was a necessity (*edei*) that he did not see. *The bankers* (*tois trapezeitais*). The benchers, money-changers, brokers, who exchanged money for a fee and who paid interest on money. Word common in late Greek. *I should have received back* (*egō ekomisamēn an*). Conclusion of a condition of the second class (determined as unfulfilled). The condition is not expressed, but it is implied. "If you had done that." *With interest* (*sun tokōi*). Not with "usury" in the sense of extortion or oppression. Usury only means "use" in itself. The word is from *tiktō*, to bring forth. Compound interest at six per cent doubles the principal every twenty years. It is amazing how rapidly that piles up if one carries it on for centuries and millenniums. "In the early Roman Empire legal interest was eight per cent, but in usurious transactions it was lent at twelve, twenty-four, and even forty-eight" (Vincent). Such practices exist today in our cities. The Mosaic law did not allow interest in dealings between Hebrews, but only with strangers (Deut. 23:19 & 20; Psa. 15:5).

30. *The unprofitable* (*ton achreion*). Useless (*a* privative and *chreios*, useful) and so unprofitable, injurious. Doing nothing is doing harm.

32. *All the nations* (*panta ta ethnē*). Not just Gentiles, but Jews also. Christians and non-Christians. This program for the general judgment has been challenged by some scholars who regard it as a composition by the evangelist to exalt Christ. But why should not Christ say this if he is the Son of Man and the Son of God and realized it? A "reduced" Christ has trouble with all the Gospels, not merely with the Fourth Gospel, and no less with Q and Mark than with Matthew and Luke. This is a majestic picture with which to close the series of parables about readiness for the second coming. Here is the program when he does come. "I am aware that doubt is thrown on this passage by some critics. But the doubt is most wanton.

Where is the second brain that could have invented anything so original and so sublime as vv. 35-40, 42-5?"
(Sanday, *Life of Christ in Recent Research*, p. 128). *As the
shepherd separates* (*hōsper ho poimēn aphorizei*). A common
figure in Palestine. The sheep are usually white and the
goats black. There are kids (*eriphōn, eriphia*) which have
grazed together. The goats devastate a field of all herbage.
"Indeed they have extirpated many species of trees which
once covered the hills" (Tristram, *Natural History of the
Bible*, pp. 89f.). The shepherd stands at the gate and taps
the sheep to go to the right and the goats to the left.

34. *From the foundation of the world* (*apo katabolēs kos-
mou*). The eternal purpose of the Father for his elect in all
the nations. The Son of Man in verse 31 is the King here
seated on the throne in judgment.

36. *Clothed me* (*periebalete me*). Second aorist middle
indicative, cast something around me. *Visited me* (*epeskep-
sasthe me*). Looked after, came to see. Our "visit" is from
Latin *viso, video*. Cf. our English "go to see."

40. *Ye did it unto me* (*emoi epoiēsate*). Dative of personal
interest. Christ identifies himself with the needy and the
suffering. This conduct is proof of possession of love for
Christ and likeness to him.

42. *No meat* (*ouk edōkate moi phagein*). You did not give
me anything to eat. The repetition of the negative *ou* in 42
and 43 is like the falling of clods on the coffin or the tomb.
It is curious the surprise here shown both by the sheep and
the goats. Some sheep will think that they are goats and
some goats will think that they are sheep.

46. *Eternal punishment* (*kolasin aiōnion*). The word
kolasin comes from *kolazō*, to mutilate or prune. Hence those
who cling to the larger hope use this phrase to mean age-long
pruning that ultimately leads to salvation of the goats, as
disciplinary rather than penal. There is such a distinction
as Aristotle pointed out between *mōria* (vengeance) and

kolasis. But the same adjective *aiōnios* is used with *kolasin* and *zōēn*. If by etymology we limit the scope of *kolasin*, we may likewise have only age-long *zōēn*. There is not the slightest indication in the words of Jesus here that the punishment is not coeval with the life. We can leave all this to the King himself who is the Judge. The difficulty to one's mind about conditional chastisement is to think how a life of sin in hell can be changed into a life of love and obedience. The word *aiōnios* (from *aiōn*, age, *aevum*, *aei*) means either without beginning or without end or both. It comes as near to the idea of eternal as the Greek can put it in one word. It is a difficult idea to put into language. Sometimes we have "ages of ages" (*aiōnes tōn aiōnōn*).

CHAPTER XXVI

2. *Cometh* (*ginetai*). Futuristic use of the present middle indicative. This was probably our Tuesday evening (beginning of Jewish Wednesday). The passover began on our Thursday evening (beginning of Jewish Friday). *After two days* (*meta duo hēmeras*) is just the familiar popular mode of speech. The passover came technically on the second day from this time. *Is delivered up* (*paradidotai*). Another instance of the futuristic present passive indicative. The same form occurs in verse 24. Thus Jesus sets a definite date for the coming crucifixion which he has been predicting for six months.

3. *Then were gathered together the chief priests and elders of the people* (*Tote sunēchthēsan hoi archiereis kai hoi presbuteroi tou laou*). A meeting of the Sanhedrin as these two groups indicate (cf. 21:23). *Unto the court* (*eis tēn aulēn*). The *atrium* or court around which the palace buildings were built. Here in this open court this informal meeting was held. Caiaphas was high priest A.D. 18 to 36. His father-in-law Annas had been high priest A.D. 6 to 15 and was still called high priest by many.

4. *They took counsel together* (*sunebouleusanto*). Aorist middle indicative, indicating their puzzled state of mind. They have had no trouble in finding Jesus (John 11:57). Their problem now is how to *take Jesus by subtilty and kill him* (*hina ton Iēsoun dolōi kratēsosin kai apokteinōsin*). The Triumphal Entry and the Tuesday debate in the temple revealed the powerful following that Jesus had among the crowds from Galilee.

5. *A tumult* (*thorubos*). They feared the uprising in behalf of Jesus and were arguing that the matter must be postponed till after the feast was over when the crowds had scattered. Then they could catch him "by craft" (*dolōi*) as they would trap a wild beast.

6. *In the house of Simon the leper* (*en oikiāi Simōnos tou leprou*). Evidently a man who had been healed of his leprosy by Jesus who gave the feast in honour of Jesus. All sorts of fantastic theories have arisen about it. Some even identify this Simon with the one in Luke 7:36ff., but Simon was a very common name and the details are very different. Some hold that it was Martha's house because she served (John 12:2) and that Simon was either the father or husband of Martha, but Martha loved to serve and that proves nothing. Some identify Mary of Bethany with the sinful woman in Luke 7 and even with Mary Magdalene, both gratuitous and groundless propositions. For the proof that Mary of Bethany, Mary Magdalene, and the sinful woman of Luke 7 are all distinct see my *Some Minor Characters in the New Testament.* John (12:1) apparently locates the feast six days before the passover, while Mark (14:3) and Matthew (26:6) seem to place it on the Tuesday evening (Jewish Wednesday) just two days before the passover meal. It is possible that John anticipates the date and notes the feast at Bethany at this time because he does not refer to Bethany again. If not, the order of Mark must be followed. According to the order of Mark and Matthew, this feast took place at the very time that the Sanhedrin was plotting about the death of Jesus (Mark 14:1f.).

7. *An alabaster cruse of exceeding precious ointment* (*alabastron murou barutimou*). The flask was of alabaster, a carbonate of lime or sulphate of lime, white or yellow stone, named alabaster from the town in Egypt where it was chiefly found. It was used for a phial employed for precious ointments in ancient writers, inscriptions and papyri just as we speak of a glass for the vessel made of glass. It had a

cylindrical form at the top, as a rule, like a closed rosebud (Pliny). Matthew does not say what the ointment (*murou*) was, only saying that it was "exceeding precious" (*barutimou*), of weighty value, selling at a great price. Here only in the N.T. "An alabaster of nard (*murou*) was a present for a king" (Bruce). It was one of five presents sent by Cambyses to the King of Ethiopia (Herodotus, iii. 20). *She poured it upon his head* (*katecheen epi tēs kephalēs autou*). So Mark (14:3), while John (12:3) says that she "anointed the feet of Jesus." Why not both? The verb *katecheen* is literally to pour down. It is the first aorist active indicative, unusual form.

8. *This waste* (*hē apōleia hautē*). Dead loss (*apōleia*) they considered it, nothing but sentimental aroma. It was a cruel shock to Mary of Bethany to hear this comment. Matthew does not tell as John does (12:4) that it was Judas who made the point which the rest endorsed. Mark explains that they mentioned "three hundred pence," while Matthew (26:9) only says "for much" (*pollou*).

10. *Why trouble ye the woman?* (*ti kopous parechete tēi gunaiki?*) A phrase not common in Greek writers, though two examples occur in the papyri for giving trouble. *Kopos* is from *koptō*, to beat, smite, cut. It is a beating, trouble, and often work, toil. Jesus champions Mary's act with this striking phrase. It is so hard for some people to allow others liberty for their own personalities to express themselves. It is easy to raise small objections to what we do not like and do not understand. *A good work upon me* (*ergon kalon eis eme*). A beautiful deed upon Jesus himself.

12. *To prepare me for burial* (*pros to entaphiasai me*). Mary alone had understood what Jesus had repeatedly said about his approaching death. The disciples were so wrapped up in their own notions of a political kingdom that they failed utterly to sympathize with Jesus as he faced the cross.

But Mary with the woman's fine intuitions did begin to understand and this was her way of expressing her high emotions and loyalty. The word here is the same used in John 19:40 about what Joseph of Arimathea and Nicodemus did for the body of Jesus before burial with the addition of *pros to* showing the purpose of Mary (the infinitive of purpose). Mary was vindicated by Jesus and her noble deed has become a "memorial of her" (*eis mnēmosumon autēs*) as well as of Jesus.

15. *What are ye willing to give me?* (*ti thelete moi dounai?*) This "brings out the *chaffering* aspect of the transaction" (Vincent). "Mary and Judas extreme opposites: she freely spending in love, he willing to sell his Master for money" (Bruce). And her act of love provoked Judas to his despicable deed, this rebuke of Jesus added to all the rest. *And I will deliver him unto you* (*kàgō hūmin paradōsō auton*). The use of *kai* with a co-ordinate clause is a colloquialism (common in the *Koinê* as in the Hebrew use of *wav*. "A colloquialism or a Hebraism, the traitor mean in style as in spirit" (Bruce). The use of *egō* seems to mean "I though one of his disciples will hand him over to you if you give me enough." *They weighed unto him* (*hoi de estēsan auto*). They placed the money in the balances or scales. "Coined money was in use, but the shekels may have been weighed out in antique fashion by men careful to do an iniquitous thing in the most orthodox way" (Bruce). It is not known whether the Sanhedrin had offered a reward for the arrest of Jesus or not. *Thirty pieces of silver* (*triakonta arguria*). A reference to Zech. 11:12. If a man's ox gored a servant, he had to pay this amount (Ex. 21:32). Some manuscripts have *statēras* (staters). These thirty silver shekels were equal to 120 *denarii*, less than five English pounds, less than twenty-five dollars, the current price of a slave. There was no doubt contempt for Jesus in the minds of both the Sanhedrin and Judas in this bargain.

16. *Sought opportunity* (*ezētei eukarian*). A good chance.
Note imperfect tense. Judas went at his business and stuck
to it.

17. *To eat the passover* (*phagein to pascha*). There were
two feasts rolled into one, the passover feast and the feast
of unleavened bread. Either name was employed. Here
the passover meal is meant, though in John 18:28 it is
probable that the passover feast is referred to as the passover meal (the last supper) had already been observed.
There is a famous controversy on the apparent disagreement
between the Synoptic Gospels and the Fourth Gospel on
the date of this last passover meal. My view is that the five
passages in John (13:1f., 27; 18:28; 19:14, 31) rightly interpreted agree with the Synoptic Gospels (Matt. 26:17,
20 = Mark 14:12, 17 = Luke 22:7, 14) that Jesus ate the
passover meal at the regular time about 6 P.M. beginning of
15 Nisan. The passover lamb was slain on the afternoon of
14 Nisan and the meal eaten at sunset the beginning of 15
Nisan. According to this view Jesus ate the passover meal
at the regular time and died on the cross the afternoon of
15 Nisan. See my *Harmony of the Gospels for Students of
the Life of Christ*, pp. 279–284. The question of the disciples
here assumes that they are to observe the regular passover
meal. Note the deliberative subjunctive (*hetoimasōmen*)
after *theleis* with *hina*. For the asyndeton see Robertson,
Grammar, p. 935.

18. *To such a man* (*pros ton deina*). The only instance in
the N.T. of this old Attic idiom. The papyri show it for
"Mr. X" and the modern Greek keeps it. Jesus may have
indicated the man's name. Mark (14:13) and Luke (22:10)
describe him as a man bearing a pitcher of water. It may
have been the home of Mary the mother of John Mark.
I keep the passover at thy house (*pros se poiō to pascha*).
Futuristic present indicative. The use of *pros se* for "at
thy house" is neat Greek of the classic period. Evidently

there was no surprise in this home at the command of Jesus. It was a gracious privilege to serve him thus.

20. *He was sitting at meat* (*anekeito*). He was reclining, lying back on the left side on the couch with the right hand free. Jesus and the Twelve all reclined. The paschal lamb had to be eaten up entirely (Ex. 12:4, 43).

21. *One of you* (*heis ex humōn*). This was a bolt from the blue for all except Judas and he was startled to know that Jesus understood his treacherous bargain.

22. *Is it I, Lord?* (*mēti egō eimi, Kurie;*). The negative expects the answer No and was natural for all save Judas. But he had to bluff it out by the same form of question (verse 25). The answer of Jesus, *Thou hast said* (*su eipas*), means Yes.

23. *He that dipped* (*ho embapsas*). They all dipped their hands, having no knives, forks, or spoons. The aorist participle with the article simply means that the betrayer is the one who dips his hand in the dish (*en tōi trubliōi*) or platter with the broth of nuts and raisins and figs into which the bread was dipped before eating. It is plain that Judas was not recognized by the rest as indicated by what Jesus has said. This language means that one of those who had eaten bread with him had violated the rights of hospitality by betraying him. The Arabs today are punctilious on this point. Eating one's bread ties your hands and compels friendship. But Judas knew full well as is shown in verse 25 though the rest apparently did not grasp it.

24. *Good were it for that man* (*kalon ēn autōi*). Conclusion of second-class condition even though *an* is not expressed. It is not needed with verbs of obligation and necessity. There are some today who seek to palliate the crime of Judas. But Jesus here pronounces his terrible doom. And Judas heard it and went on with his hellish bargain with the Sanhedrin. Apparently Judas went out at this stage (John 13:31).

26. *And blessed and brake it (eulogēsas eklasen)*. Special "Grace" in the middle of the passover meal, "as they were eating," for the institution of the Supper. Jesus broke one of the passover wafers or cakes that each might have a piece, not as a symbol of the breaking of his body as the Textus Receptus has it in I Cor. 11:24. The correct text there has only *to huper humōn* without *klōmenon*. As a matter of fact the body of Jesus was not "broken" (John 19:33) as John expressly states. *This is my body (touto estin to sōma mou)*. The bread as a symbol *represents* the body of Jesus offered for us, "a beautifully simple, pathetic, and poetic symbol of his death" (Bruce). But some have made it "run into fetish worship" (Bruce). Jesus, of course, does not mean that the bread actually becomes his body and is to be worshipped. The purpose of the memorial is to remind us of his death for our sins.

28. *The Covenant (tēs diathēkēs)*. The adjective *kainēs* in Textus Receptus is not genuine. The covenant is an agreement or contract between two (*dia, duo, thēke, from tithēmi*). It is used also for will (Latin, *testamentum*) which becomes operative at death (Heb. 9:15–17). Hence our *New Testament*. Either covenant or will makes sense here. Covenant is the idea in Heb. 7:22; 8:8 and often. In the Hebrew to make a covenant was to cut up the sacrifice and so ratify the agreement (Gen. 15:9–18). Lightfoot argues that the word *diathēke* means covenant in the N.T. except in Heb. 9:15–17. Jesus here uses the solemn words of Ex. 24:8 "the blood of the covenant" at Sinai. "My blood of the covenant" is in contrast with that. This is the New Covenant of Jeremiah 38; Heb. 8. *Which is shed for many (to peri pollōn ekchunnomenon)*. A prophetic present passive participle. The act is symbolized by the ordinance. Cf. the purpose of Christ expressed in 20:28. There *anti* and here *peri*. *Unto remission of sins (eis aphesin hamartiōn)*. This clause is in Matthew alone but it is not to be restricted for

that reason. It is the truth. This passage answers all the modern sentimentalism that finds in the teaching of Jesus only pious ethical remarks or eschatological dreamings. He had the definite conception of his death on the cross as the basis of forgiveness of sin. The purpose of the shedding of his blood of the New Covenant was precisely to remove (forgive) sins.

29. *When I drink it new with you* (*hotan auto pinō meth' humōn kaimon*). This language rather implies that Jesus himself partook of the bread and the wine, though it is not distinctly stated. In the Messianic banquet it is not necessary to suppose that Jesus means the language literally, "the fruit of the vine." Deissmann (*Bible Studies*, pp. 109f.) gives an instance of *genēma* used of the vine in a papyrus 230 B.C. The language here employed does not make it obligatory to employ wine rather than pure grape juice if one wishes the other.

30. *Sang a hymn* (*humnēsantes*). The *Hallel*, part of Psa. 115–118. But apparently they did not go out at once to the Garden of Gethsemane. Jesus tarried with them in the Upper Room for the wonderful discourse and prayer in John 14 to 17. They may have gone out to the street after John 14:31. It was no longer considered obligatory to remain in the house after the passover meal till morning as at the start (Ex. 12:22). Jesus went out to Gethsemane, the garden of the agony, outside of Jerusalem, toward the Mount of Olives.

33. *I will never be offended* (*egō oudepote skandalisthēsomai*). "Made to stumble," not "offended." Volitive future passive indicative. Peter ignored the prophecy of the resurrection of Jesus and the promised meeting in Galilee (32). The quotation from Zech. 13:7 made no impression on him. He was intent on showing that he was superior to "all" the rest. Judas had turned traitor and all were weak, Peter in particular, little as he knew it. So Jesus has to make it

plainer by pointing out "this night" as the time (34). *Before the cock crows* (*prin alektora phōnēsai*). No article in the Greek, "before a cock crow." Mark (14:30) says that Peter will deny Jesus thrice before the cock crows twice. When one cock crows in the morning, others generally follow. The three denials lasted over an hour. Some scholars hold that chickens were not allowed in Jerusalem by the Jews, but the Romans would have them.

35. *Even if I must die with thee* (*kàn deēi me sun soi apothanein*). Third-class condition. A noble speech and meant well. His boast of loyalty is made still stronger by *ou mē se aparnēsomai*. The other disciples were undoubtedly embarrassed by Peter's boast and lightheartedly joined in the same profession of fidelity.

36. *Gethsemane* (*Gethsēmanei*). The word means oil-press in the Hebrew, or olive vat. The place (*chōrion*) was an enclosed plot or estate, "garden," or orchard (*kēpos*). It is called *villa* in the Vulgate according to John 18:1. It was beyond the torrent Kedron at the foot of the Mount of Olives about three-fourths of a mile from the eastern walls of Jerusalem. There are now eight old olive trees still standing in this enclosure. One cannot say that they are the very trees near which Jesus had his Agony, but they are very old. "They will remain so long as their already protracted life is spared, the most venerable of their race on the surface of the earth. Their guarded trunks and scanty foliage will always be regarded as the most affecting of the sacred memorials in or about Jerusalem" (Stanley, *Sinai and Palestine*). *Here* (*autou*), *Yonder* (*ekei*). Jesus clearly pointed to the place where he would pray. Literally "there."

37. *He took with him* (*paralabōn*). *Taking along*, by his side (*para-*), as a mark of special favour and privilege, instead of leaving this inner circle of three (Peter, James, and John) with the other eight. The eight would serve as a sort of outer guard to watch by the gate of the garden for the com-

ing of Judas while the three would be able to share the agony of soul already upon Jesus so as at least to give him some human sympathy which he craved as he sought help from the Father in prayer. These three had been with Jesus on the Mount of Transfiguration and now they are with him in this supreme crisis. The grief of Christ was now severe. The word for *sore troubled* (*adēmonein*) is of doubtful etymology. There is an adjective *adēmos* equal to *apodēmos* meaning "not at home," "away from home," like the German *unheimisch, unheimlich*. But whatever the etymology, the notion of intense discomfort is plain. The word *adēmonein* occurs in P. Oxy. II, 298, 456 of the first century A.D. where it means "excessively concerned." See Phil. 2:26 where Paul uses it of Epaphroditus. Moffatt renders it here "agitated." The word occurs sometimes with *aporeō* to be at a loss as to which way to go. The *Braid Scots* has it "sair putten-aboot." Here Matthew has also "to be sorrowful" (*lupeisthai*), but Mark (14:33) has the startling phrase *greatly amazed and sore troubled* (*ekthambeisthai kai adēmonein*), a "feeling of terrified surprise."

38. *Watch with me* (*grēgoreite met' emou*). This late present from the perfect *egrēgora* means to keep awake and not go to sleep. The hour was late and the strain had been severe, but Jesus pleaded for a bit of human sympathy as he wrestled with his Father. It did not seem too much to ask. He had put his sorrow in strong language, "even unto death" (*heōs thanatou*) that ought to have alarmed them.

39. *He went forward a little* (*proelthōn mikron*). As if he could not fight the battle in their immediate presence. He was on his face, not on his knees (McNeile). *This cup* (*to potērion touto*). The figure can mean only the approaching death. Jesus had used it of his coming death when James and John came to him with their ambitious request, "the cup which I am about to drink" (Matt. 20:22). But now the Master is about to taste the bitter dregs in the cup

of death for the sin of the world. He was not afraid that he would die before the Cross, though he instinctively shrank from the cup, but instantly surrendered his will to the Father's will and drank it to the full. Evidently Satan tempted Christ now to draw back from the Cross. Here Jesus won the power to go on to Calvary.

40. *What* (*houtōs*). The Greek adverb is not interrogation or exclamatory *ti*, but only "so" or "thus." There is a tone of sad disappointment at the discovery that they were asleep after the earnest plea that they keep awake (verse 38). "Did you not thus have strength enough to keep awake one hour?" Every word struck home.

41. *Watch and pray* (*grēgoreite kai proseuchesthe*). Jesus repeats the command of verse 38 with the addition of prayer and with the warning against the peril of temptation. He himself was feeling the worst of all temptations of his earthly life just then. He did not wish then to enter such temptation (*peirasmon*, here in this sense, not mere trial). Thus we are to understand the prayer in Matt. 6:13 about leading (being led) into temptation. Their failure was due to weakness of the flesh as is often the case. *Spirit* (*pneuma*) here is the moral life (intellect, will, emotions) as opposed to the flesh (cf. Isa. 31:3; Rom. 7:25). *Except I drink it* (*ean mē auto piō*). Condition of the third class undetermined, but with likelihood of determination, whereas *if this cannot pass away* (*ei ou dunatai touto parelthein*) is first-class condition, determined as fulfilled, assumed to be true. This delicate distinction accurately presents the real attitude of Jesus towards this subtle temptation.

43. *For their eyes were heavy* (*ēsan gar autōn hoi ophthalmoi bebarēmenoi*). Past perfect passive indicative periphrastic. Their eyes had been weighted down with sleep and still were as they had been on the Mount of Transfiguration (Luke 9:32).

45. *Sleep on now and take your rest* (*katheudete loipon kai*

anapauesthe). This makes it "mournful irony" (Plummer) or reproachful concession: "Ye may sleep and rest indefinitely so far as I am concerned; I need no longer your watchful interest" (Bruce). It may be a sad query as Goodspeed: "Are you still sleeping and taking your rest?" So Moffatt. This use of *loipon* for now or henceforth is common in the papyri. *The hour is at hand* (*ēggiken hē hōra*). Time for action has now come. They have missed their chance for sympathy with Jesus. He has now won the victory without their aid. "The Master's time of weakness is past; He is prepared to face the worst" (Bruce). *Is betrayed* (*paradidotai*). Futuristic present or inchoative present, the first act in the betrayal is at hand. Jesus had foreseen his "hour" for long and now he faces it bravely.

46. *He is at hand* (*ēggiken*). The same verb and tense used of the hour above, present perfect active of *eggizō*, to draw near, the very form used by John the Baptist of the coming of the kingdom of heaven (Matt. 3:2). Whether Jesus heard the approach of the betrayer with the crowd around him or saw the lights or just felt the proximity of the traitor before he was there (J. Weiss), we do not know and it matters little. The scene is pictured as it happened with lifelike power.

47. *While he yet spake* (*eti autou lalountos*). It was an electric moment as Jesus faced Judas with his horde of helpers as if he turned to meet an army. *Let us go* (*agōmen*), Jesus had said. And here he is. The eight at the gate seemed to have given no notice. Judas is described here as "one of the twelve" (*heis tōn dōdeka*) in all three Synoptic Gospels (Mark 14:43; Matt. 26:47; Luke 22:47). The very horror of the thing is thus emphasized, that one of the chosen twelve apostles should do this dastardly deed. *A great multitude* (*ochlos polus*). The chief priests and Pharisees had furnished Judas a band of soldiers from the garrison in Antonia (John 18:3) and the temple police (Luke 22:52)

with swords (knives) and staves (clubs) with a hired rabble
who had lanterns also (John 18:3) in spite of the full moon.
Judas was taking no chances of failure for he well knew the
strange power of Jesus.

48. *Gave them a sign* (*edōken autois sēmeion*). Probably
just before he reached the place, though Mark (14:44) has
"had given" (*dedōkei*) which certainly means before arrival
at Gethsemane. At any rate Judas had given the leaders
to understand that he would kiss (*philēsō*) Jesus in order to
identify him for certain. The kiss was a common mode of
greeting and Judas chose that sign and actually "kissed him
fervently" (*katephilēsen*, verse 49), though the compound
verb sometimes in the papyri has lost its intensive force.
Bruce thinks that Judas was prompted by the inconsistent
motives of smouldering love and cowardice. At any rate
this revolting ostentatious kiss is "the most terrible instance of the *hekousia philēmata echthrou* (Prov. 27:6),"
the profuse kisses of an enemy (McNeile). This same compound verb occurs in Luke 7:38 of the sinful woman, in
Luke 15:20 of the Father's embrace of the Prodigal Son,
and in Acts 20:37 of the Ephesian elders and Paul.

50. *Do that for which thou art come* (*eph' ho parei*). Moffatt and Goodspeed take it: "Do your errand." There has
been a deal of trouble over this phrase. Deissmann (*Light
from the Ancient East*, pp. 125 to 131) has proven conclusively
that it is a question, *eph' ho* in late Greek having the interrogative sense of *epi ti* (Robertson, *Grammar*, p. 725). The
use of *eph' ho* for "why here" occurs on a Syrian tablet of
the first century A.D. so that it "was current coin in the
language of the people" (Deissmann). Most of the early
translations (Old Latin, Old Syriac) took it as a question.
So the Vulgate has *ad quid venisti*. In this instance the
Authorized Version is correct against the Revised. Jesus
exposes the pretence of Judas and shows that he does not
believe in his paraded affection (Bruce).

51. *One of them that were with Jesus (heis tōn meta Iēsou).*
Like the other Synoptics Matthew conceals the name of
Peter, probably for prudential reasons as he was still living
before A.D. 68. John writing at the end of the century mentions Peter's name (John 18:10). The sword or knife was
one of the two that the disciples had (Luke 22:38). Bruce
suggests that it was a large knife used in connexion with
the paschal feast. Evidently Peter aimed to cut off the
man's head, not his ear (*ōtion* is diminutive in form, but not
in sense, as often in the *Koinê*). He may have been the
leader of the band. His name, Malchus, is also given by
John (18:10) because Peter was then dead and in no danger.

52. *Put up again thy sword (apostrepson tēn machairan
sou).* Turn back thy sword into its place. It was a stern
rebuke for Peter who had misunderstood the teaching of
Jesus in Luke 22:38 as well as in Matt. 5:39 (cf. John 18:36).
The reason given by Jesus has had innumerable illustrations
in human history. The sword calls for the sword. Offensive
war is here given flat condemnation. The Paris Pact of
1928 (the Kellogg Treaty) is certainly in harmony with
the mind of Christ. The will to peace is the first step towards peace, the outlawing of war. Our American cities
are often ruled by gangsters who kill each other off.

53. *Even now (arti).* Just now, at this very moment.
Legions (legiōnas). A Latin word. Roman soldiers in large
numbers were in Palestine later in A.D. 66, but they were
in Caesarea and in the tower of Antonia in Jerusalem. A
full Roman legion had 6,100 foot and 726 horse in the time
of Augustus. But Jesus sees more than twelve legions at
his command (one for each apostle) and shows his undaunted
courage in this crisis. One should recall the story of Elisha
at Dothan (II Kings 6:17).

54. *Must be (dei).* Jesus sees clearly his destiny now that
he has won the victory in Gethsemane.

55. *As against a robber (hōs epi lēistēn).* As a robber, not

as a thief, but a robber hiding from justice. He will be crucified between two robbers and on the very cross planned for
their leader, Barabbas. They have come with no warrant
for any crime, but with an armed force to seize Jesus as if a
highway robber. Jesus reminds them that he used to sit
(imperfect, *ekathezomēn*) in the temple and teach. But he
sees God's purpose in it all for the prophets had foretold his
"cup." The desertion of Jesus by the disciples followed
this rebuke of the effort of Peter. Jesus had surrendered.
So they fled.

58. *To see the end* (*idein to telos*). Peter rallied from the
panic and followed afar off (*makrothen*), "more courageous
than the rest and yet not courageous enough" (Bruce).
John the Beloved Disciple went on into the room where
Jesus was. The rest remained outside, but Peter "sat with
the officers" to see and hear and hoping to escape notice.

59. *Sought false witness against Jesus* (*ezētoun pseudomar-
turian*). Imperfect tense, kept on seeking. Judges have no
right to be prosecutors and least of all to seek after false
witness and even to offer bribes to get it.

60. *They found it not* (*kai ouch heuron*). They found
false witnesses in plenty, but not the false witness that would
stand any sort of test.

61. *I am able to destroy the temple of God* (*dunamai katalusai
ton naon tou theou*). What he had said (John 2:19) referred
to the temple of his body which they were to destroy (and
did) and which he would raise again in three days as he did.
It was a pitiful perversion of what Jesus had said and even
so the two witnesses disagreed in their misrepresentation
(Mark 14:59).

63. *Held his peace* (*esiōpa*). Kept silent, imperfect tense.
Jesus refused to answer the bluster of Caiaphas. *I adjure
thee by the living God* (*exorkizō se kata tou theou tou zōntos*).
So Caiaphas put Jesus on oath in order to make him incrimi-
nate himself, a thing unlawful in Jewish jurisprudence. He

had failed to secure any accusation against Jesus that would stand at all. But Jesus did not refuse to answer under solemn oath, clearly showing that he was not thinking of oaths in courts of justice when he prohibited profanity. The charge that Caiaphas makes is that Jesus claims to be the Messiah, the Son of God. To refuse to answer would be tantamount to a denial. So Jesus answered knowing full well the use that would be made of his confession and claim.

64. *Thou hast said* (*su eipas*). This is a Greek affirmative reply. Mark (14:62) has it plainly, "I am" (*eimi*). But this is not all that Jesus said to Caiaphas. He claims that the day will come when Jesus will be the Judge and Caiaphas the culprit using the prophetic language in Dan. 7:13 and Psa. 109:1. It was all that Caiaphas wanted.

65. *He hath spoken blasphemy* (*eblasphēmēsen*). There was no need of witnesses now, for Jesus had incriminated himself by claiming under oath to be the Messiah, the Son of God. Now it would not be blasphemy for the real Messiah to make such a claim, but it was intolerable to admit that Jesus could be the Messiah of Jewish hope. At the beginning of Christ's ministry he occasionally used the word Messiah of himself, but he soon ceased, for it was plain that it would create trouble. The people would take it in the sense of a political revolutionist who would throw off the Roman yoke. If he declined that rôle, the Pharisees would have none of him for that was the kind of a Messiah that they desired. But the hour has now come. At the Triumphal Entry Jesus let the Galilean crowds hail him as Messiah, knowing what the effect would be. Now the hour has struck. He has made his claim and has defied the High Priest.

66. *He is worthy of death* (*enochos thanatou estin*). Held in the bonds of death (*en, echō*) as actually guilty with the genitive (*thanatou*). The dative expresses liability as in Matt. 5:21 (*tēi krisei*) and as *eis* and the accusative (Matt. 5:22). They took the vote though it was at night and they

no longer had the power of death since the Romans took it away from them. Death was the penalty of blasphemy (Lev. 24:15). But they enjoyed taking it as their answer to his unanswerable speeches in the temple that dreadful Tuesday a few days before. It was unanimous save that Joseph of Arimathea and Nicodemus did not agree. They were probably absent and not even invited as being under suspicion for being secret disciples of Christ.

68. *Thou Christ (Christe)*. With definite sneer at his claims under oath in 26:63. With uncontrolled glee and abandon like a lot of hoodlums these doctors of divinity insulted Jesus. They actually spat in his face, buffeted him on the neck (*ekolaphisan*, from *kolaphos* the fist), and struck him in the face with the palms of their hands (*erapisan*, from *rapis*, a rod), all personal indignities after the legal injustice already done. They thus gave vent to their spite and hatred.

69. *Thou also (kai su)*. Peter had gone *within* (*esō*) the palace (26:58), but was sitting *without* (*exō*) the hall where the trial was going on in the open central court with the servants or officers (*hupēretōn*, under rowers, literally, 26:58) of the Sanhedrin. But he could possibly see through the open door above what was going on inside. It is not plain at what stage of the Jewish trial the denials of Peter took place nor the precise order in which they came as the Gospels give them variously. This maid (*paidiskē*, slave girl) stepped up to Peter as he was sitting in the court and pointedly said: "Thou also wast with Jesus the Galilean." Peter was warming himself by the fire and the light shone in his face. She probably had noticed Peter come in with John the Beloved Disciple who went on up into the hall of trial. Or she may have seen Peter with Jesus on the streets of Jerusalem.

70. *I know not what thou sayest (ouk oida ti legeis)*. It was an affectation of extreme ignorance (Bruce) that deceived no one. It was an easy and ancient dodge and easy subterfuge. Dalman (*Words of Jesus*, 80f.) suggests that Peter

used the Galilean Aramaean word for know instead of the Judean Aramaean word which betrayed at once his Galilean residence.

71. *Into the porch* (*eis ton pulōna*). But Peter was not safe out here, for another maid recognized him and spoke of him as "this fellow" (*houtos*) with a gesture to those out there.

72. *With an oath* (*meta horkou*). This time Peter added an oath, probably a former habit so common to the Jews at that time, and denied acquaintance with Jesus. He even refers to Jesus as "the man" (*ton anthrōpon*), an expression that could convey contempt, "the fellow."

73. *They that stood by* (*hoi hestōtes*). The talk about Peter continued. Luke (22:59) states that the little while was about an hour. The bystanders came up to Peter and bluntly assert that he was "of a truth" (*alēthōs*) one of the followers of Jesus for his speech betrayed him. Even the Revised Version retains "bewrayeth," quaint old English for "betrayeth." The Greek has it simply "makes thee evident" (*dēlon se poiei*). His dialect (*lalia*) clearly revealed that he was a Galilean. The Galileans had difficulty with the gutterals and Peter's second denial had exposed him to the tormenting raillery of the loungers who continued to nag him.

74. *Then began he to curse and to swear* (*tote ērxato katathematizein kai omnuein*). He repeated his denial with the addition of profanity to prove that he was telling the truth instead of the lie that they all knew. His repeated denials gave him away still more, for he could not pronounce the Judean gutterals. He called down on himself (*katathematizein*) imprecations in his desperate irritation and loss of self-control at his exposure. *The cock crew* (*alektōn ephōnēsen*). No article in the Greek, just "a cock crew" at that juncture, "straightway" (*euthus*). But it startled Peter.

75. Peter remembered (*emnēsthē ho Petros*). A small

thing, but *magna circumstantia* (Bengel). In a flash of lightning rapidity he recalled the words of Jesus a few hours
before (Matt. 26:34) which he had then scouted with the
proud boast that "even if I must die with thee, yet will I not
deny thee" (26:35). And now this triple denial was a fact.
There is no extenuation for the base denials of Peter. He had
incurred the dread penalty involved in the words of Jesus in
Matt. 10:33 of denial by Jesus before the Father in heaven.
But Peter's revulsion of feeling was as sudden as his sin.
He went out and wept bitterly (*exelthōn exō eklausen pikrōs*).
Luke adds that the Lord turned and looked upon Peter (Luke
22:61). That look brought Peter back to his senses. He
could not stay where he now was with the revilers of Jesus.
He did not feel worthy or able to go openly into the hall
where Jesus was. So outside he went with a broken heart.
The constative aorist here does not emphasize as Mark's
imperfect does (Mark 14:72, *eklaien*) the continued weeping
that was now Peter's only consolation. The tears were
bitter, all the more so by reason of that look of understanding pity that Jesus gave him. One of the tragedies of the
Cross is the bleeding heart of Peter. Judas was a total wreck
and Peter was a near derelict. Satan had sifted them all
as wheat, but Jesus had prayed specially for Peter (Luke
22:31f.). Will Satan show Peter to be all chaff as Judas was?

CHAPTER XXVII

1. *Now when morning was come (prōias de genomenēs)*. Genitive absolute. After dawn came the Sanhedrin held a formal meeting to condemn Jesus and so ratify the illegal trial during the night (Mark 15:1; Luke 22:66–71). Luke gives the details of this second ratification consultation. The phrase used, *took counsel (sumboulion elabon)* is a Latin idiom (*consilium ceperunt*) for *sunebouleusanto*.

2. *Delivered him up to Pilate the governor (paredōkan Peilatōi tōi hēgemoni)*. What they had done was all a form and a farce. Pilate had the power of death, but they had greatly enjoyed the condemnation and the buffeting of Jesus now in their power bound as a condemned criminal. He was no longer the master of assemblies in the temple, able to make the Sanhedrin cower before him. He had been bound in the garden and was bound before Annas (John 18:12, 24), but may have been unbound before Caiaphas.

3. *Repented himself (metamelētheis)*. Probably Judas saw Jesus led away to Pilate and thus knew that the condemnation had taken place. This verb (first aorist passive participle of *metamelomai*) really means to be sorry afterwards like the English word *repent* from the Latin *repoenitet*, to have pain again or afterwards. See the same verb *metamelētheis* in Matt. 21:30 of the boy who became sorry and changed to obedience. The word does not have an evil sense in itself. Paul uses it of his sorrow for his sharp letter to the Corinthians, a sorrow that ceased when good came of the letter (II Cor. 7:8). But mere sorrow avails nothing unless it leads to change of mind and life (*metanoia*), the sorrow according to God (II Cor. 7:9). This sorrow Peter had when he wept

bitterly. It led Peter back to Christ. But Judas had only remorse that led to suicide.

4. *See thou to it* (*su opsēi*). Judas made a belated confession of his sin in betraying innocent blood to the Sanhedrin, but not to God, nor to Jesus. The Sanhedrin ignore the innocent or righteous blood (*haima athōion* or *dikaion*) and tell Judas to look after his own guilt himself. They ignore also their own guilt in the matter. The use of *su opsēi* as a volitive future, an equivalent of the imperative, is commoner in Latin (*tu videris*) than in Greek, though the *Koiné* shows it also. The sentiment is that of Cain (Grotius, Bruce).

5. *Hanged himself* (*apēgxato*). Direct middle. His act was sudden after he hurled the money into the sanctuary (*eis ton naon*), the sacred enclosure where the priests were. The motives of Judas in the betrayal were mixed as is usually the case with criminals. The money cut a small figure with him save as an expression of contempt as the current price of a slave.

6. *Into the treasury* (*eis ton korbanān*). Josephus (*War* II. 9, 4) uses this very word for the sacred treasury. *Korban* is Aramaic for *gift* (*dōron*) as is plain in Mark 7:11. The price of blood (blood-money) was pollution to the treasury (Deut. 23:18f.). So they took the money out and used it for a secular purpose. The rabbis knew how to split hairs about *Korban* (Mark 7:1–23; Matt. 15:1–20), but they balk at this blood-money.

7. *The potter's field* (*tou agrou tou kerameōs*). Grotius suggests that it was a small field where potter's clay was obtained, like a brickyard (Broadus). Otherwise we do not know why the name exists. In Acts 1:18 we have another account of the death of Judas by bursting open (possibly falling after hanging himself) after he obtained the field by the wages of iniquity. But it is possible that *ektēsato* there refers to the rabbinical use of *Korban*, that the money was

still that of Judas though he was dead and so he really "acquired" the field by his blood-money.

8. *The field of blood* (*agros haimatos*). This name was attached to it because it was the price of blood and that is not inconsistent with Acts 1:18f. Today potter's field carries the idea here started of burial place for strangers who have no where else to lie (*eis taphēn tois xenois*), probably at first Jews from elsewhere dying in Jerusalem. In Acts 1:19 it is called *Aceldama* or *place of blood* (*chōrion haimatos*) for the reason that Judas' blood was shed there, here because it was purchased by blood money. Both reasons could be true.

9. *By Jeremiah the prophet* (*dia Ieremiou*). This quotation comes mainly from Zech. 11:13 though not in exact language. In Jer. 18:18 the prophet tells of a visit to a potter's house and in 32:6ff. of the purchase of a field. It is in Zechariah that the thirty pieces of silver are mentioned. Many theories are offered for the combination of Zechariah and Jeremiah and attributing it all to Jeremiah as in Mark 1:2f. the quotation from Isaiah and Malachi is referred wholly to Isaiah as the more prominent of the two. Broadus and McNeile give a full discussion of the various theories from a mere mechanical slip to the one just given above. Matthew has here (27:10) "the field of the potter" (*eis ton agron tou kerameōs*) for "the potter the house of the Lord" in Zech. 11:13. That makes it more parallel with the language of Matt. 27:7.

11. *Now Jesus stood before the governor* (*ho de Iēsous estathē emprosthen tou hēgemonos*). Here is one of the dramatic episodes of history. Jesus stood face to face with the Roman governor. The verb *estathē*, not *estē* (second aorist active), is first aorist passive and can mean "was placed" there, but he stood, not sat. The term *hēgemōn* (from *hēgeomai*, to lead) was technically a *legatus Caesaris*, an officer of the Emperor, more exactly procurator, ruler under the

Emperor of a less important province than propraetor (as over Syria). The senatorial provinces like Achaia were governed by proconsuls. Pilate represented Roman law. *Art thou the King of the Jews?* (*Su ei ho basileus tōn Ioudaiōn;*). This is what really mattered. Matthew does not give the charges made by the Sanhedrin (Luke 23:2) nor the private interview with Pilate (John 18:28–32). He could not ignore the accusation that Jesus claimed to be King of the Jews. Else he could be himself accused to Caesar for disloyalty. Rivals and pretenders were common all over the empire. So here was one more. By his answer (*thou sayest*) Jesus confesses that he is. So Pilate has a problem on his hands. What sort of a king does this one claim to be? *Thou* (*su*) the King of the Jews?

14. *And he gave him no answer, not even to one word* (*kai ouk apekrithē autōi pros oude hen rhēma*). Jesus refused to answer the charges of the Jews (verse 12). Now he continued silent under the direct question of Pilate. The Greek is very precise besides the double negative. "He did not reply to him up to not even one word." This silent dignity amazed Pilate and yet he was strangely impressed.

17. *Barabbas or Jesus which is called Christ?* (*Barabbān ē Iēsoun ton legomenon Christon;*). Pilate was catching at straws or seeking any loophole to escape condemning a harmless lunatic or exponent of a superstitious cult such as he deemed Jesus to be, certainly in no political sense a rival of Caesar. The Jews interpreted "Christ" for Pilate to be a claim to be King of the Jews in opposition to Caesar, "a most unprincipled proceeding" (Bruce). So he bethought him of the time-honoured custom at the passover of releasing to the people "a prisoner whom they wished" (*desmion hon ēthelon*). No parallel case has been found, but Josephus mentions the custom (*Ant.* xx. 9, 3). Barabbas was for some reason a popular hero, a notable (*episēmon*), if not notorious, prisoner, leader of an insurrection or revolution (Mark

15·7) probably against Rome, and so guilty of the very crime that they tried to fasten on Jesus who only claimed to be king in the spiritual sense of the spiritual kingdom. So Pilate unwittingly pitted against each other two prisoners who represented the antagonistic forces of all time. It is an elliptical structure in the question, "whom do you wish that I release?" (*tina thelete apolusō;*), either two questions in one (asyndeton) or the ellipse of *hina* before *apolusō*. See the same idiom in verse 21. But Pilate's question tested the Jews as well as himself. It tests all men today. Some manuscripts add the name Jesus to Barabbas and that makes it all the sharper. Jesus Barabbas or Jesus Christ?

18. *For envy* (*dia phthonon*). Pilate was dense about many things, but he knew that the Jewish leaders were jealous of the power of Jesus with the people. He may have heard of the events of the Triumphal Entry and the Temple Teaching. The envy, of course, came primarily from the leaders.

19. *His wife* (*hē gunē autou*). Poor Pilate was getting more entangled every moment as he hesitated to set Jesus free whom he knew to be free of any crime against Caesar. Just at the moment when he was trying to enlist the people in behalf of Jesus against the schemes of the Jewish leaders, his wife sent a message about her dream concerning Jesus. She calls Jesus "that righteous man" (*tōi dikaiōi ekeinōi*) and her psychical sufferings increased Pilate's superstitious fears. Tradition names her Procla and even calls her a Christian which is not probable. But it was enough to unnerve the weak Pilate as he sat on the judgment-seat (*epi tou bēmatos*) up over the pavement.

20. *Persuaded* (*epeisan*). The chief priests (Sadducees) and elders (Pharisees) saw the peril of the situation and took no chances. While Pilate wavered in pressing the question, they used all their arts to get the people to "ask for themselves" (*aitēsōntai*, indirect middle ingressive aorist subjunctive) and to choose Barabbas and not Jesus.

22. *What then shall I do unto Jesus which is called Christ?*
(*ti oun poiēsō Iēsoun ton legomenon Christon;*). They had
asked for Barabbas under the tutelage of the Sanhedrin,
but Pilate pressed home the problem of Jesus with the dim
hope that they might ask for Jesus also. But they had
learned their lesson. Some of the very people who shouted
"Hosannah" on the Sunday morning of the Triumphal
Entry now shout *Let him be crucified* (*staurōthētō*). The tide
has now turned against Jesus, the hero of Sunday, now the
condemned criminal of Friday. Such is popular favour. But
all the while Pilate is shirking his own fearful responsibility
and trying to hide his own weakness and injustice behind
popular clamour and prejudice.

23. *Why, what evil hath he done?* (*ti gar kakon epoiēsen;*).
This was a feeble protest by a flickering conscience. Pilate
descended to that level of arguing with the mob now in-
flamed with passion for the blood of Jesus, a veritable lynch-
ing fiasco. But this exhibition of weakness made the mob
fear refusal by Pilate to proceed. So they "kept crying exceedingly" (*perissōs ekrazon*, imperfect tense of repeated
action and vehemently) their demand for the crucifixion of
Jesus. It was like a gladiatorial show with all thumbs turned
down.

24. *Washed his hands* (*apenipsato tas cheiras*). As a last
resort since the hubbub (*thorubos*) increased because of his
vacillation. The verb *aponiptō* means to wash off and the
middle voice means that he washed off his hands for himself
as a common symbol of cleanliness and added his pious claim
with a slap at them. *I am innocent of the blood of this righteous
man* (or *this blood*); *see ye to it.* (*Athōios eimi apo tou haimatos tou dikaiou toutou* or *tou haimatos toutou* as some manuscripts have it, *humeis opsesthe.*) The Jews used this symbol
(Deut. 21:6; Psa. 26:6; 73:13). Plummer doubts if Pilate
said these words with a direct reference to his wife's message
(26:19), but I fail to see the ground for that scepticism.

The so-called *Gospel of Peter* says that Pilate washed his hands because the Jews refused to do so.

25. *His blood be upon us and upon our children* (*to haima autou kai epi ta tekna hēmōn*). These solemn words do show a consciousness that the Jewish people recognized their guilt and were even proud of it. But Pilate could not wash away his own guilt that easily. The water did not wash away the blood of Jesus from his hands any more than Lady Macbeth could wash away the blood-stains from her lily-white hands. One legend tells that in storms on Mt. Pilatus in Switzerland his ghost comes out and still washes his hands in the storm-clouds. There was guilt enough for Judas, for Caiaphas and for all the Sanhedrin both Sadducees and Pharisees, for the Jewish people as a whole (*pas ho laos*), and for Pilate. At bottom the sins of all of us nailed Jesus to the Cross. This language is no excuse for race hatred today, but it helps explain the sensitiveness between Jew and Christians on this subject. And Jews today approach the subject of the Cross with a certain amount of prejudice.

26. *Scourged* (*phragellōsas*). The Latin verb *flagellare*. Pilate apparently lost interest in Jesus when he discovered that he had no friends in the crowd. The religious leaders had been eager to get Jesus condemned before many of the Galilean crowd friendly to Jesus came into the city. They had apparently succeeded. The scourging before the crucifixion was a brutal Roman custom. The scourging was part of the capital punishment. Deissmann (*Light from the Ancient East*, p. 269) quotes a Florentine papyrus of the year 85 A.D. wherein G. Septimius Vegetus, governor of Egypt, says of a certain Phibion: "Thou hadst been worthy of scourging . . . but I will give thee to the people."

27. *Into the palace* (*eis to praitōrion*). In Rome the praetorium was the camp of the praetorian (from praetor) guard of soldiers (Phil. 1:13), but in the provinces it was the palace in which the governor resided as in Acts 23:35 in Caesarea.

So here in Jerusalem Pilate ordered Jesus and all the band or cohort (*holēn tēn speiran*) of soldiers to be led into the palace in front of which the judgment-seat had been placed. The Latin *spira* was anything rolled into a circle like a twisted ball of thread. These Latin words are natural here in the atmosphere of the court and the military environment. The soldiers were gathered together for the sport of seeing the scourging. These heathen soldiers would also enjoy showing their contempt for the Jews as well as for the condemned man.

28. *A scarlet robe* (*chlamuda kokkinēn*). A kind of short cloak worn by soldiers, military officers, magistrates, kings, emperors (II Macc. 12:35; Josephus, *Ant.* V. 1, 10), a soldier's *sagum* or scarf. Carr (*Cambridge Gk. Test.*) suggests that it may have been a worn-out scarf of Pilate's. The scarlet colour (*kokkinēn*) was a dye derived from the female insect (*kermes*) which gathered on the *ilex coccifera* found in Palestine. These dried clusters of insects look like berries and form the famous dye. The word occurs in Plutarch, Epictetus, Herodas, and late papyri besides the Septuagint and New Testament. Mark (15:17) has "purple" (*porphuran*). There are various shades of purple and scarlet and it is not easy to distinguish these colours or tints. The manuscripts vary here between "stripped" (*ekdusantes*) and "clothed" (*endusantes*). He had been stripped for the scourging. If "clothed" is correct, the soldiers added the scarlet (purple) mantle. Herodotus (iii. 139) relates that Darius richly rewarded a Samian exile for a rare scarlet robe which he obtained from him. This scarlet mantle on Jesus was mock imitation of the royal purple.

29. *A crown of thorns* (*stephanon ex akanthōn*). They wove a crown out of thorns which would grow even in the palace grounds. It is immaterial whether they were young and tender thorn bushes, as probable in the spring, or hard bushes with sharp prongs. The soldiers would not care, for

they were after ridicule and mockery even if it caused pain. It was more like a victor's garland (*stephanon*) than a royal diadem (*diadēma*), but it served the purpose. So with the reed (*kalamon*), a stalk of common cane grass which served as sceptre. The soldiers were familiar with the *Ave Caesar* and copy it in their mockery of Jesus: *Hail, King of the Jews* (*chaire, Basileu tōn Ioudaiōn*). The soldiers added the insults used by the Sanhedrin (Matt. 26:67), spitting on him and smiting him with the reed. Probably Jesus had been unbound already. At any rate the garments of mockery were removed before the *via dolorosa* to the cross (verse 31).

32. *Compelled* (*ēggareusan*). This word of Persian origin was used in Matt. 5:41, which see. There are numerous papyri examples of Ptolemaic date and it survives in modern Greek vernacular. So the soldiers treat Simon of Cyrene (a town of Libya) as a Persian courier (*aggaros*) and impress him into service, probably because Jesus was showing signs of physical weakness in bearing his own Cross as the victims had to do, and not as a mere jest on Simon. "Gethsemane, betrayal, the ordeal of the past sleepless night, scourging, have made the flesh weak" (Bruce). Yes, and the burden of sin of the world that was breaking his heart. *His cross* (*ton stauron autou*). Jesus had used the term cross about himself (16:24). It was a familiar enough picture under Roman rule. Jesus had long foreseen and foretold this horrible form of death for himself (Matt. 20:19; 23:24; 26:2). He had heard the cry of the mob to Pilate that he be crucified (27:22) and Pilate's surrender (27:26) and he was on the way to the Cross (27:31). There were various kinds of crosses and we do not know precisely the shape of the Cross on which Jesus was crucified, though probably the one usually presented is correct. Usually the victim was nailed (hands and feet) to the cross before it was raised and it was not very high. The crucifixion was done by the soldiers

(27:35) in charge and two robbers were crucified on each side of Jesus, three crosses standing in a row (27:38).

33. *Golgotha* (*Golgotha*). Chaldaic or Aramaic *Gulgatha*, Hebrew *Gulgoleth*, place of a skull-shaped mount, not place of skulls. Latin Vulgate *Calvariae locus*, hence our Calvary. Tyndale misunderstood it as a place of dead men's skulls. Calvary or Golgotha is not the traditional place of the Holy Sepulchre in Jerusalem, but a place outside of the city, probably what is now called Gordon's Calvary, a hill north of the city wall which from the Mount of Olives looks like a skull, the rock-hewn tombs resembling eyes in one of which Jesus may have been buried.

34. *Wine mingled with gall* (*oinon meta cholēs memigmenon*). Late MSS. read *vinegar* (*oxos*) instead of wine and Mark (15:23) has myrrh instead of gall. The myrrh gave the sour wine a better flavour and like the bitter gall had a narcotic and stupefying effect. Both elements may have been in the drink which Jesus tasted and refused to drink. Women provided the drink to deaden the sense of pain and the soldiers may have added the gall to make it disagreeable. Jesus desired to drink to the full the cup from his Father's hand (John 18:11).

36. *Watched him there* (*etēroun auton ekei*). Imperfect tense descriptive of the task to prevent the possibility of rescue or removal of the body. These rough Roman soldiers casting lots over the garments of Christ give a picture of comedy at the foot of the Cross, the tragedy of the ages.

37. *His accusation* (*tēn aitian autou*). The title (*titlos*, John 19:19) or placard of the crime (the inscription, *hē epigraphē*) which was carried before the victim or hung around his neck as he walked to execution was now placed above (*ep' anō*) the head of Jesus on the projecting piece (*crux immurus*). This inscription gave the name and home, *Jesus of Nazareth*, and the charge on which he was convicted, *the King of the Jews* and the identification, *This is*. The four

reports all give the charge and vary in the others. The inscription in full was: This is Jesus of Nazareth the King of the Jews. The three languages are mentioned only by John (19:20), Latin for law, Hebrew (Aramaic) for the Jews, Greek for everybody. The accusation (charge, cause, *aitia*) correctly told the facts of the condemnation.

38. *Robbers* (*lēistai*). Not thieves (*kleptai*) as in Authorized Version. See Matt. 26:55. These two robbers were probably members of the band of Barabbas on whose cross Jesus now hung.

39. *Wagging their heads* (*kinountes tas kephalas autōn*). Probably in mock commiseration. "Jews again appear on the scene, with a malice like that shewn in the trial before the Sanhedrin" (McNeile). "To us it may seem incredible that even his worst enemies could be guilty of anything so brutal as to hurl taunts at one suffering the agonies of crucifixion" (Bruce). These passers-by (*paratēroumenoi*) look on Jesus as one now down and out. They jeer at the fallen foe.

40. *If thou art the Son of God* (*ei huios ei tou theou*). More exactly, "If thou art a son of God," the very language of the devil to Jesus (Matt. 4:3) in the early temptations, now hurled at Jesus under the devil's prompting as he hung upon the Cross. There is allusion, of course, to the claim of Jesus under oath before the Sanhedrin "the Son of God" (*ho huios tou theou*) and a repetition of the misrepresentation of his words about the temple of his body. It is a pitiful picture of human depravity and failure in the presence of Christ dying for sinners.

41. *The chief priests mocking* (*hoi archiereis empaizontes*). The Sanhedrin in fact, for "the scribes and elders" are included. The word for mocking (*empaizontes*, *en*, and *paizō*, from *pais*, child) means acting like silly children who love to guy one another. These grave and reverend seniors had already given vent to their glee at the condemnation of Jesus by themselves (Matt. 26:67f.).

42. *He saved others; himself he cannot save (allous esōsen; heauton ou dunatai sōsai).* The sarcasm is true, though they do not know its full significance. If he had saved himself now, he could not have saved any one. The paradox is precisely the philosophy of life proclaimed by Jesus himself (Matt. 10:39). *Let him now come down (katabatō nun).* Now that he is a condemned criminal nailed to the Cross with the claim of being "the King of Israel" (the Jews) over his head. Their spiteful assertion that they would then believe upon Jesus (*ep' auton*) is plainly untrue. They would have shifted their ground and invented some other excuse. When Jesus wrought his greatest miracles, they wanted "a sign from heaven." These "pious scoffers" (Bruce) are like many today who make factitious and arbitrary demands of Christ whose character and power and deity are plain to all whose eyes are not blinded by the god of this world. Christ will not give new proofs to the blind in heart.

43. *Let him deliver him now (rhusasthō nun).* They add the word "now" to Psalm 21 (22):9. That is the point of the sneer at Christ's claim to be God's son thrown in his teeth again and at the willingness and power of God to help his "son." The verb *thelō* here may mean *love* as in the Septuagint (Psa. 18:20; 41:12) or "cares for" (Moffatt), "gin he cares ocht for him" (*Braid Scots*).

44. *The robbers also (kai hoi lēistai).* Probably "even the robbers" (Weymouth) who felt a momentary superiority to Jesus thus maligned by all. So the inchoative imperfect *ōneidizon* means "began to reproach him."

45. *From the sixth hour (apo hektēs hōras).* Curiously enough McNeile takes this to mean the trial before Pilate (John 18:14). But clearly John uses Roman time, writing at the close of the century when Jewish time was no longer in vogue. It was six o'clock in the morning Roman time when the trial occurred before Pilate. The crucifixion began at the third hour (Mark 15:25) Jewish time or nine A.M.

The darkness began at noon, the sixth hour Jewish time and lasted till 3 P.M. Roman time, the ninth hour Jewish time (Mark 15:33 = Matt. 27:45 = Luke 23:44). The dense darkness for three hours could not be an eclipse of the sun and Luke (23:45) does not so say, only "the sun's light failing." Darkness sometimes precedes earthquakes and one came at this time or dense masses of clouds may have obscured the sun's light. One need not be disturbed if nature showed its sympathy with the tragedy of the dying of the Creator on the Cross (Rom. 8:22), groaning and travailing until now.

46. *My God, My God, why hast thou forsaken me?* (*Thee mou, thee mou, hina ti me egkatelipes;*). Matthew first transliterates the Aramaic, according to the Vatican manuscript (B), the words used by Jesus: *Elōi, elōi, lema sabachthanei;* Some of the MSS. give the transliteration of these words from Psa. 22:1 in the Hebrew (*Eli, Eli, lama Zaphthanei*). This is the only one of the seven sayings of Christ on the Cross given by Mark and Matthew. The other six occur in Luke and John. This is the only sentence of any length in Aramaic preserved in Matthew, though he has Aramaic words like amen, corban, mammon, pascha, raca, Satan, Golgotha. The so-called Gospel of Peter preserves this saying in a Docetic (Cerinthian) form: "My power, my power, thou hast forsaken me!" The Cerinthian Gnostics held that the *aeon* Christ came on the man Jesus at his baptism and left him here on the Cross so that only the man Jesus died. Nothing from Jesus so well ill strates the depth of his suffering of soul as he felt himself regarded as sin though sinless (II Cor. 5:21). John 3:16 comes to our relief here as we see the Son of God bearing the sin of the world. This cry of desolation comes at the close of the three hours of darkness.

48. *Gave him to drink* (*epotizen*). Imperfect of conative action, *offered him a drink* of vinegar on the sponge on a reed.

Others interrupted this kindly man, but Jesus did taste this mild stimulant (John 19:30) for he thirsted (John 19:28).

49. *Whether Elijah cometh to save him* (*ei erchetai Ēleias sōsōn auton*). The excuse had a pious sound as they misunderstood the words of Jesus in his outcry of soul anguish. We have here one of the rare instances (*sōsōn*) of the future participle to express purpose in the N.T. though a common Greek idiom. Some ancient MSS. add here what is genuine in John 19:34, but what makes complete wreck of the context for in verse 50 Jesus cried with a loud voice and was not yet dead in verse 49. It was a crass mechanical copying by some scribe from John 19:34. See full discussion in my *Introduction to the Textual Criticism of the N.T.*

50. *Yielded up his spirit* (*aphēken to pneuma*). The loud cry may have been Psa. 31:5 as given in Luke 23:46: "Father, into thy hands I commend my spirit." John (19:30) gives *It is finished* (*tetelestai*), though which was actually last is not clear. Jesus did not die from slow exhaustion, but with a loud cry. *He breathed out* (*exepneusen*, Mark 15:37), *sent back his spirit* (Matt. 27:50), *gave up his spirit* (*paredōken to pneuma*, John 19:30). "He gave up his life because he willed it, when he willed it, and as he willed it" (Augustine). Stroud (*Physical Cause of the Death of Christ*) considers the loud cry one of the proofs that Jesus died of a ruptured heart as a result of bearing the sin of the world.

51. *Was rent* (*eschisthē*). Both Mark (15:38) and Luke (23:45) mention also this fact. Matthew connects it with the earthquake, "the earth did quake" (*hē gē eseisthē*). Josephus (*War* VI. 299) tells of a quaking in the temple before the destruction and the Talmud tells of a quaking forty years before the destruction of the temple. Allen suggests that "a cleavage in the masonry of the porch, which rent the outer veil and left the Holy Place open to view, would account for the language of the Gospels, of Josephus, and of the Talmud." This veil was a most elaborately

woven fabric of seventy-two twisted plaits of twenty-four threads each and the veil was sixty feet long and thirty wide. The rending of the veil signified the removal of the separation between God and the people (Gould).

52. *The tombs were opened* (*ta mnēmeia aneōichthēsan*). First aorist passive indicative (double augment). The splitting of the rocks by the earthquake and the opening of tombs can be due to the earthquake. But the raising of the bodies of the dead after the resurrection of Jesus which appeared to many in the holy city puzzles many today who admit the actual bodily resurrection of Jesus. Some would brand all these portents as legends since they appear in Matthew alone. Others would say that "after his resurrection" should read "after their resurrection," but that would make it conflict with Paul's description of Christ as the first fruits of them that sleep (I Cor. 15:20). Some say that Jesus released these spirits after his descent into Hades. So it goes. We come back to miracles connected with the birth of Jesus, God's Son coming into the world. If we grant the possibility of such manifestations of God's power, there is little to disturb one here in the story of the death of God's Son.

54. *Truly this was the Son of God* (*alēthōs theou huios ēn houtos*). There is no article with God or Son in the Greek so that it means "God's Son," either "the Son of God" or "a Son of God." There is no way to tell. Evidently the centurion (*hekatontarchos* here, ruler of a hundred, Latin word *kenturiōn* in Mark 15:39) was deeply moved by the portents which he had witnessed. He had heard the several flings at Jesus for claiming to be the Son of God and may even have heard of his claim before the Sanhedrin and Pilate. How much he meant by his words we do not know, but probably he meant more than merely "a righteous man" (Luke 23:47). Petronius is the name given this centurion by tradition. If he was won now to trust in Christ, he came as a pagan and, like the robber who believed, was saved as

Jesus hung upon the Cross. All who are ever saved in truth
are saved because of the death of Jesus on the Cross. So
the Cross began to do its work at once.

55. *Many women* (*gunaikes pollai*). We have come to
expect the women from Galilee to be faithful, last at the
Cross and first at the tomb. Luke (23:49) says that "all his
acquaintance" (*pantes hoi gnōstoi autōi*) stood at a distance
and saw the end. One may hope that the apostles were in
that sad group. But certainly many women were there.
The Mother of Jesus had been taken away from the side
of the Cross by the Beloved Disciple to his own home (John
19:27). Matthew names three of the group by name. Mary
Magdalene is mentioned as a well-known person though not
previously named in Matthew's Gospel. Certainly she is
not the sinful woman of Luke 7 nor Mary of Bethany.
There is another Mary, the mother of James and Joseph
(Joses) not otherwise known to us. And then there is the
mother of the sons of Zebedee (James and John), usually
identified with Salome (Mark 15:40). These noble and
faithful women were "beholding from afar" (*apo makrothen
theōrousai*). These three women may have drawn nearer
to the Cross for Mary the Mother of Jesus stood beside the
Cross (*para tōi staurōi*) with Mary of Clopas and Mary
Magdalene (John 19:25) before she left. They had once
ministered unto Jesus (*diakonousai autōi*) and now he is
dead. Matthew does not try to picture the anguish of heart
of these noble women nor does he say as Luke (23:48) does
that "they returned smiting their breasts." He drops the
curtain on that saddest of all tragedies as the loyal band
stood and looked at the dead Christ on Golgotha. What
hope did life now hold for them?

57. *And when even was come* (*opsias de genomenēs*). It
was the Preparation (*paraskeuē*), the day before the sabbath
(Mark 15:42; Luke 23:54; John 31:42). *Paraskeuē* is the
name in modern Greek today for Friday. The Jews were

anxious that these bodies should be taken down before the sabbath began at 6 P.M. The request of Joseph of Arimathea for the body of Jesus was a relief to Pilate and to the Jews also. We know little about this member of the Sanhedrin save his name Joseph, his town Arimathea, that he was rich, a secret disciple, and had not agreed to the death of Jesus. Probably he now wished that he had made an open profession. But he has courage now when others are cowardly and asked for the personal privilege (*ēitēsato*, middle voice, asked for himself) of placing the body of Jesus in his new tomb. Some today identify this tomb with one of the rock tombs now visible under Gordon's Calvary. It was a mournful privilege and dignity that came to Joseph and Nicodemus (John 19:39-41) as they wrapped the body of Jesus in clean linen cloth and with proper spices placed it in this fresh (*kainōi*) tomb in which no body had yet been placed. It was cut in the rock (*elatomēsen*) for his own body, but now it was for Jesus. But now (verse 60) he rolled a great stone to the door of the tomb and departed. That was for safety. But two women had watched the sad and lonely ceremony, Mary Magdalene and the other Mary (mother of James and Joseph). They were sitting opposite and looking in silence.

63. *Sir, we remember* (*kurie, emnesthēmen*). This was the next day, on our Saturday, the Jewish Sabbath, the day after the Preparation (Matt. 27:62). Ingressive aorist indicative, we have just recalled. It is objected that the Jewish rulers would know nothing of such a prediction, but in Matt. 12:40 he expressly made it to them. Meyer scouts as unhistorical legend the whole story that Christ definitely foretold his resurrection on the third day. But that is to make legendary much of the Gospels and to limit Jesus to a mere man. The problem remains why the disciples forgot and the Jewish leaders remembered. But that is probably due on the one hand to the overwhelming grief of the dis-

ciples coupled with the blighting of all their hopes of a political Messiah in Jesus, and on the other hand to the keen nervous fear of the leaders who dreaded the power of Jesus though dead. They wanted to make sure of their victory and prevent any possible revival of this pernicious heresy. *That deceiver* (*ekeinos ho planos*) they call him, a vagabond wanderer (*planos*) with a slur in the use of *that* (*ekeinos*), a picturesque sidelight on their intense hatred of and fear of Jesus.

64. *The last error* (*hē eschatē planē*). The last delusion, imposture (Weymouth), fraud (Moffatt). Latin *error* is used in both senses, from *errare*, to go astray. The first fraud was belief in the Messiahship of Jesus, the second belief in his resurrection.

65. *Make it as sure as you can* (*asphalisasthe hōs oidate*). "Make it secure for yourselves (ingressive aorist middle) as you know how." *Have a guard* (*echete koustōdian*), present imperative, a guard of Roman soldiers, not mere temple police. The Latin term *koustōdia* occurs in an Oxyrhynchus papyrus of A.D. 22. "The curt permission to the Jews whom he despised is suitable in the mouth of the Roman official" (McNeile).

66. *Sealing the stone, the guard being with them* (*sphragisantēs ton lithon meta tēs koustōdias*). Probably by a cord stretched across the stone and sealed at each end as in Dan. 6:17. The sealing was done in the presence of the Roman guard who were left in charge to protect this stamp of Roman authority and power. They did their best to prevent theft and the resurrection (Bruce), but they overreached themselves and provided additional witness to the fact of the empty tomb and the resurrection of Jesus (Plummer).

CHAPTER XXVIII

1. *Now late on the sabbath as it began to dawn toward the first day of the week (opse de sabbatōn, tēi epiphōskousēi eis mian sabbatōn).* This careful chronological statement according to Jewish days clearly means that before the sabbath was over, that is before six P.M., this visit by the women was made "to see the sepulchre" (*theorēsai ton taphon*). They had seen the place of burial on Friday afternoon (Mark 15:47; Matt. 27:61; Luke 23:55). They had rested on the sabbath after preparing spices and ointments for the body of Jesus (Luke 23:56), a sabbath of unutterable sorrow and woe. They will buy other spices after sundown when the new day has dawned and the sabbath is over (Mark 16:1). Both Matthew here and Luke (23:54) use dawn (*epiphōskō*) for the dawning of the twenty-four hourday at sunset, not of the dawning of the twelve-hour day at sunrise. The Aramaic used the verb for dawn in both senses. The so-called Gospel of Peter has *epiphōskō* in the same sense as Matthew and Luke as does a late papyrus. Apparently the Jewish sense of "dawn" is here expressed by this Greek verb. Allen thinks that Matthew misunderstands Mark at this point, but clearly Mark is speaking of sunrise and Matthew of sunset. Why allow only one visit for the anxious women?

2. *There was a great earthquake (seismos egeneto megas).* Clearly not the earthquake of 27:51. The precise time of this earthquake is not given. It was before sunrise on the first day of the week when the women made the next visit. Matthew alone relates the coming of the angel of the Lord who rolled away the stone and was sitting upon it (*apekulise ton lithon kai ekathēto epanō autou*). If one is querulous

about these supernatural phenomena, he should reflect that
the Resurrection of Jesus is one of the great supernatural
events of all time. Cornelius à Lapide dares to say: "The
earth, which trembled with sorrow at the Death of Christ
as it were leaped for joy at His Resurrection." The Angel
of the Lord announced the Incarnation of the Son of God
and also His Resurrection from the grave. There are apparent inconsistencies in the various narratives of the
Resurrection and the appearances of the Risen Christ. We
do not know enough of the details to be able to reconcile
them. But the very variations strengthen the independent
witness to the essential fact that Jesus rose from the grave.
Let each writer give his own account in his own way. The
stone was rolled away not to let the Lord out, but to let the
women in to prove the fact of the empty tomb (McNeile).

3. *Appearance* (*eidea*). Here only in the N.T. Compare
morphē and *schēma*.

4. *The watchers did quake* (*eseisthēsan hoi tērountes*). And
no wonder that they became as dead men and fled before
the women came.

5. *Unto the women* (*tais gunaixin*). According to John,
Mary Magdalene had left to go and tell Peter and John of
the supposed grave robbery (John 20:1f.). But the other
women remained and had the interview with the angel (or
men, Luke) about the empty tomb and the Risen Christ.
Jesus the Crucified (*Iēsoun ton estaurōmenon*). Perfect passive participle, state of completion. This he will always be.
So Paul will preach as essential to his gospel "and this one
crucified" (*kai touton estaurōmenon*, I Cor. 2:2).

6. *Risen from the dead* (*ēgerthē apo tōn nekrōn*). *Jesus the
Risen*. This is the heart of the testimony of the angel to the
women. It is what Paul wishes Timothy never to forget (II
Tim. 2:8), "Jesus Christ risen from the dead" (*Iēsoun Christon egēgermenon ek nekrōn*). They were afraid and dazzled
by the glory of the scene, but the angel said, "Come, see the

place where the Lord lay" (*deute idete ton topon hopou ekeito ho Kurios*). Some MSS. do not have *ho Kurios*, but he is the subject of *ekeito*. His body was not there. It will not do to say that Jesus arose in spirit and appeared alive though his body remained in the tomb. The empty tomb is the first great fact confronting the women and later the men. Various theories were offered then as now. But none of them satisfy the evidence and explain the survival of faith and hope in the disciples that do not rest upon the fact of the Risen Christ whose body was no longer in the tomb.

7. *He goeth before you into Galilee* (*proagei humas eis tēn Galilaian*). Jesus did appear to the disciples in Galilee on two notable occasions (by the beloved lake, John 21, and on the mountain, Matt. 28:16–20). Probably before the women were permitted to tell this story in full to the disciples who scouted as idle talk (John 24:11) their first accounts, Jesus appeared to various disciples in Jerusalem on this first great Sunday. Jesus did not say that he would not see any of them in Jerusalem. He merely made a definite appointment in Galilee which he kept.

8. *With fear and great joy* (*meta phobou kai charas megalēs*). A touch of life was this as the excited women ran quickly (*tachu edramon*) as they had been told "to bring his disciples word" (*apaggeilai tois mathētais autou*). They had the greatest piece of news that it was possible to have. Mark calls it fear and ecstasy. Anything seemed possible now. Mark even says that at first they told no one anything for they were afraid (Mark 16:9), the tragic close of the text of Mark in Aleph and B, our two oldest manuscripts. But these mingled emotions of ecstasy and dread need cause no surprise when all things are considered.

9. *Jesus met them* (*Iēsous hupēntēsen autais*). Came suddenly face to face (*antaō, hupo*) with them as they brooded over the message of the angel and the fact of the empty

tomb (associative instrumental, *autais*). Cf. 8:34; 24:1–6.
Probably the lost portion of Mark's Gospel contained the
story of this meeting with Jesus which changed their fears
into joy and peace. His greeting was the ordinary "Hail"
(*chairete*). They fell at his feet and held them in reverence
while they worshipped him. Jesus allowed this act of
worship though he forbade eager handling of his body by
Mary Magdalene (John 20:17). It was a great moment of
faith and cheer.

10. *Fear not* (*mē phobeisthe*). They were still afraid for
joy and embarrassment. Jesus calms their excitement by
the repetition of the charge from the angel for the disciples
to meet him in Galilee. There is no special mention of Peter
("and Peter") as in Mark 16:7, but we may be sure that
the special message to Peter was delivered.

11. *Told unto the chief priests* (*apēggeilan tois archiereusin*).
These Roman soldiers had been placed at the disposal of
the Sanhedrin. They were probably afraid also to report
to Pilate and tell him what had happened. They apparently
told a truthful account as far as they understood it. But
were the Sanhedrin convinced of the resurrection of Jesus?

12. *They gave large money* (*arguria hikana edōkan*). The
use of the plural for pieces of silver (*arguria*) is common.
The papyri have many instances of *hikana* for considerable
(from *hikanō*, to reach to, attain to). These pious Sanhe-
drists knew full well the power of bribes. They make a contract with the Roman soldiers to tell a lie about the resurrection of Jesus as they paid Judas money to betray him.
They show not the slightest tendency to be convinced by
the facts though one had risen from the dead.

13. *Stole him away while we slept* (*eklepsan auton hēmōn
koimōmenōn*). Genitive absolute. An Irish bull on the
face of it. If they were asleep they would not know anything about it.

14. *We will persuade him, and rid you of care* (*hēmeis*

peisomen kai humās amerimnous poiēsomen). They would try money also on Pilate and assume all responsibility. Hence the soldiers have no anxiety (*amerimnous*, alpha privative and *merimnaō*, to be anxious). They lived up to their bargain and this lie lives on through the ages. Justin (*Dial.* 108) accuses the Jews of spreading the charge. Bengel: *Quam laboriosum bellum mendacii contra veritatem. It was spread about* (*diephēmisthē*) diligently by the Jews to excuse their disbelief in the Messiahship of Jesus.

17. *But some doubted* (*hoi de edistasan*). From *dis* (in two, divided in mind). Cf. Matt. 14:31. The reference is not to the eleven who were all now convinced after some doubt, but to the others present. Paul states that over five hundred were present, most of whom were still alive when he wrote (I Cor. 15:6). It is natural that some should hesitate to believe so great a thing at the first appearance of Jesus to them. Their very doubt makes it easier for us to believe. This was the mountain where Jesus had promised to meet them. This fact explains the large number present. Time and place were arranged beforehand. It was the climax of the various appearances and in Galilee where were so many believers. They worshipped (*prosekunēsan*) Jesus as the women had done (28:9). He is now their Risen Lord and Saviour.

18. *All authority* (*pāsa exousia*). Jesus came close to them (*proselthōn*) and made this astounding claim. He spoke as one already in heaven with a world-wide outlook and with the resources of heaven at his command. His authority or power in his earthly life had been great (7:29; 11:27; 21:23f.). Now it is boundless and includes earth and heaven. *Hath been given* (*edothē*) is a timeless aorist (Robertson, *Grammar*, pp. 836f.). It is the sublimist of all spectacles to see the Risen Christ without money or army or state charging this band of five hundred men and women with world conquest and bringing them to believe it possible and to undertake it

with serious passion and power. Pentecost is still to come, but dynamic faith rules on this mountain in Galilee.

19. *All the nations* (*panta ta ethnē*). Not just the Jews scattered among the Gentiles, but the Gentiles themselves in every land. And not by making Jews of them, though this point is not made plain here. It will take time for the disciples to grow into this *Magna Charta* of the missionary propaganda. But here is the world program of the Risen Christ and it should not be forgotten by those who seek to foreshorten it all by saying that Jesus expected his second coming to be very soon, even within the lifetime of those who heard. He did promise to come, but he has never named the date. Meanwhile we are to be ready for his coming at any time and to look for it joyfully. But we are to leave that to the Father and push on the campaign for world conquest. This program includes making disciples or learners (*mathēteu-sate*) such as they were themselves. That means evangelism in the fullest sense and not merely revival meetings. Baptism in (*eis*, not *into*) the name of the Father, the Son, and the Holy Spirit, in the name of the Trinity. Objection is raised to this language in the mouth of Jesus as too theological and as not a genuine part of the Gospel of Matthew for the same reason. See Matt. 11:27, where Jesus speaks of the Father and the Son as here. But it is all to no purpose. There is a chapter devoted to this subject in my *The Christ of the Logia* in which the genuineness of these words is proven. The name of Jesus is the essential part of it as is shown in the Acts. Trine immersion is not taught as the Greek Church holds and practices, baptism in the name of the Father, then of the Son, then of the Holy Spirit. The use of name (*onoma*) here is a common one in the Septuagint and the papyri for power or authority. For the use of *eis* with *onoma* in the sense here employed, not meaning *into*, see Matt. 10:41f. (cf. also 12:41).

20. *Teaching them* (*didaskontes autous*). Christians have

been slow to realize the full value of what we now call religious education. The work of teaching belongs to the home, to the church (sermon, Sunday school, young people's work, prayer-meeting, study classes, mission classes), to the school (not mixing of church and state, but moral instruction if not the reading of the Bible), good books which should be in every home, reading of the Bible itself. Some react too far and actually put education in the place of conversion or regeneration. That is to miss the mark. But teaching is part, a weighty part, of the work of Christians.

I am with you (*egō meta humōn*). This is the amazing and blessed promise. He is to be with the disciples when he is gone, with all the disciples, with all knowledge, with all power, with them all the days (all sorts of days, weakness, sorrows, joy, power), till the consummation of the age (*heōs tēs sunteleias tou aiōnos*). That goal is in the future and unknown to the disciples. This blessed hope is not designed as a sedative to an inactive mind and complacent conscience, but an incentive to the fullest endeavor to press on to the farthest limits of the world that all the nations may know Christ and the power of his Risen Life. So Matthew's Gospel closes in a blaze of glory. Christ is conqueror in prospect and in fact. Christian history from that eventful experience on the Mountain in Galilee has been the fulfilment of that promise in as far as we allow God's power to work in us for the winning of the world to Christ, the Risen, all powerful Redeemer, who is with his people all the time. Jesus employs the prophetic present here (*eimi*, I am). He is with us all the days till he comes in glory.

THE GOSPEL
ACCORDING TO MARK

BY WAY OF INTRODUCTION

One of the clearest results of modern critical study of the Gospels is the early date of Mark's Gospel. Precisely how early is not definitely known, but there are leading scholars who hold that A.D. 50 is quite probable. My own views are given in detail in my *Studies in Mark's Gospel*. Zahn still argues that the Gospel according to Matthew is earlier than that according to Mark, but the arguments are against him. The framework of Mark's Gospel lies behind both Matthew and Luke and nearly all of it is used by one or the other. One may satisfy himself on this point by careful use of a Harmony of the Gospels in Greek or English. Whether Mark made use of Q (*Logia of Jesus*) or not is not yet shown, though it is possible. But Mark and Q constitute the two oldest known sources of our Matthew and Luke. We have much of Q preserved in the Non-Markan portions of both Matthew and Luke, though the document itself has disappeared. But Mark's work has remained in spite of its exhaustive use by Matthew and Luke, all except the disputed close. For this preservation we are all grateful. Streeter (*The Four Gospels*) has emphasized the local use of texts in preserving portions of the New Testament. If Mark wrote in Rome, as is quite possible, his book was looked upon as the Roman Gospel and had a powerful environment in which to take root. It has distinctive merits of its own that helped to keep it in use. It is mainly narrative and the style is direct and simple with many vivid touches, like the historical present of an eyewitness. The early writers all agree that Mark was the interpreter for Simon Peter with whom he was at one time, according to Peter's own statement, either in Babylon or Rome (I Peter 5:13).

This Gospel is the briefest of the four, but is fullest of striking details that apparently came from Peter's discourses which Mark heard, such as green grass, flower beds (6:38), two thousand hogs (5:13), looking round about (3:5, 34). Peter usually spoke in Aramaic and Mark has more Aramaic phrases than the others, like *Boanerges* (3:17), *Talitha cumi* (5:41), *Korban* (7:11), *Ephphatha* (7:34), *Abba* (14:36). The Greek is distinctly vernacular *Koiné* like one-eyed (*monophthalmon*, 9:47) as one would expect from both Peter and Mark. There are also more Latin phrases and idioms like *centurio* (15:39), *quadrans* (12:42), *flagellare* (15:15), *speculator* (6:27), *census* (12:14), *sextarius* (7:4), *praetorium* (15:6), than in the other Gospels, so much so that C. H. Turner raises the question whether Mark wrote first in Latin, or at any rate in Rome. There are some who hold that Mark wrote first in Aramaic, but the facts are sufficiently accounted for by the fact of Peter's preaching and the activity in Rome. Some even think that he wrote the Gospel in Rome while with Peter who suggested and read the manuscript. B. W. Bacon holds that this Gospel has a distinct Pauline flavour and may have had several recensions. The Ur-Marcus theory does not have strong support now. Mark was once a co-worker with Barnabas and Paul, but deserted them at Perga. Paul held this against Mark and refused to take him on the second mission tour. Barnabas took Mark, his cousin, with him and then he appeared with Simon Peter with whom he did his greatest work. When Mark had made good with Barnabas and Peter, Paul rejoiced and commends him heartily to the Colossians (Col. 4:10). In the end Paul will ask Timothy to pick up Mark and bring him along with him to Paul in Rome, for he has found him useful for ministry, this very young man who made such a mistake that Paul would have no more of him. This tribute to Mark by Paul throws credit upon both of them as is shown in my *Making Good in the Ministry*. The character of the Gospel of Mark is determined largely by the scope of Peter's preaching as we see it in Acts 10:36–42, covering the period in outline from John the Baptist to the Resurrection of Jesus. There is nothing about the birth of the Baptist or of Jesus. This peculiarity of Mark's Gospel cannot be used against the narratives of the Virgin Birth of Jesus in Matthew and Luke, since Mark tells nothing whatever about his birth at all.

The closing passage in the Textus Receptus, Mark 16: 9–20, is not found in the oldest Greek Manuscripts, Aleph and B, and is probably not genuine. A discussion of the evidence will appear at the proper place. Swete points out that Mark deals with two great themes, the Ministry in Galilee (Chs. 1 to 9) and the Last Week in Jerusalem (11 to 16) with a brief sketch of the period of withdrawal from Galilee (ch. 10). The first fourteen verses are introductory as 16:9–20 is an appendix. The Gospel of Mark pictures Christ in action. There is a minimum of discourse and a maximum of deed. And yet the same essential pictures of Christ appear here as in the Logia, in Matthew, in Luke, in John, in Paul, in Peter, in Hebrews as is shown in my *The Christ of the Logia.* The cry of the critics to get back to the Synoptics and away from Paul and John has ceased since it is plain that the Jesus of Mark is the same as the Christ of Paul. There is a different shading in the pictures, but the same picture, Son of God and Son of Man, Lord of life and death, worker of miracles and Saviour from sin. This Gospel is the one for children to read first and is the one that we should use to lay the foundation for our picture of Christ. In my *Harmony of the Gospels* I have placed Mark first in the framework since Matthew, Luke, and John all follow in broad outline his plan with additions and supplemental material. Mark's Gospel throbs with life and bristles with vivid details. We see with Peter's eyes and catch almost the very look and gesture of Jesus as he moved among men in his work of healing men's bodies and saving men's souls.

CHAPTER I

1. *The beginning (archē).* There is no article in the Greek. It is possible that the phrase served as a heading or title for the paragraph about the ministry of the Baptist or as the superscription for the whole Gospel (Bruce) placed either by Mark or a scribe. And then the Gospel of Jesus Christ means the Message about Jesus Christ (objective genitive). The word Gospel here (*euaggelion*) comes close to meaning the record itself as told by Mark. Swete notes that each writer has a different starting point (*archē*). Mark, as the earliest form of the evangelic tradition, begins with the work of the Baptist, Matthew with the ancestry and birth of the Messiah, Luke with the birth of the Baptist, John with the Preincarnate Logos, Paul with the foundation of each of the churches (Phil. 4:15). *The Son of God (Huiou theou).* Aleph 28, 255 omit these words, but B, D, L, have them and the great mass of the manuscripts have *huiou tou theou.* If this is a heading added to what Mark wrote, the heading may have existed early in two forms, one with, one without "Son of God." If Mark wrote the words, there is no reason to doubt the genuineness since he uses the phrase elsewhere.

2. *In Isaiah, the prophet (en tōi Ēsaiāi tōi prophētēi).* The quotation comes from Mal. 3:1 and Isa. 40:3. The Western and Neutral classes read Isaiah, the Alexandrian and Syrian, "the prophets," an evident correction because part of it is from Malachi. But Isaiah is mentioned as the chief of the prophets. It was common to combine quotations from the prophets in *testimonia* and *catenae* (chains of quotations). This is Mark's only prophetic quotation on his own account (Bruce).

3. *The voice of one crying (phonē boōntos).* God is coming

to his people to deliver them from their captivity in Babylon. So the prophet cries like a voice in the wilderness to make ready for the coming of God. When the committee from the Sanhedrin came to ask John who he was, he used this very language of Isaiah (John 1:23). He was only a voice, but we can still hear the echo of that voice through the corridor of the centuries. *Paths straight (eutheias tas tribous)*. Automobile highways today well illustrate the wonderful Persian roads for the couriers of the king and then for the king himself. The Roman Empire was knit together by roads, some of which survive today. John had a high and holy mission as the forerunner of the Messiah.

4. *John came (egeneto Iōanēs)*. His coming was an epoch *(egeneto)*, not a mere event *(ēn)*. His coming was in accordance with the prophetic picture *(kathōs, 1:2)*. Note the same verb about John in John 1:6. The coming of John the Baptizer was the real beginning of the spoken message about Christ. He is described as *the baptizing one (ho haptizōn)* in the wilderness *(en tēi erēmōi)*. The baptizing took place in the River Jordan (Mark 1:5, 9) which was included in the general term the wilderness or the deserted region of Judea. *Preached the baptism of repentance (kērussōn baptisma metanoias)*. Heralded a repentance kind of baptism (genitive case, genus case), a baptism marked by repentance. See on Matt. 3:2 for discussion of repent, an exceedingly poor rendering of John's great word *metanoias*. He called upon the Jews to change their minds and to turn from their sins, "confessing their sins" *(exomologoumenoi tas hamartias autōn)*. See Matt. 3:16. The public confessions produced a profound impression as they would now. *Unto remission of sins (eis aphesin hamartiōn)*. This is a difficult phrase to translate accurately. Certainly John did not mean that the baptism was the means of obtaining the forgiveness of their sins or necessary to the remission of sins. The trouble lies in the use of *eis* which sometimes is used when purpose is

expressed, but sometimes when there is no such idea as in Matt. 10:41 and 12:41. Probably "with reference to" is as good a translation here as is possible. The baptism was on the basis of the repentance and confession of sin and, as Paul later explained (Rom. 6:4), was a picture of the death to sin and resurrection to new life in Christ. This symbol was already in use by the Jews for proselytes who became Jews. John is treating the Jewish nation as pagans who need to repent, to confess their sins, and to come back to the kingdom of God. The baptism in the Jordan was the objective challenge to the people.

5. *Then went out unto him* (*exeporeueto pros auton*). Imperfect indicative describing the steady stream of people who kept coming to the baptism (*ebaptizonto*, imperfect passive indicative, a wonderful sight). *In the river Jordan* (*en tōi Iordanēi potamōi*). In the Jordan river, literally.

6. *Clothed with camel's hair* (*endedumenos trichas kamēlou*). Matthew (3:4) has it a garment (*enduma*) of camel's hair. Mark has it in the accusative plural the object of the perfect passive participle retained according to a common Greek idiom. It was, of course, not camel's skin, but rough cloth woven of camel's hair. For the locusts and wild honey, see on Matt. 3:4. Dried locusts are considered palatable and the wild honey, or "mountain honey" as some versions give it (*meli agrion*), was bountiful in the clefts of the rocks. Some Bedouins make their living yet by gathering this wild honey out of the rocks.

7. *Mightier than I* (*ho ischuroteros mou*). In each of the Synoptics. Gould calls it a skeptical depreciation of himself by John. But it was sincere on John's part and he gives a reason for it. *The Latchet* (*ton himanta*). The thong of the sandal which held it together. When the guest comes into the house, performed by a slave before one enters the bath. Mark alone gives this touch.

8. *With water* (*hudati*). So Luke (3:16) the locative case,

in water. Matthew (3:11) has *en* (in), both with (in) water
and the Holy Spirit. The water baptism by John was a
symbol of the spiritual baptism by Jesus.

9. *In the Jordan* (*eis ton Iordanēn*). So in verse 10, *ek
tou hudatos*, out of the water, after the baptism into the
Jordan. Mark is as fond of "straightway" (*euthus*) as
Matthew is of "then" (*tote*). *Rent asunder* (*schizomenous*).
Split like a garment, present passive participle. Jesus saw
the heavens parting as he came up out of the water, a more
vivid picture than the "opened" in Matthew 3:16 and Luke
3:21. Evidently the Baptist saw all this and the Holy
Spirit coming down upon Jesus as a dove because he later
mentions it (John 1:32). The Cerinthian Gnostics took the
dove to mean the heavenly *aeon Christ* that here descended
upon the man Jesus and remained with him till the Cross
when it left him, a sort of forecast of the modern distinction
between the Jesus of history and the theological Christ.

11. *Thou art* (*su ei*). So Luke 3:22. Matthew 3:17 has
this is (*houtos estin*) which see. So both Mark and Luke
have "in thee," while Matthew has "in whom."

12. *Driveth him forth* (*auton ekballei*). Vivid word, bolder
than Matthew's "was led up" (*anēchthē*) and Luke's "was
led" (*ēgeto*). It is the same word employed in the driving
out of demons (Mark 1:34, 39). Mark has here "straightway" where Matthew has "then" (see on verse 9). The
forty days in the wilderness were under the direct guidance
of the Holy Spirit. The entire earthly life of Jesus was
bound up with the Holy Spirit from his birth to his death
and resurrection.

13. *With the wild beasts* (*meta tōu thēriōn*). Mark does
not give the narrative of the three temptations in Matthew
and Luke (apparently from the Logia and originally, of
course, from Jesus himself). But Mark adds this little touch
about the wild beasts in the wilderness. It was the haunt at
night of the wolf, the boar, the hyena, the jackal, the leop-

ard. It was lonely and depressing in its isolation and even dangerous. Swete notes that in Psa. 90:13 the promise of victory over the wild beasts comes immediately after that of angelic guardianship cited by Satan in Matt. 4:6. The angels did come and minister (*diēkonoun*), imperfect tense, kept it up till he was cheered and strengthened. Dr. Tristram observes that some Abyssinian Christians are in the habit of coming to the Quarantania during Lent and fasting forty days on the summit amid the ruins of its ancient cells and chapels where they suppose Jesus was tempted. But we are all tempted of the devil in the city even worse than in the desert.

14. *Jesus came into Galilee* (*ēlthen ho Iēsous eis tēn Galilaian*). Here Mark begins the narrative of the active ministry of Jesus and he is followed by Matthew and Luke. Mark undoubtedly follows the preaching of Peter. But for the Fourth Gospel we should not know of the year of work in various parts of the land (Perea, Galilee, Judea, Samaria) preceding the Galilean ministry. John supplements the Synoptic Gospels at this point as often. The arrest of John had much to do with the departure of Jesus from Judea to Galilee (John 4:1–4). *Preaching the gospel of God* (*kērussōn to euaggelion tou theou*). It is the subjective genitive, the gospel that comes from God. Swete observes that repentance (*metanoia*) is the keynote in the message of the Baptist as gospel (*euaggelion*) is with Jesus. But Jesus took the same line as John and proclaimed both repentance and the arrival of the kingdom of God. Mark adds to Matthew's report the words "the time is fulfilled" (*peplērōtai ho kairos*). It is a significant fact that John looks backward to the promise of the coming of the Messiah and signalizes the fulfilment as near at hand (perfect passive indicative). It is like Paul's fulness of time (*plērōma tou chronou*) in Gal. 4:4 and fulness of the times (*plērōma tōn kairōn*) in Eph. 1:10 when he employs the word *kairos*, opportunity or crisis

as here in Mark rather than the more general term *chronos*.
Mark adds here also: "and believe in the gospel" (*kai
pisteuete en tōi euaggeliōi*). Both repent and believe in the
gospel. Usually faith in Jesus (or God) is expected as in
John 14:1. But this crisis called for faith in the message
of Jesus that the Messiah had come. He did not use here
the term Messiah, for it had come to have political connota-
tions that made its use at present unwise. But the kingdom of God had arrived with the presence of the King. It
does make a difference what one believes. Belief or disbelief in the message of Jesus made a sharp cleavage in
those who heard him. "Faith in the message was the first
step; a creed of some kind lies at the basis of confidence in
the Person of Christ, and the occurrence of the phrase
pistuete en tōi euaggeliōi in the oldest record of the teaching
of our Lord is a valuable witness to this fact" (Swete).

16. *And passing along by the Sea of Galilee* (*kai paragōn
para tēn thalassan tēs Galilaias*). Mark uses *para* (along,
beside) twice and makes the picture realistic. He catches
this glimpse of Christ in action. Casting a *net* (*amphiballon-
tas*). Literally casting on both sides, now on one side, now
on the other. Matthew (4:18) has a different phrase which
see. There are two papyri examples of the verb *amphiballō*,
one verb absolutely for fishing as here, the other with the
accusative. It is fishing with a net, making a cast, a haul.
These four disciples were fishermen (*halieis*) and were *part-
ners* (*metochoi*) as Luke states (5:7).

17. *Become* (*genesthai*). Mark has this word not in
Matthew. It would be a slow and long process, but Jesus
could and would do it. He would undertake to make fishers
of men out of fishermen. Preachers are made out of laymen who are willing to leave their business for service for
Christ.

19. *A little further* (*oligon*). A Marcan detail. *Mending
their nets* (*katartizontas ta diktua*). See on Matt. 4:21.

Getting ready that they might succeed better at the next haul.

20. *With the hired servants* (*meta tōn misthōtōn*). One hired for wages (*misthos*), a very old Greek word. Zebedee and his two sons evidently had an extensive business in co-operation with Andrew and Simon (Luke 5:7, 10). Mark alone has this detail of the hired servants left with Zebedee. They left the boat and their father (Matt. 4:22) with' the hired servants. The business would go on while they left all (Luke 5:11) and became permanent followers of Jesus. Many a young man has faced precisely this problem when he entered the ministry. Could he leave father and mother, brothers and sisters, while he went forth to college and seminary to become a fisher of men? Not the least of the sacrifices made in the education of young preachers is that made by the home folks who have additional burdens to bear because the young preacher is no longer a bread-winner at home. Most young preachers joyfully carry on such burdens after entering the ministry.

21. *And taught* (*edidasken*). Inchoative imperfect, began to teach as soon as he entered the synagogue in Capernaum on the sabbath. The synagogue in Capernaum afforded the best opening for the teaching of Jesus. He had now made Capernaum (Tell Hum) his headquarters after the rejection in Nazareth as explained in Luke 4:16–31 and Matt. 4:13–16. The ruins of this synagogue have been discovered and there is even talk of restoring the building since the stones are in a good state of preservation. Jesus both taught (*didaskō*) and preached (*kērussō*) in the Jewish synagogues as opportunity was offered by the chief or leader of the synagogue (*archisunagōgos*). The service consisted of prayer, praise, reading of scripture, and exposition by any rabbi or other competent person. Often Paul was invited to speak at such meetings. In Luke 4:20 Jesus gave back the roll of Isaiah to the attendant or beadle (*tōi hupēretēi*) whose busi-

ness it was to bring out the precious manuscript and return it to its place. Jesus was a preacher of over a year when he began to teach in the Capernaum synagogue. His reputation had preceded him (Luke 4:14).

22. *They were astonished* (*exeplēssonto*). Pictorial imperfect as in Luke 4:32 describing the amazement of the audience, "meaning strictly to strike a person out of his senses by some strong feeling, such as fear, wonder, or even joy" (Gould). *And not as their scribes* (*kai ouch hōs hoi grammateis*). Luke 4:32 has only "with authority" (*en exousiāi*). Mark has it "as having authority" (*hōs echōn exousian*). He struck a note not found by the rabbi. They quoted other rabbis and felt their function to be expounders of the traditions which they made a millstone around the necks of the people. By so doing they set aside the word and will of God by their traditions and petty legalism (Mark 7:9, 13). They were casuists and made false interpretations to prove their punctilious points of external etiquette to the utter neglect of the spiritual reality. The people noticed at once that here was a personality who got his power (authority) direct from God, not from the current scribes. "Mark omits much, and is in many ways a meagre Gospel, but it makes a distinctive contribution to the evangelic history *in showing by a few realistic touches* (this one of them) *the remarkable personality of Jesus*" (Bruce). See on Matt. 7:29 for the like impression made by the Sermon on the Mount where the same language occurs. The chief controversy in Christ's life was with these scribes, the professional teachers of the oral law and mainly Pharisees. At once the people see that Jesus stands apart from the old group. He made a sensation in the best sense of that word. There was a buzz of excitement at the new teacher that was increased by the miracle that followed the sermon.

23. *With an unclean spirit* (*en pneumati akathartōi*). This use of *en* "with" is common in the Septuagint like the He-

brew *be*, but it occurs also in the papyri. It is the same idiom as "in Christ," "in the Lord" so common with Paul. In English we speak of our being in love, in drink, in his cups, etc. The unclean spirit was in the man and the man in the unclean spirit, a man in the power of the unclean spirit. Luke has "having," the usual construction. See on Matt. 22:43. Unclean spirit is used as synonymous with *demon* (*daimonion*). It is the idea of estrangement from God (Zech. 13:2). The whole subject of demonology is difficult, but no more so than the problem of the devil. Jesus distinguishes between the man and the unclean spirit. Usually physical or mental disease accompanied the possession by demons. One wonders today if the degenerates and confirmed criminals so common now are not under the power of demons. The only cure for confirmed criminals seems to be conversion (a new heart).

24. *What have we to do with thee?* (*ti hēmin kai soi?*) The same idiom in Matt. 8:29. Ethical dative. Nothing in common between the demon and Jesus. Note "we." The man speaks for the demon and himself, double personality. The recognition of Jesus by the demons may surprise us since the rabbis (the ecclesiastics) failed to do so. They call Jesus "The Holy One of God" (*ho hagios tou theou*). Hence the demon feared that Jesus was come to destroy him and the man in his power. In Matt. 8:29 the demon calls Jesus "Son of God." Later the disciples will call Jesus "The Holy One of God" (John 6:69). The demon cried out aloud (*anekraxen*, late first aorist form, *anekragen*, common second aorist) so that all heard the strange testimony to Jesus. The man says "I know" (*oida*), correct text, some manuscripts "we know" (*oidamen*), including the demon.

25. *Hold thy peace* (*phimōthēti*). First aorist passive imperative of *phimoō*. "Be quiet," Moffatt translates it. But it is a more vigorous word, "Be muzzled" like an ox. So literally in Deut. 25:4, I Cor. 9:9; I Tim. 5:18. It is com-

mon in Josephus, Lucian, and the LXX. See Matt. 22:12, 34. Gould renders it "Shut up." "Shut your mouth" would be too colloquial. Vincent suggests "gagged," but that is more the idea of *epistomazein* in Titus 1:11, to stop the mouth.

26. *Tearing him* (*sparaxan auton*). Margin, *convulsing him* like a spasm. Medical writers use the word for the rotating of the stomach. Luke 4:35 adds "when the demon had thrown him down in the midst." Mark mentions the "loud voice" (*phonēi megalēi*), a screech, in fact. It was a moment of intense excitement.

27. *They questioned among themselves* (*sunzētein autous*). By look and word. *A new teaching* (*didachē kainē*). One surprise had followed another this day. The teaching was fresh (*kainē*), original as the dew of the morning on the blossoms just blown. That was a novelty in that synagogue where only staid and stilted rabbinical rules had been heretofore droned out. This new teaching charmed the people, but soon will be rated as heresy by the rabbis. And it was with authority (*kat' exousian*). It is not certain whether the phrase is to be taken with "new teaching," "It's new teaching with authority behind it," as Moffatt has it, or with the verb; "with authority commandeth even the unclean spirits" (*kai tois pneumasin tois akathartois epitassei*). The position is equivocal and may be due to the fact that "Mark gives the incoherent and excited remarks of the crowd in this natural form" (Swete). But the most astonishing thing of all is that the demons "obey him" (*hupakouousin autōi*). The people were accustomed to the use of magical formulae by the Jewish exorcists (Matt. 12:27; Acts 19:13), but here was something utterly different. Simon Magus could not understand how Simon Peter could do his miracles without some secret trick and even offered to buy it (Acts 8:19).

28. *The report of him* (*hē akoē autou*). Vulgate, *rumor*. See Matt. 14:1; 24:6. They had no telephones, telegraphs,

newspapers or radio, but news has a marvellous way of
spreading by word of mouth. The fame of this new teacher
went out "everywhere" (*pantachou*) throughout all Galilee.

29. *The house of Simon and Andrew* (*tēn oikian Simōnos
kai Andreou*). Peter was married and both he and Andrew
lived together in "Peter's house" (Matt. 8:14) with Peter's
wife and mother-in-law. Peter was evidently married before
he began to follow Jesus. Later his wife accompanied him
on his apostolic journeys (I Cor. 9:5). This incident followed immediately after the service in the synagogue on the
sabbath. All the Synoptics give it. Mark heard Peter tell
it as it occurred in his own house where Jesus made his home
while in Capernaum. Each Gospel gives touches of its own
to the story. Mark has "lay sick of a fever" (*katekeito
puressousa*), lay prostrate burning with fever. Matthew
puts it "stretched out (*beblēmenēn*) with a fever." Luke
has it "holden with a great fever" (*ēn sunechomenē puretōi
megalōi*), a technical medical phrase. They all mention the
instant recovery and ministry without any convalescence.
Mark and Matthew speak of the touch of Jesus on her hand
and Luke speaks of Jesus standing over her like a doctor.
It was a tender scene.

32. *When the sun did set* (*hote edusen ho hēlios*). This
picturesque detail Mark has besides "at even" (*opsias
genomenēs*, genitive absolute, evening having come). Matthew has "when even was come," Luke "when the sun was
setting." The sabbath ended at sunset and so the people
were now at liberty to bring their sick to Jesus. The news
about the casting out of the demon and the healing of Peter's
mother-in-law had spread all over Capernaum. They
brought them in a steady stream (imperfect tense, *epheron*).
Luke (4:40) adds that Jesus laid his hand on every one of
them as they passed by in grateful procession.

33. *At the door* (*pros tēn thuran*). At the door of Peter's
house. The whole city was gathered together there (*ēn*

episunēgmenē, past perfect passive periphrastic indicative, double compound *epi* and *sun*). Mark alone mentions this vivid detail. He is seeing with Peter's eyes again. Peter no doubt watched the beautiful scene with pride and gratitude as Jesus stood in the door and healed the great crowds in the glory of that sunset. He loved to tell it afterwards. *Divers diseases (poikilais nosois)*. See Matt. 4:24 about *poikilos* meaning many-coloured, variegated. All sorts of sick folk came and were healed.

34. *Devils (daimonia)*. Demons it should be translated always. *Suffered not (ouk ēphien)*. Would not allow, imperfect tense of continued refusal The reason given is "because they knew him" (*hoti ēideisan auton*). Whether "to be Christ" (*Christon einai*) is genuine or not, that is the meaning and is a direct reference to 1:24 when in the synagogue the demon recognized and addressed Jesus as the Holy One of God. Testimony from such a source was not calculated to help the cause of Christ with the people. He had told the other demon to be silent. See on Matt. 8:29 for discussion of the word demon.

35. *In the morning, a great while before day (prōi ennucha lian)*. Luke has only "when it was day" (*genomenēs hēmeras*). The word *prōi* in Mark means the last watch of the night from three to six A.M. *Ennucha lian* means in the early part of the watch while it was still a bit dark (cf. Mark 16:2 *lian prōi*). *Rose up and went out (anastas exēlthen)*. Out of the house and out of the city, off (*apēlthen*, even if not genuine, possibly a conflate reading from 6:32, 46). "Flight from the unexpected reality into which His ideal conception of His calling had brought Him" (H. J. Holtzmann). Gould notes that Jesus seems to retreat before his sudden popularity, to prayer with the Father "that he might not be ensnared by this popularity, or in any way induced to accept the ways of ease instead of duty." But Jesus also had a plan for a preaching tour of Galilee and "He felt He could not begin

too soon. He left in the night, fearing opposition from the people" (Bruce). Surely many a popular preacher can understand this mood of Jesus when in the night he slips away to a solitary place for prayer. Jesus knew what it was to spend a whole night in prayer. He knew the blessing of prayer and the power of prayer. *And there prayed (kåkei prosēucheto)*. Imperfect tense picturing Jesus as praying through the early morning hours.

36. *Followed after him (katedīōxen auton)*. Hunted him out (Moffatt). Perfective use of the preposition *kata* (down to the finish). The verb *dīōkō* is used for the hunt or chase, pursuit. Vulgate has *persecutus est*. The personal story of Peter comes in here. "Simon's intention at least was good; the Master seemed to be losing precious opportunities and must be brought back" (Swete). Peter and those with him kept up the search till they found him. The message that they brought would surely bring Jesus back to Peter's house.

38. *Into the next towns (eis tas echomenas kōmopoleis)*. It was a surprising decision for Jesus to leave the eager, excited throngs in Capernaum for the country town or village cities without walls or much importance. Only instance of the word in the N.T. Late Greek word. The use of *echomenas* for next is a classic use meaning clinging to, next to a thing. So in Luke 13:33; Acts 13:44; 20:15; Heb. 6:9. "D" here has *eggus* (near).

39. *Throughout all Galilee (Eis holēn tēn Galilaian)*. The first tour of Galilee by Jesus. We are told little about this great preaching tour.

40. *Kneeling down to him (kai gonupetōn)*. Picturesque detail omitted by some MSS. Luke 5:12 has "fell on his face."

41. *Being moved with compassion (splagchnistheis)*. Only in Mark. First aorist passive participle.

43. *Strictly charged (embrimēsamenos)*. Only in Mark.

Luke 5:14 has *pareggeilen* (commanded). Mark's word occurs also in 14:5 and in Matt. 9:30 and John 11:38. See on Matt. 9:30. It is a strong word for the snorting of a horse and expresses powerful emotion as Jesus stood here face to face with leprosy, itself a symbol of sin and all its train of evils. The command to report to the priests was in accord with the Mosaic regulations and the prohibition against talking about it was to allay excitement and to avoid needless opposition to Christ.

44. *For a testimony unto them* (*eis marturion autois*). Without the formal testimony of the priests the people would not receive the leper as officially clean.

45. *Began to publish it much* (*erxato kerussein polla*). Luke 5:15 puts it, "so much the more" (*mallon*). One of the best ways to spread a thing is to tell people not to tell. It was certainly so in this case. Soon Jesus had to avoid cities and betake himself to desert places to avoid the crowds and even then people kept coming to Jesus (*erchonto*, imperfect tense). Some preachers are not so disturbed by the onrush of crowds.

CHAPTER II

1. *Again into Capernaum after some days (palin eis Kapharnaoum di' hēmerōn).* After the first tour of Galilee when
Jesus is back in the city which is now the headquarters for
the work in Galilee. The phrase *di' hēmerōn* means days
coming in between (*dia, duo,* two) the departure and return.
In the house (en oikōi). More exactly, *at home,* in the home
of Peter, now the home of Jesus. Another picture directly
from Peter's discourse. Some of the manuscripts have here
eis oikon, illustrating the practical identity in meaning of
en and *eis* (Robertson, *Grammar,* pp. 591–6). *It was noised*
(*ēkousthē*). It was heard (first aorist, passive indicative
from *akouō,* to hear). People spread the rumour, "He is at
home, he is indoors."

2. *So that there was no longer room for them, no, not even
about the door (hōste mēketi chōrein mēde ta pros tēn thuran).*
Another graphic Markan detail seen through Peter's eyes.
The double compound negative in the Greek intensifies the
negative. This house door apparently opened into the
street, not into a court as in the larger houses. The house
was packed inside and there was a jam outside. *And he
spake the word unto them (kai elalei autois ton logon).* And
he was speaking the word unto them, Mark's favourite descriptive imperfect tense (*elalei*). Note this word *laleō*
about the preaching of Jesus (originally just sounds like the
chatter of birds, the prattling of children, but here of the
most serious kind of speech. As contrasted with *legō* (to say)
it is rather an onomatopoetic word with some emphasis
on the sound and manner of speaking. The word is common in the vernacular papyri examples of social inter-course.

3. *And they come (kai erchontai).* Fine illustration of

266

Mark's vivid dramatic historical present preserved by Luke 5:18, but not by Matt. 9:2 (imperfect). *Borne by four* (*airomenon hupo tessarōn*). Another picturesque Markan detail not in the others.

4. *Come nigh* (*proseggisai*). But Westcott and Hort read *prosenegkai*, to bring to, after Aleph, B, L, 33, 63 (cf. John 5:18). *They uncovered the roof* (*apestegasan tēn stegēn*). They unroofed the roof (note paronomasia in the Greek and cognate accusative). The only instance of this verb in the N.T. A rare word in late Greek, no papyrus example given in Moulton and Milligan *Vocabulary*. They climbed up a stairway on the outside or ladder to the flat tile roof and dug out or broke up (*exoruxantes*) the tiles (the roof). There were thus tiles (*dia tōn keramōn*, Luke 5:19) of laths and plaster and even slabs of stone stuck in for strength that had to be dug out. It is not clear where Jesus was (*hopou ēn*), either downstairs, (Holtzmann) or upstairs (Lightfoot), or in the quadrangle (*atrium* or *compluvium*, if the house had one). "A composition of mortar, tar, ashes and sand is spread upon the roofs, and rolled hard, and grass grows in the crevices. On the houses of the poor in the country the grass grows more freely, and goats may be seen on the roofs cropping it" (Vincent). *They let down the bed* (*chalōsi ton krabatton*), historical present again, aorist tense in Luke 5:19 (*kathēkan*). The verb means to lower from a higher place as from a boat. Probably the four men had a rope fastened to each corner of the pallet or poor man's bed (*krabatton*, Latin *grabatus*. So one of Mark's Latin words). Matthew (9:2) has *klinē*, general term for bed. Luke has *klinidion* (little bed or couch). Mark's word is common in the papyri and is spelled also *krabbatos*, sometimes *krabatos*, while W, Codex Washingtonius, has it *krabbaton*.

5. *Their faith* (*tēn pistin autōn*). The faith of the four men and of the man himself. There is no reason for excluding his faith. They all had confidence in the power

and willingness of Jesus to heal this desperate case. *Are forgiven* (*aphientai*, aoristic present passive, cf. punctiliar action, Robertson's *Grammar*, pp. 864ff.). So Matt. 9:3, but Luke 5:20 has the Doric perfect passive *apheōntai*. The astonishing thing both to the paralytic and to the four friends is that Jesus forgave his sins instead of healing him. The sins had probably caused the paralysis.

6. *Sitting there, and reasoning in their hearts* (*ekei kathēmenoi kai dialogizomenoi en tais kardiais autōn*). Another of Mark's pictures through Peter's eyes. These scribes (and Pharisees, Luke 5:21) were there to cause trouble, to pick flaws in the teaching and conduct of Jesus. His popularity and power had aroused their jealousy. There is no evidence that they spoke aloud the murmur in their hearts, "within themselves" (Matt. 9:3). It was not necessary, for their looks gave them away and Jesus knew their thoughts (Matt. 9:4) and perceived their reasoning (Luke 5:22). *Instantly Jesus recognized it in his own spirit* (*euthus epignous ho Iēsous tōi pneumati autou*, Mark 2:8). The Master at once recognizes the hostile atmosphere in the house. The debate (*dialogizomenoi*) in their hearts was written on their faces. No sound had come, but feeling did.

7. *He blasphemeth* (*blasphēmei*). This is the unspoken charge in their hearts which Jesus read like an open book. The correct text here has this verb. They justify the charge with the conviction that God alone has the power (*dunatai*) to forgive sins. The word *blasphēmeō* means injurious speech or slander. It was, they held, blasphemy for Jesus to assume this divine prerogative. Their logic was correct. The only flaw in it was the possibility that Jesus held a peculiar relation to God which justified his claim. So the two forces clash here as now on the deity of Christ Jesus. Knowing full well that he had exercised the prerogative of God in forgiving the man's sins he proceeds to justify his claim by healing the man.

10. *That ye may know* (*hina eidēte*). The scribes could
have said either of the alternatives in verse 9 with equal
futility. Jesus could say either with equal effectiveness.
In fact Jesus chose the harder first, the forgiveness which
they could not see. So he now performs the miracle of healing which all could see, that all could know that (the Son of
Man, Christ's favourite designation of himself, a claim to be
the Messiah in terms that could not be easily attacked) he
really had the authority and power (*exousian*) to forgive sins.
He has the right and power here on earth to forgive sins, here
and now without waiting for the day of judgment. *He saith
to the sick of the palsy* (*legei*). This remarkable parenthesis
in the middle of the sentence occurs also in Matt. 9:6 and
Luke 5:24, proof that both Matthew and Luke followed
Mark's narrative. It is inconceivable that all three writers
should independently have injected the same parenthesis
at the same place.

12. *Before them all* (*emprosthen pantōn*). Luke 5:25 follows Mark in this detail. He picked up (*aras*) his pallet and
walked and went home as Jesus had commanded him to do
(Mark 2:11). It was an amazing proceeding and made it
unnecessary for Jesus to refute the scribes further on this
occasion. The amazement (*existasthai*, our *ecstasy*, as Luke
5:26 has it), was too general and great for words. The people
could only say: "We never saw it on this fashion" (*Houtōs
oudepote eidamen*). Jesus had acted with the power of God
and claimed equality with God and had made good his
claim. They all marvelled at the *paradoxes* (*paradoxa*, Luke
5:26) of that day. For it all they glorified God.

13. *By the seaside* (*para tēn thalassan*). A pretty picture of
Jesus walking by the sea and a walk that Jesus loved (Mark
1:16; Matt. 4:18). Probably Jesus went out from the crowd
in Peter's house as soon as he could. It was a joy to get a
whiff of fresh air by the sea. But it was not long till all the
crowd began to come to Jesus (*ērcheto*, imperfect) and Jesus

was teaching them (*edidasken*, imperfect). It was the old story over again, but Jesus did not run away.

14. *And as he passed by* (*kai paragōn*). Present participle active, was passing by. Jesus was constantly on the alert for opportunities to do good. An unlikely specimen was Levi (Matthew), son of Alpheus, sitting at the toll-gate (*telōnion*) on the Great West Road from Damascus to the Mediterranean. He was a publican (*telōnēs*) who collected toll for Herod Antipas. The Jews hated or despised these publicans and classed them with sinners (*hamartōloi*). The challenge of Jesus was sudden and sharp, but Levi (Matthew) was ready to respond at once. He had heard of Jesus and quickly decided. Great decisions are often made on a moment's notice. Levi is a fine object lesson for business men who put off service to Christ to carry on their business.

16. *The scribes of the Pharisees* (*hoi grammateis tōn Pharisaiōn*). This is the correct text. Cf. "their scribes" in Luke 5:30. Matthew gave a great reception (*dochēn*, Luke 5:29) in his house (Mark 2:15). These publicans and sinners not simply accepted Levi's invitation, but they imitated his example "and were following Jesus" (*kai ēkolouthoun autōi*). It was a motly crew from the standpoint of these young theologues, scribes of the Pharisees, who were on hand, being invited to pick flaws if they could. It was probably in the long hall of the house where the scribes stood and ridiculed Jesus and the disciples, unless they stood outside, feeling too pious to go into the house of a publican. It was an offence for a Jew to eat with Gentiles as even many of the early Jewish Christians felt (Acts 11:3) and publicans and sinners were regarded like Gentiles (I Cor. 5:11).

17. *The righteous* (*dikaious*). Jesus for the sake of argument accepts the claim of the Pharisees to be righteous, though, as a matter of fact, they fell very far short of it. Elsewhere (Matt. 23) Jesus shows that the Pharisees were

extortionate and devoured widows' houses and wore a cloak of pride and hypocritical respectability. The words "unto repentance" (*eis metanoian*) are not genuine in Mark, but are in Luke 5:32. Jesus called men to new spiritual life and away from sin and so to repentance. But this claim stopped their mouths against what Jesus was doing. The well or the strong (*ischuontes*) are not those who need the physician in an epidemic.

18. *John's disciples and the Pharisees were fasting* (*ēsan hoi mathētai Iōanou kai hoi Pharisaioi nēsteuontes*). The periphrastic imperfect, so common in Mark's vivid description. Probably Levi's feast happened on one of the weekly fast-days (second and fifth days of the week for the stricter Jews). So there was a clash of standpoints. The disciples of John sided with the Pharisees in the Jewish ceremonial ritualistic observances. John was still a prisoner in Machaerus. John was more of an ascetic than Jesus (Matt. 18f.; Luke 7:33–35), but neither one pleased all the popular critics. These learners (*mathētai*) or disciples of John had missed the spirit of their leader when they here lined up with the Pharisees against Jesus. But there was no real congeniality between the formalism of the Pharisees and the asceticism of John the Baptist. The Pharisees hated John who had denounced them as broods of vipers. Here the disciples of John and the disciples of the Pharisees (*hoi mathētai Iōanou kai hoi mathētai tōn Pharisaiōn*) join in criticizing Jesus and his disciples. Later we shall see Pharisees, Sadducees, and Herodians, who bitterly detested each other, making common cause against Jesus Christ. So today we find various hostile groups combining against our Lord and Saviour. See on Matt. 9:14–17 for comments. Matthew has here followed Mark closely.

19. *The sons of the bridechamber* (*hoi huioi tou numphōnos*). Not merely the groomsmen, but the guests also, the *para-nymphs* (*paranumphoi* of the old Greek). Jesus here adopts

the Baptist's own metaphor (John 3:29), changing the friend of the bridegroom (*ho philos tou numphiou*) to sons of the bridechamber. Jesus identifies himself with the bridegroom of the O.T. (Hos. 2:21), God in his covenant relation with Israel (Swete). Mourning does not suit the wedding feast. Mark, Matthew, and Luke all give the three parables (bridegroom, unfulled cloth, new wineskins) illustrating and defending the conduct of Jesus in feasting with Levi on a Jewish fast-day. Luke 5:36 calls these parables. Jesus here seems iconoclastic to the ecclesiastics and revolutionary in emphasis on the spiritual instead of the ritualistic and ceremonial.

21. *Seweth on* (*epirhaptei*). Here only in the N.T. or elsewhere, though the uncompounded verb *rhaptō* (to sew) is common enough, *sews upon*:in Matt. 9:16 and Luke 5:37 use *epiballei*, put upon or clap upon.

22. *But new wine into fresh wineskins* (*alla oinon neon eis askous kainous*). Westcott and Hort bracket this clause as a Western non-interpolation though omitted only in D and some old Latin MSS. It is genuine in Luke 5:38 and may be so here.

23. *Through the cornfields* (*dia tōn sporimōn*). See on Matt. 12:1. So Matt. and Luke 6:1. But Mark uses *paraporeuesthai*, to go along beside, unless *diaporeuesthai* (BCD) is accepted. Perhaps now on the edge, now within the grain. Mark uses also *hodon poiein*, to *make a way* like the Latin *iter facere*, as if through the standing grain, *plucking the ears* (*tillontes tous stachuas*). Work of preparing food the rabbis called it. The margin of the Revised Version has it correctly: They began to make their way plucking the ears of corn (grain, wheat or barley, we should say). See on Matt. 12:1–8 for discussion of this passage, parallel also in Luke 6:15.

26. *The house of God* (*ton oikon tou theou*). The tent or tabernacle at Nob, not the temple in Jerusalem built

by Solomon. *When Abiathar was high priest (epi Abiathar archiereōs).* Neat Greek idiom, in the time of Abiathar as high priest. There was confusion in the Massoretic text and in the LXX about the difference between Ahimelech (Abimelech) and Abiathar (II Sam. 8:17), Ahimelech's son and successor (I Sam. 21:2; 22:20). Apparently Ahimelech, not Abiathar was high priest at this time. It is possible that both father and son bore both names (I Sam. 22:20; II Sam. 8:17; I Chron. 18:16), Abiathar mentioned though both involved. *Epi* may so mean in the passage about Abiathar. Or we may leave it unexplained. They had the most elaborate rules for the preparation of the shewbread (*tous artous tēs protheseōs*), the loaves of presentation, the loaves of the face or presence of God. It was renewed on the commencement of the sabbath and the old bread deposited on the golden table in the porch of the Sanctuary. This old bread was eaten by the priests as they came and went. This is what David ate.

27. *For man (dia ton anthrōpon).* Mark alone has this profound saying which subordinates the sabbath to man's real welfare (mankind, observe, generic article with *anthrōpos*, class from class). Man was not made for the sabbath as the rabbis seemed to think with all their petty rules about eating an egg laid on the sabbath or looking in the glass, *et cetera.* See II Macc. 5:19 and *Mechilta* on Ex. 31:13: "The sabbath is delivered unto you and ye are not delivered unto the sabbath." Christianity has had to fight this same battle about institutionalism. The church itself is for man, not man for the church.

28. *Even of the sabbath (kai tou sabbatou).* Mark, Matthew (12:8), and Luke (6:5) all give this as a climax in the five reasons given by Christ on the occasion for the conduct of the disciples, but Mark has the little word "even" (*kai*) not in the others, showing that Jesus knew that he was making a great claim as the Son of Man, the Representative

Man, the Messiah looked at from his human interest, to lordship (*kurios*) even of the sabbath. He was not the slave of the sabbath, but the master of it. "Even of the sabbath, so invaluable in your eyes. Lord, not to abolish, but to interpret and keep in its own place, and give it a new name" (Bruce).

CHAPTER III

1. *Had his hand withered* (*exērammenēn echōn tēn cheira*).
He had his (*the* in the Greek, common idiom with article as
possessive) hand (right hand, Luke 6:6) in a withered state,
perfect passive participle (adjective *xēran* in Matthew and
Luke), showing that it was not congenital, but the result of
injury by accident or disease. Bengel: *Non ex utero, sed
morbo aut vulnere*.

2. *They watched* (*paretēroun*). Imperfect tense, were
watching on the side (or sly). Luke uses the middle voice,
paretērounto, to accent their personal interest in the proceed-
ings. It was the sabbath day and in the synagogue and
they were there ready to catch him in the act if he should
dare to violate their rules as he had done in the wheat fields
on the previous sabbath. Probably the same Pharisees are
present now as then. *That they might accuse him* (*hina
katēgorēsōsin autou*). So Matt. 12:10. Luke has it "that
they might find how to accuse him" (*hina heurōsin katēgorein
autou*). They were determined to accuse him. The sabbath
controversy offered the best opening. So here they are ready
for business.

3. *Stand forth* (*egeire eis to meson*). Step into the middle
of the room where all can see. It was a bold defiance of the
Christ's spying enemies. Wycliff rightly puts it: *They
aspieden him*. They played the spy on Jesus. One can see
the commotion among the long-bearded hypocrites at this
daring act of Jesus.

4. *But they held their peace* (*hoi de esiōpōn*). Imperfect
tense. In sullen silence and helplessness before the merciless
questions of Jesus as the poor man stood there before them
all. Jesus by his pitiless alternatives between doing good

275

(*agathopoieō*, late Greek word in LXX and N.T.) and doing evil (*kakopoieō*, ancient Greek word), to this man, for instance, *to save a life or to kill* (*psuchēn sōsai ē apokteinai*), as in this case. It was a terrible exposure.

5. *When he had looked round on them with anger* (*periblepsamenos autous met' orgēs*). Mark has a good deal to say about the looks of Jesus with this word (3:5, 34; 5:37; 9:8; 10:23; 11:11) as here. So Luke only once, 6:10. The eyes of Jesus swept the room all round and each rabbinical hypocrite felt the cut of that condemnatory glance. This indignant anger was not inconsistent with the love and pity of Jesus. Murder was in their hearts and Jesus knew it. Anger against wrong as wrong is a sign of moral health (Gould). *Being grieved at the hardness of their hearts* (*sunlupoumenos epi tēi pōrōsei tēs kardias autōn*). Mark alone gives this point. The anger was tempered by grief (Swete). Jesus is the Man of Sorrows and this present participle brings out the continuous state of grief whereas the momentary angry look is expressed by the aorist participle above. Their own heart or attitude was in a state of moral ossification (*pōrōsis*) like hardened hands or feet. *Pōros* was used of a kind of marble and then of the *callus* on fractured bones. "They were hardened by previous conceptions against this new truth" (Gould). See also on Matt. 12:9–14.

6. *And straightway with the Herodians took council* (*euthus meta tōn Hērōidianōn*). The Pharisees could stand no more. So out they stalked at once in a rage of madness (Luke 6:11) and outside of the synagogue took counsel (*sumboulion epoiēsan*) or gave counsel (*sumboulion edidoun*, as some MSS. have it, imperfect tense, offered counsel as their solution of the problem) with their bitter enemies, the Herodians, on the sabbath day still "how they might destroy him" (*hopōs auton apolesōsin*), a striking illustration of the alternatives of Jesus a few moments before, "to save life or to kill." This is the first mention of the Herodians or adherents of

Herod Antipas and the Herod family rather than the Romans. The Pharisees would welcome the help of their rivals to destroy Jesus. In the presence of Jesus they unite their forces as in Mark 8:15; 12:13; Matt. 22:16.

7. *Withdrew to the sea (anechōrēsen eis tēn thalassan).* Evidently Jesus knew of the plot to kill him, "perceiving it" (Matt. 12:15). "He and His would be safer by the open beach" (Swete). He has the disciples with him. Vincent notes that on eleven occasions Mark mentions the withdrawals of Jesus to escape his enemies, for prayer, for rest, for private conference with his disciples (1:12; 3:7; 6:31, 46; 7:24, 31; 9:2; 10:1; 14:34). But, as often, a great multitude (*polu plēthos*) from Galilee followed him.

8. *Hearing what great things he did (akouontes hosa poiei).* Masculine plural present participle, though *plēthos* is neuter singular (construction according to sense in both number and gender). This crowd by the sea came from Galilee, Judea, Jerusalem, Idumea, beyond Jordan (Decapolis and Perea), Tyre and Sidon, Phoenicia, North, South, East, and Northwest, even from Idumea (mentioned here alone in the N.T.) won by John Hyrcanus to Palestine. "In our Lord's time Idumea was practically a part of Judea with a Jewish circumcised population" (George Adam Smith). Many of these were probably Gentiles (Phoenicia and Decapolis) and may have known only the Greek language. The fame of Jesus had spread through all the regions round about. There was a jam as the crowds came to Jesus by the Sea of Galilee.

9. *That a little boat should wait on him (hina ploiarion proskarterēi autōi).* The boat was to keep close (note present tense subjunctive of *proskartereō*) to the shore in constant readiness and move as Jesus did. Whether he needed it or not is not told, but it was there at hand. *Lest they should throng him (hina mē thlibōsin auton).* Press or crush him. Jesus stayed with the crowds for they needed him. Present subjunctive again.

10. *Pressed upon him* (*epipiptein autōi*). Were falling upon him to such an extent that it was dangerous. They were not hostile, but simply intensely eager, each to have his own case attended to by Jesus. *That they might touch him* (*hina autou hapsōntai*). If only that much. They hoped for a cure by contact with Christ. Aorist subjunctive. It was a really pathetic scene and a tremendous strain on Jesus. *As many as had plagues* (*hosoi eichon mastigas*). Strokes or scourges, terms used by us today as a paralytic stroke, the influenza scourge. Our word plague is from *plēgē* (Latin *plaga*), from *plēgnumi*, to strike a blow. Common in ancient Greek in this sense. See Mark 5:29, 34; Luke 7:21 for the same use of *mastiges* and also II Macc. 9:11.

11. *Whensoever they beheld him* (*hotan auton etheōroun*). Imperfect indicative with *hotan* of repeated action. They kept falling down before him (*prosepipton*) and crying, (*ekrazon*) and he kept charging or rebuking (*epitimā*) them, all imperfects. The unclean spirits (demons) recognize Jesus as the Son of God, as before. Jesus charged them not to make him known as he had also done before. He did not wish this testimony. It was a most exciting ordeal and is given only by Mark. Note non-final use of *hina*.

13. *He goeth up into the mountain* (*anabainei eis to oros*). So Matthew (5:1) and Luke (6:12), "to pray" Luke adds. Historical present so common in Mark's vivid narrative. Neither Gospel gives the name of the mountain, assuming it as well known, probably not far from the lake. *Whom he himself would* (*hous ēthelen autos*). Emphatic use of *autos* (himself) at end of sentence. Whether by personal imitation or through the disciples Jesus invites or calls to himself (*proskaleitai*, historical middle present indicative) a select number out of the vast crowds by the sea, those whom he really wished to be with him. *They went off to him* (*apēlthon pros auton*). Luke states that Jesus "continued all night in prayer, to God." It was a crisis in the ministry of Christ.

This select group up in the hills probably respected the long agony of Jesus though they did not comprehend his motive. They formed a sort of spiritual body-guard around the Master during his night vigil in the mountain.

14. *He appointed twelve* (*epoiēsen dōdeka*). This was a second selection out of those invited to the hills and after the night of prayer and after day came (Luke 6:13). Why he chose twelve we are not told, probably because there were twelve tribes in Israel. It was a good round number at any rate. They were to be princes in the new Israel (cf. Matt. 19:28; Luke 22:30; Rev. 21:14, 15). Luke (6:13-16) also gives the list of the twelve at this point while Matthew (10:1-4) postpones giving the names till they are sent out in Galilee. There is a fourth list in Acts 1:13. See discussion of the names of the apostles on Matthew 10:1-4 and pp. 271-3 of my *Harmony of the Gospels for Students of the Life of Christ.* The three groups of four begin alike (Simon, Philip, James). There are some difficulties. *Whom he also named apostles* (*hous kai apostolous ōnomasen*). Margin of Revised Version, the text of Westcott and Hort after Aleph, B, C, etc. Genuine in Luke 6:13 and probably so here. The meaning is that Jesus himself gave the name apostle or missionary (*apostellō*, to send) to this group of twelve. The word is applied in the New Testament to others besides as delegates or messengers of churches (II Cor. 8:23; Phil. 2:25), and messenger (John 13:16). It is applied also to Paul on a par with the twelve (Gal. 1:1, 11f., etc.) and also to Barnabas (Acts 14:14), and perhaps also to Timothy and Silas (I Tim. 2:6f.). Two purposes of Jesus are mentioned by Mark in the choice of these twelve, *that they might be with him* (*hina ōsin met' autou*), *and that he might send them forth* (*kai hina apostellēi autous*). They were not ready to be sent forth till they had been with Jesus for some time. This is one of the chief tasks of Christ to train this group of men. See Bruce's *The Training of the Twelve.* The very

word *apostolos* is from *apostellō*. There were two purposes
in sending them forth expressed by two infinitives, one to
preach (*kērussein*, from *kērux*, herald), the other to have
power to cast out demons (*echein exousian ekballein ta daimonia*). This double ministry of preaching and healing was
to mark their work. The two things are, however, different,
and one does not necessarily involve the other.

16. *Simon he surnamed Peter* (*epethēken onoma tōi Simōni
Petron*). The Greek idiom seems awkward, but it is not.
Peter is in apposition with *name* or *onoma* (accusative).
This surname Jesus gave in addition (*epethēken*) to Simon
(dative case). Here then is a direct reference to what is
told in John 1:42 when Jesus met Simon for the first time.
Mark here reflects Peter's own words. Luke (6:14) simply
says "Whom he also surnamed Peter." See Matt. 16:18 for
the full explanation of the name Peter, a Rock, Cephas.

17. *Boanerges, which is Sons of thunder* (*Boanērges ho
estin huioi brontēs*). This Hebrew nickname is given only
by Mark and the reason for it is not clear. It may refer to
the fiery temperament revealed in Luke 9:34 when James
and John wanted to call down fire on the Samaritan villages
that were unfriendly to them. The word literally means
sons of tumult, sons of thunder in Syriac. No other epithets
are given by Mark save descriptions to distinguish as Simon
the Cananaean (or Zealot) and Judas Iscariot, who also betrayed him (verse 19). Andrew, (from *anēr*, a man) and Philip
(Philippos, fond of horses) are both Greek names. Bartholomew, son of Tolmai, is the Nathanael of John's Gospel
(John 21:2). He probably had both names. Matthew is a
Hebrew name meaning gift of God (*Maththaios*). Thomas
is Hebrew and means Twin (Didymus, John 11:16). There
are two uses of the name of James (*Iacōbos*, Jacob). Thad-
deus is another name for Lebbaeus.

19. *He cometh into a house* (*erchetai eis oikon*). Historical
present again and no article with noun. He comes home

from the mountain, probably the house of Simon as in 1:29. Mark passes by the Sermon on the Mount given by Matthew and Luke on the mountain (plateau on the mountain in Luke). We have to allow a reasonable interval for Mark's narrative. Mark's Gospel is full of action and does not undertake to tell all that Jesus did and said.

20. *So that they could not so much as eat bread* (*hōste mē dunasthai autous mēde arton phagein*). Note infinitive with *hōste*. Apparently Jesus and the disciples·indoors with the great crowd in the house and at the door as in 1:32; 2:2 to which Mark refers by "again." The jam was so great that they could not rest, could not eat, and apparently Jesus could not even teach. The crowd reassembled at once on Christ's return from the mountain.

21. *His friends* (*hoi par' autou*). The phrase means literally "those from the side of him (Jesus)." It could mean another circle of disciples who had just arrived and who knew of the crowds and strain of the Galilean ministry who now come at this special juncture. But the idiom most likely means the kinspeople or family of Jesus as is common in the LXX. The fact that in verse 31 "his mother and his brothers" are expressly mentioned would indicate that they are "the friends" alluded to in verse 21. It is a mournful spectacle to think of the mother and brothers saying, *He is beside himself* (*exestē*). Second aorist active indicative intransitive. The same charge was brought against Paul (Acts 26:24; II Cor. 5:13). We say that one is out of his head. Certainly Mary did not believe that Jesus was in the power of Beelzebub as the rabbis said already. The scribes from Jerusalem are trying to discount the power and prestige of Jesus (3:22). See on Matt. 9:32–34; 10:25 and 12:24 for Beelzebub and Beelzebul. Mary probably felt that Jesus was overwrought and wished to take him home out of the excitement and strain that he might get rest and proper food. See my *The Mother of Jesus: Her Prob-*

lems and Her Glory. The brothers did not as yet believe the pretensions and claims of Jesus (John 7:5). Herod Antipas will later consider Jesus as John the Baptist *redivivus,* the scribes treat him as under demonic possession, even the family and friends fear a disordered mind as a result of overstrain. It was a crucial moment for Jesus. His family or friends came to take him home, to lay hold of him (*kratēsai*), forcibly if need be.

23. *In parables* (*en parabolais*). In crisp pungent thrusts that exposed the inconsistencies of the scribes and Pharisees. See on Matt. 13 for discussion of the word *parable* (*parabolē,* placing beside for comparison). These short parabolic quips concern Satan's casting out (*ekballei,* the very word used of casting out demons) Satan (rhetorical question), a kingdom divided (*meristhēi,* for a mere portion) against itself, a house divided (*meristhēi*) against itself, two conditions of the third class undetermined, but with prospect of determination.

27. *Spoil* (*diarpasai*). Plunder, compound verb, thoroughly ransack. Picture of Satan plundering the demons, the very tools (*skeuē*) by which he carried on his business. A *reductio ad absurdum.* Jesus is the conqueror of Satan, not in league with him.

29. *Guilty of an eternal sin* (*enochos estin aiōniou hamartēmatos*). The genitive of the penalty occurs here with *enochos.* In saying that Jesus had an unclean spirit (verse 30) they had attributed to the devil the work of the Holy Spirit. This is the unpardonable sin and it can be committed today by men who call the work of Christ the work of the devil Nietzsche may be cited as an instance in point. Those who hope for a second probation hereafter may ponder carefully how a soul that eternally sins in such an environment can ever repent. That is eternal punishment. The text here is *hamartēmatos* (sin), not *kriseōs* (judgment), as the Textus Receptus has it.

31. *Standing without* (*exō stēkontes*). A late present from the perfect *hestēka*. Pathetic picture of the mother and brothers standing on the outside of the house thinking that Jesus inside is beside himself and wanting to take him home. They were crowded out. *They sent unto him, calling him* (*apesteilan pros auton kalountes auton*). They were unwilling to disclose their errand to take him home (Swete) and so get the crowd to pass word unto Jesus on the inside, "calling him" through others. Some of the MSS. add "sisters" to mother and brothers as seeking Jesus.

32. *Was sitting about him* (*ekathēto peri auton*). They sat in a circle (*kuklōi*) around Jesus with the disciples forming a sort of inner circle.

34. *Looking round on them* (*periblepsamenos*). Another of Mark's life-like touches. Jesus calls those who do the will of God his mother, brothers, and sisters. This does not prove that the sisters were actually there. The brothers were hostile and that gives point to the tragic words of Jesus. One's heart goes out to Mary who has to go back home without even seeing her wondrous Son. What did it all mean to her at this hour?

CHAPTER IV

1. *Sat in the sea* (*kathēsthai en tēi thalassēi*). In the boat, of course, which was in the sea. He first sat by the beach (Matt. 13:1) and then a very great multitude (*ochlos pleistos*) made him enter a boat in which he sat and taught. It was a common experience now to teach the crowds on the beach (2:1, 13; 3:7–9). *There is gathered* (*sunagetai*). Graphic pictorial present again. See the crowds pressing Jesus into the sea.

2. *He taught them* (*edidasken autous*). Imperfect tense describing it as going on. *In parables* (*en parabolais*). As in 3:23, only here more extended parables. See on Matt. 13 for discussion concerning Christ's use of parables. Eight are given there, one (the Lamp both in Mark 4:21 and Luke 8:16 (both Sower and the Lamp in Luke), one alone in Mark 4:26–29 (seed growing of itself) not in Matthew or Luke, ten on this occasion. Only four are mentioned in Mark 4:1–34 (The Sower, the Lamp, the Seed Growing of Itself, the Mustard Seed). But Mark adds (4:34) "without a parable spake he not unto them," clearly meaning that Jesus spoke many others on this occasion and Matt. after mentioning eight (13:34) makes the same statement. Manifestly, therefore, Jesus spoke many parables on this day and all theories of exegesis or dispensations on the basis of the number of these kingdom parables are quite beside the mark. In beginning Jesus said: *Hearken* (*Akouete*). It is significant that even Jesus had to ask people to listen when he spoke. See also verse 9.

7. *Choked* (*sunepnixan*). *Pnigō* means to strangle, throttle. Mark has the compounded form with *sun-*, squeezed together. Matt. 13:7 has *apepnixan*, *choked off*. *Yielded*

284

no fruit (karpon ouk edōkan.) In Mark alone. Barren in results.

8. *Growing up and increasing (anabainonta kai auxanomena).* In Mark alone. A vivid detail enlarging on the continued growth implied in the imperfect "yielded fruit" *(edidou karpon).* It kept on yielding as it grew. Fruit is what matters.

10. *When he was alone (hote egeneto kata monas).* Only in Mark. Vivid recollection of Peter. Mark has also "they that were about him with the twelve" *(hoi peri auton sun tois dōdeka),* Matthew and Luke simply "the disciples." They did not want the multitude to see that they did not understand the teaching of Jesus.

11. *Unto you is given the mystery of the kingdom of God (Humin to mustērion dedotai tēs basileias tou theou).* See on Matt. 13:11 for word *mustērion.* Here (Mark 4:11-Matt. 13:11-Luke 8:10) alone in the Gospels, but in Paul 21 times and in the Revelation 4 times. It is frequent in Daniel and O.T. Apocrypha. Matthew and Luke use it here in the plural. Matthew and Luke add the word *to know (gnōnai),* but Mark's presentation covers a wider range than growing knowledge, the permanent possession of the mystery even before they understand it. The secret is no longer hidden from the initiated. Discipleship means initiation into the secret of God's kingdom and it will come gradually to these men. *But unto them that are without (ekeinois de tois exō).* Peculiar to Mark, those outside our circle, the uninitiated, the hostile group like the scribes and Pharisees, who were charging Jesus with being in league with Beelzebub. Luke 8:10 has "to the rest" *(tois loipois),* Matt. 13:11 simply "to them" *(ekeinois)* Without the key the parables are hard to understand, for parables veil the truth of the kingdom being stated in terms of another realm. Without a spiritual truth and insight they are unintelligible and are often today perverted. The parables are thus a condemna-

tion on the wilfully blind and hostile, while a guide and blessing to the enlightened. *That* (*hina*). Mark has the construction of the Hebrew "lest" of Isa. 6:9f. with the subjunctive and so Luke 8:10, while Matt. 13:13 uses causal *hoti* with the indicative following the LXX. See on Matt. 13:13 for the so-called causal use of *hina*. Gould on Mark 4:12 has an intelligent discussion of the differences between Matthew and Mark and Luke. He argues that Mark here probably "preserves the original form of Jesus' saying." God ironically commands Isaiah to harden the hearts of the people. If the notion of purpose is preserved in the use of *hina* in Mark and Luke, there is probably some irony also in the sad words of Jesus. If *hina* is given the causative use of *hoti* in Matthew, the difficulty disappears. What is certain is that the use of parables on this occasion was a penalty for judicial blindness on those who will not see.

12. *Lest haply they should turn again, and it should be forgiven them* (*mēpote epistrepsōsin kai aphethēi autois*). Luke does not have these difficult words that seem in Isaiah to have an ironical turn, though Matthew 13:15 does retain them even after using *hoti* for the first part of the quotation. There is no way to make *mēpote* in Mark 4:12 and Matt. 13:15 have a causal sense. It is the purpose of condemnation for wilful blindness and rejection such as suits the Pharisees after their blasphemous accusation against Jesus. Bengel says: *iam ante non videbant, nunc accedit iudicium divinum.* Jesus is pronouncing their doom in the language of Isaiah. It sounds like the dirge of the damned.

13. *Know ye not this parable?* (*ouk oidate tēn parabolēn tautēn;*). They had asked Jesus his reasons for using parables. This question implies surprise at their dulness though initiated into the secret of God's Kingdom. Incapacity to comprehend this parable of the sower raises doubt about all the others on this day and at all times.

14. *The sower soweth the word* (*ho speirōn ton logon speirei*). Not put thus clearly and simply in Matt. 13:19 or Luke 8:11.

15. *Where the word is sown* (*hopou speiretai ho logos*). Explanatory detail only in Mark. *Satan* (*Satanās*) where Matt. 13:19 has *the evil one* (*ho ponēros*) and Luke 8:12 *the devil* (*ho diabolos*). *Sown in them* (*esparmenon eis autous*). Within them, not just among them, "in his heart" (Matt.).

19. *The lusts of other things* (*hai peri ta loipa epithumiai*). All the passions or longings, sensual, worldly, "pleasures of this life" (*hēdonōn tou biou*) as Luke has it (8:14), the world of sense drowning the world of spirit. The word *epithumia* is not evil in itself. One can yearn (this word) for what is high and holy (Luke 22:15; Phil. 1:23).

20. *Bear fruit* (*karpophorousin*). Same word in Matt. 13:23 and Luke 8:15. Mark gives the order from thirty, sixty, to a hundred, while Matt. 13:23 has it reversed.

21. *Not to be put on the stand?* (*ouch hina epi tēn luchnian tethēi;*). First aorist passive subjunctive of *tithēmi* with *hina* (purpose). The lamp in the one-room house was a familiar object along with the bushel, the bed, the lampstand. Note article with each. *Mēti* in the Greek expects the answer no. It is a curious instance of early textual corruption that both Aleph and B, the two oldest and best documents, have *hupo tēn luchnian* (under the lampstand) instead of *epi tēn luchnian*, making shipwreck of the sense. Westcott and Hort actually put it in the margin but that is sheer slavery to Aleph and B. Some of the crisp sayings were repeated by Jesus on other occasions as shown in Matthew and Luke. To put the lamp under the bushel (*modion*) would put it out besides giving no light. So as to the bed or table-couch (*klinēn*) if it was raised above the floor and liable to be set on fire.

22. *Save that it should be manifested* (*ean mē hina phanerōthēi*). Note *ean mē* and *hina*. Luke 8:17 has it *that shall not be made manifest* (*ho ou phaneron genēsetai*). Here

in Mark it is stated that the temporary concealment is for final manifestation and a means to that end. Those who are charged with the secret at this time are given the set responsibility of proclaiming it on the housetops after Ascension (Swete). The hidden (*krupton*) and the *secret* (*apokruphon*) are to be revealed in due time.

23. Repeats verse 9 with conditional form instead of a relative clause. Perhaps some inattention was noted.

24. *What ye hear* (*ti akouete*). Luke 8:18 has it "how ye hear" (*pōs akouete*). Both are important. Some things should not be heard at all for they besmirch the mind and heart. What is worth hearing should be heard rightly and heeded. *With what measure* (*en hōi metrōi*). See already in the Sermon on the Mount (Matt. 7:2; Luke 6:38).

25. *Even that which he hath* (*kai ho echei*). Luke 8:18 has *even that which he thinketh that he hath or seemeth to have* (*kai ho dokei echein*). It is possible that *echei* here has the notion of acquiring. The man who does not acquire soon loses what he thinks that he has. This is one of the paradoxes of Jesus that repay thought and practice.

26. *As if a man should cast* (*hōs anthrōpos balēi*). Note *hōs* with the aorist subjunctive without *an*. It is a supposable case and so the subjunctive and the aorist tense because a single instance. Blass considers this idiom "quite impossible," but it is the true text here and makes good sense (Robertson, *Grammar*, p. 968). The more common idiom would have been *hōs ean* (or *an*).

27. *Should sleep and rise* (*katheudēi kai egeirētai*). Present subjunctive for continued action. So also *spring up and grow* (*blastāi kai mēkunētai*) two late verbs. The process of growth goes on all night and all day (*nukta kai hēmeran*, accusative of time). *He knoweth not how* (*hōs ouk oiden autos*). Note position of *hōs* (beginning) and *autos* (end) of clause: *How knows not he*. The mystery of growth still puzzles farmers and scientists of today with all our modern

knowledge. But nature's secret processes do not fail to
operate because we are ignorant. This secret and mysterious
growth of the kingdom in the heart and life is the point of
this beautiful parable given only by Mark. "When man
has done his part, the actual process of growth is beyond
his reach or comprehension" (Swete).

28. *Of herself* (*automatē*). Automatically, we say. The
secret of growth is in the seed, not in the soil nor in the
weather nor in the cultivating. These all help, but the seed
spontaneously works according to its own nature. The word
automatē is from *autos* (self) and *memaa* desire eagerly from
obsolete *maō*. Common word in all Greek history. Only
one other example in N.T., in Acts 12:10 when the city gate
opens to Peter of its own accord. "The mind is adapted to
the truth, as the eye to the light" (Gould). So we sow the
seed, God's kingdom truth, and the soil (the soul) is ready
for the seed. The Holy Spirit works on the heart and uses
the seed sown and makes it germinate and grow, "first the
blade, then the ear, then the full corn in the ear" (*prōton
chorton, eiten stachun, eiten plērē siton en tōi stachui*). This
is the law and order of nature and also of grace in the kingdom of God. Hence it is worth while to preach and teach.
"This single fact creates the confidence shown by Jesus in
the ultimate establishment of his kingdom in spite of the
obstacles which obstruct its progress" (Gould).

29. *Is ripe* (*paradoi*, second aorist subjunctive with
hotan). Whenever the fruit yields itself or permits. *Putteth
forth* (*apostellei*). Sends forth the sickle. The word for
apostle comes from this verb. See John 4:38: "I sent you
forth to reap" (*ego apesteila humās therizein*). Sickle (*dre-
panon*) here by metonymy stands for the reapers who use
it when the harvest stands ready for it (*parestēken*, stands
by the side, present perfect indicative).

30. *How shall we liken?* (*Pōs homoiōsōmen?*) Deliberative
first aorist subjunctive. This question alone in Mark. So

with the other question: *In what parable shall we set it forth?* (*en tini autēn parabolēi thōmen;*). Deliberative second aorist subjunctive. The graphic question draws the interest of the hearers (*we*) by fine tact. Luke 13:18f. retains the double question which Matt. 13:31f. does not have, though he has it in a very different context, probably an illustration of Christ's favourite sayings often repeated to different audiences as is true of all teachers and preachers.

31. *When it is sown* (*hotan sparēi*). Second aorist passive subjunctive of *speirō*. Alone in Mark and repeated in verse 32. *Less than all the seeds* (*mikroteron pantōn tōn spermatōn*). Comparative adjective with the ablative case after it. Hyperbole, of course, but clearly meaning that from a very small seed a large plant grows, the gradual pervasive expansive power of the kingdom of God.

32. *Groweth up* (*anabainei*). Matt. 13:32 *When it is grown* (*hotan auxēthēi*). *Under the shadow thereof* (*hupo tēn skian autou*). A different picture from Matthew's *in the branches thereof* (*en tois kladois autou*). But both use *kataskēnoin*, to tent or camp down, make nests in the branches in the shade or hop on the ground under the shade just like a covey of birds. In Matt. 8:20 the birds have nests (*kataskēnōseis*). The use of the mustard seed for smallness seems to have been proverbial and Jesus employs it elsewhere (Matt. 17:20; Luke 17:6).

33. *As they were able to hear it* (*kathōs ēdunanto akouein*). Only in Mark. Imperfect indicative. See John 16:12 for *ou dunasthe bastazein*, not able to bear. Jesus used parables now largely, but there was a limit even to the use of them to these men. He gave them the mystery of the kingdom in this veiled parabolic form which was the only feasible form at this stage. But even so they did not understand what they heard.

34. *But privately to his disciples he expounded all things* (*kat' idian de tois idiois mathētais epeluen panta*). To his own

(*idiois*) disciples in private, in distinction from the mass of
the people Jesus was in the habit (imperfect tense, *epeluen*)
of *disclosing*, revealing, all things (*panta*) in plain language
without the parabolic form used before the crowds. This
verb *epiluō* occurs in the N.T. only here and in Acts 19:39
where the town-clerk of Ephesus says of the troubles by the
mob: "It shall be settled in the regular assembly" (*en tēi
ennomōi ekklēsiāi epiluthēsetai*). First future passive indicative from *epiluō*. The word means to give additional (*epi*)
loosening (*luō*), so to explain, to make plainer, clearer, even
to the point of revelation. This last is the idea of the substantive in II Pet. 1:20 where even the Revised Version has
it: "No prophecy of scripture is of private interpretation"
(*pāsa prophēteia graphēs idias epiluseōs ou ginetai*). Here the
use of *ginetai* (comes) with the ablative case (*epiluseōs*) and
the explanation given in verse 21 shows plainly that disclosure or revelation to the prophet is what is meant, not interpretation of what the prophet said. The prophetic impulse
and message came from God through the Holy Spirit. In
private the further disclosures of Jesus amounted to fresh
revelations concerning the mysteries of the kingdom of
God.

35. *When even was come* (*opsias genomenēs*). Genitive
absolute. It had been a busy day. The blasphemous accusation, the visit of the mother and brothers and possibly
sisters, to take him home, leaving the crowded house for the
sea, the first parables by the sea, then more in the house,
and now out of the house and over the sea. *Let us go over
unto the other side* (*dielthōmen eis to peran*). Hortatory
(volitive) subjunctive, second aorist active tense. They
were on the western side and a row over to the eastern shore
in the evening would be a delightful change and refreshing
to the weary Christ. It was the only way to escape the
crowds.

36. *Even as he was* (*hōs ēn*). Vulgate, *ita ut erat*. Bengel

says: *sine apparatu.* That is, they take Jesus along (*para-lambanousin*) without previous preparation. *Other boats* (*alla ploia*). This detail also is given only by Mark. Some people had got into boats to get close to Jesus. There was a crowd even on the lake.

37. *There ariseth a great storm of wind* (*ginetai lailaps megalē anemou*). Mark's vivid historical present again. Matt. 8:24 has *egeneto* (arose) and Luke 8:23 *katebē* (came down). Luke has also *lailaps*, but Matthew *seismos* (tempest), a violent upheaval like an earthquake. *Lailaps* is an old word for these cyclonic gusts or storms. Luke's "came down" shows that the storm fell suddenly from Mount Hermon down into the Jordan Valley and smote the Sea of Galilee violently at its depth of 682 feet below the Mediterranean Sea. The hot air at this depth draws the storm down with sudden power. These sudden storms continue to this day on the Sea of Galilee. The word occurs in the LXX of the whirlwind out of which God answered Job (Job 38:1) and in Jonah 1:4. *The waves beat into the boat* (*ta kumata epeballen eis to ploion*). Imperfect tense (were beating) vividly picturing the rolling over the sides of the boat "so that the boat was covered with the waves" (Matt. 8:24). Mark has it: "insomuch that the boat was now filling" (*hōste ēdē gemizesthai to ploion*). Graphic description of the plight of the disciples.

38. *Asleep on the cushion* (*epi to proskephalaion katheudōn*). Mark also mentions the cushion or bolster and the stern of the boat (*en tēi prumnēi*). Matt. 8:24 notes that Jesus was sleeping (*ekatheuden*), Luke that *he fell asleep* (*aphupnōsen*, ingressive aorist indicative). He was worn out from the toil of this day. *They awake him* (*egeirousin auton*). So Mark's graphic present. Matthew and Luke both have "awoke him." Mark has also what the others do not: "Carest thou not?" (*ou melei soi;*). It was a rebuke to Jesus for sleeping in such a storm. We are perishing (*apollumetha*, linear pres-

ent middle). Precisely this same form also in Matt. 8:25 and Luke 8:24.

39. *Rebuked the wind* (*epetimēsen tōi anemōi*) as in Matt. 8:26 and Luke 8:24. He spoke to the sea also. All three Gospels speak of the sudden calm (*galēnē*) and the rebuke to the disciples for this lack of faith.

40. *Why are ye fearful?* (*Ti deiloi este;*). They had the Lord of the wind and the waves with them in the boat. He was still Master even if asleep in the storm. *Have ye not yet faith?* (*Oupō echete pistin;*). Not yet had they come to feel that Jesus was really Lord of nature. They had accepted his Messiaship, but all the conclusions from it they had not yet drawn. How like us in our troubles they were!

41. *They feared exceedingly* (*ephobēthēsan phobon megan*). Cognate accusative with the first aorist passive indicative. They feared a great fear. Matt. 8:27 and Luke 8:22 mention that "they marvelled." But there was fear in it also. *Who then is this?* (*Tis ara houtos estin;*). No wonder that they feared if this One could command the wind and the waves at will as well as demons and drive out all diseases and speak such mysteries in parables. They were growing in their apprehension and comprehension of Jesus Christ. They had much yet to learn. There is much yet for us today to learn or seek to grow in the knowledge of our Lord Jesus Christ. This incident opened the eyes and minds of the disciples to the majesty of Jesus.

CHAPTER V

1. *The Gerasenes* (*tōn Gerasēnōn*). Like Luke 8:26 while Matt. 8:28 has "the Gadarenes." The ruins of the village Khersa (Gerasa) probably point to this site which is in the district of Gadara some six miles southeastward, not to the city of Gerasa some thirty miles away.

2. *Out of the boat* (*ek tou ploiou*). Straightway (*euthus*) Mark says, using the genitive absolute (*exelthontos autou*) and then repeating *autōi* associative instrumental after *apēntēsen*. The demoniac greeted Jesus at once. Mark and Luke 9:27 mention only one man while Matthew notes two demoniacs, perhaps one more violent than the other. Each of the Gospels has a different phrase. Mark has "a man with an unclean spirit" (*en pneumati akathartōi*), Matt. 8:28 "two possessed with demons" (*duo daimonizomenoi*), Luke 8:27 "one having demons" (*tis echōn daimonia*). Mark has many touches about this miracle not retained in Matthew and Luke. See on Matt. 8:28.

3. *No man could any more bind him, no, not with a chain* (*oude halusei oudeis edunato auton dēsai*). Instrumental case *halusei*, a handcuff (*a* privative and *luō*, to loosen). But this demoniac snapped a handcuff as if a string.

4. *Often bound* (*pollakis dedesthai*). Perfect passive infinitive, state of completion. With fetters (*pedais*, from *peza*, foot, instep) and chains, bound hand and foot, but all to no purpose. The English plural of foot is feet (Anglo-Saxon *fot, fet*) and fetter is *feeter*. *Rent asunder* (*diespāsthai*). Drawn (*spaō*) in two (*dia*- same root as *duo*, two). Perfect passive infinitive. *Broken in pieces* (*suntetriphthai*.) Perfect passive infinitive again, from *suntribō*, to rub together. Rubbed together, crushed together. Perhaps the neighbours

who told the story could point to broken fragments of chains
and fetters. The fetters may have been cords, or even
wooden stocks and not chains. *No man had strength to tame
him (oudeis ischuen auton damasai).* Imperfect tense. He
roamed at will like a lion in the jungle.

5. *He was crying out, and cutting himself with stones (ēn
krazōn kai katakoptōn heauton lithois).* Further vivid details
by Mark. Night and day his loud scream or screech could
be heard like other demoniacs (cf. 1:26; 3:11; 9:26). The
verb for cutting himself occurs here only in the N.T., though
an old verb. It means to *cut down* (perfective use of *kata-*).
We say *cut up*, gash, hack to pieces. Perhaps he was scarred
all over with such gashes during his moments of wild frenzy
night and day in the tombs and on the mountains. Periphrastic imperfect active with *ēn* and the participles.

6. *Ran and worshipped (edramen kai prosekunēsen).* "At
first perhaps with hostile intentions. The onrush of the
naked yelling maniac must have tried the newly recovered
confidence of the Twelve. We can imagine their surprise
when, on approaching, he threw himself on his knees"
(Swete).

7. *I adjure thee by God (horkizō se ton theon).* The demoniac puts Jesus on oath (two accusatives) after the startled
outcry just like the one in 1:24, which see. He calls Jesus
here "son of the Most High God" *(huie tou theou tou hupsis-
tou)* as in Luke 8:28 (cf. Gen. 14:18f.). *Torment me not (mē
me basaniseis).* Prohibition with *mē* and the ingressive
aorist subjunctive. The word means to test metals and then
to test one by torture (cf. our "third degree"). Same word
in all three Gospels.

8. *For he said (elegen gar).* For he had been saying (pro-
gressive imperfect). Jesus had already repeatedly ordered
the demon to come out of the man whereat the demon
made his outcry to Jesus and protested. Matt. 8:29 had
"before the time" *(pro kairou)* and 8:31 shows that the

demons did not want to go back to the abyss (*tēn abusson*) right now. That was their real home, but they did not wish to return to the place of torment just now.

9. *My name is Legion* (*Legiōn onoma moi*). So Luke 8:30, but not Matthew. Latin word (*legio*). A full Roman legion had 6,826 men. See on Matt. 26:53. This may not have been a full legion, for Mark 5:13 notes that the number of hogs was "about two thousand." Of course, a stickler for words might say that each hog had several demons.

13. *And he gave them leave* (*kai epetrepsen autois*). These words present the crucial difficulty for interpreters as to why Jesus allowed the demons to enter the hogs and destroy them instead of sending them back to the abyss. Certainly it was better for hogs to perish than men, but this loss of property raises a difficulty of its own akin to the problem of tornadoes and earthquakes. The question of one man containing so many demons is difficult also, but not much more so than how one demon can dwell in a man and make his home there. One is reminded of the man out of whom a demon was cast, but the demon came back with seven other demons and took possession. Gould thinks that this man with a legion of demons merely makes a historical exaggeration. "I feel as if I were possessed by a thousand devils." That is too easy an explanation. See on Matt. 8:32 for "rushed down the steep." *They were choked* (*epnigonto*). Imperfect tense picturing graphically the disappearance of pig after pig in the sea. Luke 8:33 has *apegnigē, choked off*, constative second aorist passive indicative, treated as a whole, Matt. 8:32 merely has "perished" (*apethanon*; died).

14. *And in the country* (*kai eis tous agrous*). Mark adds this to "the city." In the fields and in the city as the excited men ran they told the tale of the destruction of the hogs. They came to see (*ēlthon idein*). All the city came out (Matthew), they went out to see (Luke).

15. *They come to Jesus* (*erchontai pros ton Iēsoun*). Vivid

present. To Jesus as the cause of it all, "to meet Jesus" (*eis hupantēsin Iēsou*, Matt. 8:34). *And behold* (*theōrousin*). Present tense again. *And they were afraid* (*kai ephobēthēsan*). They became afraid. Mark drops back to the ingressive aorist tense (passive voice). They had all been afraid of the man, but there he was "sitting clothed and in his right mind," (*kathēmenon himatismenon kai sōphronounta*. Note the participles). "At the feet of Jesus," Luke adds (8:35). For a long time he had worn no clothes (Luke 8:17). Here was the healing of the wild man and the destruction of the hogs all by this same Jesus.

17. *To depart from their borders* (*apelthein apo tōn horiōn*). Once before the people of Nazareth had driven Jesus out of the city (Luke 4:16–31). Soon they will do it again on his return there (Mark 6:1–6; Matt. 13:3–4–58). Here in Decapolis pagan influence was strong and the owners of the hogs cared more for the loss of their property than for the healing of the wild demoniac. In the clash between business and spiritual welfare business came first with them as often today. All three Gospels tell of the request for Jesus to leave. They feared the power of Jesus and wanted no further interference with their business affairs.

18. *As he was entering* (*embainontos autou*). The man began to beseech him (*parekalei*) before it was too late.

19. *Go to thy house unto thy friends* (*Hupage eis ton oikon sou pros tous sous*). "To thy own folks" rather than "thy friends." Certainly no people needed the message about Christ more than these people who were begging Jesus to leave. Jesus had greatly blessed this man and so gave him the hardest task of all, to go home and witness there for Christ. In Galilee Jesus had several times forbidden the healed to tell what he had done for them because of the undue excitement and misunderstanding. But here it was different. There was no danger of too much enthusiasm for Christ in this environment.

20. *He went his way* (*apēlthen*). He went off and did as
Jesus told him. He heralded (*kērussein*) or published the
story till all over Decapolis men marvelled (*ethaumazon*) at
what Jesus did, kept on marvelling (imperfect tense). The
man had a greater opportunity for Christ right in his home
land than anywhere else. They all knew this once wild
demoniac who now was a new man in Christ Jesus. Thousands of like cases of conversion under Christ's power have
happened in rescue missions in our cities.

23. *My little daughter* (*to thugatrion mou*). Diminutive of
thugatēr (Matt. 9:18). "This little endearing touch in the
use of the diminutive is peculiar to Mark" (Vincent). "Is
at the point of death" (*eschatōs echei*). Has it in the last
stages. Matt. 9:18 has: "has just died" (*arti eteleusen*),
Luke "she lay a dying" (*apethnēsken*, imperfect, she was
dying). It was a tragic moment for Jairus. *I pray thee*, not
in the Greek. This ellipsis before *hina* not uncommon,
a sort of imperative use of *hina* and the subjunctive in the
Koiné (Robertson, *Grammar*, p. 943).

24. *He went with him* (*apēlthen*). Aorist tense. Went off
with him promptly, but a great multitude followed him
(*ēkolouthei*), was following, kept following (imperfect tense).
They thronged him (*sunethlibon auton*). Imperfect tense
again. Only example of (here and in verse 31) this compound verb in the N.T., common in old Greek. Were pressing Jesus so that he could hardly move because of the jam,
or even to breathe (*sunepnigon*, Luke 8:42).

26. *Had suffered many things of many physicians* (*polla
pathousa hupo pollōn iatrōn*). A pathetic picture of a woman
with a chronic case who had tried doctor after doctor. *Had
spent all that she had* (*dapanēsasa ta par' autēs panta*). Having spent the all from herself, all her resources. For the
idiom with *para* see Luke 10:7; Phil. 4:18. The tragedy of
it was that she "was nothing bettered, but rather grew
worse" (*mēden ōphelētheisa alla mallon eis to cheiron elthousa*).

Her money was gone, her disease was gaining on her, her one chance came now with Jesus. Matthew says nothing about her experience with the doctors and Luke 8:43 merely says that she "had spent all her living upon physicians and could not be healed of any," a plain chronic case. Luke the physician neatly takes care of the physicians. But they were not to blame. She had a disease that they did not know how to cure. Vincent quotes a prescription for an issue of blood as given in the Talmud which gives one a most grateful feeling that he is not under the care of doctors of that nature. The only parallel today is Chinese medicine of the old sort before modern medical schools came.

28. *If I touch but his garments* (*Ean hapsōmai kàn tōn himatiōn autou*). She was timid and shy from her disease and did not wish to attract attention. So she crept up in the crowd and touched the hem or border of his garment (*kraspedon*) according to Matt. 9:20 and Luke 8:44.

29. *She felt in her body* (*egnō tōi sōmati*). She knew, the verb means. She said to herself, *I am healed* (*iāmai*). *Iātai* retains the perfect passive in the indirect discourse. It was a vivid moment of joy for her. The plague (*mastigos*) or scourge was a whip used in flagellations as on Paul to find out his guilt (Acts 22:24, cf. Heb. 11:26). It is an old word that was used for afflictions regarded as a scourge from God. See already on Mark 3:10.

30. *Perceiving in himself* (*epignous en heautōi*). She thought, perhaps, that the touch of Christ's garment would cure her without his knowing it, a foolish fancy, no doubt, but one due to her excessive timidity. Jesus felt in his own consciousness. The Greek idiom more exactly means: "Jesus perceiving in himself the power from him go out" (*tēn ex autou dunamin exelthousan*). The aorist participle here is punctiliar simply and timeless and can be illustrated by Luke 10:18: "I was beholding Satan fall" (*etheōroun ton Satanān pesonta*), where *pesonta* does not mean *fallen* (*pep-*

tōkota) as in Rev. 9:1 nor falling (*piptonta*) but simply the constative aorist *fall* (Robertson, *Grammar*, p. 684). So here Jesus means to say: "I felt in myself the power from me go." Scholars argue whether in this instance Jesus healed the woman by conscious will or by unconscious response to her appeal. Some even argue that the actual healing took place after Jesus became aware of the woman's reaching for help by touching his garment. What we do know is that Jesus was conscious of the going out of power from himself. Luke 8:46 uses *egnōn* (personal knowledge), but Mark has *epignous* (personal and additional, clear knowledge). One may remark that no real good can be done without the outgoing of power. That is true of mother, preacher, teacher, doctor. *Who touched my garments?* (*Tis mou hēpsato tōn himatiōn;*). More exactly, *Who touched me on my clothes;* The Greek verb uses two genitives, of the person and the thing. It was a dramatic moment for Jesus and for the timid woman. Later it was a common practice for the crowds to touch the hem of Christ's garments and be healed (Mark 6:56). But here Jesus chose to single out this case for examination. There was no magic in the garments of Jesus. Perhaps there was superstition in the woman's mind, but Jesus honoured her darkened faith as in the case of Peter's shadow and Paul's handkerchief.

31. *Thronging thee* (*sunthlibonta se*). See verse 24. The disciples were amazed at the sensitiveness of Jesus to the touch of the crowd. They little understood the drain on Jesus from all this healing that pulled at his heart-strings and exhausted his nervous energy even though the Son of God. He had the utmost human sympathy.

32. *And he looked round about* (*kai perieblepeto*). Imperfect middle indicative. He kept looking around to find out. The answer of Jesus to the protest of the disciples was this scrutinizing gaze (see already 3:5, 34). Jesus knew the difference between touch and touch (Bruce).

33. *Fearing and trembling, knowing (phobētheisa kai tremousa, eiduia)*. These participles vividly portray this woman who had tried to hide in the crowd. She had heard Christ's question and felt his gaze. She had to come and confess, for something "has happened" (*gegonen*, second perfect active indicative, still true) to her. *Fell down before him (prosepesen autōi)*. That was the only proper attitude now. *All the truth (pāsan tēn alētheian)*. Secrecy was no longer possible. She told "the pitiful tale of chronic misery" (Bruce).

34. *Go in peace (Hupage eis eirēnēn)*. She found sympathy, healing, and pardon for her sins, apparently. Peace here may have more the idea of the Hebrew *shalōm*, health of body and soul. So Jesus adds: "Be whole of thy plague" (*isthi hugiēs apo tēs mastigos sou*). Continue whole and well.

35. *While he yet spake (Eti autou lalountos)*. Genitive absolute. Another vivid touch in Mark and Luke 8:49. The phrase is in Gen. 29:9. Nowhere does Mark preserve better the lifelike traits of an eyewitness like Peter than in these incidents in chapter 5. The arrival of the messengers from Jairus was opportune for the woman just healed of the issue of blood (*en husei haimatos*) for it diverted attention from her. Now the ruler's daughter has died (*apethane*). *Why troublest thou the master any further? (Ti eti skulleis ton didaskalon;)*. It was all over, so they felt. Jesus had raised from the dead the son of the widow of Nain (Luke 7:11–17), but people in general did not expect him to raise the dead. The word *skullō*, from *skulon (skin, pelt, spoils)*, means to skin, to flay, in Aeschylus. Then it comes to mean to vex, annoy, distress as in Matt. 9:36, which see. The middle is common in the papyri for bother, worry, as in Luke 7:6. There was no further use in troubling the Teacher about the girl.

36. *Not heeding (parakousas)*. This is the sense in Matt. 18:17 and uniformly so in the LXX. But here the other

sense of hearing aside, overhearing what was not spoken
directly to him, probably exists also. "Jesus might overhear
what was said and disregard its import" (Bruce). Certainly
he ignored the conclusion of the messengers. The present
participle *laloumenon* suits best the idea of overhearing.
Both Mark and Luke 8:50 have "Fear not, only believe"
(*mē phobou, monon pisteue*). This to the ruler of the synagogue (*tōi archisunagōgōi*) who had remained and to whom
the messenger had spoken.

37. *Save Peter, and James, and John* (*ei mē Petron kai
Iakōbon kai Iōanēn*). Probably the house was too small for
the other disciples to come in with the family. The first
instance of this inner circle of three seen again on the Mount
of Transfiguration and in the Garden of Gethsemane. The
one article in the Greek treats the group as a unit.

38. *Wailing greatly* (*alalazontas polla*). An onomatopoetic word from Pindar down. The soldiers on entering
battle cried *Alála*. Used of clanging cymbals (I Cor. 13:1).
Like *ololuzō* in James 5:1. It is used here of the monotonous
wail of the hired mourners.

39. *Make a tumult* (*thorubeisthe*). Middle voice. Jesus
had dismissed one crowd (verse 37), but finds the house occupied by the hired mourners making bedlam (*thorubos*) as
if that showed grief with their ostentatious noise. Matt.
9:23 spoke of flute-players (*aulētas*) and the hubbub of the
excited throng (*thoruboumenon*. Cf. Mark 14:2; Acts 20:1, 21;
34). Mark, Matthew, and Luke all quote Jesus as saying
that "the child is not dead, but sleepeth." Jesus undoubtedly meant that she was not dead to stay dead, though some
hold that the child was not really dead. It is a beautiful word (she is *sleeping, katheudei*) that Jesus uses of
death.

40. *And they laughed him to scorn* (*kai kategelōn*). "They
jeered at him" (Weymouth). Note imperfect tense. They
kept it up. And note also *kat-* (perfective use). Exactly

the same words in Matt. 9:24 and Luke 8:53. The loud laughter was ill suited to the solemn occasion. But Jesus on his part (*autos de*) took charge of the situation. *Taketh the father of the child and her mother and them that were with him* (*paralambanei ton patera tou paidiou kai tēn mētera kai tous met' autou*). Having put out (*ekbalōn*) the rest by a stern assertion of authority as if he were master of the house, Jesus takes along with him these five and enters the chamber of death "where the child was" (*hopou ēn to paidion*). He had to use pressure to make the hired mourners leave. The presence of some people will ruin the atmosphere for spiritual work.

41. *Talitha cumi.* These precious Aramaic words, spoken by Jesus to the child, Peter heard and remembered so that Mark gives them to us. Mark interprets the simple words into Greek for those who did not know Aramaic (*to korasion, egeire*), that is, *Damsel, arise.* Mark uses the diminutive *korasiōn*, a little girl, from *korē*, girl. *Braid Scots* has it: "*Lassie, wauken.*" Luke 8:5–9 has it *Hē pais, egeire, Maiden, arise.* All three Gospels mention the fact that Jesus took her by the hand, a touch of life (*kratēsas tēs cheiros*), giving confidence and help.

42. *Rose up, and walked* (*anestē kai periepatei*). Aorist tense (single act) followed by the imperfect (*the walking went on*). *For she was twelve years old* (*ēn gar etōn dōdeka*). The age mentioned by Mark alone and here as explanation that she was old enough to walk. *Amazed* (*exestēsan*). We have had this word before in Matt. 12:23 and Mark 2:12, which see. Here the word is repeated in the substantive in the associative instrumental case (*ekstasei megalēi*), with a great ecstasy, especially on the part of the parents (Luke 8:56), and no wonder.

43. *That no one should know this* (*hina mēdeis gnoi touto*). Second aorist active subjunctive, *gnoi.* But would they keep still about it? There was the girl besides. Both Mark and

Luke note that Jesus ordered that food be given to the child *given her to eat*, (*dothēnai autēi phagein*), a natural care of the Great Physician. Two infinitives here (first aorist passive and second aorist active). "She could walk and eat; not only alive, but well" (Bruce).

CHAPTER VI

1. *Into his own country (eis tēn patrida autou).* So Matt. 13:54. There is no real reason for identifying this visit to Nazareth with that recorded in Luke 4:16–31 at the beginning of the Galilean Ministry. He was rejected both times, but it is not incongruous that Jesus should give Nazareth a second chance. It was only natural for Jesus to visit his mother, brothers, and sisters again. Neither Mark nor Matthew mention Nazareth here by name, but it is plain that by *patrida* the region of Nazareth is meant. He had not lived in Bethlehem since his birth.

2. *Began to teach (ērxato didaskein).* As was now his custom in the synagogue on the sabbath. The ruler of the synagogue (*archisunagōgos*, see Matt. 5:22) would ask some one to speak whensoever he wished. The reputation of Jesus all over Galilee opened the door for him. Jesus may have gone to Nazareth for rest, but could not resist this opportunity for service. *Whence hath this man these things? (Pothen toutōi tauta;).* Laconic and curt, *Whence these things to this fellow?* With a sting and a fling in their words as the sequel shows. They continued to be amazed (*exeplēssonto*, imperfect tense passive). They challenge both the apparent *wisdom (sophia)* with which he spoke and *the mighty works* or powers (*hai dunameis*) *such as those (toiautai) coming to pass (ginomenai*, present middle participle, repeatedly wrought) *by his hands (dia tōn cheirōn).* They felt that there was some hocus-pocus about it somehow and somewhere. They do not deny the wisdom of his words, nor the wonder of his works, but the townsmen knew Jesus and they had never suspected that he possessed such gifts and graces.

3. *Is not this the carpenter?* (*Ouch houtos estin ho tektōn;*).
Matt. 13:55 calls him "the carpenter's son" (*ho tou tek-tonos huios*). He was both. Evidently since Joseph's death he had carried on the business and was "the carpenter" of Nazareth. The word *tektōn* comes from *tekein, tiktō,* to beget, create, like *technē* (craft, art). It is a very old word, from Homer down. It was originally applied to the worker in wood or builder with wood like our carpenter. Then it was used of any artisan or craftsman in metal, or in stone as well as in wood and even of sculpture. It is certain that Jesus worked in wood. Justin Martyr speaks of ploughs, yokes, et cetera, made by Jesus. He may also have worked in stone and may even have helped build some of the stone synagogues in Galilee like that in Capernaum. But in Nazareth the people knew him, his family (no mention of Joseph), and his trade and discounted all that they now saw with their own eyes and heard with their own ears. This word carpenter "throws the only flash which falls on the continuous tenor of the first thirty years from infancy to manhood, of the life of Christ" (Farrar). That is an exaggeration for we have Luke 2:41–50 and "as his custom was" (Luke 4:16), to go no further. But we are grateful for Mark's realistic use of *tektōn* here. *And they were offended in him* (*kai eskandalizonto en autōi*). So exactly Matt. 13:56, *were made to stumble in him,* trapped like game by the *skandalon* because they could not explain him, having been so recently one of them. "The Nazarenes found their stumbling block in the person or circumstances of Jesus. He became—*petra skandalou* (I Pet. 2:7, 8; Rom. 9:33) to those who disbelieved" (Swete). Both Mark and Matt. 13:57, which see, preserve the retort of Jesus with the quotation of the current proverb about a prophet's lack of honour in his own country. John 4:44 quoted it from Jesus on his return to Galilee long before this. It is to be noted that Jesus here makes a definite claim to being a prophet (*prophētēs,* for-

speaker for God), a seer.   He was much more than this as he
had already claimed to be Messiah (John 4:26 = Luke 4:21),
the Son of man with power of God (Mark 1:10 = Matt.
9:6 = Luke 5:24), the Son of God (John 5:22).   They stumble at
Jesus today as the townspeople of Nazareth did.   *In his own
house* (*en tēi oikiāi autou*).   Also in Matt. 13:57.   This was
the saddest part of it all, that his own brothers in his own
home disbelieved his Messianic claims (John 7:5).   This
puzzle was the greatest of all.

6.   *And he marvelled because of their unbelief* (*kai ethauma-
sen dia tēn apistian autōn*).   Aorist tense, but Westcott and
Hort put the imperfect in the margin.   Jesus had divine
knowledge and accurate insight into the human heart, but
he had human limitations in certain things that are not
clear to us.   He marvelled at the faith of the Roman centurion where one would not expect faith (Matt. 8:10 =
Luke 7:9).   Here he marvels at the lack of faith where he
had a right to expect it, not merely among the Jews, but
in his own home town, among his kinspeople, even in his
own home.   One may excuse Mary, the mother of Jesus,
from this unbelief, puzzled, as she probably was, by his
recent conduct (Mark 3:21, 31).   There is no proof that she
ever lost faith in her wonderful Son.   *He went round about
the villages teaching* (*periēgen tās kōmas kuklōi didaskōn*).
A good illustration of the frequent poor verse division.   An
entirely new paragraph begins with these words, the third
tour of Galilee.   They should certainly be placed with
verse 7.   The Revised Version would be justified if it had
done nothing else than give us paragraphs according to
the sense and connection.   "Jesus resumes the rôle of a
wandering preacher in Galilee" (Bruce).   Imperfect tense,
periēgen.

7.   *By two and two* (*duo duo*).   This repetition of the
numeral instead of the use of *ana duo* or *kata duo* is usually
called a Hebraism.   The Hebrew does have this idiom, but

it appears in Aeschylus and Sophocles, in the vernacular *Koiné* (Oxyrhynchus Papyri No. 121), in Byzantine Greek, and in modern Greek (Deissmann, *Light from the Ancient East*, pp. 122f.). Mark preserves the vernacular *Koiné* better than the other Gospels and this detail suits his vivid style. The six pairs of apostles could thus cover Galilee in six different directions. Mark notes that he "began to send them forth" (*ērxato autous apostellein*). Aorist tense and present infinitive. This may refer simply to this particular occasion in Mark's picturesque way. But the imperfect tense *edidou* means he kept on giving them all through the tour, a continuous power (authority) over unclean spirits singled out by Mark as representing "all manner of diseases and all manner of sickness" (Matt. 10:1), "to cure diseases" (*iasthai*, Luke 9:1), healing power. They were to preach and to heal (Luke 9:1; Matt. 10:7). Mark does not mention preaching as a definite part of the commission to the twelve on this their first preaching tour, but he does state that they did preach (6:12). They were to be missioners or missionaries (*apostellein*) in harmony with their office (*apostoloi*).

8. *Save a staff only* (*ei mē rabdon monon*). Every traveller and pilgrim carried his staff. Bruce thinks that Mark has here preserved the meaning of Jesus more clearly than Matt. 10:10 (nor staff) and Luke 9:3 (neither staff). This discrepancy has given trouble to commentators. Grotius suggests no second staff for Matthew and Luke. Swete considers that Matthew and Luke report "an early exaggeration of the sternness of the command." "Without even a staff is the *ne plus ultra* of austere simplicity, and self-denial. Men who carry out the spirit of these precepts will not labour in vain" (Bruce).

9. *Shod with sandals* (*hupodedemenous sandalia*). Perfect passive participle in the accusative case as if with the infinitive *poreuesthai* or *poreuthēnai*, (*to go*). Note the aorist infinitive middle, *endusasthai* (text of Westcott and Hort),

but *endusēsthe* (aorist middle subjunctive) in the margin. Change from indirect to direct discourse common enough, not necessarily due to "disjointed notes on which the Evangelist depended" (Swete). Matt. 10:10 has "nor shoes" (*mēde hupodēmata*), possibly preserving the distinction between "shoes" and "sandals" (worn by women in Greece and by men in the east, especially in travelling). But here again extra shoes may be the prohibition. See on Matt. 10:10 for this. *Two coats* (*duo chitōnas*). Two was a sign of comparative wealth (Swete). The mention of "two" here in all three Gospels probably helps us to understand that the same thing applies to shoes and staff. "In general, these directions are against luxury in equipment, and also against their providing themselves with what they could procure from the hospitality of others" (Gould).

10. *There abide* (*ekei menete*). So also Matt. 10:11; Luke 9:4. Only Matthew has city or village (10:11), but he mentions house in verse 12. They were to avoid a restless and dissatisfied manner and to take pains in choosing a home. It is not a prohibition against accepting invitations.

11. *For a testimony unto them* (*eis marturion autois*). Not in Matthew. Luke 9:5 has "for a testimony against them" (*eis marturion epi autous*). The dative *autois* in Mark is the dative of disadvantage and really carries the same idea as *epi* in Luke. The dramatic figure of *shaking out* (*ektinaxate*, effective aorist imperative, Mark and Matthew), *shaking off* (*apotinassete*, present imperative, Luke).

12. *Preached that men should repent* (*ekēruxan hina metanoōsin*). Constative aorist (*ekēruxan*), summary description. This was the message of the Baptist (Matt. 3:2) and of Jesus (Mark 1:15).

13. *They cast out many demons and they anointed with oil* (*exeballon kai ēleiphon elaiōi*). Imperfect tenses, continued repetition. Alone in Mark. This is the only example in the N.T. of *aleiphō elaiōi* used in connection with healing

save in James 5:14. In both cases it is possible that the use of oil (olive oil) as a medicine is the basis of the practice. See Luke 10:34 for pouring oil and wine upon the wounds. It was the best medicine of the ancients and was used internally and externally. It was employed often after bathing. The papyri give a number of examples of it. The only problem is whether *aleiphō* in Mark and James is used wholly in a ritualistic and ceremonial sense or partly as medicine and partly as a symbol of divine healing. The very word *aleiphō* can be translated rub or anoint without any ceremony. "Traces of a ritual use of the unction of the sick appear first among Gnostic practices of the second century" (Swete). We have today, as in the first century, God and medicine. God through nature does the real healing when we use medicine and the doctor.

14. *Heard* (*ēkousen*). This tour of Galilee by the disciples in pairs wakened all Galilee, for the name of Jesus thus became known (*phaneron*) or known till even Herod heard of it in the palace. "A palace is late in hearing spiritual news" (Bengel). *Therefore do these powers work in him* (*dia touto energousin hai dunameis en autōi*). "A snatch of Herod's theology and philosophy" (Morison). John wrought no miracles (John 10:41), but if he had risen from the dead perhaps he could. So Herod may have argued. "Herod's superstition and his guilty conscience raised this ghost to plague him" (Gould). Our word *energy* is this same Greek word here used (*energousin*). It means at work. Miraculous powers were at work in Jesus whatever the explanation. This all agreed, but they differed widely as to his personality, whether Elijah or another of the prophets or John the Baptist. Herod was at first much perplexed (*diēporei*, Luke 9:7 and Mark 6:20).

16. *John, whom I beheaded* (*hon ego apekephalisa Iōanēn*). His fears got the best of him and so Herod settled down on this nightmare. He could still see that charger containing

John's head coming towards him in his dreams. The late verb *apokephalizō* means to cut off the head. Herod had ordered it done and recognizes his guilt.

17. *For Herod himself* (*Autos gar ho Hērōidēs*). Mark now proceeds to give the narrative of the death of John the Baptist some while before these nervous fears of Herod. But this *post eventum* narrative is very little out of the chronological order. The news of John's death at Machaerus may even have come at the close of the Galilean tour. "The tidings of the murder of the Baptist seem to have brought the recent circuit to an end" (Swete). The disciples of John "went and told Jesus. Now when Jesus heard it, he withdrew from thence in a boat" (Matt. 14:12f.). See on Matt. 14:3-12 for the discussion about Herod Antipas and John and Herodias.

18. *Thy brother's wife* (*tēn gunaika tou adelphou*). While the brother was alive (Lev. 18:16; 20:21). After a brother's death it was often a duty to marry his widow.

19. *And Herodias set herself against him* (*Hē de Hērōidias eneichen autōi*). Dative of disadvantage. Literally, *had it in for him*. This is modern slang, but is in exact accord with this piece of vernacular *Koiné*. No object of *eichen* is expressed, though *orgēn* or *cholon* may be implied. The tense is imperfect and aptly described the feelings of Herodias towards this upstart prophet of the wilderness who had dared to denounce her private relations with Herod Antipas. Gould suggests that she "kept her eye on him" or kept up her hostility towards him. She never let up, but bided her time which, she felt sure, would come. See the same idiom in Gen. 49:23. She *desired to kill him* (*ēthelen auton apokteinai*). Imperfect again. *And she could not* (*kai ouk ēdunato*). *Kai* here has an adversative sense, but she could not. That is, not yet. "The power was wanting, not the will" (Swete).

20. *Feared John* (*ephobeito ton Iōanēn*). Imperfect tense,

continual state of fear. He feared John and also Herodias. Between the two Herod vacillated. He knew him to be righteous and holy (*dikaion kai hagion*) and so innocent of any wrong. So he *kept him safe* (*suneterei*). Imperfect tense again. Late Greek verb. From the plots and schemes of Herodias. She was another Jezebel towards John and with Herod. *Much perplexed* (*polla ēporei*). This the correct text not *polla epoiei*, did many things. Imperfect tense again. *He heard him gladly* (*hēdeōs ēkouen*). Imperfect tense again. This is the way that Herod really felt when he could slip away from the meshes of Herodias. These interviews with the Baptist down in the prison at Machaerus during his occasional visits there braced "his jaded mind as with a whiff of fresh air" (Swete). But then he saw Herodias again and he was at his wits' end (*ēporei*, lose one's way, *a* privative and *poros*, way), for he knew that he had to live with Herodias with whom he was hopelessly entangled.

21. *When a convenient day was come* (*genomenēs hēmeras eukairou*). Genitive absolute. A day well appointed (*eu*, well, *kairos*, time) for the purpose, the day for which she had long waited. She had her plans all laid to spring a trap for her husband Herod Antipas and to make him do her will with the Baptist. Herod was not to know that he was the mere catspaw of Herodias till it was all over. See on Matt. 14:6 for discussion of Herod's birthday (*genesiois*, locative case or associative instrumental of time). *Made a supper* (*deipnon epoiēsen*). Banquet. *To his lords* (*tois megistāsin autou*). From *megistan* (that from *megas*, great), common in the LXX and later Greek. Cf. Rev. 6:15; 18:23. In the papyri. The grandees, magnates, nobles, the chief men of civil life. *The high captains* (*tois chiliarchois*). Military tribunes, commanders of a thousand men. *The chief men of Galilee* (*tois prōtois tēs Galilaias*). The first men of social importance and prominence. A notable gathering that

included these three groups at the banquet on Herod's birthday.

22. *The daughter of Herodias herself* (*tēs thugatros autēs Hērōidiados*). Genitive absolute again. Some ancient manuscripts read *autou* (his, referring to Herod Antipas. So Westcott and Hort) instead of *autēs* (herself). In that case the daughter of Herodias would also have the name Herodias as well as Salome, the name commonly given her. That is quite possible in itself. It was toward the clòse of the banquet, when all had partaken freely of the wine, that Herodias made her daughter come in and dance (*eiselthousēs kai orchēsamenēs*) in the midst (Matthew). "Such dancing was an almost unprecedented thing for women of rank, or even respectability. It was mimetic and licentious, and performed by professionals" (Gould). Herodias stooped thus low to degrade her own daughter like a common *hetaira* in order to carry out her set purpose against John. *She pleased Herod and them that sat at meat* (*ēresen Hērōidēi kai tois sunanakeimenois*). The maudlin group lounging on the divans were thrilled by the licentious dance of the half-naked princess. *Whatsoever thou wilt* (*ho ean theleis*) The drunken Tetrarch had been caught in the net of Herodias. It was a public promise.

23. *And he sware unto her* (*kai ōmosen autēi*). The girl was of marriageable age though called *korasion* (cf. Esther 2:9). Salome was afterward married to Philip the Tetrarch. The swaggering oath to the half of the kingdom reminds one of Esther 5:3f., the same oath made to Esther by Ahasuerus.

24. *What shall I ask?* (*Ti aitēsōmai;*). The fact that she went and spoke to her mother proves that she had not been told beforehand what to ask. Matt. 14:8 does not necessarily mean that, but he simply condenses the account. The girl's question implies by the middle voice that she is thinking of something for herself. She was no doubt unprepared for her mother's ghastly reply.

25. *Straightway with haste* (*euthus meta spoudēs*). Before the king's rash mood passed and while he was still under the spell of the dancing princess. Herodias knew her game well. See on Matt. 14:8f.

26. *He would not reject her* (*ouk ēthelēsen athetēsai autēn*). He was caught once again between his conscience and his environment. Like many since his day the environment stifled his conscience.

27. *A soldier of his guard* (*spekoulatora*). Latin word *speculator*. A spy, scout, lookout, and often executioner. It was used of the bodyguard of the Roman emperor and so for one of Herod's spies. He was used to do errands of this sort and it was soon done. It was a gruesome job, but he soon brought John's head to the damsel, apparently in the presence of all, and she took it to her mother. This miserable Tetrarch, the slave of Herodias, was now the slave of his fears. He is haunted by the ghost of John and shudders at the reports of the work of Jesus.

29. *His corpse* (*to ptōma autou*). See on Matt. 24:28. It was a mournful time for the disciples of John. "They went and told Jesus" (Matt. 14:12). What else could they do?

30. *And the apostles gather themselves together unto Jesus* (*kai sunagontai hoi apostoloi pros ton Iēsoun*). Vivid historical present. *All things whatsoever they had done and whatsoever they had taught* (*panta hosa epoiēsan kai hosa edidaxan*). Not past perfect in the Greek, just the aorist indicative, constative aorist that summed it all up, the story of this their first tour without Jesus. And Jesus listened to it all (Luke 9:10). He was deeply concerned in the outcome.

31. *Come ye yourselves apart into a desert place and rest awhile* (*Deute humeis autoi kat' idian eis erēmon topon kai anapauesthe oligon*). It was plain that they were overwrought and excited and needed refreshment (*anapauesthe*, middle voice, refresh yourselves, "rest up" literally). This is one of the needed lessons for all preachers and teachers,

occasional change and refreshment. Even Jesus felt the need of it. *They had no leisure so much as to eat (oude phagein eukairoun).* Imperfect tense again. Crowds were coming and going. Change was a necessity.

32. *And they went away in a boat (kai apēlthon en tōi ploiōi).* They accepted with alacrity and off they went.

33. *Outwent them (proēlthon autous).* The crowds were not to be outdone. They recognized *(egnōsan)* Jesus and the disciples and ran around the head of the lake on foot *(pezēi)* and got there ahead of Jesus and were waiting for Him when the boat came.

34. *They were as sheep not having a shepherd (ēsan hōs probata mē echonta poimena).* Matthew has these words in another context (9:26), but Mark alone has them here. *Mē* is the usual negative for the participle in the *Koiné*. These excited and exciting people (Bruce) greatly needed teaching. Matt. 14:14 mentions healing as does Luke 9:11 (both preaching and healing). But a vigorous crowd of runners would not have many sick. The people had plenty of official leaders but these rabbis were for spiritual matters blind leaders of the blind. Jesus had come over for rest, but his heart was touched by the pathos of this situation. So "he began to teach them many things" *(ērxato didaskein autous polla).* Two accusatives with the verb of teaching and the present tense of the infinitive. He kept it up.

35. *When the day was now far spent (ēdē hōras pollēs genomenēs).* Genitive absolute. *Hōra* used here for day-time (so Matt. 14:15) as in Polybius and late Greek. *Much day-time already gone.* Luke 9:12 has it began to *incline (klinein)* or wear away. It was after 3 p.m., the first evening. Note second evening or sunset in Mark 6:47 = Matt. 14:23 = John 6:16. The turn of the afternoon had come and sunset was approaching. The idiom is repeated at the close of the verse. See on Matt. 14:15.

36. *Into the country and villages round about (eis tous kuklōi*

agrous kai kōmas). The fields (*agrous*) were the scattered farms (Latin, *villae*). The villages (*kōmas*) may have included Bethsaida Julias not far away (Luke 9:10). The other Bethsaida was on the Western side of the lake (Mark 6:45). *Somewhat to eat* (*ti phagōsin*). Literally, *what to eat, what they were to eat*. Deliberative subjunctive retained in the indirect question.

38. *Go and see* (*hupagete idete*). John says that Jesus asked Philip to find out what food they had (John 6:5f.) probably after the disciples had suggested that Jesus send the crowd away as night was coming on (Mark 6:35f.). On this protest to his command that they feed the crowds (Mark 6:37 = Matt. 14:16 = Luke 9:13) Jesus said "Go see" how many loaves you can get hold of. Then Andrew reports the fact of the lad with five barley loaves and two fishes (John 6:8f.). They had suggested before that two hundred pennyworth (*dēnariōn diakosiōn*. See on Matt. 18:28) was wholly inadequate and even that (some thirty-five dollars) was probably all that or even more than they had with them. John's Gospel alone tells of the lad with his lunch which his mother had given him.

39. *By companies* (*sumposia sumposia*). Distribution expressed by repetition as in Mark 6:7 (*duo duo*) instead of using *ana* or *kata*. Literally our word *symposium* and originally a drinking party, Latin *convivium*, then the party of guests of any kind without the notion of drinking. So in Plutarch and the LXX (especially I Macca.). *Upon the green grass* (*epi tōi chlōrōi chortōi*). Another Markan touch. It was passover time (John 6:4) and the afternoon sun shone upon the orderly groups upon the green spring grass. See on Matt. 14:15. They may have been seated like companies at tables, open at one end.

40. *They sat down in ranks* (*anepesan prasiai prasiai*). They half-way reclined (*anaklithēnai*, verse 39). Fell up here (we have to say fell down), the word *anepesan* means.

But they were arranged in groups by hundreds and by fifties and they looked like garden beds with their many-coloured clothes which even men wore in the Orient. Then again Mark repeats the word, *prasiai prasiai*, in the nominative absolute as in verse 39 instead of using *ana* or *kata* with the accusative for the idea of distribution. Garden beds, garden beds. Peter saw and he never forgot the picture and so Mark caught it. There was colour as well as order in the grouping. There were orderly walks between the rows on rows of men reclining on the green grass. The grass is not green in Palestine much of the year, mainly at the pass-over time. So here the Synoptic Gospels have an indication of more than a one-year ministry of Jesus (Gould). It is still one year before the last passover when Jesus was crucified.

41. *Brake the loaves; and he gave to the disciples* (*kai apo tōn ichthuōn*). Apparently the fishes were in excess of the twelve baskets full of broken pieces of bread. See on Matt. 14:20 for discussion of *kophinos* and *sphuris*, the two kinds of baskets.

44. *Men* (*andres*). Men as different from women as in Matt. 14:21. This remarkable miracle is recorded by all Four Gospels, a nature miracle that only God can work. No talk about accelerating natural processes will explain this miracle. And three eyewitnesses report it the Logia of Matthew, the eyes of Peter in Mark, the witness of John the Beloved Disciple (Gould). The evidence is overwhelming.

45. *To Bethsaida* (*pros Bēthsaidan*). This is Bethsaida on the Western side, not Bethsaida Julias on the Eastern side where they had just been (Luke 9:10). *While he himself sendeth the multitude away* (*heōs autos apoluei ton ochlon*). Matt. 14:22 has it "till he should send away" (*heōs hou apolusēi*) with the aorist subjunctive of purpose. Mark with the present indicative *apoluei* pictures Jesus as personally engaged in persuading the crowds to go away now. John 6:41f. explains this activity of Jesus. The crowds had become so excited that they were in the mood to start a revolution against the Roman government and proclaim Jesus king. He had already forced in reality the disciples to leave in a boat *to go before him* (*proagein*) in order to get them out of this atmosphere of overwrought excitement with a political twist to the whole conception of the Messianic Kingdom. They were in grave danger of being swept off their feet and falling heedlessly into the Pharisaic conception and so defeating the whole teaching and training of Jesus with them. See on Matt. 14:22 and 23. To this pass things had come one year before the Crucifixion. He had done his best to help and bless the crowds and lost his chance to rest. No one really understood Jesus, not the crowds, not the disciples. Jesus needed the Father to stay and steady him. The devil had come again to tempt him with world dominion in league with the Pharisees, the populace, and the devil in the background.

47. *When even was come* (*opsias genomenēs*). The second or late evening, six P.M. at this season, or sunset on. *He alone on the land* (*kai autos monos ēpi tēs gēs*). Another Markan touch. Jesus had come down out of the mountain where he had prayed to the Father. He is by the sea again in the late twilight. Apparently Jesus remained quite a while, some hours, on the beach. "It was now dark and Jesus had not yet come to them" (John 6:17).

48. *Seeing them distressed in rowing* (*idōn autous basanizomenous en tōi elaunein*). See also Matt. 8:29 for the word *basanizō*, to torture, torment (Matt. 4:24) with a touchstone, then to distress as here. Papyri have *dia basanōn* used on slaves like our third degree for criminals. *Elaunein* is literally to drive as of ships or chariots. They drove the boat with oars. Common in Xenophon for marching. *About the fourth watch of the night* (*peri tetartēn phulakēn tēs*

nuktos). That is, between three and six A.M. The wind was *contrary to them* (*enantios autois*), that is in their faces and rowing was difficult, "a great wind" (John 6:18), and as a result the disciples had made little progress. They should have been over long before this. *And he would have passed by them* (*kai ēthelen parelthein autous*). Only in Mark. He wished to pass by them, *praeterire eos* (Vulgate). Imperfect tense *ēthelen*. *They thought* (*edoxan*). A natural conclusion. *And cried out* (*anekraxan*). *Cried up*, literally, a shriek of terror, or scream.

50. *It is I* (*ego eimi*). These were the astounding words of cheer. They did not recognize Jesus in the darkness. They had never seen him or any one walk on the water. His voice reassured them.

51. *They were sore amazed in themselves* (*lian en heautois existanto*). Only in Mark. Imperfect tense picturing vividly the excited disciples. Mark does not give the incident of Peter's walking on the water and beginning to sink. Perhaps Peter was not fond of telling that story.

52. *For they understood not* (*ou gar sunēkan*). Explanation of their excessive amazement, viz., their failure to grasp the full significance of the miracle of the loaves and fishes, a nature miracle. Here was another, Jesus walking on the water. Their reasoning process (*kardia* in the general sense for all the inner man) *was hardened* (*ēn pepōrōmenē*). See on 3:5 about *pōrōsis*. Today some men have such intellectual hardness or denseness that they cannot believe that God can or would work miracles, least of all nature miracles.

53. *And moored to the shore* (*kai prosōrmisthēsan*). Only here in the New Testament, though an old Greek verb and occurring in the papyri. *Hormos* is roadstead or anchorage. They cast anchor or lashed the boat to a post on shore. It was at the plain of Gennesaret several miles south of Bethsaida owing to the night wind.

54. *Knew him* (*epignontes auton*). Recognizing Jesus, knowing fully (*epi*) as nearly all did by now. Second aorist active participle.

55. *Ran about* (*periedramon*). Vivid constative aorist picturing the excited pursuit of Jesus as the news spread that he was in Gennesaret. *On their beds* (*epi tois krabattois*). Pallets like that of the man let down through the roof (Mark 2:4). *Where they heard he was* (*hopou ēkouon hoti estin*). Imperfect tense of *akouō* (repetition), present indicative *estin* retained in indirect discourse.

56. *Wheresoever he entered* (*hopou an eiseporeueto*). The imperfect indicative with *an* used to make a general indefinite statement with the relative adverb. See the same construction at the close of the verse, *hosoi an hēpsanto auton* (aorist indicative and *an* in a relative clause), *as many as touched him*. One must enlarge the details here to get an idea of the richness of the healing ministry of Jesus. We are now near the close of the Galilean ministry with its many healing mercies and excitement is at the highest pitch (Bruce).

CHAPTER VII

2. *With defiled, that is unwashen hands (koinais chersin, tout' estin aniptois)*. Associative instrumental case. Originally *koinos* meant what was common to everybody like the *Koiné* Greek. But in later Greek it came also to mean as here what is vulgar or profane. So Peter in Acts 10:14 "common and unclean." The next step was the ceremonially unclean. The emissaries of the Pharisees and the scribes from Jerusalem had seen "some of the disciples" eat without washing their hands, how many we are not told. Swete suggests that in going through the plain the disciples were seen eating some of the bread preserved in the twelve baskets the afternoon before across the lake. There was no particular opportunity to wash the hands, a very proper thing to do before eating for sanitary reasons. But the objection raised is on ceremonial, not sanitary, grounds.

3. *Diligently (pugmēi)*. Instrumental case, *with the fist*, up to the elbow, rubbing one hand and arm with the other hand clenched. Aleph had *pukna* probably because of the difficulty about *pugmēi* (kin to Latin *pugnus*). Schultess considers it a dry wash or rubbing of the hands without water as a ritualistic concession. The middle voice *nipsōntai* means their own hands. This verb is often used for parts of the body while *louō* is used of the whole body (John 13:10). On the tradition of the elders see on Matt. 15:2.

4. *From the marketplace (ap' agoras)*. Ceremonial defilement was inevitable in the mixing with men in public. This *agora* from *ageirō* to collect or gather, was a public forum in every town where the people gathered like the courthouse square in American towns. The disciples were already ceremonially defiled. *Wash themselves (baptisōntai)*. First

aorist middle subjunctive of *baptizō*, dip or immerse. West-cott and Hort put *rantisōntai* in the text translated "sprinkle themselves" in the margin of the Revised Version, because Aleph, B, and some of the best cursives have it. Gould terms *rantisōntai* "a manifest emendation," to get rid of the difficulty of dipping or bathing the whole body. Meyer says: "The statement proceeds by way of climax: before eating they wash the hands always. When they come from market they take a bath before eating." This is not the place to enter into any controversy about the meaning of *baptizō*, to dip, *rantizō*, to sprinkle, and *eccheō*, to pour, all used in the New Testament. The words have their distinctive meanings here as elsewhere. Some scribes felt a difficulty about the use of *baptisōntai* here. The Western and Syrian classes of manuscripts add "and couches" (*kai klinōn*) at the end of the sentence. Swete considers the immersions of beds (*baptismous klinōn*) "an incongruous combination." But Gould says: "Edersheim shows that the Jewish ordinance required immersions, *baptismous*, of these vessels." We must let the Jewish scrupulosity stand for itself, though "and couches" is not supported by Aleph, B L D Bohairic, probably not genuine.

6. *Well* (*kalōs*). Appositely here, but ironical sarcasm in verse 9. Note here "you hypocrites" (*humōn tōn hupokritōn*).

8. *Ye leave the commandment of God* (*aphentes tēn entolēn tou theou*). Note the sharp contrast between the command of God and the traditions of men. Jesus here drives a keen wedge into the Pharisaic contention. They had covered up the Word of God with their oral teaching. Jesus here shows that they care more for the oral teaching of the scribes and elders than for the written law of God. The Talmud gives abundant and specific confirmation of the truthfulness of this indictment.

9. *Full well do ye reject the commandment of God that ye*

may keep your traditions (kalōs atheteite tēn entolēn tou theou hina tēn paradosin humōn tērēsēte). One can almost see the scribes withering under this terrible arraignment. It was biting sarcasm that cut to the bone. The evident irony should prevent literal interpretation as commendation of the Pharisaic pervasion of God's word. See my *The Pharisees and Jesus* for illustrations of the way that they placed this oral tradition above the written law. See on Matt. 15:7.

11. *Corban (korban ho estin dōron).* See on Matt. 15:5. Mark preserves the Hebrew word for a gift or offering to God (Ex. 21:17; Lev. 20:9), indeclinable here, meaning *gift* (*dōron*), but declinable *korbanas* in Matt. 27:6, meaning sacred treasury. The rabbis (*but ye say, humeis de legete*) actually allowed the mere saying of this word by an unfaithful son to prevent the use of needed money for the support of father or mother. It was a home thrust to these pettifogging sticklers for ceremonial punctilios. They not only justified such a son's trickery, but held that he was prohibited from using it for father or mother, but he might use it for himself.

13. *Making void the word of God by your tradition (akurountes ton logon tou theou tēi paradosei humōn).* See on Matt. 15:6 for the word *akurountes*, invalidating, a stronger word than *athetein*, to set aside, in verse 9. See both used in Gal. 3:15, 17. Setting aside does invalidate.

14. *And he called to him the multitude again (kai proskalesamenos palin ton ochlon).* Aorist middle participle, calling to himself. The rabbis had attacked the disciples about not washing their hands before eating. Jesus now turned the tables on them completely and laid bare their hollow pretentious hypocrisy to the people. *Hear me all of you and understand (akousate mou pantes kai suniete).* A most pointed appeal to the people to see into and see through the chicanery of these ecclesiastics. See on Matt. 15:11 for discussion.

17. *When he was entered into the house from the multitude* (*hote eiselthen eis oikon apo tou ochlou*). This detail in Mark alone, probably in Peter's house in Capernaum. To the crowd Jesus spoke the parable of corban, but the disciples want it interpreted (cf. 4:10ff., 33ff.). Matt. 15:15 represents Peter as the spokesman as was usually the case.

18. *Are ye so without understanding also?* (*Houtōs kai humeis asunetoi este;*). See on Matt. 15:16. You also as well as the multitude. It was a discouraging moment for the great Teacher if his own chosen pupils (disciples) were still under the spell of the Pharisaic theological outlook. It was a riddle to them. "They had been trained in Judaism, in which the distinction between clean and unclean is ingrained, and could not understand a statement abrogating this" (Gould). They had noticed that the Pharisees stumbled at the parable of Jesus (Matt. 15:12). They were stumbling themselves and did not know how to answer the Pharisees. Jesus charges the disciples with intellectual dulness and spiritual stupidity.

19. *Making all meats clean* (*katharizōn panta ta brōmata*). This anacoluthon can be understood by repeating *he says* (*legei*) from verse 18. The masculine participle agrees with Jesus, the speaker. The words do not come from Jesus, but are added by Mark. Peter reports this item to Mark, probably with a vivid recollection of his own experience on the housetop in Joppa when in the vision Peter declined three times the Lord's invitation to kill and eat unclean animals (Acts 10:14-16). It was a riddle to Peter as late as that day. "Christ asserts that *Levitical* uncleanness, such as eating with unwashed hands, is of small importance compared with *moral* uncleanness" (Vincent). The two chief words in both incidents, here and in Acts, are *defile* (*koinoō*) and *cleanse* (*katharizō*). "What God cleansed do not thou treat as defiled" (Acts 10:15). It was a revolutionary declaration by Jesus and Peter was slow to understand

it even after the coming of the Holy Spirit at Pentecost. Jesus was amply justified in his astonished question: *Perceive ye not?* (*ou noeite;*). They were making little use of their intelligence in trying to comprehend the efforts of Jesus to give them a new and true spiritual insight.

21. *Evil thoughts* (*hoi dialogismoi hoi kakoi*). These come out of the heart (*ek tēs kardias*), the inner man, and lead to the dreadful list here given like the crimes of a modern police court: *fornications* (*porneiai*, usually of the unmarried), *adulteries* (*moichaiai*, of the married), *thefts* (*klopai*, stealings), *covetings* (*pleonexiai*, craze for more and more), *murders* (*phonoi*, growing out of the others often), *wickednesses* (*ponēriai*, from *ponos*, toil, then drudge, bad like our *knave*, serving boy like German *Knabe*, and then criminal), *deceit* (*dolos*, lure or snare with bait), *lasciviousness* (*aselgeia*, unrestrained sex instinct), *evil eye* (*ophthalmos ponēros*) or eye that works evil and that haunts one with its gloating stare, *railing* (*blasphēmia*, blasphemy, hurtful speech), *pride* (*huperēphania*, holding oneself above others, stuck up), *foolishness* (*aphrosunē*, lack of sense), a fitting close to it all.

24. *Into the borders of Tyre and Sidon* (*eis ta horia Turou kai Sidōnos*). The departure from Capernaum was a withdrawal from Galilee, the second of the four withdrawals from Galilee. The first had been to the region of Bethsaida Julias in the territory of Herod Philip. This is into distinctly heathen land. It was not merely the edge of Phoenicia, but into the parts of Tyre and Sidon (Matt. 15:21). There was too much excitement among the people, too much bitterness among the Pharisees, too much suspicion on the part of Herod Antipas, too much dulness on the part of the disciples for Jesus to remain in Galilee. *And he could not be hid* (*kai ouk ēdunasthē lathein*). Jesus wanted to be alone in the house after all the strain in Galilee. He craved a little privacy and rest. This was his purpose in going into Phoenicia. Note the adversative sense of *kai* here = "but."

25. *Whose little daughter* (*hēs to thugatrion autēs*). Diminutive with tender touch. Note "whose" and "her" like vernacular today. *Having heard of him* (*akousasa peri autou*). Even in this heathen territory the fame of Jesus was known. When the Sermon on the Mount was preached people were there from "the sea coast of Tyre and Sidon" (Luke 6:17).

26. *A Greek, a Syro-Phoenician by race* (*Hellēnis, Surophoinikissa tōi genei*). "A Greek in religion, a Syrian in tongue, a Phoenician in race" (Bruce), from Euthymius Zigabenus. She was not a Phoenician of Carthage. *She besought* (*ērōta*). Imperfect tense. She kept at it. This verb, as in late Greek, is here used for a request, not a mere question. Abundant examples in the papyri in this sense.

27. *Let the children first be filled* (*aphes prōton chortasthēnai ta paidia*). The Jews had the first claim. See the command of Jesus in the third tour of Galilee to avoid the Gentiles and the Samaritans (Matt. 10:5). Paul was the Apostle to the Gentiles, but he gave the Jew the first opportunity (Rom. 2:9f.). See on Matt. 15:24f.

28. *Even the dogs under the table* (*kai ta kunaria hupokatō tēs trapezēs*). A delightful picture. Even the little dogs (*kunaria*) under the table *eat of the children's crumbs* (*esthiousin apo tōn psichiōn tōn paidiōn*). Little dogs, little scraps of bread (*psichion*, diminutive of *psichos*, morsel), little children (*paidia*, diminutive of *pais*). Probably the little children purposely dropped a few little crumbs for the little dogs. These household dogs, pets of and loved by the children. *Braid Scots* has it: "Yet the wee dowgs aneath the table eat o' the moole o' the bairns." "A unique combination of faith and wit" (Gould). Instead of resenting Christ's words about giving the children's bread to the dogs (Gentiles) in verse 27, she instantly turned it to the advantage of her plea for her little daughter.

29. *For this saying* (*dia touton ton logon*). She had faith,

great faith as Matt. 15:28 shows, but it was her quick and
bright repartee that pleased Jesus. He had missed his rest,
but it was worth it to answer a call like this.

30. *And the demon gone out (kai to daimonion exelēluthos).*
This was her crumb from the children's table. The perfect
active participle expresses the state of completion. The
demon was gone for good and all.

31. *Through the midst of the borders of Decapolis (ana meson
tōn horiōn Dekapoleōs).* Jesus left Phoenicia, but did not go
back into Galilee. He rather went east and came down east
of the Sea of Galilee into the region of the Greek cities of
Decapolis. He thus kept out of the territory of Herod Antipas. He had been in this region when he healed the Gadarene
demoniac and was asked to leave.

32. *And they bring unto him (kai pherousin autōi).* Another of Mark's dramatic presents. This incident only in
Mark.

33. *Took him aside (apolabomenos auton).* The secrecy
here observed was partly to avoid excitement and partly to
get the attention of the deaf and dumb demoniac. He could
not hear what Jesus said. So Jesus put his fingers into his
ears, spat, and touched his tongue. There was, of course, no
virtue in the spittle and it is not clear why Jesus used it.
Saliva was by some regarded as remedial and was used by
exorcists in their incantations. Whether this was a concession to the man's denseness one does not know. But it
all showed the poor man that Jesus healed him in his own
way.

34. *Ephphatha (dianoichthēti,* be opened). Another one
of Mark's Aramaic words preserved and transliterated and
then translated into Greek. "Be thou unbarred" (*Braid
Scots*). Jesus sighed (*estenaxen*) as he looked up into heaven
and spoke the word *ephphatha.* Somehow he felt a nervous
strain in this complex case (deaf, dumb, demoniac) that we
may not quite comprehend.

35. *He spake plain (elalei orthōs).* He began to speak correctly. Inchoative imperfect tense.

36. *So much the more a great deal they published it (autoi māllon perissoteron ekērusson).* Imperfect tense, continued action. Double comparative as occurs elsewhere for emphasis as in Phil. 1:23 "much more better" (*pollōi māllon kreisson*). See Robertson's *Grammar,* pp. 663f. Human nature is a peculiar thing. The command not to tell provoked these people to tell just as the leper had done (Mark 1:44f.). The more Jesus commanded (*hoson autois diestelleto*) them not to tell the more they told. It was a continuous performance. Prohibitions always affect some people that way, especially superficial and light-headed folks. But we have to have prohibitions or anarchy.

37. *He hath done all things well (Kalōs panta pepoiēken).* The present perfect active shows the settled convictions of these people about Jesus. Their great amazement (*huperperissōs exeplēssonto*), imperfect passive and compound adverb, thus found expression in a vociferous championship of Jesus in this pagan land.

CHAPTER VIII

1. *Had nothing to eat (mē echontōn ti phagōsin)*. Genitive absolute and plural because *ochlou* a collective substantive. Not having what to eat (deliberative subjunctive retained in indirect question). The repetition of a nature miracle of feeding four thousand in Decapolis disturbs some modern critics who cannot imagine how Jesus could or would perform another miracle elsewhere so similar to the feeding of the five thousand up near Bethsaida Julias. But both Mark and Matthew give both miracles, distinguish the words for baskets (*kophinos, sphuris*), and both make Jesus later refer to both incidents and use these two words with the same distinction (Mark 8:19f.; Matt. 16:9f.). Surely it is easier to conceive that Jesus wrought two such miracles than to hold that Mark and Matthew have made such a jumble of the whole business.

2. *Now three days (ēdē hēmerai treis)*. This text preserves a curious parenthetic nominative of time (Robertson, *Grammar*, p. 460). See on Matt. 15:32.

3. *Are come from far (apo makrothen eisin)*. This item alone in Mark.

4. *Here (hōde)*. Of all places, in this desert region in the mountains. The disciples feel as helpless as when the five thousand were fed. They do not rise to faith in the unlimited power of Jesus after all that they have seen.

6. *Brake and gave (eklasen kai edidou)*. Constative aorist followed by imperfect. The giving kept on. *To set before them (hina paratithōsin)*. Present subjunctive describing the continuous process.

7. *A few small fishes (ichthudia oliga)*. Mark mentions

them last as if they were served after the food, but not so Matt. 15:34f.

8. *Broken pieces that remained over* (*perisseumata klasmatōn*). Overplus, abundance, remains of broken pieces not used, not just scraps or crumbs.

10. *Into the parts of Dalmanutha* (*eis ta merē Dalmanoutha*). Matt. 15:39 calls it "the borders of Magadan." Both names are unknown elsewhere, but apparently the same region of Galilee on the western side of the lake not far from Tiberias. Mark here uses "parts" (*merē*) in the same sense as "borders" (*horia*) in 7:24 just as Matthew reverses it with "parts" in 15:21 and "borders" here in 15:39. Mark has here "with his disciples" (*meta tōn mathētōn autou*) only implied in Matt. 15:39.

11. *And the Pharisees came forth* (*kai exēlthon hoi Pharisaioi*). At once they met Jesus and opened a controversy. Matt. 16:1 adds "and Sadducees," the first time these two parties appear together against Jesus. See discussion on Matt. 16:1. The Pharisees and Herodians had already joined hands against Jesus in the sabbath controversy (Mark 3:6). They *began to question with him* (*ērxanto sunzētein autōi*). Dispute, not mere inquiry, associative instrumental case of *autōi*. They began at once and kept it up (present infinitive).

12. *He sighed deeply in his spirit* (*anastenaxas tōi pneumati*). The only instance of this compound in the N.T. though in the LXX. The uncompounded form occurs in Mark 7:34 and it is common enough. The preposition *ana*- intensifies the meaning of the verb (perfective use). "The sigh seemed to come, as we say, from the bottom of his heart, the Lord's human spirit was stirred to its depths" (Swete). Jesus resented the settled prejudice of the Pharisees (and now Sadducees also) against him and his work. *There shall no sign be given unto this generation* (*ei dothēsetai tēi geneāi tautēi sēmeion*). Matt. 16:4 has simply *ou do-*

thēsetai, plain negative with the future passive indicative. Mark has *ei* instead of *ou,* which is technically a conditional clause with the conclusion unexpressed (Robertson, *Grammar,* p. 1024), really aposiopesis in imitation of the Hebrew use of *im.* This is the only instance in the N.T. except in quotations from the LXX (Heb. 3:11; 4:3, 5). It is very common in the LXX. The rabbis were splitting hairs over the miracles of Jesus as having a possible natural explanation (as some critics do today) even if by the power of Beelzebub, and those not of the sky (from heaven) which would be manifested from God. So they put up this fantastic test to Jesus which he deeply resents. Matt. 16:4 adds "but the sign of Jonah" mentioned already by Jesus on a previous occasion (Matt. 12:39-41) at more length and to be mentioned again (Luke 11:32). But the mention of the sign of Jonah was "an absolute refusal of signs in their sense" (Bruce). And when he did rise from the dead on the third day, the Sanhedrin refused to be convinced (see Acts 3 to 5).

14. *Bread (artous). Loaves,* plural. *More than one loaf (ei mē hina arton).* Except one loaf. Detail only in Mark. Practically for thirteen men when hungry.

15. *Take heed, beware of the leaven of the Pharisees, and the leaven of Herod (Horāte, blepete apo tēs zumēs tōn Pharisaiōn kai tēs zumēs Hērōidou).* Present imperatives. Note *apo* and the ablative case. *Zumē* is from *zumoō* and occurs already in Matt. 13:33 in a good sense. For the bad sense see I Cor. 5:6. He repeatedly charged (*diestelleto,* imperfect indicative), showing that the warning was needed. The disciples came out of a Pharisaic atmosphere and they had just met it again at Dalmanutha. It was insidious. Note the combination of Herod here with the Pharisees. This is after the agitation of Herod because of the death of the Baptist and the ministry of Jesus (Mark 6:14-29 = Matt. 14:1-12 = Luke 9:7-9). Jesus definitely warns the disciples against "the leaven of Herod" (bad politics) and the leaven of the

Pharisees and Sadducees (bad theology and also bad politics).

16. *They reasoned one with another* (*dielogizonto pros allēlous*), implying discussion. Imperfect tense, kept it up. Matt. 16:7 has *en heautois*, in themselves or among themselves.

17–20. Mark here gives six keen questions of Jesus while Matt. 16:8–11 gives as four that really include the six of Mark running some together. The questions reveal the disappointment of Jesus at the intellectual dulness of his pupils. The questions concern the intellect (*noeite*, from *nous, suniete*, comprehend), the heart in a *hardened state* (*pepōrōmenēn*, perfect passive predicate participle as in Mark 6:52, which see), the eyes, the ears, the memory of both the feeding of the five thousand and the four thousand here sharply distinguished even to the two kinds of baskets (*kophinous, sphuridōn*). The disciples did recall the number of baskets left over in each instance, twelve and seven. Jesus "administers a sharp rebuke for their preoccupation with mere temporalities, as if there were nothing higher to be thought of *than bread*" (Bruce). "For the time the Twelve are wayside hearers, with hearts like a beaten path, into which the higher truths cannot sink so as to germinate" (Bruce).

21. *Do ye not yet understand?* (*oupō suniete;*). After all this rebuke and explanation. The greatest of all teachers had the greatest of all classes, but he struck a snag here. Matt. 16:12 gives the result: "Then they understood how that he bade them not beware of the loaves of bread, but of the teaching of the Pharisees and Sadducees." They had once said that they understood the parables of Jesus (Matt. 13:51). But that was a long time ago. The teacher must have patience if his pupils are to understand.

22. *Unto Bethsaida* (*eis Bēthsaidan*). On the Eastern side not far from the place of the feeding of the five thousand, Bethsaida Julias. Note dramatic presents *they come* (*erchon-*

tai), *they bring* (*pherousin*). This incident in Mark alone
(verses 22–26).

23. *Brought him out of the village* (*exēnegken auton exō tēs
kōmēs*). It had been a village, but Philip had enlarged it
and made it a town or city (*polis*), though still called a village (verses 23, 26). As in the case of the deaf and dumb
demoniac given also alone by Mark (7:31–37), so here Jesus
observes the utmost secrecy in performing the miracle for
reasons not given by Mark. It was the season of retirement
and Jesus is making the fourth withdrawal from Galilee.
That fact may explain it. The various touches here are of
interest also. Jesus led him out by the hand, put spittle on
his eyes (using the poetical and *Koiné* papyri word *ommata*
instead of the usual *opthalmous*), and laid his hands upon
him, perhaps all this to help the man's faith.

24. *I see men, for I behold them as trees walking* (*Blepō
tous anthrōpous hoti hōs dendra horō peripatountas*). A vivid
description of dawning sight. His vision was incomplete
though he could tell that they were men because they were
walking. This is the single case of a gradual cure in the
healings wrought by Jesus. The reason for this method in
this case is not given.

25. *He looked steadfastly* (*dieblepsen*). He saw thoroughly
now, effective aorist (*dieblepsen*), he was completely restored
(*apekatestē*, second aorist, double compound and double
augment), and kept on seeing (*eneblepen*, imperfect, continued action) all things clearly or at a distance (*tēlaugōs*,
common Greek word from *tēle*, afar, and *augē*, radiance, far-
shining). Some manuscripts (margin in Westcott and Hort)
read *dēlaugōs*, from *dēlos*, plain, and *augē*, radiance.

26. *To his home* (*eis oikon autou*). A joyful homecoming
that. He was not allowed to enter the village and create
excitement before Jesus moved on to Caesarea Philippi.

27. *Into the villages of Caesarea Philippi* (*eis tās kōmas
Kaisarias tēs Philippou*). *Parts* (*merē*) Matt. 16:13 has,

the Caesarea of Philippi in contrast to the one down on the Mediterranean Sea. Mark means the villages belonging to the district around Caesarea Philippi. This region is on a spur of Mount Hermon in Iturea ruled by Herod Philip so that Jesus is safe from annoyance by Herod Antipas or the Pharisees and Sadducees. Up here on this mountain slope Jesus will have his best opportunity to give the disciples special teaching concerning the crucifixion just a little over six months ahead. So Jesus asked (*epērotā*, descriptive imperfect) *Who do men say that I am?* (*Tina me legousin hoi anthrōpoi einai;*). Matt. 16:13 has "the Son of Man" in place of "I" here in Mark and in Luke 9:18. He often described himself as "the Son of Man." Certainly here the phrase could not mean merely "a man." They knew the various popular opinions about Jesus of which Herod Antipas had heard (Mark 3:21, 31). It was time that the disciples reveal how much they had been influenced by their environment as well as by the direct instruction of Jesus.

28. *And they told him* (*hoi de eipan*). They knew only too well. See on Matt. 16:14, 28 for discussion.

29. *Thou art the Christ* (*Su ei ho Christos*). Mark does not give "the Son of the living God" (Matt. 16:16) or "of God" (Luke 9:20). The full confession is the form in Matthew. Luke's language means practically the same, while Mark's is the briefest. But the form in Mark really means the full idea. Mark omits all praise of Peter, probably because Peter had done so in his story of the incident. For criticism of the view that Matthew's narrative is due to ecclesiastical development and effort to justify ecclesiastical prerogatives, see discussion on Matt. 16:16, 18. The disciples had confessed him as Messiah before. Thus John 1:41; 4:29; 6:69; Matt. 14:33. But Jesus had ceased to use the word Messiah to avoid political complications and a revolutionary movement (John 6:14f.). But did the disciples still believe in

Jesus as Messiah after all the defections and oppositions
seen by them? It was a serious test to which Jesus now put
them.

30. *Of him* (*peri autou*). As being the Messiah, that he
was the Christ (Matt. 16:20). Not yet, for the time was not
yet ripe. When that comes, the triumphal entry into Jerusalem, the very stones will cry out, if men will not (Luke
19:40).

31. *He began to teach them* (*ērxato didaskein autous*).
Mark is fond of this idiom, but it is not a mere rhetorical
device. Matt. 16:21 expressly says "from that time."
They had to be told soon about the approaching death of
Jesus. The confession of faith in Jesus indicated that it was
a good time to begin. Death at the hands of the Sanhedrin
(elders, chief priests, and scribes) in which Pharisees and Sadducees had about equal strength. The resurrection on the
third day is mentioned, but it made no impression on their
minds. This rainbow on the cloud was not seen. *After
three days* (*meta treis hēmeras*). Matt. 16:21 has "the
third day" (*tēi tritēi hēmerāi*) in the locative case of point
of time (so also Luke 9:22). There are some people who
stickle for a strict interpretation of "after three days"
which would be "on the fourth day," not "on the third day."
Evidently Mark's phrase here has the same sense as that in
Matthew and Luke else they are hopelessly contradictory.
In popular language "after three days" can and often does
mean "on the third day," but the fourth day is impossible.

32. *Spake the saying openly* (*parrēsiāi ton logon elalei*).
He held back nothing, told it all (*pān*, all, *rēsia*, from *eipon*,
say), without reserve, to all of them. Imperfect tense
elalei shows that Jesus did it repeatedly. Mark alone gives
this item. Mark does not give the great eulogy of Peter in
Matt. 16:17, 19 after his confession (Mark 8:29; Matt. 16:16;
Luke 9:20), but he does tell the stinging rebuke given Peter
by Jesus on this occasion. See discussion on Matt. 16:21, 26.

33. *He turning about and seeing his disciples* (*epistrapheis kai idōn tous mathētās autou*). Peter had called Jesus off to himself (*proskalesamenos*), but Jesus quickly wheeled round on Peter (*epistrapheis*, only *strapheis* in Matthew). In doing that the other disciples were in plain view also (this touch only in Mark). Hence Jesus rebukes Peter in the full presence of the whole group. Peter no doubt felt that it was his duty as a leader of the Twelve to remonstrate with the Master for this pessimistic utterance (Swete). It is even possible that the others shared Peter's views and were watching the effect of his daring rebuke of Jesus. It was more than mere officiousness on the part of Peter. He had not risen above the level of ordinary men and deserves the name of Satan whose rôle he was now acting. It was withering, but it was needed. The temptation of the devil on the mountain was here offered by Peter. It was Satan over again. See on Matt. 16:23.

34. *And he called unto him the multitude with his disciples* (*kai proskalesamenos ton ochlon sun tois mathētais autou*). Mark alone notes the unexpected presence of a crowd up here near Caesarea Philippi in heathen territory. In the presence of this crowd Jesus explains his philosophy of life and death which is in direct contrast with that offered by Peter and evidently shared by the disciples and the people. So Jesus gives this profound view of life and death to them all. *Deny himself* (*aparnēsasthō heauton*). Say no to himself, a difficult thing to do. Note reflexive along with the middle voice. Ingressive first aorist imperative. See on Matt. 16:24 about taking up the Cross. The shadow of Christ's Cross was already on him (Mark 8:31) and one faces everyone.

35. *And the gospel's sake* (*kai tou euaggeliou*). In Mark alone. See on Matt. 16:25f. for this paradox. Two senses of "life" and "save." For the last "save" (*sōsei*) Matt. 16:25 has "find" (*heurēsei*). See on Matt. 16:26 for "gain," "profit," and "exchange."

38. *For whosoever shall be ashamed of me and my words (hos gar ean epaischunthēi me kai tous emous logous).* More exactly, *whosoever is ashamed* (first aorist passive subjunctive with indefinite relative and *ean = an.* See Robertson, *Grammar,* pp. 957–9. It is not a statement about the future conduct of one, but about his present attitude toward Jesus. The conduct of men toward Christ now determines Christ's conduct then (*epaischunthēsetai,* first future passive indicative). This passive verb is transitive and uses the accusative (*me, auton*). *In this adulterous and sinful generation (en tēi geneāi tautēi tēi moichalidi kai hamartōlōi).* Only in Mark. *When he cometh (hotan elthēi).* Aorist active subjunctive with reference to the future second coming of Christ with the glory of the Father with his holy angels (cf. Matt. 16:27). This is a clear prediction of the final eschatological coming of Christ. This verse could not be separated from Mark 9:1 as the chapter division does. These two verses in Mark 8:38 and 9:1 form one paragraph and should go together.

CHAPTER IX

1. *Till they see the kingdom of God come with power* (*heōs an idōsin tēn basileian tou theou elēluthuian en dunamei*). In 8:38 Jesus clearly is speaking of the second coming. To what is he referring in 9:1? One is reminded of Mark 13:32 = Matt. 24:36 where Jesus expressly denies that anyone save the Father himself (not even the Son) knows the day or the hour. Does he contradict that here? It may be observed that Luke has only "see the kingdom of God," while Matthew has "see the Son of man coming" (*erchomenon*, present participle, a process). Mark has "see the kingdom of God come" (*elēluthuian*, perfect active participle, already come) and adds "with power." Certainly the second coming did not take place while some of those standing there still lived. Did Jesus mean that? The very next incident in the Synoptic Gospels is the Transfiguration on Mount Hermon. Does not Jesus have that in mind here? The language will apply also to the coming of the Holy Spirit on the great Day of Pentecost. Some see in it a reference to the destruction of the temple. It is at least open to question whether the Master is speaking of the same event in Mark 8:38 and 9:1.

2. *By themselves* (*monous*). Alone. This word only in Mark. See on Matt. 17:1–8 for discussion of the Transfiguration. Luke 9:28 adds "to pray" as the motive of Jesus in taking Peter, James, and John into the high mountain.

3. *Glistering, exceeding white* (*stilbonta leuka lian*). Old words, all of them. Matt. 17:2 has *white as the light* (*leuka hōs to phōs*), Luke 9:29 "white and dazzling" (*leukos exastraptōn*) like lightning. *So as no fuller on earth can*

338

whiten them (*hoia gnapheus epi tēs gēs ou dunatai houtōs leukānai*). *Gnaphō* is an old word to card wool. Note *houtōs*, so, so white. Some manuscripts in Matthew add *hōs chiōn*, as snow. Probably the snow-capped summit of Hermon was visible on this very night. See on Matt. 17:2 for "transfigured."

4. *Elijah with Moses* (*Ēleias sun Mōusei*). Matthew and Luke have "Moses and Elijah." Both, as a matter of fact were prophets and both dealt with law. Both had mysterious deaths. The other order in Mark 9:5.

6. *For he wist not what to answer* (*ou gar ēidei ti apokrithēi*). Deliberative subjunctive retained in indirect question. But why did Peter say anything? Luke says that he spoke, "not knowing what he said," as an excuse for the inappropriateness of his remarks. Perhaps Peter felt embarrassed at having been asleep (Luke 9:32) and the feast of tabernacles or booths (*skēnai*) was near. See on Matt. 17:4. Peter and the others apparently had not heard the talk of Moses and Elijah with Jesus about his decease (*exodon*, exodus, departure) and little knew the special comfort that Jesus had found in this understanding of the great approaching tragedy concerning which Peter had shown absolute stupidity (Mark 8:32f.) so recently. See on Matt. 17:5 about the overshadowing and the voice.

8. *Suddenly looking round about* (*exapina periblepsamenoi*). Matt. 17:8 has it "lifting up their eyes." Mark is more graphic. The sudden glance around on the mountain side when the cloud with Moses and Elijah was gone. *Jesus only with themselves* (*meth' heautōn ei mē Iēsoun monon*). Mark shows their surprise at the situation. They were sore afraid (Matt. 17:6) before Jesus touched them.

9. *Save when* (*ei mē hotan*). Matthew has "until" (*heōs hou*). *Should have risen* (*anastēi*). Second aorist active subjunctive. More exactly, "should rise" (punctiliar aorist and futuristic, not with any idea of perfect tense).

Luke 9:36 merely says that they told no man any of these things. It was a high and holy secret experience that the chosen three had had for their future good and for the good of all.

10. *They kept the saying* (*ton logon ekratēsan*) to themselves as Jesus had directed, but *questioning among themselves* (*pros heautous sunzētountes*). Now they notice his allusion to rising from the dead which had escaped them before (Mark 8:31).

12. *Restoreth all things* (*apokatistanei panta*). This late double compound verb, usual form *apokathistēmi* in the papyri, is Christ's description of the Baptist as the promised Elijah and Forerunner of the Messiah. See on Matt. 17:10–13. The disciples had not till now understood that the Baptist fulfilled the prophecy in Mal. 3:5f. They had just seen Elijah on the mountain, but Jesus as Messiah preceded this coming of Elijah. But Jesus patiently enlightens his dull pupils as they argue about the exegesis of the scribes.

14. *And scribes questioning with them* (*kai grammateis sunzētountes pros autous*). Mark alone gives this item. He is much fuller on this incident (9:14–29) than either Matthew (17:14–20) or Luke (9:37–43). It was just like the professional scribes to take keen interest in the failure of the nine disciples to cure this poor boy. They gleefully nagged and quizzed them. Jesus and the three find them at it when they arrive in the plain.

15. *Were greatly amazed* (*exethambēthēsan*). First aorist passive ingressive aorist with perfective compound *ex-*. The sudden and opportune appearance of Jesus in the midst of the dispute when no one was looking for him turned all eyes to him. He would not fail, however the disciples might do so. The people were awed for the moment and then running began to welcome him (*protrechontes ēspazonto*). Present participle and imperfect middle indicative.

16. *What question ye with them?* (*Ti sunzēteite pros*

autous;). Jesus had noticed the embarrassment of the nine and at once takes hold of the situation.

17. *I brought unto thee my son (ēnegka ton huion mou pros se).* The father stepped out and gave the explanation of the excited dispute in direct and simple pathos.

18. *Wheresoever it taketh him (hopou ean auton katalabēi).* Seizes him down. Our word catalepsy is this same word. The word is used by Galen and Hippocrates for fits. The word is very common in the papyri in various senses as in the older Greek. Each of the verbs here in Mark is a graphic picture. *Dashes down (rēssei).* Also *rēgnumi, mi* form. Convulses, rends, tears asunder. Old and common word. *Foameth (aphrizei).* Here only in the N.T. Poetic and late word. *Grindeth (trizei).* Another *hapax legomenon* in the N.T. Old word for making a shrill cry or squeak. *Pineth away (xērainetai).* Old word for drying or withering as of grass in James. 1:11. *And they were not able (kai ouk ischusan).* They did not have the strength *(ischus)* to handle this case. See Matt. 17:16 = Luke 9:40 *(kai ouk edunēthēsan,* first aorist passive). It was a tragedy.

19. *Bring him unto me (pherete auton pros me).* The disciples had failed and their unbelief had led to this fiasco. Even the disciples were like and part of the *faithless (apistos,* unbelieving) generation in which they lived. The word *faithless* does not here mean treacherous as it does with us. But Jesus is not afraid to undertake this case. We can always come to Jesus when others fail us.

20. *Tare him grievously (sunesparaxen auton).* Luke 9:42 has both *errēxen* (dashed down, like Mark 9:18, *rēssei*) and *sunesparaxen* (convulsed). This compound with *sun-* (together with), strengthens the force of the verb as in *sunpnigō* (Mark 4:7) and *suntēreō* (6:20). The only other instance of this compound verb known is in Maximus Tyrius (second century B.C.). *Wallowed (ekulieto).* Imperfect passive, was rolled. A pitiful sight. Late form of the old *kulindō.*

22. *But if thou canst* (*all 'ei ti dunēi*). Jesus had asked (verse 21) the history of the case like a modern physician. The father gave it and added further pathetic details about the fire and the water. The failure of the disciples had not wholly destroyed his faith in the power of Jesus, though the conditional form (first class, assuming it to be true) does suggest doubt whether the boy can be cured at all. It was a chronic and desperate case of epilepsy with the demon possession added. *Help us* (*boethēson hemin*). Ingressive aorist imperative. Do it now. With touching tenderness he makes the boy's case his own as the Syrophoenician woman had said, "Have mercy on me" (Matt. 15:21). The leper had said: "If thou wilt" (Mark 1:40). This father says: "If thou canst."

23. *If thou canst* (*to ei dunēi*). The Greek has a neat idiom not preserved in the English translation. The article takes up the very words of the man and puts the clause in the accusative case of general reference. "As to the 'if thou canst,' all things can (*dunata*) to the one who believes." The word for "possible" is *dunata*, the same root as *dunēi* (canst). This quick turn challenges the father's faith. On this use of the Greek article see Robertson, *Grammar*, p. 766.

24. *Cried out* (*kraxas*). Loud outcry and at once (*euthus*). The later manuscripts have "with tears" (*meta dakruōn*), not in the older documents. *I believe; help my unbelief* (*Pisteuō: boēthei tēi apistiāi*). An exact description of his mental and spiritual state. He still had faith, but craved more. Note present imperative here (continuous help) *boēthei*, while aorist imperative (instant help) *boēthēson*, verse 22. The word comes from *boē*, a cry and *theō*, to run, to run at a cry for help, a vivid picture of this father's plight.

25. *A multitude came running together* (*episuntrechei ochlos*). A double compound here alone in the N.T. and not in the old Greek writers. *Epitrechō* occurs in the papyri, but not *episuntrechō*. The double compound vividly describes the

rapid gathering of the crowd to Jesus and the epileptic boy
to see the outcome. *Come out of him* (*exelthe ex autou*).
Jesus addresses the demon as a separate being from the
boy as he often does. This makes it difficult to believe that
Jesus was merely indulging popular belief in a superstition.
He evidently regards the demon as the cause in this case
of the boy's misfortune.

26. *Having torn much* (*sparaxas*). The uncompounded
verb used in verse 20. *Became as one dead* (*egeneto hōsei
nekros*). As if dead from the violence of the spasm. The
demon did him all possible harm in leaving him.

28. *Privately, saying* (*kat' idian hoti*). Indoors the nine
disciples seek an explanation for their colossal failure. They
had cast out demons and wrought cures before. The Re-
visers are here puzzled over Mark's use of *hoti* as an interrogative particle meaning *why* where Matt. 17:19 has
dia ti. Some of the manuscripts have *dia ti* here in Mark
9:28 as all do in Matt. 17:19. See also Mark 2:16 and 9:11.
It is probable that in these examples *hoti* really means *why*.
See Robertson, *Grammar*, p. 730. The use of *hos* as interrogative "is by no means rare in the late Greek" (Deissmann, *Light from the Ancient East*, p. 126).

29. *Save by prayer* (*ei mē en proseuchēi*). The addition
of "and of fasting" does not appear in the two best Greek
manuscripts (Aleph and B). It is clearly a late addition to
help explain the failure. But it is needless and also untrue.
Prayer is what the nine had failed to use. They were power-
less because they were prayerless. Their self-complacency
spelled defeat. Matt. 17:20 has "because of your little
faith" (*oligopistian*). That is true also. They had too much
faith in themselves, too little in Christ. "They had trusted
to the semi-magical power with which they thought themselves invested" (Swete). "Spirits of such malignity were
quick to discern the lack of moral power and would yield
to no other" (*ibid.*).

30. *He would not that any man should know it* (*ouk ēthelen hina tis gnoi*). Imperfect tense followed by ingressive aorist subjunctive (*gnoi = gnōi*, the usual form). He was not willing that any one should learn it. Back in Galilee Jesus was, but he was avoiding public work there now (cf. 7:24). He was no longer the hero of Galilee. He had left Caesarea Philippi for Galilee.

31. *For he taught* (*edidasken gar*). Imperfect tense, and the reason given for secrecy. He was renewing again definitely the prediction of his death in Jerusalem some six months ahead as he had done before (Mark 8:31 = Matt. 16:21 = Luke 9:22). Now as then Jesus foretells his resurrection "after three days" ("the third day," Matt. 17:23).

32. *But they understood not the saying* (*hoi de ēgnooun to rhēma*). An old word. Chiefly in Paul's Epistles in the N.T. Imperfect tense. They continued not to understand. They were agnostics on the subject of the death and resurrection even after the Transfiguration experience. As they came down from the mountain they were puzzled again over the Master's allusion to his resurrection (Mark 9:10). Matt. 17:23 notes that "they were exceeding sorry" to hear Jesus talk this way again, but Mark adds that they "were afraid to ask him" (*ephobounto auton eperōtēsai*). Continued to be afraid (imperfect tense), perhaps with a bitter memory of the term "Satan" hurled at Peter when he protested the other time when Jesus spoke of his death (Mark 8:33 = Matt. 16:23). Luke 9:45 explains that "it was concealed from them," probably partly by their own preconceived ideas and prejudices.

33. *In the house* (*en tēi oikiāi*). Probably Peter's house in Capernaum which was the home of Jesus when in the city. *What were ye reasoning in the way?* (*Ti en tēi hodōi dielogizesthe;*). Imperfect tense. They had been disputing (verse 34), not about the coming death of the Master, but about the relative rank of each of them in the political king-

dom which they were expecting him to establish. Jesus
had suspected the truth about them and they had apparently
kept it up in the house. See on Matt. 18:1 where the disciples are represented as bringing the dispute to Jesus while
here Jesus asks them about it. Probably they asked Jesus
first and then he pushed the matter further and deeper to
see if this had not been the occasion of the somewhat heated
discussion on the way in.

34. *But they held their peace* (*Hoi de esiōpōn*). Imperfect
tense. Put thus to them, they felt ashamed that the Master
had discovered their jealous rivalry. It was not a mere
abstract query, as they put it to Jesus, but it was a canker
in their hearts.

35. *He sat down and called the twelve* (*kathisas ephōnēsen
tous dōdeka*). Deliberate action of Jesus to handle this
delicate situation. Jesus gives them the rule of greatness:
"If any man would be first (*prōtos*) he shall be last (*eschatos*)
of all, and minister (*diakonos*) of all." This saying of
Christ, like many others, he repeated at other times (Mark
10:43f.; Matt. 23:8ff.; Luke 22:24f.). Matt. 18:2 says that
he called a little child, one there in the house, perhaps
Peter's child. Luke 9:47 notes that he "set him by his side."
Then Jesus *taking him in his arms* (*enagkalisamenos*, aorist
middle participle, late Greek word from *agkalē* as in Luke
2:28) spoke again to the disciples.

37. *One of such little children* (*hen tōn toioutōn paidiōn*).
Matt. 18:5 has "one such little child" and Luke 9:48
"this little child." It was an object lesson to the arrogant
conceit of the twelve apostles contending for primacy. They
did not learn this lesson for they will again wrangle over
primacy (Mark 10:33–45 =Matt. 20:20–28) and they will be
unable to comprehend easily what the attitude of Jesus
was toward children (Mark 10:13–16 =Matt. 19:13–15 =Luke
18:15–17). The child was used as a rebuke to the apostles.

38. *Because he followed not us* (*hoti ouk ēkolouthei hēmin*).

Note vivid imperfect tense again. John evidently thought to change the subject from the constraint and embarrassment caused by their dispute. So he told about a case of extra zeal on his part expecting praise from Jesus. Perhaps what Jesus had just said in verse 37 raised a doubt in John's mind as to the propriety of his excessive narrowness. One needs to know the difference between loyalty to Jesus and stickling over one's own narrow prejudices.

39. *Forbid him not* (*mē kōluete*). Stop hindering him (*mē* and the present imperative) as John had been doing.

40. *He that is not against us is with us* (*hos ouk estin kath' hēmōn huper hēmōn estin*). This profound saying throws a flood of light in every direction. The complement of this logion is that in Matt. 12:30: "He that is not with me is against me." Both are needed. Some people imagine that they are really for Christ who refuse to take a stand in the open with him and for him.

41. *Because ye are Christ's* (*hoti Christou este*). Predicate genitive, belong to Christ. See Rom. 8:9; I Cor. 1:12; II Cor. 10:7. That is the bond of universal brotherhood of the redeemed. It breaks over the lines of nation, race, class, sex, everything. No service is too small, even a cup of cold water, if done for Christ's sake. See on Matt. 18:6f. for discussion on stumbling-blocks for these little ones that believe on Jesus (Mark 9:42), a loving term of all believers, not just children.

43. *Into hell, into the unquenchable fire* (*eis tēn geennan, eis to pūr to asbeston*). Not Hades, but Gehenna. *Asbeston* is alpha privative and *sbestos* from *sbennumi* to quench. It occurs often in Homer. Our word asbestos is this very word. Matt. 18:8 has "into the eternal fire." The Valley of Hinnom had been desecrated by the sacrifice of children to Moloch so that as an accursed place it was used for the city garbage where worms gnawed and fires burned. It is thus a vivid picture of eternal punishment.

44 and 46. The oldest and best manuscripts do not give these two verses. They came in from the Western and Syrian (Byzantine) classes. They are a mere repetition of verse 48. Hence we lose the numbering 44 and 46 in our verses which are not genuine.

47. *With one eye* (*monophthalmon*). Literally one-eyed. See also Matt. 18:9. Vernacular *Koinê* and condemned by the Atticists. See Matt. 18:8f. Mark has here "kingdom of God" where Matt. 18:9 has "life."

48. *Their worm* (*ho skōlēx autōn*). "The worm, i.e. that preys upon the inhabitants of this dread realm" (Gould). Two bold figures of Gehenna combined (the gnawing worm, the burning flame). No figures of Gehenna can equal the dread reality which is here described. See Isa. 66:24.

50. *Have salt in yourselves* (*echete en heautois hala*). Jesus had once called them the salt of the earth (Matt. 5:13) and had warned them against losing the saltness of the salt. If it is *analon*, nothing can *season* (*artuō*) it and it is of no use to season anything else. It is like an exploded shell, a burnt-out crater, a spent force. This is a warning for all Christians.

CHAPTER X

1. *Into the border of Judea and beyond Jordan (eis ta horia tēs Ioudaias kai peran tou Iordanou).* See on Matt. 19:1 for discussion of this curious expression. Matthew adds "from Galilee" and Luke 17:11 says that Jesus "was passing through the midst of Samaria and Galilee" after leaving Ephraim (John 11:54). A great deal has intervened between the events at the close of Mark 9 and those in the beginning of Mark 10. For these events see Matt. 18, John 7 to 11, Luke 9:57 to 18:14 (one-third of Luke's Gospel comes in here). It was a little over six months to the end at the close of Mark 9. It is just a few weeks now in Mark 10. Jesus has begun his last journey to Jerusalem going north through Samaria, Galilee, across the Jordan into Perea, and back into Judea near Jericho to go up with the passover pilgrims from Galilee. *Multitudes (ochloi).* Caravans and caravans journeying to Jerusalem. Many of them are followers of Jesus from Galilee or at least kindly disposed towards him. They go together *(sunporeuontai)* with Jesus. Note dramatic historical present. *As he was wont (hōs eiōthei).* Second past perfect used like an imperfect from *eiōtha,* second perfect active. Jesus *was teaching (edidasken,* imperfect, no longer present tense) this moving caravan.

2. *Tempting him (peirazontes).* As soon as Jesus appears in Galilee the Pharisees attack him again (cf. 7:5; 8:11). Gould thinks that this is a test, not a temptation. The word means either (see on Matt. 4:1), but their motive was evil. They had once involved the Baptist with Herod Antipas and Herodias on this subject. They may have some such hopes about Jesus, or their purpose may have been to see if Jesus will be stricter than Moses taught. They knew

that he had already spoken in Galilee on the subject (Matt.
5:31f.).

3. *What did Moses command you?* (*Ti humin eneteilato
Mōusēs;*). Jesus at once brought up the issue concerning
the teaching of Moses (Deut. 24:1). But Jesus goes back
beyond this concession here allowed by Moses to the ideal
state commanded in Gen. 1:27.

4. *To write a bill of divorcement and to put her away* (*biblion
apostasiou grapsai kai apolusai*). The word for "bill"
(*biblion*) is a diminutive and means "little book," like the
Latin *libellus*, from which comes our word *libel* (Vincent).
Wycliff has it here "a libel of forsaking." This same point
the Pharisees raise in Matt. 19:7, showing probably that
they held to the liberal view of Hillel, easy divorce for almost
any cause. That was the popular view as now. See on Matt.
19:7 for this and for discussion of "for your hardness of
heart" (*sklērokardia*). Jesus expounds the purpose of marriage (Gen. 2:24) and takes the stricter view of divorce, that
of the school of Shammai. See on Matt. 19:1–12 for discussion. Mark 10:10 notes that the disciples asked Jesus
about this problem "in the house" after they had gone away
from the crowd.

11. Mark does not give the exception stated in Matt.
19:9 "except for fornication" which see for discussion,
though the point is really involved in what Mark does record.
Mere formal divorce does not annul actual marriage con-
summated by the physical union. Breaking that bond does
annul it.

12. *If she herself shall put away her husband and marry
another* (*ean autē apolusasa ton andra autēs gamēsei*). Condition of the third class (undetermined, but with prospect
of determination). Greek and Roman law allowed the divorce of the husband by the wife though not provided for
in Jewish law. But the thing was sometimes done as in the
case of Herodias and her husband before she married Herod

Antipas. So also Salome, Herod's sister, divorced her husband. Both Bruce and Gould think that Mark added this item to the words of Jesus for the benefit of the Gentile environment of this Roman Gospel. But surely Jesus knew that the thing was done in the Roman world and hence prohibited marrying such a "grass widow."

13. *They brought* (*prosepheron*). Imperfect active tense, implying repetition. So also Luke 18:15, though Matt. 19:13 has the constative aorist passive (*prosēnechthēsan*). "This incident follows with singular fitness after the Lord's assertion of the sanctity of married life" (Swete). These children (*paidia*, Mark and Matthew; *brephē* in Luke) were of various ages. They were brought to Jesus for his blessing and prayers (Matthew). The mothers had reverence for Jesus and wanted him to touch (*hapsētai*) them. There was, of course, no question of baptism or salvation involved, but a most natural thing to do.

14. *He was moved with indignation* (*ēganaktēsen*). In Mark alone. The word is ingressive aorist, became indignant, and is a strong word of deep emotion (from *agan* and *achthomai*, to feel pain). Already in Matt. 21:15; 26:8. Old and common word. *Suffer the little children to come unto me* (*aphete ta paidia erchesthai pros me*). Mark has the infinitive *erchesthai* (come) not in Matthew, but in Luke. Surely it ought to be a joy to parents to bring their children to Jesus, certainly to allow them to come, but to hinder their coming is a crime. There are parents who will have to give answer to God for keeping their children away from Jesus.

15. *As a little child* (*hōs paidion*). How does a little child receive the kingdom of God? The little child learns to obey its parents simply and uncomplainingly. There are some new psychologists who argue against teaching obedience to children. The results have not been inspiring. Jesus here presents the little child with trusting and simple and loving obedience as the model for adults in coming into the king-

dom. Jesus does not here say that children are in the kingdom of God because they are children.

16. *He took them in his arms* (*enagkalisamenos*). A distinct rebuke to the protest of the over-particular disciples. This word already in Mark 9:36. In Luke 2:28 we have the full idiom, to receive into the arms (*eis tās agkalas dechesthai*). So with tender fondling Jesus repeatedly blessed (*kateulogei*, imperfect), laying his hands upon each of them (*titheis*, present participle). It was a great moment for each mother and child.

17. *Ran* (*prosdramōn*). Jesus had left the house (10:10) and was proceeding with the caravan on the way (*eis hodon*) when this ruler eagerly ran and kneeled (*gonupetēsas*) and was asking (*epērōtā*, imperfect) Jesus about his problem. Both these details alone in Mark.

18. *Why callest thou me good?* (*Ti me legeis agathon;*). So Luke 18:19. Matt. 19:17 has it: "Why asketh thou concerning that which is good?" The young ruler was probably sincere and not using mere fulsome compliment, but Jesus challenges him to define his attitude towards him as was proper. Did he mean "good" (*agathos*) in the absolute sense as applied to God? The language is not a disclaiming of deity on the part of Jesus. *That I may inherit* (*hina klēronomēsō*). Matt. 16 has (*schō*), that I may "get."

20. *All these* (*tauta panta*). Literally, *these all* (of them).

21. *Looking upon him loved him* (*emblepsas autōi ēgapēsen*). Mark alone mentions this glance of affection, ingressive aorist participle and verb. Jesus fell in love with this charming youth. *One thing thou lackest* (*Hen se husterei*). Luke 18:22 has it: "One thing thou lackest yet" (*Eti hen soi leipei*). Possibly two translations of the same Aramaic phrase. Matt. 19:20 represents the youth as asking "What lack I yet?" (*Ti eti husterō;*). The answer of Jesus meets that inquiry after more than mere outward obedience to laws and regulations. The verb *husterō* is from the adjec-

tive *husteros* (behind) and means to be too late, to come short, to fail of, to lack. It is used either with the accusative, as here, or with the ablative as in II Cor. 11:5, or the dative as in Textus Receptus here, *soi*.

22. *But his countenance fell* (*ho de stugnasas*). In the LXX and Polybius once and in Matt. 16:3 (passage bracketed by Westcott and Hort). The verb is from *stugnos*, sombre, gloomy, like a lowering cloud. See on Matt. 19:22 for discussion of "sorrowful" (*lupoumenos*).

23. *Looked round about* (*periblepsamenos*). Another picture of the looks of Jesus and in Mark alone as in 3:5, 34. "To see what impression the incident had made on the Twelve" (Bruce). "When the man was gone the Lord's eye swept round the circle of the Twelve, as he drew for them the lesson of the incident" (Swete). *How hardly* (*Pōs duskolōs*). So Luke 18:24. Matt. 19:23 has it: "With difficulty (*duskolōs*) shall a rich man." See on Matthew for this word.

24. *Were amazed* (*ethambounto*). Imperfect passive. A look of blank astonishment was on their faces at this statement of Jesus. They in common with other Jews regarded wealth as a token of God's special favour. *Children* (*tekna*). Here alone to the Twelve and this tender note is due to their growing perplexity. *For them that trust in riches* (*tous pepoithotas epi tois chrēmasin*). These words do not occur in Aleph B Delta Memphitic and one Old Latin manuscript. Westcott and Hort omit them from their text as an evident addition to explain the difficult words of Jesus.

25. *Needle's eye* (*trumaliās rhaphidos*). See on Matt. 19:24 for discussion. Luke uses the surgical needle, *belonēs*. Matthew has the word *rhaphis* like Mark from *rhaptō*, to sew, and it appears in the papyri. Both Matthew and Luke employ *trēmatos* for eye, a perforation or hole from *titraō*, to bore. Mark's word *trumalias* is from *truō*, to wear away, to perforate. In the LXX and Plutarch.

26. *Then who* (*kai tis*). Matt. 19:25 has *Tis oun*. Evidently *kai* has here an inferential sense like *oun*.

27. *Looking on them* (*emblepsas autois*). So in Matt. 19:26. Their amazement increased (26). *But not with God* (*all' ou para theōi*). Locative case with *para* (beside). The impossible by the side of men (*para anthrōpois*) becomes possible by the side of God. That is the whole point and brushes to one side all petty theories of a gate called needle's eye, etc.

28. *Peter began to say* (*ērxato legein ho Petros*). It was hard for Peter to hold in till now. Matt. 19:27 says that "Peter answered" as if the remark was addressed to him in particular. At any rate Peter reminds Jesus of what they had left to follow him, four of them that day by the sea (Mark 1:20 = Matt. 4:22 = Luke 5:11). It was to claim obedience to this high ideal on their part in contrast with the conduct of the rich young ruler.

30. *With persecutions* (*meta diōgmōn*). This extra touch is in Mark alone. There is a reminiscence of some of "the apocalyptic of the familiar descriptions of the blessings of the Messianic kingdom. But Jesus uses such language from the religious idiom of this time only to idealize it" (Gould). The apostles were soon to see the realization of this foreshadowing of persecution. Vincent notes that Jesus omits "a hundred wives" in this list, showing that Julian the Apostate's sneer on that score was without foundation.

31. See on Matt. 19:30 for the use of the paradox about *first* and *last*, probably a rebuke here to Peter's boast.

32. *And they were amazed* (*kai ethambounto*). Imperfect tense describing the feelings of the disciples as Jesus was walking on in front of them (*ēn proagōn autous*, periphrastic imperfect active), an unusual circumstance in itself that seemed to bode no good as they went on through Perea towards Jerusalem. In fact, *they that followed were afraid* (*hoi de akolouthountes ephobounto*) as they looked at Jesus walking

ahead in solitude. The idiom (*hoi de*) may not mean that all the disciples were afraid, but only some of them. "The Lord walked in advance of the Twelve with a solemnity and a determination which foreboded danger" (Swete). Cf. Luke 9:5. They began to fear coming disaster as they neared Jerusalem. They read correctly the face of Jesus. *And he took again the twelve* (*kai paralabōn tous dōdeka*). Matthew has "apart" from the crowds and that is what Mark also means. Note *paralabōn*, taking to his side. *And began to tell them the things that were to happen to him* (*ērxato autois legein ta mellonta autōi sumbainein*). He had done it before three times already (Mark 8:31; 9:13; 9:31). So Jesus tries once more. They had failed utterly heretofore. How is it now? Luke adds (18:34): "They understood none of these things." But Mark and Matthew show how the minds of two of the disciples were wholly occupied with plans of their own selfish ambition while Jesus was giving details of his approaching death and resurrection.

35. *There come near unto him James and John* (*kai prosporeuontai Iakōbos kai Iōanēs*). Dramatic present tense. Matthew has *tote*, then, showing that the request of the two brothers with their mother (Matt. 20:20) comes immediately after the talk about Christ's death. *We would* (*thelomen*). We wish, we want, bluntly told. *She came worshipping* (*proskunousa*) Matthew says. The mother spoke for the sons. But they try to commit Jesus to their desires before they tell what they are, just like spoiled children.

37. *In thy glory* (*en tēi doxēi*). Matt. 20:21 has "in thy kingdom." See on Matt. 20:20 for the literal interpretation of Matt. 19:28. They are looking for a grand Jewish world empire with apocalyptic features in the eschatological culmination of the Messiah's kingdom. That dream brushed aside all the talk of Jesus about his death and resurrection as mere pessimism.

38. *Or be baptized with the baptism that I am baptized with*

(*ē to baptisma ho egō baptizomai baptisthēnai*). Cognate accusative with both passive verbs. Matt. 20:22 has only the cup, but Mark has both the cup and the baptism, both referring to death. Jesus in the Garden of Gethsemane will refer to his death again as "the cup" (Mark 14:36 = Matt. 26:39 = Luke 22:42). He had already used baptism as a figure for his death (Luke 12:50). Paul will use it several times (I Cor. 15:29; Rom. 6:3–6; Col. 2:12).

39–45. See on Matt. 20:23 to 28 for discussion on these memorable verses identical in both Matthew and Mark. In particular in verse 45 note the language of Jesus concerning his death as "a ransom for many" (*lutron anti pollōn*), words of the Master that were not understood by the apostles when spoken by Jesus and which have been preserved for us by Peter through Mark. Some today seek to empty these words of all real meaning as if Jesus could not have or hold such a conception concerning his death for sinners.

46. *From Jericho* (*apo Iereichō*). See on Matt. 20:29 for discussion of this phrase and Luke's (18:35) "nigh unto Jericho" and the two Jerichos, the old and the new Roman (Luke). The new Jericho was "about five miles W. of the Jordan and fifteen E. of Jerusalem, near the mouth of the *Wady Kelt*, and more than a mile south of the site of the ancient town" (Swete). *Great multitude* (*ochlou hikanou*). Considerable, more than sufficient. Often in Luke and the papyri in this sense. See Matt. 3:11 for the other sense of fit for *hikanos*. *Bartimaeus* (*Bartimaios*). Aramaic name like Bartholomew, *bar* meaning son like Hebrew *bēn*. So Mark explains the name meaning "the son of Timaeus" (*ho huios Timaiou*). Mark alone gives his name while Matt. 20:30 mentions two which see for discussion. *Blind beggar* (*tuphlos prosaitēs*), "begging" (*epaitōn*) Luke has it (18:35). All three Gospels picture him as *sitting by the roadside* (*ekathēto para tēn hodon*). It was a common sight. Bartimaeus had his regular place. Vincent quotes Thomson concerning

Ramleh: "I once walked the streets counting all that were either blind or had defective eyes, and it amounted to about one-half the male population. The women I could not count, for they are rigidly veiled" (*The Land and the Book*). The dust, the glare of the sun, the unsanitary habits of the people spread contagious eye-diseases.

48. *Rebuked him* (*epetimōn autōi*). Imperfect tense. Kept rebuking repeatedly. So Luke 18:39. Aorist tense in Matt. 20:31. *Should hold his peace* (*siōpēsēi*). Ingressive aorist subjunctive, become silent. *The more a great deal* (*pollōi mȃllon*). So Luke 18:39. Only *meizon* in Matt. 20:31.

49. *Stood still* (*stas*). Second aorist active ingressive participle. So Matt. 20:32. Luke 18:40 has *statheis*, aorist passive participle. *He calleth thee* (*phōnei se*). That was joyful news to Bartimaeus. Vivid dramatic presents here in Mark.

50. *Casting away his garment* (*apobalōn to himation autou*). Second aorist active participle. Outer robe in his haste. *Sprang up* (*anapēdēsas*). Leaping up, vivid details again in Mark.

51. *That I should do* (*poiēsō*). Neat Greek idiom with aorist subjunctive without *hina* after *theleis*. For this asyndeton (or parataxis) see Robertson, *Grammar*, p. 430. *Rabboni* (*Rabbounei*). The Aramaic word translated Lord (*Kurie*) in Matt. 20:33 and Luke 18:41. This very form occurs again in John 20:16. *That I may receive my sight* (*hina anablepsō*). To recover sight (*ana-*), see again. Apparently he had once been able to see. Here *hina* is used though *thelō* is not (cf. 10:35). The Messiah was expected to give sight to the blind (Isa. 61:1; Luke 4:18; 7:22).

52. *Followed* (*ēkolouthei*). Imperfect tense picturing joyful Bartimaeus as he followed the caravan of Jesus into the new Jericho. *Made thee whole* (*sesōken*). Perfect active indicative. The word commonly means *save* and that may be the idea here.

CHAPTER XI

1. *Unto Bethphage and Bethany (eis Bēthphagē kai Bēthanian).* Both together as in Luke 19:29, though Matt. 21:1 mentions only Bethphage. See discussion in Matthew for this and the Mount of Olives.

2. *As ye enter (eisporeuomenoi).* So also Luke 19:30. Present middle participle. *Colt (pōlon).* So Luke 19:30. Matt. 21:2 speaks of the ass *(onon)* also. *Whereon no one ever yet sat (eph' hon oudeis anthrōpōn ekathisen).* So Luke 19:30.

3. *The Lord (ho Kurios).* So Matt. and Luke. See on Matt. 21:3 for discussion of this word applied to Jesus by himself. *He will send him back (apostellei).* Present indicative in futuristic sense. Matt. 21:3 has the future *apostelei.*

4. *A colt tied at the door without in the open street (pōlon dedemenon pros thuran exō epi tou amphodou).* A carefully drawn picture. The colt was outside the house in the street, but fastened (bound, perfect passive participle) to the door. "The better class of houses were built about an open court, from which a passage way under the house led to the street outside. It was at this outside opening to the street that the colt was tied" (Gould). The word *amphodos* (from *amphō*, both, and *hodos*, road) is difficult. It apparently means road around a thing, a crooked street as most of them were (cf. Straight Street in Acts 9:11). It occurs only here in the N.T. besides D in Acts 19:28. It is very common in the papyri for *vicus* or "quarter." *And they loose him (kai luousin auton).* Dramatic present tense. Perhaps Peter was one of those sent this time as he was later (Luke 22:8). If so, that explains Mark's vivid details here.

5. *Certain of those that stood there (tines tōn ekei hestēko-*

tōn). Perfect active participle, genitive plural. Bystanders. Luke 19:33 terms them "the owners thereof" (*hoi kurioi autou*). The lords or masters of the colt. They make a natural protest.

7. *They bring the colt unto Jesus* (*pherousin ton pōlon pros ton Iēsoun*). Vivid historical present. The owners acquiesced as Jesus had predicted. Evidently friends of Jesus.

8. *Branches* (*stibadas*). A litter of leaves and rushes from the fields. Textus Receptus spells this word *stoibadas*. Matt. 21:8 has *kladous*, from *klaō*, to break, branches broken or cut from trees. John 12:13 uses the branches of the palm trees (*ta baia tōn phoinikōn*), "the feathery fronds forming the tufted crown of the tree" (Vincent). That is to say, some of the crowd did one of these things, some another. See on Matt. 21:4–9 for discussion of other details. The deliberate conduct of Jesus on this occasion could have but one meaning. It was the public proclamation of himself as the Messiah, now at last for his "hour" has come. The excited crowds in front (*hoi proagontes*) and behind (*hoi akolouthountes*) fully realize the significance of it all. Hence their unrestrained enthusiasm. They expect Jesus, of course, now to set up his rule in opposition to that of Caesar, to drive Rome out of Palestine, to conquer the world for the Jews.

11. *When he had looked round about upon all things* (*periblepsamenos panta*). Another Markan detail in this aorist middle participle. Mark does not give what Luke 19:39–55 has nor what Matt. 21:10–17 does. But it is all implied in this swift glance at the temple before he went out to Bethany with the Twelve, *it being now eventide* (*opse ēdē ousēs tēs hōras*). Genitive absolute, the hour being already late. What a day it had been! What did the apostles think now?

12. *On the morrow* (*tēi epaurion*). Matt. 21:18 has "early" (*prōi*), often of the fourth watch before six A.M. This was

Monday morning. The Triumphal Entry had taken place
on our Sunday, the first day of the week.

13. *If haply he might find anything thereon* (*ei ara ti
heurēsei en autēi*). This use of *ei* and the future indicative
for purpose (to see if, a sort of indirect question) as in Acts
8:22; 17:27. Jesus was hungry as if he had had no food on the
night before after the excitement and strain of the Triumphal
Entry. The early figs in Palestine do not get ripe before
May or June, the later crop in August. It was not the
season of figs, Mark notes. But this precocious tree in a
sheltered spot had put out leaves as a sign of fruit. It had
promise without performance.

14. *No man eat fruit from thee henceforward forever* (*Mēketi
eis ton aiōna ek sou mēdeis karpon phagoi*). The verb *phagoi*
is in the second aorist active optative. It is a wish for the
future that in its negative form constitutes a curse upon the
tree. Matt. 21:19 has the aorist subjunctive with double
negative *ou mēketi genētai*, a very strong negative prediction
that amounts to a prohibition. See on Matthew. Jesus
probably spoke in the Aramaic on this occasion. *And his
disciples* heard it (*kai ēkouon hoi mathētai autou*). Imperfect
tense, "were listening to it," and evidently in amazement,
for, after all, it was not the fault of the poor fig tree that it
had put out leaves. One often sees peach blossoms nipped by
the frost when they are too precocious in the changeable
weather. But Jesus offered no explanation at this time.

15. *Began to cast out* (*ērxato ekballein*). Mark is fond of
"began." See on Matt. 21:12f. for discussion of this second
cleansing of the temple in its bearing on that in John 2:14f.

Money-changers (*kollubistōn*). This same late word in
Matt. 21:12 which see for discussion. It occurs in papyri.

16. *Through the temple* (*dia tou hierou*). The temple
authorities had prohibited using the outer court of the
temple through the Precinct as a sort of short cut or by-path
from the city to the Mount of Olives. But the rule was

neglected and all sorts of irreverent conduct was going on that stirred the spirit of Jesus. This item is given only in Mark. Note the use of *hina* after *ēphie* (imperfect tense) instead of the infinitive (the usual construction).

17. *For all the nations* (*pāsin tois ethnesin*). Mark alone has this phrase from Isa. 56:7; Jer. 7:11. The people as well as the temple authorities were guilty of graft, extortion, and desecration of the house of prayer. Jesus assumes and exercises Messianic authority and dares to smite this political and financial abuse. Some people deny the right of the preacher to denounce such abuses in business and politics even when they invade the realm of morals and religion. But Jesus did not hesitate.

18. *Sought how they might destroy him* (*ezētoun pōs auton apolesōsin*). Imperfect indicative, a continuous attitude and endeavour. Note deliberative subjunctive with *pōs* retained in indirect question. Here both Sadducees (chief priests) and Pharisees (scribes) combine in their resentment against the claims of Jesus and in the determination to kill him. Long ago the Pharisees and the Herodians had plotted for his death (Mark 3:6). Now in Jerusalem the climax has come right in the temple. *For they feared him* (*ephobounto gar*). Imperfect middle indicative. Hence in wrath they planned his death and yet they had to be cautious. The Triumphal Entry had shown his power with the people. And now right in the temple itself "all the multitude was astonished at his teaching" (*pās ho ochlos exeplēsseto epi tēi didachēi autou*). Imperfect passive. The people looked on Jesus as a hero, as the Messiah. This verse aptly describes the crisis that has now come between Christ and the Sanhedrin.

19. *Every evening* (*hotan opse egeneto*). Literally, *whenever evening came on* or more exactly *whenever it became late*. The use of *hotan* (*hote an*) with the aorist indicative is like *hopou an* with the imperfect indicative (*eiseporeueto*) and

hosoi an with the aorist indicative (*hēpsanto*) in Mark 6:56.
The use of *an* makes the clause more indefinite and general,
as here, unless it renders it more definite, a curious result, but
true. Luke 21:37 has the accusative of extent of time, "the
days," "the nights." The imperfect tense he (or they)
would go (*exeporeueto, exeporeuonto*) out of the city suggests
"whenever" as the meaning here.

20. *As they passed by in the morning* (*paraporeuomenoi
prōi*). Literally, passing by in the morning. The next
morning. They went back by the lower road up the Mount
of Olives and came down each morning by the steep and
more direct way. Hence they saw it. Matt. 21:20 does
not separate the two mornings as Mark does. *From the
roots* (*ek rizōn*). Mark alone gives this detail with *exērammenēn* perfect passive predicate participle from *xērainō*.

21. *Peter calling to remembrance* (*anamnēstheis ho Petros*).
First aorist participle, being reminded. Only in Mark and
due to Peter's story. For his quick memory see also 14:72.
Which thou cursedst (*hēn katērasō*). First aorist middle indicative second person singular from *kataraomai*. It almost
sounds as if Peter blamed Jesus for what he had done to the
fig tree.

22. *Have faith in God* (*echete pistin theou*). Objective
genitive *theou* as in Gal. 2:26; Rom. 3:22, 26. That was the
lesson for the disciples from the curse on the fig tree so
promptly fulfilled. See this point explained by Jesus in
Matt. 21:21 which see for "this mountain" also.

23. *Shall not doubt in his heart* (*mē diakrithēi en tēi kardiāi
autou*). First aorist passive subjunctive with *hos an*. The
verb means a divided judgment (*dia* from *duo*, two, and
krinō, to judge). Wavering doubt. Not a single act of
doubt (*diakrithēi*), but continued faith (*pisteuēi*). *Cometh
to pass* (*ginetai*). Futuristic present middle indicative.

24. *Believe that ye have received them* (*pisteuete hoti elabete*).
That is the test of faith, the kind that sees the fulfilment

before it happens. *Elabete* is second aorist active indicative, antecedent in time to *pisteuete*, unless it be considered the timeless aorist when it is simultaneous with it. For this aorist of immediate consequence see John 15:6.

25. *Whensoever ye stand* (*hotan stēkete*). Late form of present indicative *stēkō*, from perfect stem *hestēka*. In LXX. Note use of *hotan* as in 11:19. Jesus does not mean by the use of "stand" here to teach that this is the only proper attitude in prayer. *That your Father also may forgive you* (*hina kai ho patēr aphēi humin*). Evidently God's willingness to forgive is limited by our willingness to forgive others. This is a solemn thought for all who pray. Recall the words of Jesus in Matt. 6:12, 14f.

26. This verse is omitted by Westcott and Hort. The Revised Version puts it in a footnote.

27. *The chief priests, and the scribes, and the elders* (*hoi archiereis kai hoi grammateis kai hoi presbuteroi*). Note the article with each separate group as in Luke 20:1 and Matt. 21:23. These three classes were in the Sanhedrin. Clearly a large committee of the Sanhedrin including both Sadducees and Pharisees here confront Jesus in a formal attack upon his authority for cleansing the temple and teaching in it.

28. *By what authority* (*en poiāi exousiāi*). This question in all three Gospels was a perfectly legitimate one. See on Matt. 21:23-27 for discussion. Note present subjunctive here (*hina tauta poiēis*), that you keep on doing these things.

30. *Answer me* (*apokrithēte moi*). This sharp demand for a reply is only in Mark. See also verse 29. Jesus has a right to take this turn because of John's direct relation to himself. It was not a dodge, but a home thrust that cleared the air and defined their attitude both to John and Jesus. They rejected John as they now reject Jesus.

31. *If we say* (*ean eipōmen*). Third-class condition with aorist active subjunctive. The alternatives are sharply presented in their secret conclave. They see the two horns

of the dilemma clearly and poignantly. They know only too well what Jesus will say in reply. They wish to break Christ's power with the multitude, but a false step now will turn the laugh on them. They see it.

32. *But should we say* (*alla eipōmen*). Deliberative subjunctive with aorist active subjunctive again. It is possible to supply *ean* from verse 31 and treat it as a condition as there. So Matt. 21:26 and Luke 20:6. But in Mark the structure continues rugged after "from men" with anacoluthon or even aposiopesis—"they feared the people" Mark adds. Matthew has it: "We fear the multitude." Luke puts it: "all the people will stone us." All three Gospels state the popular view of John as a prophet. Mark's "verily" is *ontōs* really, actually. They feared John though dead as much as Herod Antipas did. His martyrdom had deepened his power over the people and disrespect towards his memory now might raise a storm (Swete).

33. *We know not* (*ouk oidamen*). It was for the purpose of getting out of the trap into which they had fallen by challenging the authority of Jesus. Their self-imposed ignorance, refusal to take a stand about the Baptist who was the Forerunner of Christ, absolved Jesus from a categorical reply. But he has no notion of letting them off at this point.

CHAPTER XII

1. *He began to speak unto them in parables* (*ērxato autois en parabolais lalein*). Mark's common idiom again. He does not mean that this was the beginning of Christ's use of parables (see 4:2), but simply that his teaching on this occasion took the parabolic turn. "The circumstances called forth the parabolic mood, that of one whose heart is chilled, and whose spirit is saddened by a sense of loneliness, and who, retiring within himself, by a process of reflection, frames for his thoughts forms which half conceal, half reveal them" (Bruce). Mark does not give the Parable of the Two Sons (Matt. 21:28-32) nor that of the Marriage Feast of the King's Son (Matt. 22:1-14). He gives here the Parable of the Wicked Husbandmen. Also in Matt. 21:33-46 and Luke 20:9-19. See discussion in Matthew. Matt. 21:33 calls the man "a householder" (*oikodespotēs*). *A pit for the winepress* (*hupolēnion*). Only here in the N.T. Common in the LXX and in late Greek. Matthew had *lēnon*, winepress. This is the vessel or trough under the winepress on the hillside to catch the juice when the grapes were trodden. The Romans called it *lacus* (lake) and Wycliff *dalf* (lake), like delved. See on Matthew for details just alike. *Husbandmen* (*geōrgois*). Workers in the ground, tillers of the soil (*ergon, gē*).

2. *At the season* (*tōi kairōi*). For fruits as in the end of the sentence. *A servant* (*doulon*). Bondslave. Matthew has plural. *That he might receive* (*hina labē*). Purpose clause with second aorist subjunctive. Matthew has infinitive *labein*, purpose also. *Wounded in the head* (*ekephaliōsan*). An old verb (*kephalaiō*), to bring under heads

364

(*kephalē*), to summarize. Then to hit on the head. Only here in the N.T.

5. *Beating some and killing some* (*hous men derontes, hous de apoktennuntes*). This distributive use of the demonstrative appears also in Matt. 21:35 in the singular (*hon men, hon de, hon de*). Originally *derō* in Homer meant to skin, flay, then to smite, to beat. *Apoktennuntes* is a *mi* form of the verb (*apoktennumi*) and means to kill off.

6. *A beloved son* (*huion agapēton*). Luke 20:13 has *ton huion ton agapēton*. Jesus evidently has in mind the language of the Father to him at his baptism (Mark 1:11 = Matt. 3:17 = Luke 3:22). *Last* (*eschaton*). Only in Mark. See on Matt. 21:37 for discussion of "reverence."

7. *Among themselves* (*pros heautous*). This phrase alone in Mark. Luke 20:14 has "with one another" (*pros allēlous*), reciprocal instead of reflexive, pronoun.

8. *Killed him and cast him forth* (*apekteinan auton, kai exebalon auton*). Matthew and Luke reverse the order, cast forth and killed.

10. *This scripture* (*tēn graphēn tautēn*). This passage of scripture (Luke 4:21; John 19:37; Acts 1:16). It is a quotation from Psa. 118:22f. See on Matt. 21:42 for discussion.

11. *This* (*hautē*). Feminine in LXX may refer to *kephalē* (head) or may be due to the Hebrew original *zōth* (this thing) which would be neuter *touto* in a Greek original, a translation Hebraism.

12. *Against them* (*pros autous*). So Luke. It was a straight shot, this parable of the Rejected Stone (12:10f.) and the longer one of the Wicked Husbandmen. There was no mistaking the application, for he had specifically explained the application (Matt. 21:43-45). The Sanhedrin were so angry that they actually started or sought to seize him, but fear of the populace now more enthusiastic for Jesus than ever held them back. They went off in disgust,

but they had to listen to the Parable of the King's Son before going (Matt. 22:1–14).

13. *That they might catch him in talk* (*hina auton agreusōsin logōi*). Ingressive aorist subjunctive. The verb is late from *agra* (a hunt or catching). It appears in the LXX and papyri. Here alone in the N.T. Luke 20:20 has the same idea, "that they may take hold of his speech" (*epilabōntai autou logon*) while Matt. 22:15 uses *pagideusōsin* (to snare or trap). See discussion in Matthew. We have seen the scribes and Pharisees trying to do this very thing before (Luke 11:33f.). Mark and Matthew note here the combination of Pharisees and Herodians as Mark did in 3:6. Matthew speaks of "disciples" or pupils of the Pharisees while Luke calls them "spies" (*enkathetous*).

14. *Shall we give or shall we not give?* (*dōmen ē mē dōmen;*). Mark alone repeats the question in this sharp form. The deliberative subjunctive, aorist tense active voice. For the discussion of the palaver and flattery of this group of theological students see on Matt. 22:16–22.

15. *Knowing their hypocrisy* (*eidōs autōn tēn hupocrisin*). Matt. 22:18 has "perceived their wickedness" (*gnous tēn ponērian autōn*) while Luke 20:23 says, "perceived their craftiness" (*katanoēsas autōn tēn panourgian*). Each of these words throws a flash-light on the spirit and attitude of these young men. They were sly, shrewd, slick, but they did not deceive Jesus with their pious palaver. See on Matthew for further details.

17. *Marvelled greatly at him* (*exethaumazon ep' autōi*). Imperfect tense with perfective use of the preposition *ex*. Both Matthew and Luke use the ingressive aorist. Luke adds that they "held their peace" (*esigēsan*) while Matthew notes that they "went their way" (*apēlthan*), went off or away.

18. *There come unto him Sadducees* (*erchontai Saddoukaioi pros auton*). Dramatic present. The Pharisees and Herodi-

ans had had their turn after the formal committee of the Sanhedrin had been so completely routed. It was inevitable that they should feel called upon to show their intellectual superiority to these raw Pharisaic and Herodian theologians. See on Matt. 22:23–33 for discussion of details. It was a good time to air their disbelief in the resurrection at the expense of the Pharisees and to score against Jesus where the Sanhedrin and then the Pharisees and Herodians had failed so ignominiously.

19. *Moses wrote* (*Mōusēs egrapsen*). So Luke 20:28 (Gen. 38:8; Deut. 25:5f.). Matthew has "said" (*eipen*).

20. *Took a wife* (*elaben gunaika*). So Luke 20:29. Matthew has "married" (*gēmas*).

22. *Last of all* (*eschaton pantōn*). Adverbial use of *eschaton*.

23. *To wife* (*gunaika*). Predicate accusative in apposition with "her" (*autēn*). So Luke, but Matthew merely has "had her" (*eschon autēn*), constative aorist indicative active.

24. *Is it not for this cause that ye err?* (*Ou dia touto planāsthe;*). Mark puts it as a question with *ou* expecting the affirmative answer. Matthew puts it as a positive assertion: "Ye are." *Planaomai* is to wander astray (cf. our word *planet*, wandering stars, *asteres planētai*, Jude 13) like the Latin *errare* (our *error*, err). *That ye know not the scriptures* (*mē eidotes tas graphas*). The Sadducees posed as men of superior intelligence and knowledge in opposition to the traditionalists among the Pharisees with their oral law. And yet on this very point they were ignorant of the Scriptures. How much error today is due to this same ignorance among the educated! *Nor the power of God* (*mēde tēn dunamin tou theou*). The two kinds of ignorance generally go together (cf. I Cor. 15:34).

25. *When they shall rise from the dead* (*hotan ek nekrōn anastōsin*). Second aorist active subjunctive with *hotan* (*hote* plus *an*). Matt. 22:30 has it "in the resurrection,"

Luke 20:35 "to attain to the resurrection." The Pharisees regarded the future resurrection body as performing marriage functions, as Mohammedans do today. The Pharisees were in error on this point. The Sadducees made this one of their objections to belief in the resurrection body, revealing thus their own ignorance of the true resurrection body and the future life where marriage functions do not exist. *As angels in heaven* (*hōs aggeloi en tōi ouranōi*). So Matt. 22:30. Luke 20:36 has "equal unto the angels" (*isaggeloi*). "Their equality with angels consists in their deliverance from mortality and its consequences" (Swete). The angels are directly created, not procreated.

26. *In the place concerning the Bush* (*epi tou batou*). This technical use of *epi* is good Greek, in the matter of, in the passage about, the Bush. *Batos* is masculine here, feminine in Luke 20:37. The reference is to Ex. 3:3-6 (in the book of Moses, *en tēi biblōi*).

27. *Ye do greatly err* (*polu planāsthe*). Only in Mark. Solemn, severe, impressive, but kindly close (Bruce).

28. *Heard them questioning together* (*akousas autōn sunzētountōn*). The victory of Christ over the Sadducees pleased the Pharisees who now had come back with mixed emotions over the new turn of things (Matt. 22:34). Luke 20:39 represents one of the scribes as commending Jesus for his skilful reply to the Sadducees. Mark here puts this scribe in a favourable light, "knowing that he had answered them well" (*eidōs hoti kalōs apekrithē autois*). "Them" here means the Sadducees. But Matt. 22:35 says that this lawyer (*nomikos*) was "tempting" (*peirazōn*) by his question. "A few, among whom was the scribe, were constrained to admire, even if they were willing to criticize, the Rabbi who though not himself a Pharisee, surpassed the Pharisees as a champion of the truth." That is a just picture of this lawyer. *The first of all* (*prōtē pantōn*). First in rank and importance. Matt. 22:36 has "great" (*megalē*). See discussion there.

Probably Jesus spoke in Aramaic. "First" and "great" in Greek do not differ essentially here. Mark quotes Deut. 6:4f. as it stands in the LXX and also Lev. 19:18. Matt. 22:40 adds the summary: "On these two commandments hangeth (*krematai*) the whole law and the prophets."

32. *And the scribe said* (*eipen autōi ho grammateus*). Mark alone gives the reply of the scribe to Jesus which is a mere repetition of what Jesus had said about the first and the second commandments with the additional allusion to I Sam. 15:22 about love as superior to whole burnt offerings. *Well* (*kalōs*). Not to be taken with "saidst" (*eipes*) as the Revised Version has it following Wycliff. Probably *kalōs* (well) is exclamatory. "Fine, Teacher. Of a truth (*ep' alētheias*) didst thou say."

34. *Discreetly* (*nounechōs*). From *nous* (intellect) and *echō*, to have. Using the mind to good effect is what the adverb means. He had his wits about him, as we say. Here only in the N.T. In Aristotle and Polybius. *Nounechontōs* would be the more regular form, adverb from a participle. *Not far* (*ou makran*). Adverb, not adjective, feminine accusative, a long way (*hodon* understood). The critical attitude of the lawyer had melted before the reply of Jesus into genuine enthusiasm that showed him to be near the kingdom of God. *No man after that* (*oudeis ouketi*). Double negative. The debate was closed (*etolma*, imperfect tense, dared). Jesus was complete victor on every side.

35. *How say the scribes* (*Pōs legousin hoi grammateis*). The opponents of Jesus are silenced, but he answers them and goes on teaching (*didaskōn*) in the temple as before the attacks began that morning (11:27). They no longer dare to question Jesus, but he has one to put to them "while the Pharisees were gathered together" (Matt. 22:41). The question is not a conundrum or scriptural puzzle (Gould), but "He contents himself with pointing out a difficulty, in the solution of which lay the key to the whole problem of His

person and work" (Swete). The scribes all taught that the Messiah was to be the son of David (John 7:41). The people in the Triumphal Entry had acclaimed Jesus as the son of David (Matt. 21:9). But the rabbis had overlooked the fact that David in Psa. 110:1 called the Messiah his Lord also. The deity and the humanity of the Messiah are both involved in the problem. Matt. 22:45 observes that "no one was able to answer him a word."

36. *The footstool* (*hupopodion*). Westcott and Hort read *hupokatō* (under) after Aleph B D L.

37. *The common people heard him gladly* (*ho polus ochlos ēkouen autou hedeōs*). Literally, the much multitude (the huge crowd) was listening (imperfect tense) to him gladly. Mark alone has this item. The Sanhedrin had begun the formal attack that morning to destroy the influence of Jesus with the crowds whose hero he now was since the Triumphal Entry. It had been a colossal failure. The crowds were drawn closer to him than before.

38. *Beware of the scribes* (*blepete apo tōn grammateōn*). Jesus now turns to the multitudes and to his disciples (Matt. 23:1) and warns them against the scribes and the Pharisees while they are still there to hear his denunciation. The scribes were the professional teachers of the current Judaism and were nearly all Pharisees. Mark (14:38-40) gives a mere summary sketch of this bold and terrific indictment as preserved in Matt. 23 in words that fairly blister today. Luke 20:45-47 follows Mark closely. See Matt. 8:15 for this same use of *blepete apo* with the ablative. It is usually called a translation-Hebraism, a usage not found with *blepō* in the older Greek. But the papyri give it, a vivid vernacular idiom. "Beware of the Jews" (*blepe saton apo tōn Ioudaiōn*, Berl. G. U. 1079. A.D. 41). See Robertson, *Grammar*, p. 577. The pride of the pompous scribes is itemized by Mark: *To walk in long robes* (*stolais*), *stoles*, the dress of dignitaries like kings and priests. *Salutations in*

the marketplaces (*aspasmous en tais agorais*), where the people could see their dignity recognized.

39. *First seats in the synagogues* (*prōtokathedrias*). As a mark of special piety, seats up in front while now the hypocrites present in church prefer the rear seats. *Chief places at feasts* (*prōtoklisias en tois deipnois*). Recognizing proper rank and station. Even the disciples fall victims to this desire for precedence at table (Luke 22:24).

40. *Devour widows' houses* (*hoi katesthontes tās oikias tōn chērōn*). New sentence in the nominative. Terrible pictures of civil wrong by graft grabbing the homes of helpless widows. They inveigled widows into giving their homes to the temple and took it for themselves. *For a pretence make long prayers* (*prophasei makra proseuchomenoi*). *Prophasei* instrumental case of the same word (*prophēmi*) from which prophet comes, but here pretext, pretence of extra piety while robbing the widows and pushing themselves to the fore. Some derive it from *prophainō*, to show forth. *Greater* (*perissoteron*). More abundant condemnation. Some comfort in that at any rate.

41. *Sat down over against the treasury* (*kathisas katenanti tou gazophulakiou*). The storm is over. The Pharisees, Sadducees, Herodians, scribes, have all slunk away in terror ere the closing words. Mark draws this immortal picture of the weary Christ sitting by the treasury (compound word in the LXX from *gaza*, Persian word for treasure, and *phulakē*, guard, so safe for gifts to be deposited). *Beheld* (*etheōrei*). Imperfect tense. He was watching *how the multitude cast money* (*pōs ho ochlos ballei*) into the treasury. The rich were casting in (*eballon*, imperfect tense) as he watched.

42. *One poor widow* (*mia chēra ptōchē*). Luke has *penichra*, a poetical late form of *penēs*. In the N.T. the *ptōchos* is the pauper rather than the mere peasant, the extreme opposite of the rich (*plousioi*). The money given by most was copper (*chalkon*). *Two mites* (*duo lepta*). *Leptos* means peeled or

stripped and so very thin. Two *lepta* were about two-fifths of a cent. *Farthing* (*kodrantes*, Latin *quadrans*, a quarter of an *as*).

43. *Called unto him* (*proskalesamenos*). Indirect middle voice. The disciples themselves had slipped away from him while the terrific denunciation of the scribes and Pharisees had gone on, puzzled at this turn of affairs. *More than all* (*pleion pantōn*). Ablative of comparison (*pantōn*). It may mean, more than all the rich put together. *All that she had* (*panta hosa eichen*). Imperfect tense. *Cast in* (*ebalen*). Aorist tense, in sharp contrast. *All her living* (*holon ton bion autēs*). Her *livelihood* (*bios*), not her *life* (*zōē*). It is a tragedy to see a stingy saint pose as giving the widow's mite when he could give thousands instead of pennies.

CHAPTER XIII

1. *Master, behold, what manner of stones and what manner of buildings* (*didaskale, ide potapoi lithoi kai potapai oikodomai*). Matt. 24:1 and Luke 21:5 tell of the fact of the comment, but Mark alone gives the precise words. Perhaps Peter himself (Swete) was the one who sought thus by a pleasant platitude to divert the Teacher's attention from the serious topics of recent hours in the temple. It was not a new observation, but the merest commonplace might serve at this crisis. Josephus (*Ant.* xv. 11, 3) speaks of the great size of these stones and the beauty of the buildings. Some of these stones at the southeastern and southwestern angles survive today and measure from twenty to forty feet long and weigh a hundred tons. Jesus had, of course, often observed them.

2. *These great buildings* (*tautas tas oikodomas*). Jesus fully recognizes their greatness and beauty. The more remarkable will be their complete demolition (*kataluthēi*), *loosened down*. Only the foundation stones remain.

3. *Over against the temple* (*katenanti tou hierou*). In full view of the temple about which they had been speaking. *Privately* (*kat' idian*). Peter and James and John and Andrew (named only in Mark) had evidently been discussing the strange comment of Jesus as they were coming out of the temple. In their bewilderment they ask Jesus a bit to one side, though probably all the rest drew up as Jesus began to speak this great eschatological discourse.

4. *Tell us, when shall these things be?* (*Eipon hēmin pote tauta estai;*). The Revised Version punctuates it as a direct question, but Westcott and Hort as an indirect inquiry. They asked about the *when* (*pote*) and the *what sign* (*ti*

sēmeion). Matt. 24:3 includes "the sign of thy coming and
the end of the world," showing that these tragic events are
brought before Jesus by the disciples. See discussion of the
interpretation of this discourse on Matt. 24:3. This chapter
in Mark is often called "The Little Apocalypse" with the
notion that a Jewish apocalypse has been here adapted by
Mark and attributed to Jesus. Many of the theories attribute grave error to Jesus or to the Gospels on this subject.
The view adopted in the discussion in Matthew is the one
suggested here, that Jesus blended in one picture his death,
the destruction of Jerusalem within that generation, the
second coming and end of the world typified by the destruction of the city. The lines between these topics are not
sharply drawn in the report and it is not possible for us to
separate the topics clearly. This great discourse is the
longest preserved in Mark and may be due to Peter. Mark
may have given it in order "to forewarn and forearm"
(Bruce) the readers against the coming catastrophe of the
destruction of Jerusalem. Both Matthew (ch. 24) and Luke
(21:5–36) follow the general line of Mark 13 though Matt.
24:43 to 25:46 presents new material (parables).

5. *Take need that no man lead you astray* (*Blepete mē tis
hūmās planēsēi*). Same words in Matt. 24:4. Luke 21:8 has
it "that ye be not led astray" (*mē planēthēte*). This word
planaō (our *planet*) is a bold one. This warning runs through
the whole discussion. It is pertinent today after so many
centuries. About the false Christs then and now see on
Matt. 24:5. It is amazing the success that these charlatans
have through the ages in winning the empty-pated to their
hare-brained views. Only this morning as I am writing a
prominent English psychologist has challenged the world to a
radio communication with Mars asserting that he has made
frequent trips to Mars and communicated with its alleged
inhabitants. And the daily papers put his ebullitions on the
front page. For discussion of the details in verses 6 to 8 see

on Matt. 24:5 to 8. All through the ages in spite of the words of Jesus men have sought to apply the picture here drawn to the particular calamity in their time.

7. *Must needs come to pass* (*dei genesthai*). Already there were outbreaks against the Jews in Alexandria, at Seleucia with the slaughter of more than fifty thousand, at Jamnia, and elsewhere. Caligula, Claudius, Nero will threaten war before it finally comes with the destruction of the city and temple by Titus in A.D. 70. Vincent notes that between this prophecy by Jesus in A.D. 30 (or 29) and the destruction of Jerusalem there was an earthquake in Crete (A.D. 46 or 47), at Rome (A.D. 51), at Apamaia in Phrygia (A.D. 60), at Campania (A.D. 63). He notes also four famines during the reign of Claudius A.D. 41–54. One of them was in Judea in A.D. 44 and is alluded to in Acts 11:28. Tacitus (*Annals* xvi. 10–13) describes the hurricanes and storms in Campania in A.D. 65.

9. *But take heed to yourselves* (*Blepete de humeis heautous*). Only in Mark, but dominant note of warning all through the discourse. Note *humeis* here, very emphatic. *Councils* (*sunedria*). Same word as the Sanhedrin in Jerusalem. These local councils (*sun, hedra,* sitting together) were modelled after that in Jerusalem. *Shall ye be beaten* (*darēsesthe*). Second future passive indicative second person plural. The word *derō* means to flay or skin and here has been softened into *beat* like our tan or skin in the vernacular. Aristophanes has it in this colloquial sense as have the papyri in the *Koiné*. *Before governors and kings* (*epi hēgemonōn kai basileōn*). Gentile rulers as well as before Jewish councils. *Shall stand* (*stathēsesthe*). First aorist passive indicative second person plural of *histēmi*.

10. *Must first be preached* (*prōton dei kēruchthēnai*). This only in Mark. It is interesting to note that Paul in Col. 1:6, 23 claims that the gospel has spread all over the world. All this was before the destruction of Jerusalem.

11. *Be not anxious beforehand what ye shall speak* (*mē promerimnāte ti lalēsēte*). Negative with present imperative to make a general prohibition or habit. Jesus is not here referring to preaching, but to defences made before these councils and governors. A typical example is seen in the courage and skill of Peter and John before the Sanhedrin in Acts 4. The verb *merimnaō* is from *merizō* (*meris*), to be drawn in opposite directions, to be distracted. See on Matt. 6:25. They are not to be stricken with fright beforehand, but to face fearlessly those in high places who are seeking to overthrow the preaching of the gospel. There is no excuse here for the lazy preacher who fails to prepare his sermon out of the mistaken reliance upon the Holy Spirit. They will need and will receive the special help of the Holy Spirit (cf. John 14–16).

13. *But he that endureth to the end* (*ho de hupomeinas eis telos*). Note this aorist participle with the future verb. The idea here is true to the etymology of the word, remaining under (*hupomenō*) until the end. The divisions in families Jesus had predicted before (Luke 12:52f.; 14:25f.). *Be saved* (*sōthēsetai*). Here Jesus means final salvation (effective aorist future passive), not initial salvation.

14. *Standing where he ought not* (*hestēkota hopou ou dei*). Matt. 24:15 has "standing in the holy place" (*hestos en topoi hagiōi*), neuter and agreeing with *bdelugma* (abomination), the very phrase applied in I Macc. 1:54 to the altar to Zeus erected by Antiochus Epiphanes where the altar to Jehovah was. Mark personifies the abomination as personal (masculine), while Luke 21:20 defines it by reference to the armies (of Rome, as it turned out). So the words of Daniel find a second fulfilment, Rome taking the place of Syria (Swete). See on Matt. 24:15 for this phrase and the parenthesis inserted in the words of Jesus ("Let him that readeth understand"). See also on Matt. 24:16 to 25 for discussion of details in Mark 13:14 to 22.

16. *In the field (eis ton agron)*. Here Matt. 24:18 has *en tōi agrōi*, showing identical use of *eis* with accusative and *en* with the locative.

19. *Which God created (hēn ektisen ho theos)*. Note this amplification to the quotation from Dan. 12:1.

20. *Whom he chose (hous exelexato)*. Indirect aorist middle indicative. In Mark alone. Explains the sovereign choice of God in the end by and for himself.

22. *That they may lead astray (pros to apoplanāin)*. With a view to leading off (*pros* and the infinitive). Matt. 24:24 has *hōste apoplāsthai*, so as to lead off.

23. *But take ye heed (Humeis de blepete)*. Gullibility is no mark of a saint or of piety. Note emphatic position of you (*humeis*). Credulity ranks no higher than scepticism. God gave us our wits for self-protection. Christ has warned us beforehand.

24. *The sun shall be darkened (ho helios skotisthēsetai)*. Future passive indicative. These figures come from the prophets (Isa. 13:9f.; Ezek. 32:7f.; Joel 2:1f., 10f.; Amos 8:9; Zeph. 1:14–16; Zech. 12:12). One should not forget that prophetic imagery was not always meant to be taken literally, especially apocalyptic symbols. Peter in Acts 2:15–21 applies the prophecy of Joel about the sun and moon to the events on the day of Pentecost. See on Matt. 24:29–31 for details of verses 24–27.

25. *The stars shall be falling (hoi asteres esontai piptontes)*. Periphrastic future indicative, *esontai*, future middle indicative and *piptontes*, present active participle.

27. *Shall gather together his elect (episunaxei tous eklektous autou)*. This is the purpose of God through the ages. *From the uttermost part of the earth to the uttermost part of heaven (ap' akrou gēs heōs akrou ouranou)*. The Greek is very brief, "from the tip of earth to the tip of heaven." This precise phrase occurs nowhere else.

28. *Coming to pass (ginomena)*. Present middle participle,

linear action. See on Matt. 24:32 to 36 for details of verses 28 to 32 (the Parable of the Fig Tree).

32. *Not even the Son* (*oude ho huios*). There is no doubt as to the genuineness of these words here such as exists in Matt. 24:36. This disclaimer of knowledge naturally interpreted applies to the second coming, not to the destruction of Jerusalem which had been definitely limited to that generation as it happened in A.D. 70.

34. *Commanded also the porter to watch* (*kai tōi thurōrōi eneteilato hina grēgorēi*). The porter or door-keeper (*thurōros*), as well as all the rest, to keep a watch (present subjunctive, *grēgorēi*). This Parable of the Porter is only in Mark. Our ignorance of the time of the Master's return is an argument not for indifference nor for fanaticism, but for alertness and eager readiness for his coming.

35. The four watches of the night are named here: evening (*opse*), midnight (*mesonuktion*), cock-crowing (*alektorophōnias*), morning (*prōi*).

37. *Watch* (*grēgoreite*). Be on the watch. Present imperative of a verb made on the second perfect, *egrēgora*, to be awake. Stay awake till the Lord comes.

CHAPTER XIV

1. *After two days* (*meta duo hēmeras*). This was Tuesday evening as we count time (beginning of the Jewish Wednesday). In Matt. 26:2 Jesus is reported as naming this same date which would put it our Thursday evening, beginning of the Jewish Friday. The Gospel of John mentions five items that superficially considered seem to contradict this definite date in Mark and Matthew, but which are really in harmony with them. See discussion on Matt. 26:17 and my *Harmony of the Gospels*, pp. 279 to 284. Mark calls it here the feast of "the passover and the unleavened bread," both names covering the eight days. Sometimes "passover" is applied to only the first day, sometimes to the whole period. No sharp distinction in usage was observed. *Sought* (*ezētoun*). Imperfect tense. They were still at it, though prevented so far.

2. *Not during the feast* (*Mē en tēi heortēi*). They had first planned to kill him at the feast (John 11:57), but the Triumphal Entry and great Tuesday debate (this very morning) in the temple had made them decide to wait till after the feast was over. It was plain that Jesus had too large and powerful a following. See on Matt. 26:47.

3. *As he sat at meat* (*katakeimenou autou*). Matt. 26:7 uses *anakeimenou*, both words meaning reclining (leaning down or up or back) and in the genitive absolute. See on Matt. 26:6 in proof that this is a different incident from that recorded in Luke 7:36–50. See on Matt. 26:6–13 for discussion of details. *Spikenard* (*nardou pistikēs*). This use of *pistikos* with *nardos* occurs only here and in John 12:3. The adjective is common enough in the older Greek and appears in the papyri also in the sense of genuine, unadulter-

379

ated, and that is probably the idea here. The word spikenard is from the Vulgate *nardi spicati*, probably from the Old Latin *nardi pistici*. *Brake* (*suntripsousa*). Only in Mark. She probably broke the narrow neck of the vase holding the ointment.

5. *Above three hundred pence* (*epanō dēnariōn triakosiōn*). Matthew has "for much" while John 12:5 has "for three hundred pence." The use of "far above" may be a detail from Peter's memory of Judas' objection whose name in this connection is preserved in John 12:4. *And they murmured against her* (*kai enebrimōnto autēi*). Imperfect tense of this striking word used of the snorting of horses and seen already in Mark 1:43; 11:38. It occurs in the LXX in the sense of anger as here (Dan. 11:30). Judas made the complaint against Mary of Bethany, but all the apostles joined in the chorus of criticism of the wasteful extravagance.

8. *She hath done what she could* (*ho eschen epoiēsen*). This alone in Mark. Two aorists. Literally, "what she had she did." Mary could not comprehend the Lord's death, but she at least showed her sympathy with him and some understanding of the coming tragedy, a thing that not one of her critics had done. *She hath anointed my body aforehand for the burying* (*proelaben murisai to sōma mou eis ton entaphiasmon*). Literally, "she took beforehand to anoint my body for the burial." She anticipated the event. This is Christ's justification of her noble deed. Matt. 26:12 also speaks of the burial preparation by Mary, using the verb *entaphiasai*.

9. *For a memorial of her* (*eis mnēmosunon autēs*). So in Matt. 26:13. There are many mausoleums that crumble to decay. But this monument to Jesus fills the whole world still with its fragrance. What a hint there is here for those who wish to leave permanent memorials.

10. *He that was one of the twelve* (*ho heis tōn dōdeka*). Note the article here, "the one of the twelve," Matthew has only *heis*, "one." Some have held that Mark here calls

Judas the primate among the twelve. Rather he means to call attention to the idea that he was the one of the twelve who did this deed.

11. *And they, when they heard it, were glad (hoi de akousantes echarēsan)*. No doubt the rabbis looked on the treachery of Judas as a veritable dispensation of Providence amply justifying their plots against Jesus. *Conveniently (eukairōs)*. This was the whole point of the offer of Judas. He claimed that he knew enough of the habits of Jesus to enable them to catch him "in the absence of the multitude" (Luke 22:6) without waiting for the passover to be over, when the crowds would leave. For discussion of the motives of Judas, see on Matt. 26:15. Mark merely notes the promise of "money" while Matthew mentions "thirty pieces of silver" (Zech. 11:12), the price of a slave.

12. *When they sacrificed the passover (hote to pascha ethuon)*. Imperfect indicative, customary practice. The paschal lamb (note *pascha*) was slain at 6 P.M., beginning of the fifteenth of the month (Ex. 12:6), but the preparations were made beforehand on the fourteenth (Thursday). See on Matt. 26:17 for discussion of "eat the passover."

13. *Two of his disciples (duo tōn mathētōn autou)*. Luke 22:8 names them, Peter and John. *Bearing a pitcher of water (keramion hudatos bastazōn)*. This item also in Luke, but not in Matthew.

14. *The goodman of the house (tōi oikodespotēi)*. A non-classical word, but in late papyri. It means master (despot) of the house, householder. The usual Greek has two separate words, *oikou despotēs* (master of the house). *My guest-chamber (to kataluma mou)*. In LXX, papyri, and modern Greek for lodging-place (inn, as in Luke 2:7 or guest-chamber as here). It was used for *khan* or *caravanserai*. *I shall eat (phagō)*. Futuristic aorist subjunctive with *hopou*.

15. *And he (kai autos)*. Emphatic, and he himself. *A large upper room (anagaion mega)*. Anything above ground

(*gē*), and particularly upstairs as here. Here and in Luke
22:12. Example in Xenophon. Jesus wishes to observe
this last feast with his disciples alone, not with others as
was often done. Evidently this friend of Jesus was a man
who would understand. *Furnished* (*estrōmenon*). Perfect
passive participle of *strōnnumi*, state of readiness. "Strewed
with carpets, and with couches properly spread" (Vincent).

17. *He cometh* (*erchetai*). Dramatic historical present.
It is assumed here that Jesus is observing the passover
meal at the regular time and hour, at 6 P.M. at the beginning
of the fifteenth (evening of our Thursday, beginning of
Jewish Friday). Mark and Matthew note the time as
evening and state it as the regular passover meal.

18. *As they sat* (*anakeimenōn autōn*). Reclined, of course.
It is a pity that these verbs are not translated properly in
English. Even Leonardo da Vinci in his immortal painting
of the Last Supper has Jesus and his apostles sitting, not
reclining. Probably he took an artist's license for effect.
Even he that eateth with me (*ho esthiōn met' emou*). See Psa.
4:9. To this day the Arabs will not violate hospitality
by mistreating one who breaks bread with them in the
tent.

20. *One of the twelve* (*heis tōn dōdeka*). It is as bad as
that. The sign that Jesus gave, *the one dipping in the dish
with me* (*ho embaptomenos met' emou eis to trublion*), escaped
the notice of all. Jesus gave the sop to Judas who understood perfectly that Jesus knew his purpose. See on Matt.
26:21-24 for further details.

23. *A cup* (*potērion*). Probably the ordinary wine of the
country mixed with two-thirds water, though the word for
wine (*oinos*) is not used here in the Gospels, but "the
fruit of the vine" (*ek tou genēmatos tēs ampelou*). See Matt.
26:26-29 for discussion of important details. Mark and
Matthew give substantially the same account of the institution of the Supper by Jesus, while Luke 22:17-20 agrees

closely with I Cor. 11:23–26 where Paul claims to have obtained his account by direct revelation from the Lord Jesus.

26. *Sung a hymn* (*humnēsantes*). See Matt. 26:30 for discussion.

29. *Yet will not I* (*all' ouk egō*). Mark records here Peter's boast of loyalty even though all desert him. All the Gospels tell it. See discussion on Matt. 26:33.

30. *Twice* (*dis*). This detail only in Mark. One crowing is always the signal for more. The Fayum papyrus agrees with Mark in having *dis*. The cock-crowing marks the third watch of the night (Mark 13:35).

31. *Exceeding vehemently* (*ekperissōs*). This strong compounded adverb only in Mark and probably preserves Peter's own statement of the remark. About the boast of Peter see on Matt. 26:35.

32. *Which was named* (*hou to onoma*). Literally, "whose name was." On Gethsemane see on Matt. 26:36. *While I pray* (*heōs proseuxōmai*). Aorist subjunctive with *heōs* really with purpose involved, a common idiom. Matthew adds "go yonder" (*apelthōn ekei*).

33. *Greatly amazed and sore troubled* (*ekthambeisthai kai adēmonein*). Matt. 26:37 has "sorrowful and sore troubled." See on Matt. about *adēmonein*. Mark alone uses *exthambeisthai* (here and in 9:15). There is a papyrus example given by Moulton and Milligan's *Vocabulary*. The verb *thambeō* occurs in Mark 10:32 for the amazement of the disciples at the look of Jesus as he went toward Jerusalem. Now Jesus himself feels amazement as he directly faces the struggle in the Garden of Gethsemane. He wins the victory over himself in Gethsemane and then he can endure the loss, despising the shame. For the moment he is rather amazed and homesick for heaven. "Long as He had foreseen the Passion, when it came clearly into view its terror exceeded His anticipations" (Swete). "He learned from what he

suffered," (Heb. 5:8) and this new experience enriched the human soul of Jesus.

35. *Fell on the ground* (*epipten epi tēs gēs*). Descriptive imperfect. See him falling. Matthew has the aorist *epesen*. *Prayed* (*proseucheto*). Imperfect, prayed repeatedly or inchoative, began to pray. Either makes good sense. *The hour* (*hē hōra*). Jesus had long looked forward to this "hour" and had often mentioned it (John 7:30; 8:20; 12:23, 27; 13:1). See again in Mark 14:41. Now he dreads it, surely a human trait that all can understand.

36. *Abba, Father* (*Abba ho patēr*). Both Aramaic and Greek and the article with each. This is not a case of translation, but the use of both terms as is Gal. 4:6, a probable memory of Paul's childhood prayers. About "the cup" see on Matt. 26:39. It is not possible to take the language of Jesus as fear that he might die before he came to the Cross. He was heard (Heb. 5:7f.) and helped to submit to the Father's will as he does instantly. *Not what I will* (*ou ti egō thelō*). Matthew has "as" (*hōs*). We see the humanity of Jesus in its fulness both in the Temptations and in Gethsemane, but without sin each time. And this was the severest of all the temptations, to draw back from the Cross. The victory over self brought surrender to the Father's will.

37. *Simon, sleepest thou?* (*Simōn, katheudeis;*). The old name, not the new name, Peter. Already his boasted loyalty was failing in the hour of crisis. Jesus fully knows the weakness of human flesh (see on Matt. 26:41).

40. *Very heavy* (*katabarunomenoi*). Perfective use of *kata-* with the participle. Matthew has the simple verb. Mark's word is only here in the N.T. and is rare in Greek writers. Mark has the vivid present passive participle, while Matthew has the perfect passive *bebarēmenoi*. *And they wist not what to answer him* (*kai ouk ēdeisan ti apokrithōsin autōi*). Deliberative subjunctive retained in the

indirect question. Alone in Mark and reminds one of the like embarrassment of these same three disciples on the Mount of Transfiguration (Mark 9:6). On both occasions weakness of the flesh prevented their real sympathy with Jesus in his highest and deepest experiences. "Both their shame and their drowsiness would make them dumb" (Gould).

41. *It is enough* (*apechei*). Alone in Mark. This impersonal use is rare and has puzzled expositors no little. The papyri (Deissmann's *Light from the Ancient East* and Moulton and Milligan's *Vocabulary*) furnish many examples of it as a receipt for payment in full. See also Matt. 6:2ff.; Luke 6:24; Phil. 4:18 for the notion of paying in full. It is used here by Jesus in an ironical sense, probably meaning that there was no need of further reproof of the disciples for their failure to watch with him. "This is no time for a lengthened exposure of the faults of friends; the enemy is at the gate" (Swete). See further on Matt. 26:45 for the approach of Judas.

43. *And the scribes* (*kai tōn grammateōn*). Mark adds this item while John 18:3 mentions "Pharisees." It was evidently a committee of the Sanhedrin for Judas had made his bargain with the Sanhedrin (Mark 14:1 = Matt. 26:3 = Luke 22:2). See discussion of the betrayal and arrest on Matt. 26:47–56 for details.

44. *Token* (*sussēmon*). A common word in the ancient Greek for a concerted signal according to agreement. It is here only in the New Testament. Matt. 26:48 has *sēmeion*, sign. The signal was the kiss by Judas, a contemptible desecration of a friendly salutation. *And lead him away safely* (*kai apagete asphalōs*). Only in Mark. Judas wished no slip to occur. Mark and Matthew do not tell of the falling back upon the ground when Jesus challenged the crowd with Judas. It is given by John alone (John 18:4–9).

47. *A certain one* (*heis tis*). Mark does not tell that it

was Peter. Only John 18:10 does that after Peter's death. He really tried to kill the man, Malchus by name, as John again tells (18:10). Mark does not give the rebuke to Peter by Jesus in Matt. 26:52ff.

48. *Against a robber* (*epi leistēn*). Highway robbers like Barabbas were common and were often regarded as heroes. Jesus will be crucified between two robbers in the very place that Barabbas would have occupied.

51. *A certain young man* (*neaniskos tis*). This incident alone in Mark. It is usually supposed that Mark himself, son of Mary (Acts 12:12) in whose house they probably had observed the passover meal, had followed Jesus and the apostles to the Garden. It is a lifelike touch quite in keeping with such a situation. Here after the arrest he was following with Jesus (*sunēkolouthei autōi*, imperfect tense). Note the vivid dramatic present *kratousin* (they seize him).

52. *Linen cloth* (*sindona*). An old Greek word of unknown origin. It was fine linen cloth used often for wrapping the dead (Matt. 27:59 = Mark 15:46 = Luke 23:53). In this instance it could have been a fine sheet or even a shirt.

54. *Peter had followed him afar off* (*Ho Petros apo makrothen ēkolouthēsen autōi*). Here Mark uses the constative aorist (*ēkolouthēsen*) where Matt. 26:58, and Luke 22:54 have the picturesque imperfect (*ēkolouthei*), was following. Possibly Mark did not care to dwell on the picture of Peter furtively following at a distance, not bold enough to take an open stand with Christ as the Beloved Disciple did, and yet unable to remain away with the other disciples. *Was sitting with* (*ēn sunkathēmenos*). Periphrastic imperfect middle, picturing Peter making himself at home with the officers (*hupēretōn*), under rowers, literally, then servants of any kind. John 18:25 describes Peter as standing (*hestōs*). Probably he did now one, now the other, in his restless weary mood. *Warming himself in the light* (*thermainomenos prōs to phōs*). Direct middle. Fire has light as well as heat and it

shone in Peter's face. He was not hidden as much as he supposed he was.

56. *Their witness agreed not together* (*isai hai marturiai ouk ēsan*). Literally, the testimonies were not equal. They did not correspond with each other on essential points. *Many were bearing false witness* (*epseudomarturoun,* imperfect, repeated action) *against him.* No two witnesses bore joint testimony to justify a capital sentence according to the law (Deut. 19:15). Note imperfects in these verses (55–57) to indicate repeated failures.

57. *Bare false witness* (*epseudomarturoun*). In desperation some attempted once more (conative imperfect).

58. *Made with hands* (*cheiropoiēton*). In Mark alone. An old Greek word. The negative form *acheiropoiēton* here occurs elsewhere only in II Cor. 5:1 and Col. 2:11. In Heb. 9:11 the negative *ou* is used with the positive form. It is possible that a real *logion* of Jesus underlies the perversion of it here. Mark and Matthew do not quote the witnesses precisely alike. Perhaps they quoted Jesus differently and therein is shown part of the disagreement, for Mark adds verse 59 (not in Matthew). "And not even so did their witness agree together," repeating the point of verse 57. Swete observes that Jesus, as a matter of fact, did do what he is quoted as saying in Mark: "He said what the event has proved to be true; His death destroyed the old order, and His resurrection created the new." But these witnesses did not mean that by what they said. The only saying of Jesus at all like this preserved to us is that in John 2:19, when he referred not to the temple in Jerusalem, but to the temple of his body, though no one understood it at the time.

60. *Stood up in the midst* (*anastas eis meson*). Second aorist active participle. For greater solemnity he arose to make up by bluster the lack of evidence. The high priest stepped out into the midst as if to attack Jesus by vehement questions. See on Matt. 26:59–68 for details here.

61. *And answered nothing* (*kai ouk apekrinato ouden*). Mark adds the negative statement to the positive "kept silent" (*esiōpā*), imperfect, also in Matthew. Mark does not give the solemn oath in Matthew under which Jesus had to answer. See on Matthew.

62. *I am* (*ego eimi*). Matthew has it, "Thou hast said," which is the equivalent of the affirmative. But Mark's statement is definite beyond controversy. See on Matt. 26:64–68 for the claims of Jesus and the conduct of Caiaphas.

64. *They all* (*hoi de pantes*). This would mean that Joseph of Arimathea was not present since he did not consent to the death of Jesus (Luke 23:51). Nicodemus was apparently absent also, probably not invited because of previous sympathy with Jesus (John 7:50). But all who were present voted for the death of Jesus.

65. *Cover his face* (*perikaluptein autou to prosōpon*). Put a veil around his face. Not in Matthew, but in Luke 22:64 where Revised Version translates *perikalupsantes* by "blindfolded." All three Gospels give the jeering demand of the Sanhedrin: "Prophesy" (*prophēteuson*), meaning, as Matthew and Luke add, thereby telling who struck him while he was blindfolded. Mark adds "the officers" (same as in verse 54) of the Sanhedrin, Roman lictors or sergeants-at-arms who had arrested Jesus in Gethsemane and who still held Jesus (*hoi sunechontes auton*, Luke 22:63). Matt. 26:67 alludes to their treatment of Jesus without clearly indicating who they were. *With blows of their hands* (*rapismasin*). The verb *rapizō* in Matt. 26:67 originally meant to smite with a rod. In late writers it comes to mean to slap the face with the palm of the hands. The same thing is true of the substantive *rapisma* used here. A papyrus of the sixth century A.D. uses it in the sense of a scar on the face as the result of a blow. It is in the instrumental case here. "They caught him with blows," Swete suggests for the unusual *elabon* in this sense. "With rods" is, of course,

possible as the lictors carried rods. At any rate it was a gross indignity.

66. *Beneath in the court* (*katō en tēi aulēi*). This implies that Jesus was upstairs when the Sanhedrin met. Matt. 22:69 has it *without in the court* (*exō en tēi aulēi*). Both are true. The open court was outside of the rooms and also below.

67. *Warming himself* (*thermainomenon*). Mark mentions this fact about Peter twice (14:54, 67) as does John (18:18, 25). He was twice beside the fire. It is quite difficult to relate clearly the three denials as told in the Four Gospels. Each time several may have joined in, both maids and men. *The Nazarene* (*tou Nazarēnou*). In Matt. 26:69 it is "the Galilean." A number were probably speaking, one saying one thing, another another.

68. *I neither know nor understand* (*oute oida oute epistamai*). This denial is fuller in Mark, briefest in John. *What thou sayest* (*su ti legeis*). Can be understood as a direct question. Note position of *thou* (*su*), proleptical. *Into the porch* (*eis to proaulion*). Only here in the New Testament. Plato uses it of a prelude on a flute. It occurs also in the plural for preparations the day before the wedding. Here it means the vestibule to the court. Matt. 26:71 has *pulōna*, a common word for gate or front porch. *And the cock crew* (*kai alektōr ephōnēsen*). Omitted by Aleph B L Sinaitic Syriac. It is genuine in verse 72 where "the second time" (*ek deuterou*) occurs also. It is possible that because of verse 72 it crept into verse 68. Mark alone alludes to the cock crowing twice, originally (Mark 14:30), and twice in verse 72, besides verse 68 which is hardly genuine.

69. *To them that stood by* (*tois parestōsin*). This talk about Peter was overheard by him. "This fellow (*houtos*) is one of them." So in verse 70 the talk is directly to Peter as in Matt. 26:73, but in Luke 22:59 it is about him. Soon the bystanders (*hoi parestōtes*) will join in the accusation to Peter

(verse 70; Matt. 26:73), with the specially pungent question in John 18:26 which was the climax. See on Matt. 26:69 to 75 for discussion of similar details.

71. *Curse* (*anathematizein*). Our word *anathema* (*ana*, *thema*, an offering, then something devoted or a curse). Finally the two meanings were distinguished by *anathēma* for offering and *anathema* for curse. Deissmann has found examples at Megara of *anathema* in the sense of curse. Hence the distinction observed in the N.T. was already in the *Koiné*. Matt. 26:74 has *katathematizein*, which is a *hapax legomenon* in the N.T., though common in the LXX. This word has the notion of calling down curses on one's self if the thing is not true.

72. *Called to mind* (*anemnēsthē*). First aorist passive indicative. Matt. 26:75 has the uncompounded verb *emnēsthē* while Luke 22:61 has another compound *hupemnēsthē*, was reminded. *When he thought thereon* (*epibalōn*). Second aorist active participle of *epiballō*. It is used absolutely here, though there is a reference to *to rhēma* above, the word of Jesus, and the idiom involves *ton noun* so that the meaning is to put the mind upon something. In Luke 15:12 there is another absolute use with a different sense. Moulton (*Prolegomena*, p. 131) quotes a Ptolemaic papyrus Tb P 50 where *epibalōn* probably means "set to," put his mind on. *Wept* (*eklaien*). Inchoative imperfect, began to weep. Matt. 26:75 has the ingressive aorist *eklausen*, burst into tears.

CHAPTER XV

1. *In the morning* (*prōi*). The ratification meeting after day. See on Matt. 26:1–5 for details. *Held a consultation* (*sumboulion poiēsantes*). So text of Westcott and Hort (Vulgate *consilium facientes*), though they give *hetoimasantes* in the margin. The late and rare word *sumboulion* is like the Latin *consilium*. If *hetoimasantes* is the correct text, the idea would be rather to prepare a concerted plan of action (Gould). But their action was illegal on the night before and they felt the need of this ratification after dawn which is described in Luke 22:66–71, who does not give the illegal night trial. *Bound Jesus* (*dēsantes ton Iēsoun*). He was bound on his arrest (John 18:12) when brought before Annas who sent him on bound to Caiaphas (John 18:24) and now he is bound again as he is sent to Pilate (Mark 15:1 = Matt. 27:2). It is implied that he was unbound while before Annas and then before Caiaphas and the Sanhedrin.

2. *Art thou the King of the Jews?* (*Su ei ho basileus tōn Ioudaiōn;*). This is the only one of the charges made by the Sanhedrin to Pilate (Luke 23:2) that he notices. He does not believe this one to be true, but he has to pay attention to it or be liable to charges himself of passing over a man accused of rivalry and revolution against Caesar. John 18:28–32 gives the interview with Jesus that convinces Pilate that he is a harmless religious fanatic. See on Matt. 26:11. *Thou sayest* (*su legeis*). An affirmation, though in John 18:34–37 there is a second and fuller interview between Pilate and Jesus. "Here, as in the trial before the Sanhedrin, this is the one question that Jesus answers. It is the only question on which his own testimony is important and

necessary" (Gould). The Jews were out on the pavement or sidewalk outside the palace while Pilate came out to them from above on the balcony (John 18:28f.) and had his interviews with Jesus on the inside, calling Jesus thither (John 18:33).

3. *Accused him of many things* (*kategoroun autou polla*). Imperfect tense, repeated accusations besides those already made. They let loose their venom against Jesus. One of the common verbs for speaking against in court (*kata* and *agoreuō*). It is used with the genitive of the person and the accusative of the thing.

5. *Marvelled* (*thaumazein*). Pilate was sure of the innocence of Jesus and saw through their envy (Mark 15:10), but he was hoping that Jesus would answer these charges to relieve him of the burden. He marvelled also at the self-control of Jesus.

6. *Used to release* (*apeluen*). Imperfect tense of customary action where Matt. 27:15 has the verb *eiōthei* (was accustomed to). *They asked of him* (*pareitounto*). Imperfect middle, expressing their habit also.

7. *Bound with them that had made insurrection* (*meta tōn stasiastōn dedemenos*). A desperate criminal, leader in the insurrection, sedition (*en tēi stasei*), or revolution against Rome, the very thing that the Jews up at Bethsaida Julias had wanted Jesus to lead (John 6:15). Barabbas was the leader of these rioters and was bound with them. *Had committed murder* (*phonon pepoiēkeisan*). Past perfect indicative without augment. Murder usually goes with such rioters and the priests and people actually chose a murderer in preference to Jesus.

8. *As he was wont to do unto them* (*kathōs epoiei autois*). Imperfect of customary action again and dative case.

9. *The King of the Jews* (*ton basilea tōn Ioudaiōn*). That phrase from this charge sharpened the contrast between Jesus and Barabbas which is bluntly put in Matt. 27:17

"Barabbas or Jesus which is called Christ." See discussion there.

10. *He perceived* (*eginōsken*). Imperfect tense descriptive of Pilate's growing apprehension from their conduct which increased his intuitive impression at the start. It was gradually dawning on him. Both Mark and Matthew give "envy" (*phthonon*) as the primary motive of the Sanhedrin. Pilate probably had heard of the popularity of Jesus by reason of the triumphal entry and the temple teaching. *Had delivered* (*paradedōkeisan*). Past perfect indicative without augment where Matt. 27:18 has the first aorist (kappa aorist) indicative *paredōkan*, not preserving the distinction made by Mark. The aorist is never used "as" a past perfect.

11. *Stirred up* (*aneseisan*). *Shook up* like an earthquake (*seismos*). Matt. 27:20 has a weaker word, "persuaded" (*epeisan*). Effective aorist indicative. The priests and scribes had amazing success. If one wonders why the crowd was fickle, he may recall that this was not yet the same people who followed him in triumphal entry and in the temple. That was the plan of Judas to get the thing over before those Galilean sympathizers waked up. "It was a case of regulars against an irregular, of priests against prophet" (Gould). "But Barabbas, as described by Mark, represented a popular passion, which was stronger than any sympathy they might have for so unworldly a character as Jesus—the passion for *political liberty*" (Bruce). "What unprincipled characters they were! They accuse Jesus to Pilate of political ambition, and they recommend Barabbas to the people for the same reason" (Bruce). The Sanhedrin would say to the people that Jesus had already abdicated his kingly claims while to Pilate they went on accusing him of treason to Caesar. *Rather* (*mallon*). Rather than Jesus. It was a gambler's choice.

12. *Whom ye call the King of the Jews* (*hon legete ton basilea tōn Ioudaiōn*). Pilate rubs it in on the Jews (cf. verse 9).

The "then" (*oun*) means since you have chosen Barabbas instead of Jesus.

13. *Crucify him* (*Staurōson auton*). Luke 23:21 repeats the verb. Matt. 27:22 has it, "Let him be crucified." There was a chorus and a hubbub of confused voices all demanding crucifixion for Christ. Some of the voices beyond a doubt had joined in the hallelujahs to the Son of David in the triumphal entry. See on Matt. 27:23 for discussion of Mark 15:14.

15. *To content the multitude* (*tōi ochlōi to hikanon poiēsai*). A Latin idiom (*satisfacere alicui*), to do what is sufficient to remove one's ground of complaint. This same phrase occurs in Polybius, Appian, Diogenes Laertes, and in late papyri. Pilate was afraid of this crowd now completely under the control of the Sanhedrin. He knew what they would tell Caesar about him. See on Matt. 27:26 for discussion of the scourging.

16. *The Praetorium* (*praitōrion*). In Matt. 27:27 this same word is translated "palace." That is its meaning here also, the palace in which the Roman provincial governor resided. In Phil. 1:13 it means the Praetorian Guard in Rome. Mark mentions here "the court" (*tēs aulēs*) inside of the palace into which the people passed from the street through the vestibule. See further on Matthew about the "band."

17. *Purple* (*porphuran*). Matt. 27:28 has "scarlet robe" which see for discussion as well as for the crown of thorns.

19. *Worshipped him* (*prosekunoun*). In mockery. Imperfect tense as are *etupton* (smote) and *eneptuon* (did spit upon). Repeated indignities.

20. *They lead him out* (*exagousin auton*). Vivid historical present after imperfects in verse 19.

21. *They compel* (*aggareuousin*). Dramatic present indicative again where Matt. 27:32 has the aorist. For this Persian word see on Matt. 5:41 and 27:32. *Coming out*

of the country (*erchomenon ap' agrou*). Hence Simon met the procession. Mark adds that he was "the father of Alexander and Rufus." Paul mentions a Rufus in Rom. 16:13, but it was a common name and proves nothing. See on Matt. 27:32 for discussion of cross-bearing by criminals. Luke adds "after Jesus" (*opisthen tou Iēsou*). But Jesus bore his own cross till he was relieved of it, and he walked in front of his own cross for the rest of the way.

22. *They bring him* (*pherousin auton*). Historical present again. See on Matt. 27:33f. for discussion of Golgotha.

23. *They offered him* (*edidoun autōi*). Imperfect tense where Matthew has the aorist *edōkan*. *Mingled with myrrh* (*esmurnismenon*). Perfect passive participle. The verb means flavoured with myrrh, myrrhed wine. It is not inconsistent with Matt. 27:34 "mingled with gall," which see. *But he received it not* (*hos de ouk elaben*. Note the demonstrative *hos* with *de*. Matthew has it that Jesus was not willing to take. Mark's statement is that he refused it.

24. *What each should take* (*tis ti ārei*). Only in Mark. Note double interrogative, Who What? The verb *ārei* is first aorist active deliberative subjunctive retained in the indirect question. The details in Mark 15:24 to 32 are followed closely by Matt. 27:35 to 44. See there for discussion of details.

25. *The third hour* (*hōra tritē*). This is Jewish time and would be nine A.M. The trial before Pilate was the sixth hour Roman time (John 19:14), six A.M.

26. The superscription (*hē epigraphē*). The writing upon the top of the cross (our word epigraph). Luke 23:38 has this same word, but Matt. 27:37 has "accusation" (*aitian*). See Matthew for discussion. John 19:19 has "title" (*titlon*).

32. *Now come down* (*katabatō nun*). Now that he is nailed to the cross. *That we may see and believe* (*hina idōmen kai pisteusōmen*). Aorist subjunctive of purpose with *hina*. They use almost the very language of Jesus in their ridicule,

words that they had heard him use in his appeals to men to
see and believe. *Reproached him (ōneidizon auton)*. Imperfect tense. They did it several times. Mark and Matthew
both fail to give the story of the robber who turned to
Christ on the Cross as told in Luke 23:39–43.

33. *The sixth hour (hōras hektēs)*. That is, noon (Jewish
time), as the third hour was nine A.M. (Mark 15:25). See
on Matt. 27:45 for discussion. Given also by Luke 23:44.
Mark gives the Aramaic transliteration as does B in Matt.
27:45, which see for discussion. *Forsaken (egkatelipes)*.
Some MSS. give *ōneidisas* (reproached). We are not able to
enter into the fulness of the desolation felt by Jesus at this
moment as the Father regarded him as sin (II Cor. 5:21).
This desolation was the deepest suffering. He did not cease
to be the Son of God. That would be impossible.

35. *He calleth Elijah (Ēleian phōnei)*. They misunderstood the *Elōi* or *Ēlei* (my God) for Elijah.

36. *To take him down (kathelein auton)*. Matt. 27:49 has
"to save him" *(sōsōn)*, which see for discussion.

37. *Gave up the ghost (exepneusen)*. Literally, breathed
out. See "yielded up his spirit" in Matt. 27:50 for discussion for details. Mark uses this word *exepneusen* again
in verse 39.

39. *The centurion (ho kenturiōn)*. A Latin word *(centurio)*
used also in verse 44 and here only in the N.T. *Which stood
by over against him (ho parestēkōs ex enantias autou)*. This
description alone in Mark, picturing the centurion "watching Jesus" (Matt. 27:54). *So (houtōs)*. With the darkness
and the earthquake. See on Matt. 27:54 for discussion of
"the Son of God," more probably "a Son of God."

40. *And Salome (kai Salōmē)*. Apparently the "mother
of the sons of Zebedee" (Matt. 27:56). Only in Mark.

41. *Followed him and ministered unto him (ēkolouthoun kai
diēkonoun autōi)*. Two imperfects describing the long Galilean ministry of these three women and many other women

in Galilee (Luke 8:1–3) who came up with him (*hai sunana-basai autōi*) to Jerusalem. This summary description in Mark is paralleled in Matt. 27:55f. and Luke 23:49. These faithful women were last at the Cross as they stood afar and saw the dreadful end to all their hopes.

42. *The preparation* (*paraskeuē*). Mark explains the term as meaning "the day before the sabbath" (*prosabbaton*), that is our Friday, which began at sunset. See discussion on Matt. 27:57. The Jews had already taken steps to get the bodies removed (John 19:31).

43. *A councillor of honourable estate* (*euschēmōn bouleutēs*). A senator or member of the Sanhedrin of high standing, rich (Matt. 27:57). *Looking for the Kingdom of God* (*ēn prosdechomenos tēn basileian tou theou*). Periphrastic imperfect. Also Luke 23:51. The very verb used by Luke of Simeon and Anna (2:25, 38). Matt. 27:57 calls him "Jesus' disciple" while John 19:38 adds "secretly for fear of the Jews." He had evidently taken no public stand for Jesus before now. *Boldly* (*tolmēsas*). Aorist (ingressive) active participle, becoming bold. It is the glory of Joseph and Nicodemus, secret disciples of Jesus, that they took a bold stand when the rest were in terror and dismay. That is love psychology, paradoxical as it may seem.

44. *If he were already dead* (*ei ēdē tethnēken*). Perfect active indicative with *ei* after a verb of wondering, a classical idiom, a kind of indirect question just as we say "I wonder if." Usually death by crucifixion was lingering. This item is only in Mark. *Whether he had been any while dead* (*ei palai apethanen*). B D read *ēdē* (already) again here instead of *palai* (a long time). Mark does not tell the request of the Jews to Pilate that the legs of the three might be broken (John 19:31–37). Pilate wanted to make sure that Jesus was actually dead by official report.

45. *Granted the corpse* (*edōrēsato to ptōma*). This official information was necessary before the burial. As a matter

of fact Pilate was probably glad to turn the body over to
Joseph else the body would go to the potter's field. This is
the only instance when *ptōma* (*cadaver*, corpse) is applied to
the body (*sōma*) of Jesus, the term used in Matt. 27:59 =
Luke 23:53 = John 19:40).

46. *Wound* (*eneilēsen*). This word is only here in the N.T.
as *entulissō* is only in Matt. 27; 59; Luke 23:53; John 20:7.
Both verbs occur in the papyri, Plutarch, etc. They both
mean to wrap, wind, roll in. The body of Jesus was wound
in the linen cloth bought by Joseph and the hundred pounds
of spices brought by Nicodemus (John 19:39) for burying
were placed in the folds of the linen and the linen was bound
around the body by strips of cloth (John 19:40). The time
was short before the sabbath began and these two reverently
laid the body of the Master in Joseph's new tomb, hewn
out of a rock. The perfect passive participle (*lelatomēmenon*)
is from *latomos*, a stonecutter (*lōs*, stone, *temnō*, to cut).
For further details see on Matt. 27:57–60. Luke 23:53 and
John 19:41 also tell of the new tomb of Joseph. Some modern scholars think that this very tomb has been identified
in Gordon's Calvary north of the city. *Against the door* (*epi
tēn thuran*). Matthew has the dative *tēi thurāi* without *epi*
and adds the adjective "great" (*megan*).

47. *Beheld* (*etheōroun*). Imperfect tense picturing the
two Marys "sitting over against the sepulchre" (Matt. 27:
61) and watching in silence as the shadows fell upon all
their hopes and dreams. Apparently these two remained
after the other women who had been beholding from afar
the melancholy end (Mark 15:40) had left and "were watching the actions of Joseph and Nicodemus" (Swete). Probably also they saw the body of Jesus carried and hence they
knew where it was laid and saw that it remained there
(*tetheitai*, perfect passive indicative, state of completion).
"It is evident that they constituted themselves a party of
observation" (Gould).

CHAPTER XVI

1. *When the sabbath was past* (*diagenomenou tou sabbatou*). Genitive absolute, the sabbath having come in between, and now over. For this sense of the verb (common from Demosthenes on) see Acts 25:13; 27:9. It was therefore after sunset. *Bought spices* (*ēgorasan arōmata*). As Nicodemus did on the day of the burial (John 19:40). Gould denies that the Jews were familiar with the embalming process of Egypt, but at any rate it was to be a reverential anointing (*hina aleipsōsin*) of the body of Jesus with spices. They could buy them after sundown. Salome in the group again as in Mark 15:40. See on Matt. 28:1 for discussion of "late on the sabbath day" and the visit of the women to the tomb before sundown. They had returned from the tomb after the watching late Friday afternoon and had prepared spices (Luke 23:56). Now they secured a fresh supply.

2. *When the sun was risen* (*anateilantos tou hēliou*). Genitive absolute, aorist participle, though some manuscripts read *anatellontos*, present participle. Luke 24:1 has it "at early dawn" (*orthrou batheos*) and John 20:1 "while it was yet dark." It was some two miles from Bethany to the tomb. Mark himself gives both notes of time, "very early" (*lian prōi*), "when the sun was risen." Probably they started while it was still dark and the sun was coming up when they arrived at the tomb. All three mention that it was on the first day of the week, our Sunday morning when the women arrive. The body of Jesus was buried late on Friday before the sabbath (our Saturday) which began at sunset. This is made clear as a bell by Luke 23:54 "and the sabbath drew on." The women rested on the sabbath (Luke 23:56). This visit of the women was in the early morning of our

399

Sunday, the first day of the week. Some people are greatly disturbed over the fact that Jesus did not remain in the grave full seventy-two hours. But he repeatedly said that he would rise on the third day and that is precisely what happened. He was buried on Friday afternoon. He was risen on Sunday morning. If he had really remained in the tomb full three days and then had risen after that, it would have been on the fourth day, not on the third day. The occasional phrase "after three days" is merely a vernacular idiom common in all languages and not meant to be exact and precise like "on the third day." We can readily understand "after three days" in the sense of "on the third day." It is impossible to understand "on the third day" to be "on the fourth day." See my *Harmony of the Gospels*, pp. 289–91.

3. *Who shall roll us away the stone?* (*Tis apokulisei hēmin ton lithon;*). Alone in Mark. The opposite of *proskuliō* in 15:46. In verse 4 *rolled back* (*anekekulistai*, perfect passive indicative) occurs also. Both verbs occur in *Koiné* writers and in the papyri. Clearly the women have no hope of the resurrection of Jesus for they were raising the problem (*elegon*, imperfect) as they walked along.

4. *Looking up they see* (*anablepsasai theōrousin*). With downcast eyes and heavy hearts (Bruce) they had been walking up the hill. Mark has his frequent vivid dramatic present "behold." Their problem is solved for the stone lies rolled back before their very eyes. Luke 24:2 has the usual aorist "found." *For* (*gar*). Mark explains by the size of the stone this sudden and surprising sight right before their eyes.

5. *Entering into the tomb* (*eiselthousai eis to mnēmeion*). Told also by Luke 24:3, though not by Matthew. *A young man* (*neaniskon*). An angel in Matt. 28:5, two men in Luke 24. These and like variations in details show the independence of the narrative and strengthen the evidence for the

general fact of the resurrection. The angel sat upon the stone (Matt. 28:2), probably at first. Mark here speaks of the young man *sitting on the right side* (*kathēmenon en tois dexiois*) inside the tomb. Luke has the two men standing by them on the inside (Luke 24:4). Possibly different aspects and stages of the incident. *Arrayed in a white robe* (*peribeblēmenon stolēn leukēn*). Perfect passive participle with the accusative case of the thing retained (verb of clothing). Luke 24:4 has "in dazzling apparel." *They were amazed* (*exethambēthēsan*). They were utterly (*ex* in composition) amazed. Luke 24:5 has it "affrighted." Matthew 28:3f. tells more of the raiment white as snow which made the watchers quake and become as dead men. But this was before the arrival of the women. Mark, like Matthew and Luke, does not mention the sudden departure of Mary Magdalene to tell Peter and John of the grave robbery as she supposed (John 20:1-10).

6. *Be not amazed* (*mē ekthambeisthe*). The angel noted their amazement (verse 5) and urges the cessation of it using this very word. *The Nazarene* (*ton Nazarēnon*). Only in Mark, to identify "Jesus" to the women. *The crucified one* (*ton estaurōmenon*). This also in Matt. 28:5. This description of his shame has become his crown of glory, for Paul (Gal. 6:14), and for all who look to the Crucified and Risen Christ as Saviour and Lord. *He is risen* (*ēgerthē*). First aorist passive indicative, the simple fact. In I Cor. 15:4 Paul uses the perfect passive indicative *egēgertai* to emphasize the permanent state that Jesus remains risen. *Behold the place* (*ide ho topos*). Here *ide* is used as an interjection with no effect on the case (nominative). In Matt. 28:6 *idete* is the verb with the accusative. See Robertson, *Grammar*, p. 302.

7. *And Peter* (*kai tōi Petrōi*). Only in Mark, showing that Peter remembered gratefully this special message from the Risen Christ. Later in the day Jesus will appear also to

Peter, an event that changed doubt to certainty with the apostles (Luke 24:34; I Cor. 15:5). See on Matt. 28:7 for discussion of promised meeting in Galilee.

8. *Had come upon them* (*eichen autas*). Imperfect tense, more exactly, *held them, was holding them fast.* *Trembling and astonishment* (*tromos kai ekstasis*, trembling and ecstasy), Mark has it, while Matt. 28:8 has "with fear and great joy" which see for discussion. Clearly and naturally their emotions were mixed. *They said nothing to any one* (*oudeni ouden eipan*). This excitement was too great for ordinary conversation. Matt. 28:8 notes that they "ran to bring his disciples word." Hushed to silence their feet had wings as they flew on. *For they were afraid* (*ephobounto gar*). Imperfect tense. The continued fear explains their continued silence. At this point Aleph and B, the two oldest and best Greek manuscripts of the New Testament, stop with this verse. Three Armenian MSS. also end here. Some documents (cursive 274 and Old Latin k) have a shorter ending than the usual long one. The great mass of the documents have the long ending seen in the English versions. Some have both the long and the short endings, like L, Psi, 0112, 099, 579, two Bohairic MSS; the Harklean Syriac (long one in the text, short one in the Greek margin). One Armenian MS. (at Edschmiadzin) gives the long ending and attributes it to Ariston (possibly the Aristion of Papias). W (the Washington Codex) has an additional verse in the long ending. So the facts are very complicated, but argue strongly against the genuineness of verses 9 to 20 of Mark 16. There is little in these verses not in Matt. 28. It is difficult to believe that Mark ended his Gospel with verse 8 unless he was interrupted. A leaf or column may have been torn off at the end of the papyrus roll. The loss of the ending was treated in various ways. Some documents left it alone. Some added one ending, some another, some added both. A full discussion of the facts is found in the last chapter of

my *Studies in Mark's Gospel* and also in my *Introduction to the Textual Criticism of the New Testament*, pp. 214–16.

9. *When he had risen early on the first day of the week* (*anastas prōi prōtēi sabbatou*). It is probable that this note of time goes with "risen" (*anastas*), though it makes good sense with "appeared" (*ephanē*). Jesus is not mentioned by name here, though he is clearly the one meant. Mark uses *mia* in verse 2, but *prōtē* in 14:12 and the plural *sabbatōn* in verse 2, though the singular here. *First* (*prōton*). Definite statement that Jesus *appeared* (*ephanē*) to Mary Magdalene first of all. The verb *ephanē* (second aorist passive of *phainō*) is here alone of the Risen Christ (cf. *Ēleias ephanē*, Luke 9:8), the usual verb being *ōphthē* (Luke 24:34; I Cor. 15:5ff.). *From whom* (*par' hēs*). Only instance of *para* with the casting out of demons, *ek* being usual (1:25, 26; 5:8; 7:26, 29; 9:25). *Ekbeblēkei* is past perfect indicative without augment. This description of Mary Magdalene is like that in Luke 8:2 and seems strange in Mark at this point, described as a new character here, though mentioned by Mark three times just before (15:40, 47; 16:1). The appearance to Mary Magdalene is given in full by John 20:11–18.

10. *She* (*ekeinē*). Only instance of this pronoun (= *illa*) absolutely in Mark, though a good Greek idiom. (See John 19:35.) See also verses 11, 20. *Went* (*poreutheisa*). First aorist passive participle. Common word for going, but in Mark so far only in 9:30 in the uncompounded form. Here also in verses 12, 15. *Them that had been with him* (*tois met' autou genomenois*). This phrase for the disciples occurs here alone in Mark and the other Gospels if the disciples (*mathētai*) are meant. All these items suggest another hand than Mark for this closing portion. *As they mourned and wept* (*penthousin kai klaiousin*). Present active participles in dative plural agreeing with *tois . . . genomenois* and describing the pathos of the disciples in their utter bereavement and woe.

11. *Disbelieved* (*ēpistēsan*). This verb is common in the ancient Greek, but rare in the N.T. and here again verse 16 and nowhere else in Mark. The usual N.T. word is *apeitheō*. Luke 24:11 uses this verb (*ēpistoun*) of the disbelief of the report of Mary Magdalene and the other women. The verb *etheathē* (from *theaōmai*) occurs only here and in verse 14 in Mark.

12. *After these things* (*meta tauta*). Only here in Mark. Luke tells us that it was on the same day (24:13). *In another form* (*en heterāi morphēi*). It was not a *metamorphōsis* or transfiguration like that described in 9:2. Luke explains that their eyes were holden so that they could not recognize Jesus (24:16). This matchless story appears in full in Luke 24:13–32.

13. *Neither believed they them* (*oude ekeinois episteusan*). The men fared no better than the women. But Luke's report of the two on the way to Emmaus is to the effect that they met a hearty welcome by them in Jerusalem (Luke 24:33–35). This shows the independence of the two narratives on this point. There was probably an element who still discredited all the resurrection stories as was true on the mountain in Galilee later when "some doubted" (Matt. 28:17).

14. *To the eleven themselves* (*autois tois hendeka*). Both terms, eleven and twelve (John 20:24), occur after the death of Judas. There were others present on this first Sunday evening according to Luke 24:33. *Afterward* (*husteron*) is here alone in Mark, though common in Matthew. *Upbraided* (*ōneidisen*). They were guilty of unbelief (*apistian*) and hardness of heart (*sklērokardian*). Doubt is not necessarily a mark of intellectual superiority. One must steer between credulity and doubt. That problem is a vital one today in all educated circles. Some of the highest men of science today are devout believers in the Risen Christ. Luke explains how the disciples were upset by the sudden appearance of Christ and were unable to believe the evidence of their own senses (24:38–43).

15. *To the whole creation* (*pāsēi tēi ktisei*). This commission in Mark is probably another report of the missionary *Magna Charta* in Matt. 28:16–20 spoken on the mountain in Galilee. One commission has already been given by Christ (John 20:21–23). The third appears in Luke 24:44–49 = Acts 1:3–8.

16. *And is baptized* (*kai baptistheis*). The omission of *baptized* with "disbelieveth" would seem to show that Jesus does not make baptism essential to salvation. Condemnation rests on disbelief, not on baptism. So salvation rests on belief. Baptism is merely the picture of the new life not the means of securing it. So serious a sacramental doctrine would need stronger support anyhow than this disputed portion of Mark.

17. *They shall speak with new tongues* (*glōssais lalēsousin* [*kainais*]). Westcott and Hort put *kainais* (new) in the margin. Casting out demons we have seen in the ministry of Jesus. Speaking with tongues comes in the apostolic era (Acts 2:3f.; 10:46; 19:6; I Cor. 12:28; ch. 14).

18. *They shall take up serpents* (*opheis arousin*). Jesus had said something like this in Luke 10:19 and Paul was unharmed by the serpent in Malta (Acts 28:3f.). *If they drink any deadly thing* (*k'an thanasimon ti piōsin*). This is the only N.T. instance of the old Greek word *thanasimos* (deadly). James 3:8 has *thanatēphoros*, deathbearing. Bruce considers these verses in Mark "a great lapse from the high level of Matthew's version of the farewell words of Jesus" and holds that "taking up venomous serpents and drinking deadly poison seem to introduce us into the twilight of apocryphal story." The great doubt concerning the genuineness of these verses (fairly conclusive proof against them in my opinion) renders it unwise to take these verses as the foundation for doctrine or practice unless supported by other and genuine portions of the N.T.

19. *Was received up into heaven* (*anelēmpthē eis ton oura-*

non). First aorist passive indicative. Luke gives the fact of the Ascension twice in Gospel (Luke 24:50f.) and Acts 1:9–11. The Ascension in Mark took place after Jesus spoke to the disciples, not in Galilee (16:15–18), nor on the first or second Sunday evening in Jerusalem. We should not know when it took place nor where but for Luke who locates it on Olivet (Luke 24:50) at the close of the forty days (Acts 1:3) and so after the return from Galilee (Matt. 28:16). *Sat down at the right hand of God* (*ekathisen ek dexiōn tou theou*). Swete notes that the author "passes beyond the field of history into that of theology," an early and most cherished belief (Acts 7:55f.; Rom. 8:34; Eph. 1:20; Col. 3:1; Heb. 1:3; 8:1; 10:12; 12:2; I Pet. 3:22; Rev. 3:21).

20. *The Lord working with them* (*tou kuriou sunergountos*). Genitive absolute. This participle not in Gospels elsewhere nor is *bebaiountos* nor the compound *epakolouthountōn*, all in Paul's Epistles. *Pantachou* once in Luke. Westcott and Hort give the alternative ending found in L: "And they announced briefly to Peter and those around him all the things enjoined. And after these things Jesus himself also sent forth through them from the east even unto the west the holy and incorruptible proclamation of the eternal salvation."